THE TEACHING METHODS OF CHRIST

by   John Harris, D.D.

WIPF & STOCK · Eugene, Oregon

Wipf and Stock Publishers
199 W 8th Ave, Suite 3
Eugene, OR 97401

The Teaching Methods of Christ
By Harris, John
ISBN 13: 978-1-55635-745-9
ISBN 10: 1-55635-745-1
Publication date 12/3/2007
Previously published by Thomas Ward and Co., 1837

FOREWORD

Christians never tire of studying the life of Christ for they can glean from His example lessons that can then be applied to their own work and service. Educators at one time were particularly fond of drawing from the pages of the Gospels truths relating to Christ's teaching methods. These pedagogical truths are still timely and relevant. They can be used by all who minister from the pulpit, teach in a Sunday school, or in other ways seek to share their faith.

The author of this volume was at one time principal of the New College, London. Born in Devonshire, John Harris (1802-1856) worked in his father's tailor shop during the day and studied by himself at night. He soon began preaching in little chapels close to his home town and people flocked to hear him.. It was not long before they began referring to him affectionately as the "boy preacher".

By age 21 John Harris had prepared himself sufficiently to be able to enter the Independent College of Hoxton. Three years later he became the pastor of a Congregational church at Epsom. Here he established his reputation as a preacher and large crowds were attracted to hear him.

It was during his stay at Epsom that Harris wrote his first book on the teaching methods of the Lord Jesus Christ (1835). Such was the acclaim that he received that, in 1837, he was appointed to the theological chair of Chestnut College. A year later he was honored with a doctorate by Brown University, Pennsylvania. Within a relatively short period of time he became principal of the New College, London, where he also served as professor of theology.

As a theologian, Dr. Harris sought to infuse more relevance into the dry dogmas of the church that were current in his day. He also urged Christians to begin applying their beliefs to the practical situations of life. Both in the classroom and the church his teaching and preaching met with a warm response.

It is a little surprising to learn that Dr. Harris' published writings became better known in the United States than in the United Kingdom. To the end of his days his best and most widely acclaimed work was *The Great Teacher* which, fortunately for us is here reproduced under the title *The Teaching Methods of Christ*.

Dr. Cyril J. Barber
Author, *The Minister's Library*

CONTENTS.

PREFACE . . . . p. vii—xvi

ESSAY I.

THE AUTHORITY OF OUR LORD'S TEACHING.

A Divine Teacher needed—Desired—Might have been expected—Was predicted—His Advent in the Person of Christ—His lowly Condition—Herald—Installation to Office—Subject proposed—A very small Proportion of his Discourses recorded—Scope of his Teaching—First Characteristic, *Authority*. I. Authority of Goodness — Invitations — Beatitudes. II. Authority of Greatness—Claims universal Audience—Superiority to Jonah, Solomon, and all the great Names of the Jewish Church—Supremacy—Central Object of the Judgment Day—Impresses his Name on every Thing—Speaks of all Things, awful and sublime, calmly, like one familiar with them—Teaching, declarative and dogmatic. III. Authority of Solemnity—His peculiar Formula—His Denunciations of Woe. IV. Legislative Authority—Revises the Mosaic Code—Asserts his Superiority to Law—Repeals existing Economy—Controls Laws of Nature himself, and confers the Power on others—" I say unto you"—His new Commandment—Not only enacts Laws, but ensures Obedience—Forgives Sin—Reposed on his own personal Authority—Conclusion—His Teaching exempt from all supposable Circumstances unfavourable to authoritative Teaching—Taught with the perfect Conviction of the Truth of his Doctrine—His Example enforced it—Cordial Sympathy with it—Knew the ultimate Principles on which his Doctrines rested—And the supreme Value of the Truth he taught—And the Purity of his own Motives—And the ultimate Triumph of his Doctrine—All this must have clothed his Teaching, especially when contrasted with the prevailing Mode of Jewish Instruction, with commanding Power—His Disciples should be distinguished by Reverence and Docility—These Dispositions to be sought and found at the Throne of Grace, p. 1—41

ESSAY II.

THE ORIGINALITY OF OUR LORD'S TEACHING.

SECTION I.— *Of God the Father.*

Originality not valuable for its own Sake—His Praise consists partly in not being more Original—Designed to adopt familiar Illustrations and Sayings in order to engage Attention and Affection—His highest Claim to Originality consists in new Disclosures of truth—To have merely interpreted the Book of Nature, unavailing—Is itself brought under the Curse—The great Truth it attests is the Existence of its Maker. I. Christ taught his Character—Prevailing Ignorance on the Subject—Even in Judea—Among the Heathens, the Epicurean System general. II. Christ taught the universal Providence and paternal Character of God. III. His Love to Man, exemplified in the Mission of Christ. IV. This, only the Means of Mercy. V. The End—Free Gift of eternal Life. VI. Offered to all. VII. Character of Christ is the Character of the Father. VIII. Taught us to call him our Father—Summary of our Lord's Teaching on this Subject—Life eternal to know God through Christ . . . . p. 42—79

SECTION II.— *Concerning Himself.*

His Person unique—Not understood by his Disciples till after his Ascension. I. The Complexity of his Person. II. Object of his Advent—Evinced the Divine Existence—Embodied the Divine Spirituality—But, chiefly, represented the Divine Character. III. Mode of Manifestation—By sensible Representation—Affirming that all he did was only in Fulfilment of the Father's Commission—Ascending the Cross—Saving the Outcast—Identifying his Interest with ours—Sending Salvation to Jerusalem—Giving his own Spirit to his Disciples—Interceding—Personally—Allowing us to plead his Name—Engaging himself to answer Prayer—Object of the Whole to demonstrate that " God is Love ;" and to make us the Heirs of that Love . . . . p. 80—131

SECTION III.— *Of the Holy Spirit.*

Difficult to discriminate between Originality and mere Novelty—New Theological Opinions sprung up between the Times of Malachi and of Christ—Though much is taught of the Holy Spirit in the Old Testament, the Doctrine of his Agency is one of the most original that came from the lips of Christ—The Study of it comparatively neglected. I. Mission of the Spirit dependent on his own Return to Heaven—the Reasons why. II. Object of the Spirit's Advent—to convince of Sin. III. Means of his Operation. IV. Necessity of Regeneration. V. Effects of it. VI. Glorifies Christ. VII. To enhance our Views and Desires of the Spirit, our Lord taught that to reject him is unpardonable—That his Presence would compensate for his own Departure—Be a Remedy for all the Miseries of Earth—God's all-comprehending Gift—Free for all . . . . p. 132—174

SECTION IV.— *Of the Doctrine of the Trinity ; and of a Spiritual Church.*

The Doctrine of the Trinity imperfectly known under the Jewish Economy—Taught by our Lord practically—In the Formula of Christian Baptism. I. The Existence of a Spiritual Church. II. Had been pre-figured—The World contains nothing like it. III. Its Simplicity. IV. Its Purpose. V. Its Spirituality—Preached Repentance as a Requisite for Membership—

Armed his Church with Power to expel Offenders—Denounced the Pharisees for "teaching as Doctrine the Commandments of Men"—The Church his earthly Kingdom . . . . p. 175—189

Section V.— *On Satanic Agency.*

Satan, the Prince of Devils—Numbers of his Agents—His Apostacy, and Ruin of Man—His Power on Earth, a Kingdom—Organized—Long almost undisputed—Christ came to dispute his Authority—Took an affecting View of human Vassalage—Satan, aware of his Advent—Undertook to conduct his Temptation—Made his Life an incessant Conflict—Compassed his Death—Defeated—The Defeat of Satan quite reconcileable with his present Prevalence—Called a Spirit, to excite our Vigilance—An unclean Spirit, to awaken our Antipathy—His Influence over the heart, great—But only exercised with our Consent—The Period of his Reign limited . p. 190—203

Section VI.— *Of the Immortality of the Soul; Resurrection of the Body.*

The Hope of Immortality reasonable—The great Instinct of Humanity—Revelation necessary to authenticate it—It did so, partially, under the last Economy—Full Revelation and Proof of the Doctrine reserved for Christ. I. Taught the Doctrine of an intermediate Existence. II. Proved a Resurrection. III. He himself will raise the Dead. IV. Resurrection universal. V. Bodies raised identical with those interred. VI. Means of a Resurrection to eternal Life, provided by Christ—He possesses the Power—By dying in our stead, has acquired the Right—Begins, even here, to make his Power and Right available, by quickening dead Souls—The final Extinction of Death so certain, that he speaks of it as already effected . p. 209—236

Section VII.— *Of the Final Judgment.*

The Judgment anticipated by the Human Mind. I. Its Publicity. II. Christ himself the Judge. III. Its solemn Pomp. IV. Its Rectitude—Hence, it will be universal—Take Cognizance of every Act— A Judgment of Comparison and Proportion—And conducted according to the known Laws of the Divine Government. V. Its Division of all intelligent Beings into Good and Bad—This Distribution commenced upon Earth—Angels will then be employed to complete it. VI. Its final Awards—These Awards everlasting—The whole Doctrine exhibits the practical Value of the Gospel, and the infinite Importance of Christ . . . . p. 237—263

ESSAY III.

SPIRITUALITY OF OUR LORD'S TEACHING.

I. The Spirituality of the Divine Nature. II. Of the Moral Law. III. Of the Worship of God—As opposed to that which is local—Ceremonial—Prescribed by Human Authority—Formal and insincere. IV. Of his Kingdom—Denounced the Temporal Hopes of the Jews—Called for Spiritual Subjects—Born from above—Disclaimed for his Kingdom all Resemblance to Earthly Governments—Conclusion—The whole reminds us of our Proneness to repose in a Form of Piety to the Neglect of Evangelical Holiness—This has originated Superstition—Neutralized the Jewish Economy—And early began to vitiate Christianity itself—Importance of exemplifying the Spiritual Nature of our Vocation . . . . p. 264—302

ESSAY IV.

ON THE TENDERNESS AND BENEVOLENCE OF OUR LORD'S TEACHING.

The Recollection of our Lord's Character necessary, to feel the Pathos of his Teaching. I. His Excellences—Loveliness of his Youth—His gracious Commission—Purity—Superiority to the Age in which he lived—Independent of all surrounding Influences—Universality of his Plans—Qualities, contrasted, but harmonized by Benevolence — Overflowing Benignity. II. His Benevolence as a Teacher—Objection answered—Employed Parables—Chose to be Poor—Preached to the Poor—Taught gratuitously—Simplified Instruction—Teaching consolatory—Places in which he preached, evinced Condescension—Always accessible—Impressed unwelcome Truths by employing affecting Signs; the little Child; washing the Disciples' Feet; the last Supper. III. Instances of the Tenderness and Benevolence of his Teaching—Predicted his own Death—Blessed the Poor in Spirit—Soothed the Anxious—Offered the Weary Rest—Parable of the Prodigal—Identifies himself with all Piety—Apostrophizes, and weeps over Jerusalem—His valedictory Discourse—His Purposes of Grace—Universality of his Offers—Expressions of his Benevolence went on increasing to the last—Conclusion; Character of Christ regarded as an Evidence for Christianity—An Example —And an Encouragement—His Expostulation with the Unbeliever,
p. 303—363

ESSAY V.

OUR LORD'S TEACHING PRACTICAL.

The Gospel more likely than ever to be studied as a practical Science. I. Our Lord evinced his Wisdom, as a Practical Teacher, by limiting his Revelation to the Measure of our real Wants—By dispensing with a cumbrous Ritual. II. His favourite Topics, Humility and Benevolence. III. Adjusted the Claims of Heaven and Earth. IV. Preferred comprehensive Rules to a detailed Enumeration of Duties. V. His Morality extends to the Thoughts. VI. To Motives—Love of God. VII. Prescribes for its End, the Glory of God. VIII. For its Standard, the Character of God. IX. Injunctions, simple and authoritative—Sanctions. X. Not only commands, but enables. XI. Objections of the Incompleteness of the Saviour's Code, answered—Happy Effects of his Gospel. XII. Impiety of those who regard it as a Dispensation *from* Holiness. XIII. Supreme Importance which he ascribed to Holiness—Aimed to make Earth resemble Heaven. p. 364—427

PREFACE.

In revising this volume for a new edition, the principal alteration made relates to the Preface. This consisted of a series of remarks on the subjects of the essays, which almost imperceptibly accumulated while the volume was first going through the press. With these remarks I have now done that which I should have done at first if I had had the opportunity—transferred them to their proper places in the body of the book.

Owing, perhaps, partly, to the absorbing attractions which invest the subject of our Lord's atoning death, and, partly, to the eclipsing flood of light which, immediately after his death, burst on the church in the ministry of the apostles, the impression which is generally entertained of the claims of Christ as a Teacher is, if I mistake not, most disproportionately inadequate. The object of the following pages is to point out and illustrate the leading features of his divine instructions; from which it will appear, that he was the best Teacher of his own religion; and that his personal ministry, as recorded in the evangelical history, dwelt on all the essential doctrines of the Christian system, as afterwards explained in the apostolic writings.

Taking it for granted that the most simple and natural method of arranging a subject is the best, I have adopted that order in the distribution of the following essays which I suppose an unprejudiced and intelligent Jew, who had enjoyed our Lord's personal ministry, would have observed, in giving a methodical account of its leading characteristics.

He would, I imagine, have spoken to the following effect:—1. " The first thing which struck me in the ministry of this Great Teacher was the air of *authority* with which he spoke. All the people were astonished at it. It was so utterly unlike the feeble, puerile, and uncertain manner of our scribes, who seem almost to invite disbelief, and so much like what I have often imagined an ancient prophet must have been, that I frequently fancied myself listening to an Elijah or an Ezekiel. 2. And then his teaching was so *original!* If he excelled our scribes in the authority with which he spoke, he equally excelled our ancient prophets—even David and Isaiah—in his originality. Whatever he uttered seemed new. Though he frequently insisted on topics familiar to our holy books, yet the flood of radiance which he threw on many of those subjects, and the great additions which he made to others, gave them the freshness and force of a new revelation. But when he spoke of the Divine Father, of Himself as the only begotten Son, and of the Holy Spirit—when he discoursed of a spiritual church, angelic agency, the immortality of the soul, the resurrection of the dead, and the judgment day, the truths which he propounded were so original and sublime, that Solomon himself might have sat at his feet as a little child. 3. And the more original his teaching was, the more was it marked by *spirituality!* Whether he adverted to the Divine Nature, the moral law, the worship of God, or to his own unearthly kingdom, his doctrine appeared like the pure and disembodied spirit escaped from the lifeless body of the Rabbinical system. 4. But etherial as it was, it was not a cold abstraction. Often would he bathe his doctrine with tears. Jeremiah himself might have learnt *tenderness* from his tones, and pathos from his passionate expostulations. And, frequently, while weeping himself, with what condescending solicitude would he wipe away the tears of others, and bind up the broken in heart! 5. And his teaching was eminently *practical.* Never did he omit an opportunity of exposing sin, or of explaining the duties, and enforcing the obligations, of universal holiness. One peculiarity there was which pervaded the whole of his wonderful ministry—he was emphatically his own theme. Every truth which he taught was, in one way or another, related to himself. As if he beheld a line drawn from himself to every object in the universe, he constantly spoke of himself—though he appeared the personification of humility—as the centre of the great system of truth and providence."

These five characteristics of our Lord's teaching were, I humbly conceive, the chief, and would have been the first to strike an intelligent hearer of the class described. But his ministry was marked by many other peculiar features; and if it were the design of the following pages to do more than present a specimen of its principal excellences, it would only be necessary to carry out and apply this principle of arrangement to those other excellences, in order to classify and comprehend the whole of his divine instructions.

When considering the evangelical nature of our Lord's teaching, one of the first thoughts perhaps which arises in the mind of the reflecting Christian relates to the fact of our Lord's discourses containing less of the peculiar doctrines of grace than the teaching of the apostles. How is the striking contrast between the gospels and epistles, in this important respect, to be accounted for? The following considerations may furnish a satisfactory reply:—1. It was only in accordance with his own arrangements and predictions that it should be so. Hence, he foretold that his first disciples should do greater works than he did; that their success should be greater; and that it was reserved for the Spirit to lead them into all truth. 2. The very limited and gross apprehensions of the disciples imposed a restraint on the teaching of Christ, and determined the measure of his divine communications. Though he had " many things to say " to them, he pronounced them unable to bear the disclosure. And what would be the things which, under these circumstances, he would necessarily withhold—what, but the more spiritual truths and peculiar doctrines of salvation? 3. The object and limit of his instructions appear to have been, to inculcate the nature and necessity of that moral excellence which God and heaven require; in order that he might make us feel the want of it, preparatory to the offer of his Holy Spirit to produce it. The full and explicit exposition of the evangelical system, therefore, did not come within the pre-determined scope of his teaching. For, 4. He came less to preach salvation than to procure it; to make known redemption, not by a verbal and detailed announcement of its plan, but by the visible accomplishment of its conditions; to be the gospel, and to make it. He came to supply the facts out of which the evangelical doctrines are deduced, and which *must* philosophically precede them. For what is the doctrinal part of the gospel but the exposition of these facts? their transplantation out of the historical or external world, into the intellectual or spiritual? 5. It might, however, be easily shewn, that whatever is essential to the Christian system is to be found, *in semine*, in our Lord's teaching. His divinity, his atonement, the influence of his Spirit, and all the leading doctrines of grace, are to be found there in a condensed state, in a quintessence. If the principles of Christianity, as taught by the apostles, form a chain of evangelical truth, the first link, the very staple ring, is to be found in the teaching of Christ. The humble incrustation cannot conceal from the eye of the mineralogist the precious gem that dwells within, and a single blow, properly given, will lay bare its peculiar primitive or fundamental form: many of our Lord's sayings have a signification and a value far beyond their unpretending appearance; nor is it difficult for the Christian disciple to discover in them the first forms, the simple elements, of evangelical truth, of which the teaching of the apostles was only the *laminæ*, the natural accretions afterwards formed. His sayings are texts; their writings are only the necessary amplification and comment. Their instructions are not so properly a new revelation, as the result of the opening of their eyes to behold the wonderful things contained in his teaching. 6. And, finally, the uniform mode of divine revelation, in all ages, required that the doctrines of grace should be gradually developed; proceeding from the obscurity of dawn in our Lord's teaching, to the radiance of noon-day in that of the apostles.

Since writing the preceding paragraph, I have been surprised at meeting with the following remarks, bearing on the same subject; which, as they occur in a popular work of the present day, deserve a moment's attention. "Others are embarrassed when they think on this subject;" (that is, on the greater prominence given to the object and efficacy of our Lord's death in the epistles compared with the gospels;) "they do not know how to reconcile the seeming inconsistency, though they endeavour to diminish it, as far as possible, *by exaggerating and emphasizing the little which Jesus Christ did say, in regard to his sufferings and death* . . . . He who cannot take the directions which Christ or John gave, for beginning a life of piety by simple repentance for the past, without adding something from his own theological stores, *or forcing the language to express what never could have been understood by those who originally heard it, he cannot be studying the gospel in the right spirit.*" To put a forced and mystical construction on any part of the oracles of God, is an act of irreverence which cannot be sufficiently deprecated. But it is one thing to put them to the torture, compelling them to utter what they never meant; to turn from them, or to drown their voice with our own, before they have uttered all the mind of the Spirit, is another.

The statements cited appear at least to be unconsidered and unguarded; and, on the principle which they seem to involve,—namely, that the understanding of our Lord's original hearers was the measure of his meaning, —I will venture to remark; First, that, in direct contradiction to this proposition, it is a well-known canon of scripture interpretation, that " the sayings of our Saviour are to be apprehended, not merely in that sense to which the views of his hearers at the time could reach, but in the sense which he himself attached to them." Second, his own practice contains a warrant for this canon; for how often do we find him applying it to the interpretation of the Old Testament; expounding some of its truths in a sense more spiritual and profound than even the original propounders themselves conceived. Third, his express declarations, and the confessions of his apostles, harmonize with it. They frankly acknowledge, that when he adverted to the nature and necessity of his sufferings, they understood not his meaning. He reproached them with their slowness of apprehension. He promised his Spirit to recal his sayings to their minds as so many lost truths. He intimated that he had left in their possession truths of which they little suspected the value. And after his resurrection, "he said unto them, These are the things which I spake unto you, while I was yet with you . . . . . . Then opened he their understanding that they might understand the Scriptures;"—obviously implying, that, up to that moment, they had not understood his evangelical expositions of them. Fourth, it seems to be necessary for the moral development of our nature, that the truth employed should be such as is itself capable of constant expansion and new developments,—that, like its Divine original, it should brighten while we are looking at it, heighten while we are aspiring to reach it, and thus elevate us to itself, the standard of perfection.

Accordingly, all the first lessons *set* us by God in nature and providence appear to be constructed on this principle. He who becomes a student of nature soon finds that he is bending over a fountain which deepens beneath his gaze. And what is the Jewish economy, if we desire to reach its interior truths, but a vast, profound, elaborated enigma,—to which the gospel indeed brings us the key, but the opening and exploration of which is yet incomplete: excusing, if not justifying, the opinion of Origen, that "a clear understanding of the reasons of the Israelitic economy, and of all the Levitical laws, belongs to the privileges of the future life." And the teaching of Christ seems to possess the same profound and comprehensive character. Comparative anatomy informs us, not only that animated nature forms an ascending series of beings, beginning with few organs, and increasing in number, complexity, and finish, up to man; but that in some of the earliest and simplest links of the living chain, there is traceable a promise, a mute prophecy, of all the rest, a rough outline of all that is to follow; that many processes are sketched in the lower animals, the completion of which is reserved for the composition of man. In like manner, the entire system of Judaism was one compacted prophecy of the gospel, a presentiment of Christianity; in which the great doctrines and virtues, which it is the province of the new dispensation to develop and mature, may be found in their embryos and elements. And on the same principle, in the sayings of Christ, the gospel may be found thrown out in its rudiments. " For Christ," saith Milton, " gives no full comments, or continued discourses, but speaks oft in monosyllables, like a master scattering the heavenly grain of his doctrine like pearls here and there, which requires a skilful and laborious gatherer." His teaching is the seed-plot in which the great doctrines of grace were first sown, to be afterwards transplanted and cultivated in the inspired ministry of the apostles, where they have room to luxuriate and yield in perfection the fruit of life.

Considerations like these warrant us to suppose, not merely that the whole evangelical system, as developed by the apostles, lies, in its germ, in the teaching of Christ, but that such is the fulness, the seminal character of his teaching, that even their epistles do not exhaust it. That they have put us in possession of every essential truth, we admit; that any fundamental doctrine remains to be discovered, cannot for a moment be imagined; but it may be suggested, that even with their inspired epistles in our hand, and regarding those epistles in the light of commentaries on the sayings of our Lord, there yet remain to be discovered in his teaching new aspects of some truths, the immeasurable compass of others, and harmonies subsisting between them all, beyond the perception of ordinary vision; and the development of which is reserved to reward the pious industry of the devout and vigorous mind.

The church of God has been too generally content

with the great surface-truths of revelation,—those which we have only to stoop for in order to possess, but which are made so obvious, and placed so near, not as a premium to indolence, but in accommodation to our moral incuriousness and necessities; not as a dispensation from diligent investigation, but as an allurement to it where it can be made, and to render it unnecessary where it cannot. "The kingdom of heaven"—in the sense of celestial truth—"is like treasure hid in a field; the which when a man hath found, he hideth; and, for joy thereof, goeth, and selleth all that he hath, and buyeth that field;" and buyeth it in order that he may ransack, and turn up every part of it, and make himself master of all its treasures. And further, it is as if the same man, while digging for more coins and concealed jewels, should unexpectedly happen on a vein of precious ore. Hitherto, we have done little more than collect, estimate, and classify, the more accessible treasures. But let the shaft which is already begun be sunk deep enough, and the labours of the mine be properly conducted, and the discovery of many a rich and precious lode will demonstrate that the great globe itself is not more interlaced with golden veins, and filled with precious things, than the field of revelation, the storehouse of the unsearchable riches of Christ.

J. H.

THE GREAT TEACHER.

ESSAY I.

ON THE AUTHORITY OF OUR LORD'S TEACHING.

When, in the fulness of time, the eternal Son came forth from the bosom of the Father, he descended to a region of spiritual darkness. Ages of inquiry, conjecture, and effort, had only served to demonstrate the fact—that man, " by searching, cannot find out God." Legislators, philosophers, and poets—the pride of their time, and the boast of the species—had toiled to construct a system whose top should reach unto heaven; but in vain; they built only to the clouds. Reason, confident in her resources, had sent forth her sons, under all auspices, and in every direction: but they returned, defeated and disheartened; the footsteps of truth could nowhere be found. In vain had generation after generation asked, in its way to oblivion, " What is truth?" The devotee had urged the inquiry at the shrine of his God; the priest, at his altar of sacrifice; the sage had repeated it as he walked amidst the works and wonders of creation; but nothing was heard in reply; nothing, but the faint and bewildering echo, " What is truth?" Darkness covered the earth, and gross darkness the minds of the people.

Nor can the state of Judea be regarded as an exception to the prevailing gloom. There, indeed, the ancient oracles of God were yet extant; but their still small voice, heard only, at any time, by the attentive listener, had been long since overpowered and silenced by the dogmas of their professed interpreters, and the clamours of rival sects. The spiritual import of the sacred volume, like the seven-sealed roll of the Apocalypse, had long been closed to the Jew; and when the Lion of the tribe of Judah prevailed to open it, the aversion with which they turned from the sight shewed how unaccustomed they were to gaze on the truth. The darkness was universal and complete. It had settled down, like a pall, over the face of the whole earth. Truth looked down from heaven; but from no part could she behold her image reflected. If she would relieve the gloom, she must descend and shine, and dissipate it by her actual presence. All things proclaimed the urgent necessity that the world should be visited by " a teacher sent from God."

Not only did this awful exigence exist, it was extensively felt and acknowledged; and by many of the more enlightened heathens, a Divine Instructor was ardently desired. In illustration of this, the language of Plato has been often cited; nor is it easy to conceive of any thing more conclusive and striking than his picture of Socrates advising his pupil to forego the usual sacrifices until a teacher should be sent from on high. In another place, speaking of such an inspired teacher, he represents, with prophetic sagacity and precision, that " he must be poor, and void of all qualifications but those of virtue alone; that a wicked world would not bear his instructions and reproofs; and therefore, within three or four years after he began to preach, he would be persecuted, imprisoned, scourged, and at last be put to death."

In this remarkable passage, we behold the divine philosopher, rising from a mournful survey of human ignorance, turning with an air of despondency from every earthly resource, yet eagerly thirsting for a knowledge of God, and virtue, and futurity, till his thirst grows into a desire for celestial aid, and his desire matures to an anticipation, and even a prediction, which God was actually intending to fulfil; perhaps, indeed, we err in not cordially recognising in his language the presence of heavenly inspiration. And in uttering the desire which his words disclose, we may take it for granted, he was clothing the thoughts of a thousand bosoms, venting the secret and cherished lodgings of unnumbered hearts. If we, though standing in the radiance of the "Sun," which has since risen on the world, are yet sometimes conscious of impatience, and complain of obscurity, what must have been the wishes and aspirations of those who, with a keen perception of their exigence, were sitting in darkness and the shadow of death?

Now the appearance of a Divine Instructor, thus absolutely necessary, and ardently desired, might have been warrantably expected. Indubitable evidence existed that God already *had* spoken to man, at sundry times, and in divers manners; and as the ignorance of the world was still unreclaimed, and there was no intimation that his voice had been final, there was ground to anticipate that, in his own time, he would break the silence again. Besides, the very presence and nature of the Jewish economy was a standing evidence that such was his gracious intention. Bearing the marks of a celestial origin, and fraught with important truth, it yet veiled its meaning in types and enigmas, the solution of which remained to be given. Here were mysteries—where was the interpreter? Here were shadows—the substance, "the very things themselves," must be at hand. Here were proofs that, in a former age, God had said, " Let there be spiritual light" —was it not likely that, in the process of his new creation, the time would come when he would collect, and embody, and augment this light into a glorious sun? Here was a system of divine intimations and unfinished economy—was it likely that he would leave it incomplete? was it not more accordant with the character of a perfect being, that, putting his hand a second time to the work, he would bring it to perfection?

But, beyond this, the spirit of prophecy had distinctly foretold that an inspired instructor should appear. " For Moses truly said unto the fathers, A prophet shall the Lord your God raise up unto you of your brethren, like unto me; him shall ye hear in all things whatsoever he shall say unto you. And it shall come to pass, that every soul which will not hear that prophet, shall be destroyed from among the people. Yea, and all the prophets from Samuel, and those that follow after, as many as have spoken, have likewise foretold of these days." Thus a prediction was to be found, at the very opening of the prophetic roll, announcing the advent of a distinguished teacher, whose words would demand universal regard; while his authority would be supreme, and his power invincible. Unfolding it farther, we read, that he should preach the gospel to the poor, and proclaim the acceptable year of the Lord; that he should set judgment in the earth, and the isles should wait for his law; that the Gentiles should come to his light, and kings to the brightness of his rising. And as *he* was its earliest, so he was also its latest theme. For, reading on to its closing lines, we find it predicting him as the Messenger of the covenant who was yet to come, and the Sun of Righteousness yet to arise. His name was the first which prophecy had uttered; as often as it spoke, it resumed the inspiring theme; and when at length it expired, his name lingered on its lips. " When the fulness of time was come, God sent forth *his Son*." " Hear, O heavens; and be astonished, O earth!" the appointed Instructor appears, and proves to be no less a being than the Son of God himself. It is true, the deep necessities of man, the riches of the divine benevolence, and the glowing colours of prophecy, might have kindled and justified the expectation of a most illustrious teacher; but that he should have appeared in the person of the Eternal Word, exceeds the highest flight of human hope; that he should have come from the bosom of the Father, was an excess of goodness,—one of those splendid surprises of grace by which mercy delights to melt the obduracy and to win the confidence of our guilty race.

The circumstances attending the advent of so illustrious a Prophet must be entitled to receive our profound attention. With the outlines of these we are all familiar. The condescending object of his mission required that, for a time, he should hold the essential glories of his nature in abeyance: accordingly, he mysteriously allied himself to our condition; " the Word was made flesh." The strain of prophecy had assigned the scene of his life and labours to Judea; and in that favoured land he appeared. That he should have *grown* in wisdom as he rose to maturity, was only according to a law of our nature—an ordinance of his own divine appointment—since it is only by a gradual development that the faculties of man arrive at perfection; but the office he had come to assume, and the divine qualifications he brought to it, supposed him superior to human tuition; and accordingly he sought it not. When, in childhood, he mingled a moment with the doctors of the temple, " they were astonished at his understanding;" his inquiries were more instructive and replete with wisdom than their replies. On an after occasion, their surprise at his stores of sacred science was augmented by the knowledge of the fact, that he had " never learned," never approached the schools of human instruction. He had access to a tree of knowledge they knew not of. As his dignity was of an order distinct from earthly pomp, incapable of being diminished by its absence, or of being embellished by its presence, he entirely dispensed with it. The various gradations of human condition were all open and free to his choice, but of these he selected the lowliest; and however astonishing the selection may appear to those who place distinction in opulence and rank, to him who had already stooped from an infinite height in becoming man, the varieties of earthly rank were as nothing, were only minute degrees of littleness. The place of his birth, like a place constructed from the very wrecks of poverty, was entirely swept of every trace of luxury, every vestige of indulgence, and seemed sacred to humility alone. And the lowliness of all his subsequent life strictly accorded with the humbleness of his birth. Had he come in the pomp of outward state, the multitude would have been debarred from his presence, and the regards of men would have been divided between the attractions of his earthly rank and the claims of celestial truth; but by choosing the low condition of the great majority, and declining the tinselled drapery which charms the eye, he graciously made himself accessible to all, while he seemed to put forward truth alone as the only object demanding their notice—to challenge their *whole* attention to the native worth, the intrinsic importance, of the doctrines he announced.

But though, for the reasons assigned, he assumed the most bare and unpretending simplicity, as the hour for opening his divine commission drew nigh, the public mind was apprized of the event by " wonders in heaven above, and signs in the earth beneath." A herald, preceding his steps, aroused the nation, by the solemn announcement that he was now at hand;—a herald, whose office was deemed so important as the precursor of Christ, that even he had been the subject of ancient prediction;—while, to prepare the minds, and to excite the expectations, of those he addressed, the burden of his message was nothing less than the stern necessity of immediate repentance, and the approaching erection of a heavenly kingdom: " Repent ye, for the kingdom of heaven is at hand." The voice came pealing from the Judean desert, peopling its path wherever it swept with echoes of astonishment and alarm; and as it passed over the banks of the Jordan, rung through the palaces and streets of Jerusalem, and startled even the distant shores: the wondering land went out in crowds; the sanguine, the envious, the devout, the anxious, the oppressed, the curious—priest, politician, populace—all flocked and thronged to the scene of this remarkable prodigy; where, having won their admiration and credence, by the severe sanctity of his life, and agitated their fears by the bold and alarming tenour of his address, he awoke in them vague but elevated anticipations of " him that should come," and took from them a solemn pledge, by baptism, that as soon as that Illustrious Personage appeared they would enrol themselves among his disciples. " Now when all the people were baptized," while the herald voice was yet ringing in their ears, and their expectation was raised to the utmost pitch, Jesus, the subject of prophecy, the object of hope, the desire of nations, appeared, and with ineffable condescension received, at the hands of John, the baptismal rite. Having thus honoured the ministry of his servant, and ratified and obeyed existing laws, he ascended from the waters, and prayed; and as he prayed, " Lo, the heavens were opened unto him, and he saw the Spirit of God descending like a dove, and lighting upon him: and lo, a voice from heaven, saying, This is my beloved Son, in whom I am well pleased." Such was the splendid scene of his divine inauguration to an office to which we behold him appointed by the concurrent suffrages of the eternal Father and the Holy Spirit; invested with the authority and enjoying the complacency of the one, anointed and endowed with the unmeasured fulness of the other; an office which was destined to absorb all moral authority, distinction, and power, and in the discharge of which whatever he uttered was henceforth to be regarded as law and life.

In the following essays, I propose to point out the *leading features* of our Lord's instructions. My object, be it remarked, is not to attempt a detailed and textual exposition of the truths he taught, the words he uttered, —though these, of necessity, will be constantly before us, as our only data and source of illustration,—but to elicit and exemplify the peculiar qualities by which these truths and words, when viewed as a whole, are distinguished. With the substance of *what* he taught we are all more or less familiar; since, in common with the stupendous miracles which marked his path, the purity and perfection of his character, his amazing death, and glorious resurrection, it forms an important part of our scripture reading, and is one of the ordinary topics of pulpit instruction: but, if I mistake not, the impression which is generally entertained of the claims of Christ as a teacher, is most disproportionately inadequate; owing, perhaps, partly to the absorbing attractions which invest the subject of his atoning death, and partly to that eclipsing flood of light which immediately afterwards burst on the church in the ministry of the apostles; for, by a known principle, truth evolved and illustrated will supplant and succeed in the mind the same truth condensed and primitive, however superior its source, and throw over it an air of undeserved disparagement. Were it proposed to magnify his office as the great Prophet of the church, it would be important to remark that the preaching of the apostles, subsequent to his ascension, was virtually the mere continuation of his own preaching; that they were simply the organs and oracles through which he spoke; as much so as when he had sent them forth, by two and two, to proclaim through Judea the kingdom of God; the only difference being, that he had now removed the scene of his instructions from earth to heaven: but, without recurring to this consideration, and confining ourselves entirely to the specimens we possess of his *personal* teaching, it may easily be made apparent that, in the most literal and comprehensive sense of the expression, "never man spake like this man." And in adopting the plan contemplated, of exemplifying the peculiar characteristics of his earthly teaching, I am principally moved by the persuasion that it is best adapted to exhibit an enlarged, connected, and impressive view of the emphatic truth of this declaration.

On meeting with an allusion to our Lord's discourses, we naturally recur, in thought, to his sermon on the Mount, to his parables, his charge to his apostles, his more lengthened vindicatory replies to the questions and imputations of his adversaries, his terrible prophetic denunciation of the Jewish priesthood and nation, and his valedictory address to his disciples on the eve of his crucifixion. These, when brought from their various detached positions in the gospels, and grouped together in the mind, assume, perhaps, a larger appearance than the cursory reader had before attached to them. He must, however, be aware that we possess but a very small proportion of what Jesus actually delivered. It is not to be imagined that he, who went about doing good, and who turned every event into an occasion of usefulness, would travel from place to place, with his disciples, in silence. Rather, we infer from the characteristic inquisitiveness which some of them shewed, and his uniform readiness to reply, that the very scenes through which he walked, if nothing else, would furnish him with a perpetual occasion of instruction; that, in traversing a land so often pressed by angels' feet, so rich in the relics of miracle and devotion, that its very soil had lost its gross materiality, and every object had acquired a supernatural aspect, he would often advert to ancient times, making them the text of hallowed remark, and thus turn the very dust he trod into the gold of wisdom. And yet, though so much of his time was necessarily occupied in frequent, circuitous, and protracted journeys, a few fragments, incidentally given, are all that we have of his divine communications by the way.

But we are not left to mere conjecture as to the probable occasions on which he taught. The scene of the first discourse he is recorded to have uttered appears to have been Jerusalem; but of that memorable unsealing of the fountains of the waters of life we only know that, in conjunction with his miracles, it was the means of inducing many to believe on him. To form an idea of the immense proportion in which the amount of his teaching must have exceeded what is on record, we have only to recal the following expressions: " And Jesus returned in the power of the Spirit into Galilee; and there went out a fame of him through all the region round about. And he taught in their synagogues, being glorified of all. And he came to Nazareth, and preached there. And he came down to Capernaum, and taught them on the Sabbath days. And he said, I must preach the kingdom of God to other cities also; for therefore am I sent. And he preached in the synagogues of Galilee." These intimations are all to be found in a single chapter, the fourth of Luke; and only refer to a single period, the opening of his ministry. But if we bear in mind that similar intimations are dispersed through the gospels, and are equally applicable to all the subsequent stages of his life, we shall be vividly impressed, that what we read is merely a hint of what he delivered. What synagogue in Galilee, if not in Judea, did not resound to his gracious voice? What Sabbath did not behold him breaking the bread of life to famishing crowds? He held the key of all the treasures of wisdom, and he distributed of its stores with the affluence and profusion of unwearied beneficence. He had come to sow the earth with truth, and wherever he went he scattered in abundance the incorruptible seed. What has been transmitted by the holy evangelists is all that is necessary to inform and to sanctify; had all that he uttered in the course of his laborious ministry been preserved—for he never pronounced an idle word—the voluminous mass would have been inaccessible to the great majority, and thus its design would have been defeated; "for I suppose the world itself would not have been able to receive the books that should be written."

We may, I think, warrantably suppose that, on commencing his public ministry, the adorable Redeemer had present to his comprehensive mind an outline of the truths which should form the scope of his teaching. The worthlessness of formal ceremonial obedience; the spirituality of the law, and its eternal obligations; the holy, benevolent, and paternal character of God; the relations in which we stand to God, and to each other; the display of his grace in the gift of his Son for human salvation; the spiritual nature of the gospel kingdom; the necessity of prayer, repentance, and holiness in those who belong to it; the agency of the Holy Spirit to enlighten, renew, and sanctify the soul; the sublime fact of his own divine appointment to be the Saviour and Judge of the world; these were the momentous truths on which he chiefly dwelt, and to these, whatever the immediate occasion of his speaking, he perpetually returned. Like some of the celestial bodies, indeed, which refuse to come under any astronomical arrangement of signs, some of the lights which he kindled and placed in the great firmament of truth stand out in isolated grandeur, and shine apart. But though this was to be expected, owing to the awful extent of that ignorance he came to enlighten from the stores of his wisdom, and the variety of occasion which called it forth, the mass of his divine instructions will be found to come under the enumeration we have specified. And it is from his discourses and discoveries on these topics that we now proceed to exhibit those distinguishing marks of his teaching on which we propose to treat.

It is impossible to peruse the instructions of Christ without remarking the tone of *authority* which pervades them: this was the characteristic by which his hearers, on several occasions, appear to have been chiefly impressed; and to this, therefore, we think it natural to advert *first*. Of his personal appearance, and general address, we are left in ignorance: nor is it necessary that, in order to form an idea of his teaching, we should be able to imagine them. For this purpose, we have only to suppose, what is surely allowable, that they were in no way unfriendly to useful effect; and that, whatever the theme which engaged his tongue,—his voice, and words, and gestures, accorded with it, being true to nature and to the eloquence of holy human feeling. And hence, the authority with which he spoke was not of one unvaried character, but was marked and modified by the nature of his subject. There was authority in his invitations and promises, not less than in his denunciations and commands, for they were uttered in the language of independent goodness and power; but while we hear in the former the overflowings of paternal tenderness and love, we recognise in the latter the tones of the lawgiver and the judge. Availing myself of this variety, it may serve to promote distinctness and easier recollection if I classify the quotations I intend to make accordingly.

I. There are passages which exhibit especially the *authority of goodness.* " Come unto me all ye that labour and are heavy laden; and I will give you rest." " If any man thirst, let him come unto me, and drink." " Him that cometh unto me, I will in nowise cast out." Who can listen to these great and gracious announcements without feeling himself standing in the presence of *superior* goodness? His first emotion may be that of admiring gratitude at the display of so much benignity and compassion; but scarcely can it fail to be followed by the delightful, yet awful impression, that he is occupying holy ground, standing near the fountain of mercy itself. What distinguished dignity and grace do we recognise in sentences such as these:—" I am the light of the world:" " I am the bread of life:" " I am the way, the truth, and the life:" " I am the good shepherd, and give unto my sheep eternal life:" " I am come that they might have life, and that they might have it more abundantly." When from the midst of the burning bush Jehovah proclaimed himself, *I am that I am*, he announced his independent existence and self-sufficient perfections; in other words, he declared *what he is in himself.* In these declarations of Jesus, we recognise the same ineffable Being describing what he is to his people; laying open the resources of his infinite nature, appropriating and applying them, with high complacency in the act, to the wants of our guilty race: in each instance the dignity addressing us is the same, only that, in the language of the Incarnate Word, the awful is exchanged for the attractive and gracious. He spoke like the soul of universal goodness, conscious of a power of breathing into prostrate humanity the breath of life; of entering the vast capacities of the world, and filling them all with a fulness of joy. And, as the only other illustration we shall adduce, think of the opening of his divine discourse on the Mount of Beatitudes. How like a cloud of goodness did he crown the honoured mount, and shower his benedictions with a copiousness which shewed that it was at once his pleasure and his prerogative to bless!—in a way which evinced that, while so employed, he was only engaged in his own peculiar province; that the treasures of eternity were at his command; that in the disposal of them he knew no control; that he thought it no robbery to enact the God; he rejected the minions and favourites of the world, and, calling authoritatively on a peculiar people, he distributed them into classes, assigned to each an appropriate award, and made them free of the universal kingdom of God. Having brought into the world the accumulated treasures of the eternal God, thus publicly did he adopt his heirs, and authoritatively assign to each his respective share. Turning to such as might suffer for his " name's sake" last, he declared that " great should be their reward in heaven;" thus disclosing the dignity which attached to his name, and the unlimited authority he possesses in heaven.

II. There were occasions when he spoke with the authority of *greatness*. " He that hath ears to hear," said he, " let him hear;" and in thus bespeaking universal and submissive attention, he was only repeating the command from the excellent glory which had summoned the world to listen while he spoke, and to receive every word he might utter as law and life. In accordance with the spirit of that command, he did not hesitate to compare himself with the most distinguished lights of the Jewish Church, and to claim pre-eminence over them all. Jonah was one of the most exalted names of which the Israelites could boast. His voice, like a blast from the trump of God, had pealed through the streets of Nineveh, and had made all its palaces tremble. his preaching had humbled the mightiest nation of the east; had instrumentally preserved an empire from destruction; had caused their religion and their laws to be revered by the surrounding lands, and had greatly exalted the God of Israel before the heathen. Yet aware that all these impressions of Jonah's greatness were vividly present to their minds, " Behold," said he, "a greater than Jonah is here!" Solomon was with them a name for glory. As the founder of their magnificent temple, as the instrument of raising their nation to the loftiest point of prosperity, as the most highly endowed and wisest of men, the depository and personification of wisdom, they hallowed his name with a reverence which fell little short of idolatry: so that to assert superiority to him was, in their eyes, to be claimed to be considered as more than a man; as passing beyond the limits of humanity, and invading the precincts of Deity. Yet aware that such was their high and jealous regard for his fame, and while standing amidst the splendid memorials of his greatness, " Behold," said he, "a greater than Solomon is here!" Not only did he claim to eclipse their brightest luminaries, he spoke of all the flower and prime of their nation as having longed to complete their earthly distinctions by sitting at his feet, and following in his train. " He turned unto his disciples, and said, Blessed are your eyes, for they see; and your ears, for they hear. For verily I say unto you, that many prophets, and kings, and righteous men, have desired to see those things which ye see, and have not seen them; and to hear those things which ye hear, and have not heard them." And, as though to extinguish with a breath, and for ever, all idea of rivalship with him, he distinctly assumed and appropriated, as his right, the title of authority his followers had placed at his feet, and affirmed his claim to the entire subjection and allegiance of their faith. " Ye call me Master and Lord, and ye say well, for so I am; one is your master, even Christ." Thus taking possession of the sacred domain of conscience in his own name, he erected a throne whose supremacy it is treason to question, and blasphemy to attempt to usurp.

In his graphic and awful allusions to the last day, in none of which he fails to make prominent the glorious tribunal of the Son of man, what a voice of authority and majesty is heard to speak! While reading, for instance, his parabolical representation of it, in the twenty-fifth of Matthew, how imperceptibly, but irresistibly, is the attention engaged, and the heart subdued; till, having marked, with conscious concern, the partition betwixt the sheep and the goats, and intensely listened to his portentous addresses to each, and trembled at the temerity evinced in the defence of the wicked, and sympathized with the characteristic reply of the righteous, we hang, with breathless anxiety, on the lips which pronounce their respective awards, and feel, at the breaking up and departure of the vast assembly to their separate states, as though we ourselves had been arraigned in his august presence, how entirely we are in his hands, and how insignificant we are there. Having amazed his hearers by the announcement of that partial resurrection which accompanied and adorned his own triumph over the grave, he bade them reserve their wonder for the far more impressive scenes of the last day:

"Marvel not at this, for the hour is coming in the which all that are in the graves shall hear the voice of the Son of man, and shall come forth." If we would recognise the authority which belongs to every part of his teaching, we have only to realize the thought, that in listening to him we are actually listening to the voice which is soon to resound through all the nations of the dead, and to which we ourselves shall reply by awaking and leaving the chambers of the grave. When all the universe shall be convened for judgment, the only parties remaining will be He who judges and they who are judged; of all the multiplied relations which now subsist, that which makes us accountable to God will alone be felt: so that, were it possible, in that awful juncture, for every order of created beings to disown and desert us, the calamity would fail, from its comparative insignificance, to attract our notice. Yet the Saviour unequivocally implies that if he alone "profess to be ashamed" of us, our doom will be sealed: that it will be only for him to disown us, happiness and hope will instantly desert us, and from that moment we shall have to date our woe. Virtue, wherever it exists, is greatness of the highest order, for it allies us to supreme greatness; but, as though he represented and embodied universal holiness in his own person, as though he were at once the author and champion of all righteousness, he engages to reward every act that befriends it, as an honour conferred on himself; while, whatever opposes it, even in thought, he describes as a violence offered to his own nature, which he feels himself bound to resent. "Ye did it *unto me*, or, ye did it *not unto me;*" these are the terms of aggravation in which he depicts himself describing every act, and by which he informs us that, as he sits on the throne of judgment, the great centre of the congregated world, every act will be seen, like a line, pointing to him as its object and end, or else, in forgetfulness and enmity, diverging from him, and losing itself in outer darkness.

The name of a person is a familiar formula to denote his character and influence. The name of God is a compendious idiom of scripture, importing his glory, the fulness and totality of his divine perfections. Hence, everything peculiar to the legal economy was prescribed in his name as the Fountain of authority, or was required to be done *to* his name, as its only legitimate object and end. In introducing the Christian economy, we find Jesus denoting his power and supremacy in the same manner. Copying the example of Deity, he impressed his *name* upon every act, and object, and office, peculiar to the new dispensation. His disciples, as often as they desired to call down spiritual blessings, were to employ his name, and their plea would prevail. They were to gather together for social worship *to* his name. They were to baptize to his name. In his name they were to summon and subvert the strongholds of idolatry and sin, and to arouse the nations from the slumbers of spiritual death. Speaking in his name, they were to find the ordinances of nature miraculously obedient to their voice. His name was to be their watchword, their badge of distinction, the principle of their piety, the bond of their union, the end of their actions, the authority for their conduct, and the source of their success. Nothing was to be recognised or received in his kingdom, which did not bear the superscription of his name; everything was to confess his supremacy, by acknowledging him for its author, or else for its ultimate design.

But these illustrations of the dignity which marked the teaching of Christ might be multiplied indefinitely. I do not profess to have selected the best; for when I have hoped the difficulty of selection was over, a new specimen has suddenly occurred, bringing in its train a host of fresh illustrations, as eligible as those already cited. It is one of the peculiarities of our Lord's teaching, that he was his own subject; and seldom does he release our attention from the exalted theme. As if he sought to be always present to our eye, he converted all nature into an index to his greatness, using it as an intended system of emblems of himself. There is a sense in which the much-admired saying of Plato, that light is "only the shadow of God," was applied by our Lord to himself. "I," said he, "am the light of the world;" the sun is only "my emblematic representative." Water, and air, and light, and life, the great elements of existence, the universal principles, were selected by him as the only adequate emblems of his greatness. How numerous the occasions in which he partially removed the veil of his greatness; heightening our conceptions of his majesty by the terms of reserve in which he spoke of it. His pre-existence, his personal dignity, his prospective glory; these were themes familiar to his tongue. "He thought it not robbery to be equal with God;" and accordingly, when he claimed the equality, he did not employ any pomp of words, he did not appoint a public occasion, and assemble the nation, and command attention by the trumpets and thunders of Sinai; like one to whom all greatness was familiar, he simply announced it in his common speech. "As the Father," said he, "knoweth me, even so know I the Father. The Son restoreth to life whom he will. All things that the Father hath are mine. I and my Father are one. I appoint unto you a kingdom." Greatness, which baffles and astonishes our conceptions, he spoke of in a tone of unmoved tranquillity. He lays his hand on the throne of God, with the spontaneous ease of an eternal habitude. Arraying himself in all the perfections of Godhead, and putting on his head the crown of Deity, he assumes his seat at the right hand of the Father, and claims a community of supreme honours. Grandeur, which the heart of man hath not imagined, and which even his apostles could not glance at without emotions of unutterable wonder, he speaks of without any effort, and distributes without any ostentation. Astonishment is only for those to whom knowledge is novelty; but " the glory which is to be revealed" to us, is " the glory which he had with the Father before the world was;" the unapproachable splendours of the celestial state he speaks of as ever present to his mind, as the natural and familiar scenes of his father's house. The heavenly heights, to which we can ascend only as we are succoured and raised by an omnipotent arm, was the state of exaltation with which he had ever moved on a level, and from which he had visited us only by accomplishing a laborious descent. He carried our views of his greatness from the present to the future; declared that his final doom of the wicked will be, " Depart from me;" importing that banishment from him will be exile from happiness, the consummation of human woe: while, on the other hand, the peculiar and eternal charm of that world where all is glorious is to consist in the manifestation and enjoyment of his presence. " Where I am, there also shall my servant be." " I will that they be with me where I am, to behold my glory."

Under this head, it is needful to remark, that the prevading style of our Lord's teaching is that of assertion and testimony. While it pre-supposes the laws of reason, it does not, nor could it without manifest incongruity, make an appeal to them. His disclosures of truth are necessarily dogmatic. But since man, if he is to be treated as a rational being, must have adequate grounds on which to rest his belief, our Lord, in the stead of arguments, constructed a basis of miracles. He claimed to be " believed for the works' sake." They were the hand of God, endorsing and attesting as true whatever he revealed. Having thus acquired a right to dictate, he could not have submitted the principles he announced to the ordinary process of argumentation without implying that human reasoning—our present impaired perceptions of truth—was a surer ground for reliance than the purest reason; he would have been expunging faith from the Christian virtues, exalting human reason, or that which stands for it, above the wisdom of God, and treating it as though in the sphere of religion it were perfect, and at home; whereas he found it prostrate and lost, and had to rekindle its extinguished torch with the very first elements of sacred knowledge. Surrounded with divine credentials, he took his stand as a living oracle, and demanded the credence of all who heard his unreasoned verities. He spake as one having authority, addressing himself to humility, obedience, and implicit faith. Every science has its data; fundamental principles, assumed to be true, on the unquestioned authority of which all its deductions and applications rest; in the science of theology, the sayings of Christ are ultimate truths. From these, as from first principles, all our reasoning in religion must proceed: to call in question their authority, would be to disturb and subvert the foundations of truth. His dictates constitute the rudiments of sacred science; and they are to be acquiesced in, as the reasons of duty, and the laws of faith.

If any are disposed to wonder why our Lord should have said so much less, in the way of direct assertion, concerning his personal dignity, than his apostles, let it be remembered, that it was not his object to give a full verbal exposition of his personal claims; that, during his earthly ministry, it was his aim, and a part of his humiliation, partially to conceal them; to observe a medium course between the extremes of a mean obscurity on the one hand, and an overwhelming grandeur on the other; to provide that human agency might be left free and unconstrained in its conduct towards him on the one hand, and that his love, on the other, might move on to the cross, unthwarted and undisturbed by man; that the solemn oblation of himself, which was the act to which all his ministry subserved,—for his whole life was only a preface to his death,—might neither be prevented nor disregarded; that he left his dignity to be inferred chiefly from his actions, and from a comparison of his life with the writings of the prophets; that his divine greatness having long been the subject of prophecy, it was not necessary for him to do more on this head than to identify himself with the prophecy. And he did this, —explicitly affirming that they wrote of him. Bringing all the rays of prophetic light together, he wreathed them into a crown of glory for his own head.

But, as if to compensate himself for the arrangement which required the temporary obscuration of his greatness, he was emphatically his own subject. He himself was almost invariably the point from which he started, the theme on which he enlarged, or the centre to which he returned. If he adverted to the great elements of nature, it was only to proclaim them emblems of himself. If he spoke of the greatness of persons and objects which his hearers reverenced next to the Deity, it was only to announce himself as greater than they. If he displaced the types and rites of the Jewish church, it was that he might occupy their place himself; clearing the entire area of the church, to fill it with his own glory. He turned all the great things of nature and of the ancient church into so many marginal references to the all-absorbing theme, *himself;* and he frequently did it in a manner which shewed that he considered them dignified by being so employed. He carried this same spirit of self-aggrandizement into the presence of God; he predicted that the Eternal Spirit himself should come and wait on his glory. He is distinguished from every other teacher by this, that while he spoke of lowliness as his chief characteristic, he seldom released the attention of his hearers from himself; and yet the heart of the Christian is sensible of no inconsistency here, for it feels that, while what he said of himself is measurable, what he left unsaid and unrevealed is immeasurable.

III. A third quality, which imparted a style of awful authority to our Lord's teaching, was *solemnity.* In the Old Testament, *As I live, saith the Lord,* is a form of divine asseveration which compels attention, and which, by giving the existence of Jehovah in pledge, imparts to sentiments already grave in themselves the exceeding awfulness of an infinite oath. Answerable to this is that remakable formula employed by Christ, and peculiar to him, with which he so often commands attention, as with the blast of a trumpet—" Verily, verily, I say unto you." The reiteration of the first word, proceeding from the lips of him who is " the truth," and " the word of God," invests the announcements which follow with a superlative sanctity and solemnity, as if they came to us legibly impressed with the stamp and seal of God. Solemnity of address, at all times affecting, is never more so than when, like elemental thunder, it proclaims the terrors of the Lord. Whoever may be the organ of divine denunciation, he has only to evince that he feels the weight and burden of his message, in order to obtain respectful audience from the conscience of the sinner, and to awaken and authenticate its most hidden forebodings. But what an appalling accession to the Redeemer's power of rebuke is derived from the consideration of his prevailing compassion, as well as of his mysterious resources to fulfil and to punish. The voice of him who was " meek and lowly in heart," uttering the hoarse and exasperated accents of wrath, is more than a recollection of Sinai. But how was it possible that even mercy itself could visit a scene like that which he traversed, and maintain a style of unmingled tenderness. Accordingly, there were occasions when, surveying the proud, hypocritical, and guilty throngs which crowded his path, he clothed himself with zeal as with a garment, and, with a consuming jealousy for the insulted majesty of God, " took them into his lips, and smote them with the sword of his mouth." Witness the cleansing of the temple. Intent on gain, the Jews had converted the holy place into a scene of sacrilegious traffic; they had turned the ancient and solemn passover itself to profit; they bartered deep in the blood of human souls; they worshipped mammon in his Father's house. But, "suddenly coming to his temple," he flamed around its hallowed walls, " like a refiner's fire," and, with the tones of injured and insulted Deity, rained on their consciences such strokes of terrible dismay that they eagerly sought refuge from his holy indignation in flight, leaving him the Lord and sole possessor of the sanctuary.

But, chiefly, let us recal to our recollection the unbroken series of pregnant woes which he denounced during his last visit to the temple. Long had he walked, like an incarnate conscience, through their guilty land; and often had they been troubled, and trembled at the rebuke of his sacred presence. Having nearly filled the capacious measure of their iniquity by rejecting him, they were about to make it overflow by his crucifixion.

Undeterred by the appalling prospect, he came with unfaltering step to the scene of his sufferings, to finish the work which was given him to do. Finding himself surrounded in the temple by a large assemblage of Jewish doctors, scribes, and lawyers and pharisees,—the very elements and essence of the nation's guilt,—he assailed and demolished the enormous fabric of sanctimonious hypocrisy which their laborious impiety had reared, and, with the fidelity and fearlessness of the king of martyrs, denounced and delivered his final protest against the pride and the power which upheld it. They had occasionally heard his fearful comminations before, and trembled for their security, for every word was a weapon; but now, having regularly invested and approached their fortified guilt, he opened on them the dreadful artillery of his divine malediction. An occasional flash had before apprized them that a storm might be near; but now, having collected together all the materials of tempest into one black and fearful mass, and having awed them to silence as nature is hushed when awaiting a crisis, he discharged its tremendous contents, in one volleyed and prolonged explosion, on their guilty and unsheltered heads. He arraigned them as though he had already ascended the seat of doom, and laid open all the sepulchral recesses of their iniquity as though he read from the book of God's remembrance. Hypocrisy was unable to conceal itself in the clouds of incense which it offered. The proud, the covetous, the intolerant, he confounded and covered with the shame of detection and conscious guilt. As they came up for judgment, in succession, he fulminated against them the woes and imprecations of his wrath, "the wrath of the Lamb," in tones anticipating those of their final sentence. "Woe unto you, scribes and pharisees, hypocrites!" "One woe is past, and behold, another woe cometh."

" Woe unto you, scribes and pharisees, hypocrites! ye serpents, ye generation of vipers, how can ye escape the damnation of hell?" That solemn scene, remembering the character of the Great Reprover, and the impending judgments of which it was prognostic, may well remind us of the seven apocalyptic thunders uttering their voices; and often, may we suppose, would the echoes of his denunciations return upon the ears of those who heard them in after years, like the distant but quailing reverberations of the mount that burned.

IV. Another characteristic of the authority which marked the teaching of our Lord, and the last I propose to illustrate, is that which he discovered in his legislative and judicial capacity. To disturb the majestic repose of the divine law, argues, on the part of him who attempts it, either the final stage of insane impiety, or an authority clothed with the prerogatives of the original lawgiver. In this latter exalted predicament the Saviour claimed to stand; " As the Father," said he, " hath life in himself, so hath he given to the Son, to have life in himself; and hath given him authority to execute judgment also, because he is the Son of man." " All things are delivered unto me of my Father." In the exercise of his legal supremacy, he may be said to have revised the laws of Heaven. Not only did he put on them his own authoritative interpretation,—from which he permits no appeal, and by which he greatly extended the sphere of their jurisdiction,—in bestowing forgiveness, he even controlled and suspended their operation; he pronounced what part of the divine code was of perpetual, and what of temporary obligation; he repealed its positive enactments, and enjoined others; while, by laying open the scenes of the final judgment, and speaking as from the mysterious cross, he placed it on another basis, infused into it a new vigour, and augmented its force in the highest degree.

When the sanctimonious pharisees, impatient to accuse him, but despairing of a charge, alleged against him the trivial act of his hungry disciples, in plucking the ears of corn on the sabbath day, he not only established the innocence of the deed, but with what an air of inimitable dignity did he cast over it the ample shield of his own prerogative: "The Son of man," said he, "is Lord even of the sabbath day." On another occasion, when the same unappeasable intolerance, and cloaked hypocrisy, construed an act of healing into a breach of the sabbath, he again asserted his superiority to the law. But, beyond this, he expounded his right to that superiority; he declared, that as the operations of the Father knew no intermission, so neither did his; that as the machinery of Providence does not pause in deference to the sabbatic law, but continues, through every moment of time, to fill the universe with its agency, so he acknowledged no restraint, but claimed the same unlimited scope, and infinite freedom of activity for his beneficence; thus clearly placing his own miraculous works on a level with the works of God; demanding the same consideration for their character, and assuming an equality, or rather an identity, with the Supreme, in will, and right, and power. "My Father worketh until now, and I work. Whatsoever things the Father doeth, those things the Son also doeth in like manner." But his dispensation with the law of the sabbath was only a specimen of his supreme authority. By issuing the final and sovereign mandate to his disciples, "Go into all the world, and preach the gospel to every creature," he virtually annulled the Jewish ritual, and repealed a whole economy, casting it back among the things that were; while, by replacing it with ordinances of his own enactment, and sacred to his worship, he proclaimed himself the founder and legislator of a new religion.

For the establishment of his religion, a display of miraculous power was necessary; and, accordingly, he not only declared his ability and right to control at pleasure the laws of nature,—he placed those laws, as he saw fit, under the subjection of his apostles also. "When he had called unto him his twelve disciples, he gave them power against unclean spirits to cast them out, and to heal all manner of sickness, and all manner of disease. And these signs shall follow them that believe; in my name shall they work miracles." "And whatsoever ye shall ask in my name that *I will* do."

The exercise of his supremacy, in the instances we have cited, was accompanied by the most illustrious displays of authority, in developing and enforcing the eternal and unchangeable laws of morality. The morality of the Mosaic code was of divine dictation; but, in revising its statutes and giving it perfection, he introduces his new prescriptions with this preamble, "Ye have heard that it was said to them of old time; but I say unto you;" thus placing his own legislation on a footing with the authority of Sinai; and, if not actually effacing the original tables, to make room for his own statutes, yet inserting and incorporating these statutes at pleasure, and publishing them as a part of the eternal law. How tender, yet inconcealable, the tone of authority in which he said to his disciples, when he was only a step from the cross, "A new commandment give I unto you, that ye love one another." To regard this as a mere republication seems to impugn the modesty which distinguished his character; for it represents him as claiming originality and novelty for that which is only the revival of an obsolete law. But with that ancient precept which enjoined love to our neighbour this new command has no affinity, except in appearance; it differs in its nature, its objects, and in the peculiar considerations by which it is enforced. *That* prescribes the love of benevolence; *this* requires the love of complacency: *that* enjoins loving kindness, the love of the kind, of man as man; *this* enjoins the love of character, of virtue, of man as Christian: while its claim to novelty is completed by the divine Legislator proposing his own example as the model and motive to obedience. But that which displays his superiority to all human, all merely delegated authority, and which places him on a level with the Supreme Power, is, that having enacted laws, he can ensure obedience. The highest praise of an earthly lawgiver is to adapt his laws as nearly as possible to the claims of abstract right, on the one hand, and to the peculiar state of the people receiving them, on the other. He can do little more to promote obedience to them, than by publicly chastising the refractory and disobedient. But the great Prophet and Lawgiver of the Christian church, having consulted our nature in the requirements he makes, can then conform our nature to his authority,—having authoritatively announced his will, he can carry it into all the recesses of the soul, and, in perfect harmony with our free volitions, can so identify it with our thoughts and aims, so blend it with the stream and current of our consciousness, that in yielding obedience to his word we are only obeying the actings and impulses of our own minds. Hence the language of conscious authority and efficient power which he employed in relation to the conversion of the Gentiles: " Other sheep I have, which are not of this fold; them also *I must bring*, and they *shall hear my voice;* and there shall be one fold, and one shepherd." Hence too, he could say, to whom he chose, " Follow me:" and the individual addressed " arose and followed him." At this disenchanting command, the spirit of the world fled from the heart—the thousand ties which bound it to the earth were snapped asunder—and the man suddenly found himself emancipated, and walking in the Saviour's train. The omnipotent effect with which he spoke to the tempestuous elements, and to demons more fierce and fearful than they, was only a type and pledge of his unlimited power over the mind of man. He speaks, and it is done; his people are " made willing in the day of his power."

But of all his displays of authority, his forgiveness of sin is immeasurably the greatest. This, according to human conceptions, is the highest and uttermost prerogative of the Supreme. It is to ascend a throne above the lawgiver, and to silence his voice, and suspend his functions, for a *reason* paramount to all law, and more comprehensive. It is to overrule the claims of justice, and, stopping it in its full career towards the sinner, to exhibit a reason for mercy, to which justice bows with reverence, and before which it retires. Law, the dictate of infinite wisdom, is the rule by which man is to act towards God; but forgiveness is a dispensation, a reason, issuing from a deeper recess of his mysterious nature, and by which he chooses to act towards us. But this prerogative, essentially divine, this high and incommunicable right, Jesus exercised, and vindicated his competence to do so. " Son," said he, to the paralytic man, " be of good cheer; thy sins are forgiven thee: and, behold, some of the scribes said within themselves, Why doth he thus speak blasphemies? who can forgive sins but God alone? But Jesus, knowing their thoughts, said, Why do ye think evil in your hearts? For which is easier to say, Thy sins are forgiven; or to say, Arise and walk? But that ye may know the Son of man upon earth hath a right to forgive sins, (he saith to the paralytic,) Arise, take up thy couch, and go to thy house." Thus, forestalling the functions of the last day, he remitted the claim of justice on a sinful being, erased his guilt from the book of God, changed the relations of an accountable creature to the Supreme Governor, and in effect, asserted that he possessed the power of taking from the inmost soul the sting of conscious guilt: while by declaring that he retained this power, though he was then the *Son of man upon earth*, he carries our thoughts to the state whence he had descended, and reminds us that no distance from his throne above, no depth of humiliation to which he might condescend, can deprive him of his right to pardon; that as it is exclusively, so it is in alienably divine; and that he is therefore free to use it as God, though for a time he may choose to rank as the Son of man.

Preceding prophets, jealous for the divine honour, had scrupulously guarded against the remotest suspicion that they spake in their own name; they distinctly confessed their delegated capacity, and perpetually appealed to the authority which sent them. But Jesus, we have seen, without any modification or reserve, employed the language of supreme personal authority. He did not, indeed, in any way impart the impression of an interest, or even an existence, detached from the Father. The authority by which he spoke, though expressly his own, was, by identity of nature, the authority of the Father also. As often as he exercised the functions of the legislator, he placed himself, if I may say so, on a level, and in a line, with the eternal throne; so that its glory fell directly upon him, and by him was again reflected back, mingled with the lustre of his own greatness. While he stood forth distinctly in his own personality, and addressed us in his own name, he stood in so perfect a conjunction with the Deity, and so far within the borders of the encircling light, that his voice came with the authority of an oracle from the central glory. " Glorify thy Son, that thy Son also may glorify thee. I am in the Father, and the Father is in me. No man knoweth the Father but the Son, neither knoweth any man the Son but the Father. Whatsoever things the Father doeth, these also doeth the Son likewise. He that hath seen me hath seen the Father also. I and my Father are one."

In closing our illustrations of the authority of the Saviour's teaching, it may not be irrelevant briefly to remark, that not only was that authority exempt from those deductions to which the force of mere human instruction is liable, but that it must have been greatly augmented by every consideration of an opposite kind.

Nothing can be imagined more fatal to the power of a public teacher than a lurking suspicion, a secret misgiving, of the truth, the value, or consistency, of his doctrine. In such a case, the mind may be said to have lost its power of projection; its professed aim will not be reached. Anything short of full conviction will betray itself to his audience, in a way inviting their suspicion and creating disbelief. Equally unfriendly to the weight of his instructions is a conscious inability to refer them to those first principles from which they derive their authority,—a want of cordial sympathy with their practical influence,—a sense of discordance between that influence and his present conduct,—a painful uncertainty concerning their success,—or, lastly, a doubt of his own eligibility and right to the office of teacher.

Now, not merely was the Saviour exempt, by necessity of nature, from each of these foes to authoritative teaching; the mount, from which he sometimes taught, was only an emblem of the moral elevation on which he always stood, where everything was present to augment the pervading power of his preaching, and from whence he spoke with an authority exclusively his own. To convince the incredulity of others that he came from God, he often referred to his being heralded by John, to his announcement by the voice from the excellent glory, and to his affluence in divine qualifications and miraculous powers. For himself, he could not have felt a stronger assurance of the fact, had all the hierarchies and state of heaven constantly and visibly stood around him, an amphitheatre of living glory, to corroborate his mission, and authenticate every sentence he uttered.

So perfect was his example, that had it been possible for the least inconsistency to have existed between his instructions and his life, we should, without hesitation, have sought the defect in his teaching. But such a discrepancy was impossible. In every precept he taught, he felt that he was only expounding his own life, reading from the holy volume of his own heart. Virtue found itself reassured in his presence; and, having imbibed courage and strength from his looks, went to complete the conquest of Sin. Instead of pointing his hearers to the tables of stone, he could invite them to learn of him; and the holy law rejoiced the while in its living representative. He could look round on a nation of witnesses, and say, " Which of you convicteth me of sin?" with the certainty that the challenge could not be accepted. But what amazing weight must this consideration have lent to his instructions, what power to his rebukes, what authority and force to his commands! Truth never languished on his lips, never suffered in his hands, from want of sympathy in its advocate. " To this end was I born," said he, " and for this cause came I into the world, that I should bear witness unto the truth." And as often as it issued from his tongue, it came with the freshness of a new revelation; was announced with an earnestness commensurate with its intrinsic importance, and with the momentous results depending on its success; and was defended with the devotedness and zeal of a champion prepared to die in its behalf.

Such is the present limitation of our knowledge, and our constant liability to err, that diffidence in the announcement of our opinions is accounted a virtue. But he, who came forth from God to be the light of the world, spoke on every subject with the unfaltering assurance of certain knowledge. To him, truth, all truth, was, in a sense, ever present and self-evident. Properly speaking, he uttered no mere sentiments, notions, or opinions, but only truths. He did not speak on probability and credit; his assertions were sustained on ultimate principles and personal knowledge. He saw intuitively, that whatever was opposed to his doctrine, however plausible as conjecture, or deeply rooted in the popular faith, was delusion and falsehood. "Every one that is of the truth," said he, "heareth my voice." And not only was he assured of the particular doctrine, he was perfectly acquainted with the general principle whence it drew its authority, and with the unchangeable position that principle holds in the system of universal truth. Having stood in the counsel of God, having dwelt in the penetralia, the innermost recesses of the eternal sanctuary, the elements and originals of all truth were familiarly present to his mind. Of his sublimest supernatural disclosures he averred, that he was speaking that which he knew, and testifying that which he had seen. He came forth from the bosom of the Father, as the Word, the Revealer of that infinite mind in which, from eternity, he had surveyed the archetype and idea of all truth; and he spoke with the authority of a divine oracle.

But, besides the consciousness that he was the Word and the Wisdom of God, his discourses must have derived an accession of power from the knowledge that he was unfolding truth of the highest order—the words of eternal life. Science of all kinds is distinction and power; and he who imparts it is a benefactor to his species: but the knowledge which Jesus came to unfold was emphatically *the gospel;* truth which God deems important, which had been revolved from eternity in his infinite mind, which enters into his purposes and involves his glory; a revelation so essential to our well-being, and every way so momentous, that it not only disdains comparison with the discoveries of man, but, engrossing to itself the undivided attention of the only begotten Son of God, would have held its majesty debased had it been mingled, even on his hallowed lips, with the meaner topics of human science. His mission contemplated our race as immortal beings labouring under the frown of incensed justice, and standing—ignorant, helpless, and exposed—on the verge of a gulf of irretrievable ruin. Alive to all the horrors of our condition, he came with the message and means of deliverance; he brought from Heaven an express assurance of complete relief. Other knowledge may be acquired by ordinary means, its worth may be computed, it may be dispensed with altogether; but the way of salvation could only be made known by God himself: while its utter indispensableness and infinite value appear from the fact, that we must have it or perish. " I am come," said Christ, " a light into the world ;" and, as he ascended the firmament of truth, he shone with the sublime consciousness that, were he to withdraw its beams, and retire, the world would be immersed in eternal night,—but that as many as should walk in his light would be brought, from the darkness and distance of sin, into the immediate vision and fruition of God. He could stand forth and challenge the profound attention of the world, with the full conviction that he was not only the greatest benefactor it would ever behold, but that he combined within himself all the several qualities of beneficence to be found in the universe; for he felt that, in imparting the gospel, he was pouring out the resources of Heaven, and conferring an antidote for all the miseries of mankind.

Add to this, the Son of God was perfectly exempt from the chilling perception that his motives were alloyed. It was peculiar to him, of all born of woman, to be entirely free from the taint of selfishness. "He pleased not himself." The whole of his course was a history of pure disinterested benevolence. He had assumed our nature for no other purpose than to display the glory of God in the happiness of man; and for this end he breathed out his life. When uttering his largest professions of sympathy and love, he rejoiced in the secret consciousness that he intended to do abundantly more than he had said,—that, besides the stream of goodness and truth which issued daily from his lips, he held within his heart a fountain of compassion, clear as crystal, as yet untouched, but which, at the appointed hour, would issue forth, far exceeding expectation, and blessing the world.

And beyond all this, what must have imparted vigour to the tone of his teaching was the unclouded prospect which he enjoyed of its ultimate and universal success. "This gospel," he could say, "shall be preached for a witness among all nations." In its immediate results, indeed, it but too fully realized the representation of the sower, that went forth to sow. But he clearly foresaw that the incorruptible seed of his word, though for a time it might seem to be lost, was destined again to spring out of the earth, producing a harvest of holiness for heaven. In praying that his church might be sanctified by the truth, he felt that he was praying with the force of an almighty decree; that, in the divine intention, his prayer was answered as soon as uttered; while he beheld, in anticipation, a number which no one could number, already encircling the throne above, robed in the purity his prayer desired. A part of the joy which was set before him consisted in the distinct perception of a scene in which his truth, armed with the omnipotence of the Holy Spirit, having completed the conquest of error, given law to the world, and impressed her image on every thing human, was receiving the homage of a renovated race, and reigning in the new heavens, and the new earth, wherein dwelleth righteousness.

Recollecting that causes such as these concurred in the teaching of the Son of God, and bearing in mind the specimens we have adduced from his divine discourses, we are fully prepared to hear it testified, that "the people were astonished at his doctrine;" and that, "when Jesus had ended these sayings, the people were astonished at his doctrine; for he taught them as one having authority, and not as the scribes." Their established teachers, having long since completed the conquest of common sense, laboured to preserve the fruits of their victory, by the endless repetition of fables and childish traditions. The loftiest models of public instruction with which they were acquainted consisted in the heartless recitement of frivolous opinions and trivial ceremonies, confirmed by quotations more jejune and frivolous still; the very essence of insipidity. What then must have been the astonishment and involuntary homage with which they listened to the discourses of the Son of God! It was an era in the history of their minds. In their opinion, he spake as never man spake. For, besides that he addressed them in his own name, as the highest authority, he laid open scenes the most novel, and subjects the most momentous; carried his appeals into their conscience; made them once more feel that they were immortal men; stripped off every mask, and conveyed them, with their sins upon them, to the throne of God; annihilated the distance between them and the judgment day; placed them on the threshold of the infinite and everlasting; and effaced the recollection of the present, by the absorbing realities of the eternal future. Some hailed his preaching as a new and glorious light, while others shunned it as the forked and fatal lightning; each class bearing involuntary testimony to its commanding power. And, associated, as it naturally would be in their minds, with the recollection of his miraculous deeds; remembering that the demons had quailed, and the tempestuous ocean grown quiet in the presence in which they were standing; that the whirlwind had revered the voice to which they were listening; they could not but tacitly confess that he spoke with an authority which, if the sun were extinguished, might say, " Let there be light," and light would be.

In concluding an essay, already, I fear, too much prolonged, the reader will allow me to suggest its practical application. Whatever may be the characteristics of a perfect instructor, he is entitled to look for the counterpart of each in those he addresses. The authority then which distinguishes the teaching of Christ should be met, by his disciples, with submission and acquiescence. It is obvious to all, that the mental impression received from any object depends materially on the state of the mind itself. " If any man will do the will of God," said Jesus, " he shall know of the doctrine whether it be of God, or whether I speak of myself." His gospel is addressed to our moral nature; and the only mind in a state to do justice to the divinity of its claims is that which is trained and disciplined to habits of holy obedience. If we take to it a spirit which it does not approve, we are likely to bring from it a spirit which it has not imparted. Even the ancient heathens, when they went to consult their idol gods, did not expect to succeed without due preparation. Their approaches were marked by acts of reverence and self-purification. Before they hoped for the least oracular intimation, days were consumed in sacrifice, ablution, and meditation. They did not degrade even their false deities by supposing they would speak in the ear of levity, or waste instruction on an irreverent and polluted mind. Were we creatures devoid of a moral nature, or did the gospel address the understanding alone, we might then approach it as we go to the study of a mathematical truth, as beings of intellect only; but its aim is the heart; it is addressed to our moral nature; and, as such, it claims a free and undisputed ingress to the throne of the will. If it flattered our importance by submitting its truths to the tribunal of reason, pride would then be no unsuitable preparation for receiving it; but, taking for granted our moral disqualification, it " casts down imaginations, and every high thing that exalteth itself against the knowledge of God, and brings into captivity every thought to the obedience of Christ." Proceeding on the supposition that it is the heart which in its fall has dragged down the faculties of the soul, it proposes to erect them again by raising and restoring the degrading cause; it requires, therefore, that in the process they be submissive and silent. If we would learn of Christ, the soul must be vacated of all its proud prepossessions, that there may be room to prepare him a seat in the will. If we would listen to his voice with effect, there must be silence in the soul: the clamorous pretensions of self-sufficiency must be rebuked; and, putting on the robe of humility, we must take our station as children at his feet.

But that submission to the authority of Christ which forms an essential qualification in his disciples is not only opposed to the pride that rejects,—it is intelligent and conscious, and therefore equally remote from that unheeding acquiescence which admits with a fatal facility, and as a matter of custom and course, whatever he inculcates: if the former of these is the disqualification of rebellion, the latter is the incapacity of death. Perhaps no greater obstacle can be named, to the proper reception of the gospel, than the error—alas! how common— of placing religion in a bare assent to its truths,—of cherishing a settled and satisfied persuasion that we are Christians, simply because we subscribe, and in proportion to the unthinking readiness with which we subscribe, to its dictates. So effectually does this delusion enclose and encase the heart, that "the arrows of the Lord," though barbed and winged by an angel's hand, would fail to "stick fast in it." So potent is the spell, that it enables us to listen, not only to truths the most pungent, but even to the description which portrays the very delusion itself, without any self-application or effect. With such certainty does it turn aside and ward off every salutary impression, that, like a building defended from the lightnings of heaven by a rod of steel, we can venture amongst the forked lightnings of the truth, and yet come out from them free, unscathed, and untouched. On such a state of mind, the voice of the Great Teacher himself—its loudest, its most solemn and authoritative tones—are dissipated and lost.

The submission, then, which he demands, is that which arises from conviction, and consists in the self-surrender of the will; that which, while it admits, at the same time "trembles at his words." But where is this preparation to be obtained? where, but at the throne of the heavenly grace? It is only at the altar, and from the hand of God, we can receive that celestial torch which reveals at once our own incompetence and the dignity and glory of Christ. That is the appointed place of meeting between God and the soul, where he puts us under the guidance of that holy Spirit who leads us into all truth,—who takes the things of Christ as they fall from his lips, and conveys them as living powers into the obedient heart,—who prepares and delivers us into the mould of the gospel, that we may take the perfect impress of its author.

ESSAY II.

ON THE ORIGINALITY OF OUR LORD'S TEACHING.

SECTION I.—OF GOD THE FATHER.

In illustrating the originality which marked the instructions of our blessed Lord, it can scarcely be necessary to premise that, as the *mode* of his teaching will receive our separate consideration, we shall now confine ourselves to its *subjects*.

Were we claiming the attribute of originality for an uninspired mind, we should feel as if we were establishing his right to fame. For he who enlarges, in the least, the narrow confines of human knowledge, is said to confer imperishable wealth,—to redeem our mental character; and thus, owing to the unfrequency of the occurrence, he renders himself an object of homage to the species. But this is a quality which, abstractedly considered, has no moral character; it is a blessing or a curse only according to the direction which it takes, and the service in which it is engaged.

As the ultimate object of our Lord's teaching was of a nature entirely practical, it requires but little effort of the imagination to conceive why, if his praise consists partly in being so original, it consists also partly in not being more original than he is. " If I have told you earthly things, and ye believe not, how shall ye believe if I tell you heavenly things?" He could unquestionably have made disclosures which would have eclipsed, and consigned to oblivion, all prior discoveries. As far as power is concerned, he could easily have embroiled the polemic world, by mystifying, without misrepresenting, every subject of earthly dispute. He could have uttered a single sentence, which, by furnishing a key to many a mystery, and affording a glimpse of arcana before unknown, would have collected and concentrated around it the busy thoughts of each successive generation to the close of time. Opening one of the numerous doors at which human curiosity has been knocking impatiently for ages, he could have admitted men to a tree of knowledge, from which, age after age, they would have continued to pluck and partake, until the trump of God surprised them at their unholy feast, and found them unprepared for the summons. But he came to plant for them the tree of life, and to give them access to its healing fruits. And as he allowed nothing to divert his own attention from the accomplishment of this object, he guarded against everything likely to beguile them from seeking the benefit resulting from it. He disdained not the repetition of old and familiar truths, provided his introduction of them would subserve his grand design; for though he proposed to erect a second temple of truth, the glory of which should eclipse the splendour of the first, he deigned to appropriate whatever of the ancient materials remained available. Truths, which the lapse of time had seen displaced and disconnected from their true position, as stars are said to have wandered from their primal signs, he recalled and established anew; and principles, which had faded, disappeared, and been lost, as stars are said to have become extinct, he rekindled and resphered, and commanded them to stand fast for ever. Such, for instance, was the golden law of wedded love; which, though coeval with paradise, and the crown of its joys, had been partially remitted by divine sufferance, and reduced to a name by human depravity, but which he restored and republished as of divine and indissoluble obligation.

The reader is probably aware that, during the interval which elapsed between the cessation of the Old Testament oracle and the advent of Christ, many new terms came into use;* especially new epithets for designating the expected Messiah and the Holy Spirit; — such, for instance, as the names Logos and Paraclete; and, also, that various theological opinions prevailed; which, while they pleaded an Old-Testament origin, were taught, if taught there at all, only by inference and suggestion. Now when a person first becomes aware of this fact, and discovers also that some of these terms and opinions were adopted by Christ, and incorporated by him into his New-Testament record, he may be tempted to depreciate in thought the divinity and originality of these particular parts of our Lord's teaching.

But let him reflect, first, that, *as to the divine origin of these particular truths,* the persons who first announced

---

* It is a favourite hypothesis of the neological school, says Tholuck, in his " Hints on the Importance of the Study of the Old Testament," that " the Jewish religion, coalescing with the Persian doctrines, was brought to perfection, and *thus* served to lay the foundation for the new order of things which Christ introduced. This appears to us to have been the true origin of these doctrines. Providence designed that they should be disseminated just before the advent of Christ, in order that he, who was merely to bring the new Spirit, and, by means of this, to destroy the veil of the law, and to illustrate these doctrines, need furnish no system of doctrines, but merely announce, by his precepts and his life, the one great doctrine— *God hath so loved the world.* Those post-Babylonian doctrines were illustrated, however, by the instructions of Jesus and the apostles, to such a degree, that they appear in an entirely new and spiritual light, as the pure and disembodied spirit escaped from the lifeless body of the rabbinical system."

The difference between this hypothesis and the statement in the text them, no doubt, derived the idea of them from the ancient scriptures, and could have pointed to the precise passage or passages which, in their opinion, warranted the idea. And, secondly, *as to our Lord's claim to originality in teaching these particular truths ;*—this becomes a question of mere words ; for though originality was no longer possible in the sense of novelty, still his office was original—he was the first to announce these truths as divine.

Suppose, for example, an inspired prophet were now to appear in the church to add a supplement to the canonical books,—what a Babel of opinions would he find existing on almost every theological subject ! — and how highly probable is it that his ministry would consist, or seem to consist, in the mere selection and ratification of such of these opinions as accorded with the mind of God. Absolute originality would seem to be almost impossible. The inventive mind of man has already bodied forth speculative opinions in almost every conceivable form,—forestalling and robbing the future of its fair proportion of novelties, and leaving little more, even to a Divine Messenger, than the office of taking some of these opinions, and impressing them with the seal of Heaven. Imagine him to choose for his theme—that

---

above is so obvious and essential, that to spend a moment in pointing it out may, perhaps, be considered superfluous. But, lest the statement in the text should have the effect, in however small a degree, of preparing the mind of an unwary reader for the reception of the neology contained in the quotation with which it is contrasted, I will take the liberty of remarking, that, while the tendency of the latter is to detract from the value both of our Lord's teaching and of the Old-Testament doctrines, by admitting the philosophy of paganism to share the honours of divine revelation, the object of the former is to vindicate to the Old Testament the claim of having suggested the various evangelical phrases and opinions which had obtained about the time of our Lord's appearance, and to assert for him the honour of having selected and authenticated such of those opinions as were true, and of having turned them into inspired doctrines.

vinum dæmonum of the church in every age—the subject of a millenium; and may it not be confidently affirmed, that, whatever his divine doctrine might be, an anticipation of it, if not the identical doctrine itself, has appeared already among the thousand theories which the church has heard on the subject? Yet how important the office which would still devolve on him, in evoking the one truth, and dispersing the multiplied attendant errors— and how worthy of a teacher sent from God! Humanly speaking, the task of the aged seer, in selecting from the eleven sons of Jesse the future king of Israel, was easy, compared with the task of him who has to choose from a multitude of speculative opinions—all of which are specious and popular, and possessed of an apparent likeness— the one heaven-born truth, and anoint it for the Lord.

Now such was the relation in which our Lord may be said to have stood to some of the doctrines of the New Testament. Originality, in the sense of novelty, was, on these particular subjects, impossible: for the teeming mind of man, quickened to activity by some hint of scripture, had already occupied the ground with theories of every grade of merit, and opinions adapted to every taste. With these, hypothetically speaking, the Saviour might be acquainted, or he might not. On the supposition that he did not know them, the doctrine he taught on either of these subjects, however familiar it might already have been to human ears, was unborrowed, original, and emphatically his own; it had no other channel, in its descent from the celestial throne to the human heart, but his own inspired lips. On the supposition that he knew them, his office at least was original, and equally dignified; for still he proclaimed the particular truth, not because man had patronized it, but because he knew it to be the true saying of God. And more than that, he redeemed it from the base companionship of error, and made it free of the universe. He not merely rescued it from the gloomy region of doubt, but enabled it to shine in its own right, and to illuminate the surrounding darkness. If he found it one of the multitude, he raised it to the throne. If he found it a guess, he left it a doctrine—a living and incorporated member of the immortal body of truth. If he found it an outcast, he took it within the pale and royalty of truth, and surrounded it with the awful sanctions of the God of truth. He proved himself to be the Word and the Wisdom of God.

The power of recasting important truths from their old and worn-out forms, and of giving them to the world again with all their original freshness and force, is the peculiar prerogative of genius; but, though our Lord must be supposed to have possessed this power in perfection, he did not exercise it for his own sake. An acquaintance with the origin of some of his parables, his prayers, and many of his most familiar sayings, will shew that he often condescended to adopt the beauties of the Talmud, which were then "floating on the lips of the wise," as well as the popular proverbs of the day, and to insert them into his own instructions. But this by no means impairs his claim to originality of the loftiest kind. Intellect of the highest earthly order, though aware that its claims to renown depended chiefly on the exercise of its own creative powers, has not feared the forfeiture of those claims for borrowing the productions of inferior minds: it was conscious of a power of falling back, at pleasure, on its own resources, and of being ably sustained. Then how much more might he do the same—He, to whom all human thought is but one idea, and that only a fractional part of the infinite whole which his mind comprehends!—He, who, in his pre-existent state, had not refused to predicate of his divine nature the parts and passions of poor humanity, though at the hazard of materializing his pure spirituality in the crude conceptions of human ignorance!—He, who had proceeded even to assume that humanity, the mere figurative assumption of which was an infinite condescension, might surely be spared the necessity of a defence for the occasional appropriation of human thoughts. If his assumption of our nature was an infinite stoop of grace demanding our adoration, his adoption of any of our thoughts (though not to be named as a comparison) was only an adjunct and continuation of that grace.

Besides, this probably is only to be regarded as one of the numerous methods by which he was constantly aiming to lessen the impression which must have frequently returned on his hearers—as far as that impression was likely to interfere with his usefulness—of his mysterious and incomprehensible character. He knew, with a perfection of knowledge, that as the great and beneficent operations of nature are produced, not by abrupt and extraordinary interpositions, but by the calm and regular movements of its appointed laws; so, ordinarily, a method of instruction which violates the sanctuary of our settled associations, though it may startle, and astonish, and even fill with wonder for the moment, is far from friendly to the lasting conviction and future improvement of the mind; and, therefore, he disturbed their accustomed trains of thought as little as was consistent with the introduction of a renovating power, a new and transforming economy of truth. He sought access to their minds by the beaten pathway of their most familiar associations; he insinuated and intertwined his divine instruction with the network of their most hallowed recollections and sympathies; thus providing for it the easiest mode of admission into their hearts, and making them feel that his identification with their nature and interest was complete. But, at the same time, whatever of their most popular and admired lore he condescended to employ, he gave them an opportunity of marking his superiority to the most approved and honoured of their rabbinical teachers; for, however great its original excellences might have been considered, it came from his hands beautified with a simplicity, dignified with a power, and invested with attractions, unknown to it before.

In order that he might obtain admission through the common avenue of our sympathies, and build himself a home in our hearts, he drew his images and illustrations from the great treasury of our household affections, and from the most familiar features of nature. But *the lily of the field*, as plucked by his hand, has the freshness of the morning, and the dew upon it; and the homeliest fact, as unfolded by him, is found to contain the most treasured truths. Thus, by deriving his illustrations from humble sources, he not only avoided taking our feelings by surprise, he shewed us how all unperverted knowledge tends towards heaven by a law, and how all unsophisticated nature, rightly construed, is only an expanded page of holy writ; how every part of Eden and of earth must have teemed, and been vocal, with wisdom to the attentive ear of unfallen man; and how, to the mind which mirrors and reflects the lines and aspects of nature, truth may still be said to spring out of the earth.

But, though we could not have passed entirely unnoticed the circumstantial originality of the Saviour's teaching, it is time to shew that his claim to this quality arises from merits peculiarly his own—from additional revelations, and momentous disclosures of divine truth. Had he only commented on the volume of nature, had he even read from the book of the universe the names and titles of its author, our advantage, comparatively, would have been small indeed. That volume was originally meant only for the eye of sinless humanity. It uttered no prediction, awoke no presentiment of the fall; in no part of its hallowed contents could a line be found foretokening woe. The morning of the day of transgression dawned on the world, unconscious of the impending change. The sun poured forth as full a flood of living light; the air was as rich in fragrance and song; earth and heaven appeared to live in each other's smiles; nature lay open at as fair and bright a page as at the moment when God complacently pronounced it to be very good. The tremendous catastrophe of that day took it by surprise. So far from furnishing man with resources for the event, it was itself involved in the calamity; it was " cursed for his sake." So far from being able to utter a consolatory truth in human ears, it required itself to be solaced and sustained, for it lay prostrate and panting under its Maker's frown. Wounded by the stroke, and cumbered with the weight of sin, it sent forth a cry, in which all its natural harmonies were drowned; a cry of helplessness and of suffering, which has never from that moment ceased, but which has gone on, from age to age, waxing louder and louder, till the whole creation has become vocal with woe, " and groaneth and travaileth in pain together until now," labouring in its pangs, and struggling to be free.

So far from shewing commiseration, and whispering hope, there is a sense in which all nature stands ready to avenge the quarrel of God with man. Take, as examples, the histories of Pharaoh and Herod. When the former refused to obey the mandates of Heaven, all nature expressed its sympathy with its injured Maker; armed in his behalf, and put itself in motion to avenge the insult. The latter, affected to be thought a god, forthwith an angel, jealous of Jehovah's honour, descends and smites him; and, at the same moment, the meanest insects begin to devour him: the highest order of created intelligence, and the lowest form of animal existence, the two extremes in the scale of creation, unite to prostrate and punish his impiety. It will be found, in the history of the divine justice, that every element of nature has taken its turn, as a minister of wrath, to assert the quarrel of God with rebellious man. And be it remembered that one of these elements is held in reserve for the destruction of the world: he has only to speak, and it will wrap the globe in living flames. Meanwhile, he may be said to have laid all nature under a solemn interdict, not to minister to our most pressing wants: he has laid it under an eternal ban. Let there be no peace to the wicked, saith my God; let everything be at war with him. If he will be the enemy of God, let him live and die amidst a universe of frowns: let everything, in heaven, earth, and hell, be armed, and ready to assail him: *let there be no peace to the wicked;* and universal nature responds, *there shall be none;* and the universal experience of sinners, as it sends up its reply from the bottomless pit, declares, in accents of terrible despair, *there is none.* Could the sinner but open his eyes to the dreadful reality of his condition, were he endowed with a power of vision like the servant of the prophet, he would find himself surrounded, not indeed with horses and chariots of fire to guard him, but with terrible forms of anger and destruction, waiting to dart on him, and make him their prey. He would find himself standing in the great theatre of the universe, with every eye that it contains fixed and frowning upon him; with every weapon in the infinite armory of God ready and levelled against him. And the hour arrives when he finds that sin has arrayed against him, not only all the universe without, but all the powers and passions within him; that it has armed him against himself; that it has given a sting to every thought, and turned his conscience into a worm that dieth not, and his depraved and ungoverned passions into fires never to be quenched.

O how unparalleled the infatuation of the man who pretends that, from the doubtful and scattered intimations of nature, he can collect the materials of a sufficient creed, when at the same time they are so obviously intermixed with the fragments of a violated law. Nature, indeed, is still an oracle on one point; and when consulted on that point, which relates to the great remedy for sin, her spontaneous response is, *it is not in me:* it is not until man has examined her by torture that he extorts some doubtful reply, which—his vanity being made the interpreter—is found to coincide with his wishes, and to flatter his pride. On the fact of the divine existence, indeed, the protestations of nature are positive, loud, and unceasing: this is a truth of which she is never making less than solemn affirmation and oath, with all her myriad voices: the unintermitting response of the living creatures heard by John is only the echo of her voice in the sanctuary above, proclaiming to the universe his eternal power and Godhead. But, however able and ready to enlighten the inquiring mind on the fact of his existence, she could do nothing to dissipate the clouds of doubt and gloom which had gathered and settled into thick darkness round about his throne: on the anxious subject of his character, and his possible conduct towards the guilty, she has received no instructions, and is silent. By the introduction of sin, our condition has become preternatural; and the wisdom that prescribes for us, therefore, must be supernatural, or it will prove a physician of no value.

I. Jesus Christ, the only begotten of the Father, came to be the light of the world; and one of the topics on which he most delighted to expatiate and dwell was, the paternal character and universal benevolence of God. This, in the form in which it came from his hands, was an original subject,—a new gift to the world.

Hear his own emphatic representations: " O righteous Father, the world hath not known thee." " No man knoweth the Father save the Son, and he to whomsoever the Son will reveal him." " I have manifested thy name unto the men whom thou gavest me out of the world." Such are the unequivocal terms in which he declares that, at the time he spoke, the world was destitute of the knowledge of God; that this inestimable knowledge was his own peculiar gift, the chief treasure which he had brought into the world; that the impartation of it was in his high prerogative alone; and that, in the sovereign exercise of that prerogative, he had given it to his disciples, by them to be communicated to the world at large.

Nor does this statement require any qualification, from the fact that God had before spoken to man, " at sundry times and in divers manners." Without any unjust depreciation of the Jewish institute, it may be boldly affirmed, that it gave but a faint and partial representation of the divine character. What must have been the views of God entertained by Solomon, who, though he had been employed to build the temple of Jehovah. could forsake that very temple for an idol's grove? What must have been the God of the prophet Jonah, when he attempted to flee from his presence, and pettishly charged him with fickleness of purpose, for not involving Nineveh in destruction? It is, indeed, impossible to state the precise amount of the knowledge of God which is essential to salvation; but there is reason to conclude that, considering the peculiar advantages of the Mosaic economy, that knowledge was generally at its minimum in Judea. It is more than probable, that when those prophetic intimations were first uttered which contain most hope for man, and which we are accustomed to admire as splendid anticipations of the gospel, and worthy the meridian of the Christian church, they were either dismissed by their hearers as unintelligible, or understood with so great a reserve in favour of Judea as virtually to annul the prophecy. Besides, between such enlarged representations, and the restrictive spirit of their economy, a conflict must necessarily have ensued, which could not fail to end in favour of the latter. And when, in addition to this, it is remembered, that the whole of their law had become rabbinized and overlaid with traditions; that, notwithstanding their sacrificial types, the doctrine of pardon procured by a vicarious expiation was " to the Jews a stumbling-block ;" that all that was supernatural in their temple worship had been long since recalled to heaven, and all that was spiritual suffered to depart; that any of their moral duties were compounded for a pecuniary consideration; that the only heaven they knew was suspended, in their imagination, over the land of Judea; and that they were actually jealous of the Divine Being, lest he should take within the pale of salvation any part of the Gentile world,—it will be admitted that, of such a people, it would be difficult to underrate their acquaintance with the divine character.

As to the state of the heathen world, it is only necessary to quote the declaration of the apostle—that it *knew not God*. In Greece, where the dialectic philosophy saw its proudest days,—at Athens, where it was enthroned,— its last effort was to rear *an altar to the unknown God*. At Rome, the asylum of deposed and fugitive gods, the pantheon of the world, the genius of Cicero, though it towered above his age, could add nothing to the religious knowledge of that age—could only speak vaguely of a *numen aliquod præstantissimæ mentis.* From the moment that philosophy touched its meridian, in the hands of Socrates, Plato, and Aristotle, it began to decline. Reason, as if blinded by excess of light, submitted to be led by any who assumed the office of a guide—revenged herself, for the prodigious effort to which she had been tasked, by abandoning herself to the sorcery of the senses. Truth was pronounced unattainable; Virtue, impracticable; the temples of Religion were ceded to Vice, who found herself consecrated and enshrined in their inmost recesses; while the phantom of Happiness (for the reality had departed with its sister fugitives, Virtue and Truth,) was chased under a thousand forms and names; till the world, having applied its fevered lips to the poisoned chalice of Epicurus, concluded, in their intoxication, that they had found it in the sensual form of unbridled pleasure.

By one class, the idea of a Deity was discarded as a baseless figment of the fancy; by another, he was multiplied into "lords many, and gods many," the patrons of as many vices; and, by a third, his throne was removed to a distance, which relieved the world of his presence, and eased him of the cares of active government. This was unquestionably the creed of the majority; for it had this irresistible recommendation, that, by admitting his existence, it preserved the mask of religion, while, by transferring his seat to some unknown region in the outskirts of the creation, it saved them the practical inconvenience of regarding his character, or consulting his will. They persuaded themselves, not only that his habitation was so immeasurably remote, but also that his dignity and felicity were so essentially dependent on undisturbed repose, that the character and condition of human beings never shared for a moment his divine regards. This was courteously deposing, and complimentally dismissing, the god of their creed beyond the circle of their society. This was "atheism with a god." This was attaining the completion of their misery and guilt. For, by this virtual annihilation of the Divine Being, they destroyed every adequate restraint on vice, every encouragement to virtue, and every ground of substantial consolation to distress. The vicious might sin on, without dreading his frown; the virtuous might sacrifice life itself in the pursuit of improvement, without hoping to obtain his smile: and had all the sufferers which the world contained sent up one united groan, one concentrated cry for relief, they would only have been giving their breath to the winds. They had reduced themselves to the blank and cheerless state of being " without hope and without God in the world."

II. How different the view of his character and conduct presented to us by the hand of Christ! Drawing aside the veil which concealed his glory from our eyes, it shews him in his high and holy place, not in a state of silence and solitude, but surrounded by ten thousand times ten thousand, and thousands of thousands of holy, happy beings, and every one of them waiting to do his bidding; not in a state of inactivity and moral indifference, but in active communication with every part of his vast dominions, through a numberless variety of channels; not in a state of apathy, regardless of the world, and all its multiplied concerns, but as actually stooping from his throne and bending towards it, listening to every sound it utters, observing the movements of every being it contains, and approving or condemning every action it exhibits; it even shews him to us in the astonishing act of raising up the fallen and prostrate children of earth, and putting them in the way of reaching his own abode.

To exalt our conceptions of the greatness of the Deity, our divine Instructor describes him as reigning sole over all the universe of matter and mind; asserts the pure spirituality of his nature, which no material images can represent; ascribes to him a power to which easy and difficult are terms alike unknown, for to him all things are possible; and raising him to an infinite height above the loftiest created intelligence, declares that he stands alone in absolute unapproachable perfection. To enlarge our views of his condescension and benevolence, he assembles the universal family of man, "the just and the unjust," and takes from each of the uncounted multitude a distinct attestation of the divine goodness to himself in particular. He leads them abroad into the open fields of nature, and, lo, on touching their eyes, he surprises them with the sight of the hand which upholds the worlds, employed in painting the lily of the field, feeding the fowls of the air, and adjusting and succouring the descent of the falling sparrow. He appeals to every drop of rain, and to every ray of light, shed on an unthankful world; and they confirm his testimony to the supreme goodness.

But he informs his disciples that the amount of divine attention bestowed on any given object is proportioned to the rank which that object occupies in the scale of creation. If the grass of the field, then, share so much of the divine attention, can we form exaggerated ideas of the regard which he bestows on man? Having thus prepared his disciples to see greater things than these, he conducts them into a higher department of truth. He lays open to their inspection the volume of providence, and turning to the name of each one in succession, shews him that in that volume each has a page—that he has never been absent from the mind of God—that the page assigned to him contains every particular of his history, even to the numbered hairs of his head.

III. From this department of truth he leads us into a higher region still; for, having elated our hopes by the minuteness of the divine attention to our temporal condition, he has prepared us to look for a far more astonishing display of divine munificence towards us, as his spiritual offspring. Having already shewn us the liberality of his hand, he encourages us to approach and take a nearer view of his character,—to look into his heart. We begin to enter into the spirit of the exercise, to feel our hope taking confidence, and our anticipations growing sanguine; we become conscious that we must give scope and wing to our expectation, and urge it to its utmost flight, to do anything like justice to the occasion. But who shall anticipate the gifts of infinite love?

"God so loved the world that he gave his only begotten Son, that whosoever believeth in him should not perish, but have everlasting life." Though sin had for ages disturbed the equable flow of the divine benevolence to man, that benevolence had never for a moment ceased to accumulate, or lost its earthward direction. Through every hour of every age it had continued to increase, and was only restrained till a suitable channel was ready, and the world prepared to receive it. And now, when the fulness of time was come, the windows of heaven, the heart of Deity itself, was opened, and poured forth on the world a healing flood of heavenly grace. *Herein is love!* We will not presume to question whether a gift of inferior value would have been adequate to relieve the world or not; but God so loved us that he could not have realized his vast propensions of grace by giving us less; he so loved us that he would not suffer it to remain possible to be said that he could love us more; he knew that a donation of calculable value would only call forth an odious spirit of fierce and jealous monopoly, but he so loved us that he resolved on a gift defying all computation, and the very mention of which should surcharge our minds with greatness, give us an idea of infinity, and impregnate our selfishness with a transforming sentiment of generous and diffusive benevolence; he so loved us, that he would leave nothing for the most apprehensive guilt to fear, nor the most capacious wishes to desire; he laid claim to the whole of our affections, by pouring out the whole treasury of Heaven—by giving us his all at once. Herein is love.

"God sent not his Son into the world to condemn the world, but that the world through him might be saved." In order to enhance our views of the divine compassion, the Saviour, in this language, reminds us of the terrible alternative which outraged Omnipotence might have adopted. He carries back our thoughts to the time when God, after looking with centuries of patience and forbearance on the unparalleled spectacle of his holy law prostrate, and broken, and trampled under foot by a confederated race of rebellious creatures, came forth out of his place, and punished the inhabitants of the earth for their iniquity—swept them away with a flood, as with a besom of destruction. But man, insensible to the lessons of chastisement, was no sooner permitted to repeople the earth than he resumed his weapons—renewed his hostility to Heaven under circumstances of aggravation unknown before— and transmitted to his posterity, as if it had been a sacred obligation, the art and spirit of the unnatural war. So deep had this infernal enmity to God struck its roots in the human heart, and so wide were its ramifications throughout the entire mass of humanity, that even a solitary indication of returning friendship towards him was denounced as treachery to a common cause; the first relaxation of this impious strife—the first relenting sigh—was instantly detected by a wakeful impiety, quickened by hatred to an instinctive vigilance, and was summarily dealt with as an enemy in the camp. Man had naturalized the principle of sin—had consecrated vice in all its forms—had opened to it all the recesses of his nature—cherished and established its dominion by every species of submission and indulgence—and boasted of his new allegiance in the face of Heaven. The only law which kept mankind united, the only sympathy which held the unnumbered parts and interests of the world in affinity, seemed to be an all-pervading principle of aversion to God: and this was sufficient to bind them fast for ages, in one great and unbroken work of prodigious guilt. The destruction of the world, therefore, so far from being an infraction of justice, was only what justice required,—would only have been the natural course of things, flowing in the unobstructed order of cause and effect. A crisis had arrived in the government of God on earth, in which something great and decisive must be done;—prolong the delay, and the character of God will be compromised and gone. The voices of the souls beneath the altar were wearied with crying for retribution—the armory of heaven was open—all its hosts and equipments ready—justice had only to speak the word, and, in a moment's flight, the panic earth would have beheld its firmament filled with the careering fires and terrific forms of descending wrath. The Son of God had only to pour out the vial of incensed wrath, and there would have been voices, and thunderings, and lightnings, and earthquakes, and universal desolation; and all the holy intelligences as they stood afar off, on the sea of glass, beholding the tremendous catastrophe, would have said, " Thou art righteous, O Lord, because thou hast judged thus."

But at that crisis of the world, when every movement in the government of God was to be watched with breathless apprehension, when, had justice made the slightest move, everything that had feeling would have veiled its eyes in fear,—then mercy prevailed to unfold the scheme of love, and it became the office of justice to wonder and attend; then, when God might have sent his Son to condemn the world, he was sent—amazing grace!—to save it. Herein is love! The apostles never touched it but they instantly kindled at the inspiration of the theme. Conscious that their language fell far below their conceptions, and their conceptions below their subject, they could only exclaim, in the impotence of overwhelming admiration, *Herein is love!* The universe is crowded with proofs of his benevolence; but here is a proof which outweighs them all! How much he loved us we can never compute; we have no line with which to fathom, no standard with which to compare it; but he so loved us, that he gave his only begotten Son, that through him he might confer on us eternal life.

IV. But, in order to raise our estimate of the divine benevolence, the Saviour not only announces that he brings from Heaven the infinite donation of eternal life; *he points our attention to the means of mercy.* " For as Moses lifted up the serpent in the wilderness, so must the Son of man be lifted up." Everlasting life is a gift so ineffably great, an alternative so vast, for creatures who had reached, who were crossing, the confines of endless death, that had it cost the Almighty but a mere volition, had it been the result of a fiat as easy and unexpensive as that which gave birth to light, it would still have rendered his grace the theme and wonder of the universe. But, however spontaneous the love which projected the plan of mercy, the execution of that plan asks for more than the simple volitions which created the world, or the unconstrained and tranquil circulation of the power which sustains it: *The Son of Man must be lifted up.* He must yield to conditions of which an infinite nature alone is capable; and, in yielding to which, all that infinite capability will be in stress. At the time he spoke, he had already made an infinite stoop, in consenting to an actual junction with the nature that had sinned, and on which sin was to be punished. But this was only the prologue of the act of mercy. He had joined the offending nature to his own, for the distinct and deliberate object of pouring out the blood which flowed through its veins, and of making its soul an offering for sin. His whole life was only a preface to his death. Having taken a survey of all that would be required from the surety of sinners,—having cast up and pondered the mighty sum of guilt to be cancelled, and measured with his eye the thunder-stores of wrath which must be exhausted, and fathomed the pit which to them was bottomless,—he pressed the entire responsibility to his heart, and addressed himself to the task. Our nature, to him, was a robe of suffering, assumed expressly that, when the crisis of our redemption came, justice might find him sacrificially attired and prepared for the altar, a substance which her sword could smite, a victim which could agonize and die. And if the human soul admits of an indefinite enlargement, in its capacity of pleasure and pain—if the admission of the purified spirit to the uncreated splendour above augments that capacity to such a degree that almost an infinite of emotion can be compressed into the space of a moment—what must have been the measureless capability of the human soul, which he took into so perfect a union with his divinity that the two natures composed only one person,—what must have been the acquired intensity of its antipathy to sin, and what the consequent intensity of his exceeding sorrow, when, being in agony, he had, in a sense, to absorb the infinite mass of human guilt, and to exhaust, in one short moment, the mighty cup of omnipotent wrath!

For the key to all this mystery of compassion, the Saviour himself refers us to the love of God. While we are standing before his cross, and musing on that amazing expedient of mercy, the holy Sufferer himself raises his eyes to heaven for its origin, and looks at the heart of God. He impresses on us the sublime fact, that the Father loves us, not in consequence of the great propitiation, but that he provided the propitiation because he loved us; because he was bent on obtaining a medium through which he could pour out the ocean-fulness of his love upon us.

Of all the remarkable declarations of Christ, when the love of God was his theme, one of the most striking, perhaps, and one which seems to place us in an unusually favourable position for looking at the divine benevolence, is the memorable sentence—" Therefore doth my Father love me, *because I lay down my life,* that I might take it again ...... because I lay down my life for the sheep :" in other words, " My Father loves you with a love so unbounded that he even loves me the more for dying to redeem you. He so loves you, that whatever facilitates the expression of his love receives an expression of his divine esteem: by sustaining your liabilities, by surrendering my life as an equivalent for your transgressions, and thus vindicating his law from all appearance of connivance at sin, I am setting his compassion at liberty; I am removing a restraint from his love, which threatened to hold it in eternal suspense; I am enabling his grace to act, to save whom it will; and for thus concurring in his benevolent purpose, and opening an ample channel for the tide of his love to flow in, the Father loves me; I receive such additional expressions of his complacency, that, though ineffably beloved from eternity, he may be said to have added infinite delight to infinite."

And how does it enhance our conceptions of the divine compassion, when we reflect that there is a sense in which the sufferings of Christ were the sufferings of the Father also. From eternity, their divine subsistence in the unity of the Godhead had been only short of identity; nor could the circumstance of the Saviour's humiliation in the slightest degree relax the bonds of this mutual in-being: while walking the earth in the form of a servant, he could still affirm, " My Father is in me, and I in him. . . . . . I and my Father are one." Once and again did the paternal complacency overflow, surprising the world with expressions of infinite delight, and inviting us to resign our hearts, at once and for ever, to his beloved Son: besides which, numerous intimations are given, that the mysterious interchange of divine affection which had existed from eternity, continued in undiminished activity; that the Incarnate Word was often surrounded as with an atmosphere instinct with love, into which God had breathed the elements of the joy which he had with the Father before the world was; that, had the great designs of mercy allowed, the parental love, as if impatient of his continuance on earth, would have borne him from the world, and resumed him to himself again.

The love of God, then, invites our adoration, not only as it, at first, sent his only begotten Son: during every moment of the Saviour's sojourn on earth, that love was repeating its gift, was making an infinite sacrifice for sinners; while every pang he endured in the prosecution of his work was the infliction of a wound in the very heart of paternal love. Who, then, shall venture to speak of the appeal which was made to that love, of the trial to which that love was put, when the blessed Jesus took into his hand the cup of suffering, when his capacity for suffering was the only limitation his sufferings knew? If it be true, that God is always in vital, sympathetic communication with every part of the suffering creation,—that, as the sensorium of the universe, he apprehends every emotion, and commiserates every thrill of anguish,—how exquisitely must he have felt the filial appeal when, in the extremity of pain, in the very crisis of his agonizing task, the Saviour cried, " My God, my God, why hast thou forsaken me!" Were it possible for a moment to occur in which the worship of Heaven could be lost on the divine attention—in which the infinite mind could be concentrated and confined to one object alone—that, surely, must have been the moment;—were it possible that any juncture could have arrived in which the paternal love could have repented the sacrifice it had made for man, that, surely, must have been the hour.

What a new and amazing insight, then, does it give us into his love for sinners, that it was able to bear the stress of that crisis, that it did not yield and give way to the incalculable power of that appeal. This is a circumstance which, if I may so say, puts into our hands a line enabling us to fathom his love to an infinite depth; but we find it immeasurably deeper still. It invests the attractions of the cross with augmented power; for in the sufferings of that scene we behold more—if more we are capable of seeing—more even than the love of Christ; in every pang which is there endured, we behold the throes of paternal love, the pulsations and tears of infinite compassion; more than the creation in travail, the divine Creator himself travailing in the greatness of almighty love.

V. But if this be an outline of the *means* of mercy, what can be the nature of that *end* which justifies the employment of such means? To enlarge our views of the divine benevolence, the Saviour announces that he brings from Heaven the vast donation of eternal life; that the sole object of God, in sending him to be lifted up, is, that we might have everlasting life. The separation which sin had effected between God and man had robbed us of a whole order of life. All that remained to us on earth was a masked and modified form of death; and, as to the future, there was nothing left us but to perish for ever. Here, then, was scope for divine benevolence to do as little or as much as it chose. Here was a wide waste of misery, inferior only to the blank and limitless desolation of hell, in which divine compassion could find room to expatiate at large; and in which, while its richest stores could be all employed, its smallest gift would be an infinite gratuity—shewing like a single star in the darkness of midnight.

But he chose it to be the theatre of his mightiest grace. As if heaven, with all its amplitude, were too confined, he sought to enlarge the sphere of his beneficence by the addition of another province; and, as if to take the universe by surprise, to put forth his grace in a form which it had not entered into the busy and far-reaching minds of angels to conceive, he chose that that province should be this sinking world. But there is suspended over it a sweeping sentence of utter condemnation; the clouds of wrath are collected around it; the materials of destruction have been piled up for ages, and still they continue to increase; it is the place where Satan's seat is, and all its population he holds in allegiance; it is the immediate precincts and neighbourhood of hell. Yes, but these are the mighty impediments which it is the glory of God to cope with and overcome; these are the hopeless materials, the elements of damnation, out of which he delights to raise the fabric of eternal life. To deliver us only from the impending evil, or to confer on us merely a limited good, could not have satisfied his paternal heart. Having committed himself to the amazing work of our redemption, he resolved that he would spare nothing, however costly,—withhold nothing, however dear,—which was essential to the consummation of the design. Having begun to bless us, he determined that he would not stop short of heaven itself,—that he would not stop even there, but would continue to surround us with favours, to heap on us gift after gift, until he had filled our capacity for enjoyment, and had opened to us all the treasures of eternal life.

For this high purpose his peculiar presence was necessary amongst us; accordingly, he erected a throne on earth, making it the scene of his especial grace, and of wonders surpassing those of heaven. The course of justice requires that sin should be, not merely pardoned, but punished, or expiated: he compasses both, by appointing his only begotten Son, first, to expiate, and then forgive. But man is severed from the life of God; his soul is so palsied and disabled by the deadly poison of sin, that his spiritual system is incapable of appropriating and circulating the element of a divine life, were it even provided; and so prone, so ingenious is he to pervert every blessing he receives, and to employ it as a weapon against the divine Bestower, that Providence can hardly dare to bless him. But God is not to be thus defeated: he sent his Son to assume our humanity; that through him he might open the springs of his life-giving nature anew, and henceforth maintain a perpetual stream of his vital and transforming spirit; that, by this mysterious adjunction of our nature to his, he himself might henceforth live through all the powers of the soul—light, in its understanding; love, in its affections; a perpetual current of blessedness and joy, blended with the stream of its own consciousness; and life to its immortality, life of the most exalted order. But the properties of that life, who on earth shall describe? It is more than a simple element of good, a single blessing; it is a vast assemblage of blessings. All other things, at best, are only accessaries to happiness; this is happiness itself. Compared with this, a bare perpetuity of existence is only a mockery of life, deserves only the name of death: this is existence enriched with the highest positive blessedness; life purified, exalted, applied to the loftiest purposes, carried out to its utmost extent of enjoyment; the very crown of being. Everlasting life is a name for a blessing which enables us to challenge with impunity the universe of evil, and to write our names, as heirs, on all the universe of good; it is God himself multiplied in the souls of his people.

VI. And, as the representative of the Father, our blessed Lord *offered this gift to all.* Human reason, arguing from the limited application of the benefit, would infer that the extent of the love which provided, and the value of the means which procured it, are limited also; would examine them by the torture of its logic, and bring its insignificant line to the measurement of boundless grace. Human selfishness would make a monopoly of eternal life. The Jewish Christians would fain have made it a local and national benefit; till the unconfinable Spirit came, and shewed them that, like the air, it belonged to the world. And the inheritors of their selfishness, in every succeeding age, have attempted to number Israel, to count the people,—have adhered to the persuasion that the great gift of eternal life is only to be offered to a party. But an attempt to imprison the air, and to enchain the light, would be wise and salutary compared with this.

Of the angels that kept not their first estate, we read, that God hath reserved them in everlasting chains, under darkness, unto the judgment of the great day. From which we learn, that when any part of the creation sins, and falls away from God, the natural, direct, and, if mercy interpose not, the inevitable consequence of such apostacy is, everlasting and remediless punishment. Why did not sin then entail this awful consequence on man? Why is it that some other race of intelligent beings is not, at this moment, reading concerning us what we have just quoted of the apostate angels—that the race of man, the inhabitants of the earth, who kept not their first estate, God hath reserved in everlasting chains of darkness against the judgment of the great day? Our only reply is, that God, having designed our salvation, devised an expedient, in the sacrifice of Christ, of unlimited value—unlimited, by right of its own nature, as God himself is infinite; so that the love of God, acting through the atonement of Christ, has been from the beginning of time, keeping all the living out of hell, and conducting multitudes to heaven; and thus operating, as it is at this moment, in favour of all mankind. To this source it is that our Lord would have us to ascribe our common mercies; he would put every individual of our race to take a census of the divine favours; to compute how many of these he enjoys in common with the species, and how many, besides, are conferred in particular on himself; and, finally, to draw the inevitable conclusion, that universality belongs to the divine goodness. And, while his ordinary blessings are chartered to the world, shall the stigma of exclusiveness be reserved for his grace alone? "I am the light of the world," said Christ; a blessing, universal as the light. He came to demolish every wall of partition, to throw open every compartment in the temple of creation, that every worshipper might have free and equal access to the God of the temple. He so unveiled and presented the character of God, that every human being should feel it to be looking on himself, casting an aspect of benignity directly on himself. The message of mercy which he brought from the Father was meant for the ear of the world; "whoso hath ears to hear, let him hear." And supposing the world to be assembled, and audience obtained, this was the music which broke from his lips— "God so loved the world, that he gave his only begotten Son, that whosoever believeth in him should not perish, but have everlasting life." He gave him, to encircle the world with an atmosphere of grace, as real and universal as the elemental air which encompasses and circulates around the globe itself; and whoever chooses to inhale it hath eternal life.

Herein is love! That he should have raised our world from the gloomy suburbs of hell, and have lifted it into the radiance of an orbit next his throne; that he should have made our hatred subserve the purposes of his love, and have educed from our evil a greater good than would otherwise have existed; that he should have adopted our nature into the person of his Son, and have carried it to the highest throne of the highest heavens; that he should confer on us an honour, to which a retinue of angels would form no comparison, no addition—himself inhabiting and possessing us with his own life, making us instinct with his own Spirit; that the origin of all this should be his spontaneous love; that the means of it should be the incarnation and death of his only begotten Son; and its consummation—but for that we have at present only a name, standing in the stead of an infinite meaning—everlasting life;—whatever the point from which we contemplate his love, the prospect widens into infinitude; the subject grows in our hands; amasses glory on glory, till it becomes too bright for contemplation, and towers as high as the heaven is above the earth. O what a God, what a Father, what an ocean of love is the God of our salvation! Having collected all the riches of the universe, and laid open all the resources of his infinite nature, he gave them all into the hands of Christ, and said, "These, all these, are for man; use them for man; distribute them to men; if necessary, confer them all upon man, in order to convince him that there is no love in the universe but mine, and that his happiness consists in loving me, and giving himself to me in return." In discharge of this momentous trust, the Word became flesh, and dwelt among us. It was to render this vast deposit available that he sprinkled it with his blood; an act, by which he, at the same time, both made it ours, and added to its original value an infinity of worth; an act, by which he created for the world a truth incomparably more precious than aught which the ark contained—that the richest gift, and the costliest sacrifice, have been selected by God as the only adequate expression of his love to man.

Our redemption by Christ is an exhibition of grace which God himself cannot surpass: unexpected developments of its relations and glories will, no doubt, through eternity, be constantly rising to view, and maintaining for it a character of ever new and increasing interest; our conceptions of its excellence will be continually receiving fresh accessions; but while its future glory may surpass its present in the eyes of the redeemed, God, if I may be allowed to say so, the blessed God, has deprived himself of the power of ever eclipsing that glory by exhibiting to the universe a richer display of love. But well may his infinite mind be satisfied with this as his crowning work; for he has now demonstrated to all his intelligent creation that there is no love but his.

VII. But the Saviour had not yet completed his representation of the divine character. He had rolled away the thick darkness from before the throne of God, and had revealed him to the world as light and love; but it remained to attemper the radiance of the light, and to soften and humanize the love. As long as we remain immersed in sense, we must be indebted for all our conceptions to sensible objects: hence the purest and most abstract of human sciences has its diagrams; and Christianity, the most spiritual form of religion, employs its symbols. The same necessity has, in every age, expressed itself in ardent desires for sensible manifestations of the Divine Being. The entreaty of Moses, " I beseech thee shew me thy glory," was again repeated by Philip, when he said, " Shew us the Father, and it sufficeth us;" and both requests were only the echo of a universal desire,—a desire of the mind for something to sustain it in its most etherial of efforts, its endeavours to think of God.

Another necessity requiring to be met, was the exaggerated fears of the penitent sinner, when interpreting the rectorial office of the Father in the covenant of grace into a proof of his avenging inexorableness. In the ministry of the gospel, the constant reference which is necessarily made to his just requirements in maintaining the rights of Deity, is extremely liable to produce on a mind perturbed with guilt an impression of dread, which no mere abstract description of the love of God can effectually remove; which makes it impossible to speak of that love in terms of excess. Now, of both these necessities, the Saviour took special cognizance; against each of them he fully provided, when, standing forth before the eye of the world, he proclaimed himself the perfect representative of the Father; and, in that capacity, challenged, for the Father, the confidence, and affection, and cordial allegiance, of mankind. " I am in the Father," said he, " and the Father is in me ;"..." from henceforth ye know him, and have seen him. Philip saith unto him, Lord, shew us the Father, and it sufficeth us. Jesus saith unto him, Have I been so long time with you, and yet hast thou not known me, Philip? He that hath seen me hath seen the Father; and how sayest thou then, Shew us the Father? Believest thou not that I am in the Father, and the Father in me? ... the Father that dwelleth in me, he doeth the works. Believe me that I am in the Father, and the Father in me: or else believe me for the very works' sake." " I and my Father are one."

Instead of leaving our faith to apprehend an infinite abstraction, he has, in his own person, invested the Deity with that power over our minds which a definite object alone can exercise. Instead of claiming our affections merely for the invisible and impalpable cause of mercy, he wrestles with our fears, and challenges our embracing affections, by protesting that there is no feature to be loved in himself which is not equally to be loved in the character of God—that if we admire the tenderness and compassion of his character, we are admiring the very same qualities in the Father—that we do injustice to his representative character if we do not receive it entire as a perfect reduplication of the mind of God. He would have us to believe, and to act on the belief, that so far from attempting to bribe and beguile our affections for God, by expressing for us a kindness to which the heart of God does not respond, he could not have omitted a single expression of that kindness without giving us a defective idea of the divine benevolence; that so utterly impossible would it be for him to give us an exaggerated conception of that benevolence, that could we by any process collect and concentrate all the varied expressions of his grace to a focal point, and receive the effect of the whole entire and at once, that effect, after all, would be a bare and inadequate impression of the love of God to man. Whatever doctrine of grace he propounds, whatever promise he gives, whatever deed of love he performs, whatever divine attractions he exhibits,—every such attraction in him is to be regarded as an index to the same quality indefinitely greater in the character of God. The conduct of Christ is a copy, a living map of the immense expanse of the divine perfections, reduced from its infinite dimensions, and subdued to a scale studiously adapted to the feeble vision of man. The character of God, so infinitely reduced, is to be seen in the life of Christ; the excellences of Christ, if infinitely magnified and restored to their original proportions, are to be found in the perfections of God. The character of Christ is the conception of a being of infinite amiableness, seeking to engage the heart of a world that reasons by analogy, and to enamour it of divine excellence. How often did he authenticate the life of Jesus, and give it currency as a copy of his own. Had the Almighty Father veiled his glories, and dwelt among us, the history which now belongs to Christ would have related, word for word, his own condescending grace; so that, in every word and act of Jesus, we are to recognise, in effect, the voice and movements of paternal love.

In the person of Christ we behold the eternal God engaged in an enterprise of boundless mercy. To aid our conceptions of his being, he clothes his spirituality in the vestments of humanity. To convince us that an unlimited concern for our souls may co-exist with the utmost hatred of our sins, he shews us that the river of the water of life takes its rise from under his throne; he plants a cross, and provides a sacrifice, and enacts before the world a prodigy of mercy, of which this is the only adequate solution, that he *so loved us.* That no unwarranted apprehensions of his greatness might efface this impression of his love from our minds, that all suspicion and distrust might be made impossible, he shews us that he can stoop from an act which saves a world to number the very hairs of our head; that his regard for the whole comprises a regard for each infinitesimal part; so that whatever has the power of raising an emotion in our breast, acquires, by that circumstance, if by nothing else, sufficient importance to receive his sympathetic attention. Disrobed of his essential glory, unattended by the train and state of heaven, as if earth was to be henceforth his adopted home, he came evidently attired for a purpose of love, mingled in our common cares, and inscribed his name on every object which speaks to the human heart. The cup of sorrow never passed him untasted; often did he exhaust the distasteful draught himself, and return the cup of gladness in its stead. The human heart, in his hands, might have become a sacred harp, every chord of which should have sent forth none but heavenly music. The history of his labours of love is the shame and condemnation of unbelief, the argument of faith and hope, the standing memorial of his claims on the undoubting trust of a dependent world: for it presents him, not barely fulfilling the conditions of our redemption, but far exceeding them,—going beyond the complement of grace, overflowing in supererogatory acts of beneficence, and anticipating the tender offices proper to Heaven by beginning even here to wipe away all tears from all faces.

VIII. Having restored our confidence in the divine character, the Saviour sought to complete our love to God, by teaching us to address him by a new name, —a name which should be at once a sign of our affection to him, and a pledge of his tender regard and relationship to us. He knew that the name which is entwined with the dearest associations of the human heart is also the name which hath most music in the ear of God, and therefore he selected and encouraged us to employ it—the endearing appellation of *Father*. And that we might not be deterred from taking it into our lips by the fear of presumption, he continues to repeat it, again and again, until it has become familiar to our ear. Thus instructed and encouraged, he leads us through a new and living way, every step of which is hung with emblems of paternal love, adorned with memorials of redeeming grace; conducts us into the holiest of all, even to our Father's throne; reveals him there, surrounded with all the heaped and opulent resources of infinite grace; and then, in order that our confidence and love might find speech, and our poverty lose itself in boundless wealth, he adds, " Ask, and ye shall receive." " If ye, being evil, know how to give good gifts unto your children; how much more shall your heavenly Father give his Holy Spirit to them that ask him ?"

It will then, I think, be conceded that the character of the Supreme Being, as it came from the hands of Christ, was an original subject—a new gift to the world. It was new in the universal aspect of benevolence which it bears towards man, as opposed to those limited conceptions of his goodness which were cherished, if not propagated, by the Jewish economy; new in its mode of exemplification—for it was seen, not in the works of nature, the operations of Providence, or the rites of religion, but in the living incarnation, the real and visible person of his only begotten Son; new in its bestowments—for hitherto, however rich its gifts to his church had been, he had always accompanied them with an assurance that he had yet a gift in reserve in which all good would be summed up; and however various they had been, they all bore some resemblance and relation to each other, in value, at least, if in nothing else; but now, in the person of Christ, he bestowed the promised gift, eclipsed his former grace, and conferred a donation, which, as it was perfectly original, so it can never be repeated or equalled ; since every subsequent donation is only a consequence and part of the gift, and eternity itself will be necessary for the full development of all it contains; new in its paternal aspect—not merely representing him as our Father, but teaching us to address him as such,—to regard him as the fountain of all that parental affection which has flown down, generation after generation, through the channel of human hearts, and to believe that all the pity, compassion, and love, which he has ever poured through parental natures, are as nothing compared with what resides in his own heart,—that however much he may have imparted, infinitely more, a reserved ocean, must ever remain behind in himself,—and that all this is in perpetual activity, interesting itself in the wants, and providing for the happiness, of his people; and new, also, in the mode of its future connexion with man, through a Mediator—for since Christ came to declare the Father unto us, it is the exalted privilege of believers to contemplate God in Christ, to approach his throne in the name, and relying on the successful intercession, of Christ.

" And this is life eternal, that they might know thee the

only true God, and Jesus Christ, whom thou hast sent." Knowledge, of all kinds, is the wealth proper to a rational nature; but to captivate us with the knowledge of God, our Lord declares that this is the only science which conducts to happiness—the only wealth which can be converted into unfading crowns and eternal life. As the whole of celestial blessedness is often, in scripture, made to consist in the vision of God, so the whole of religion on earth is represented as consisting in the knowledge of him. Because, first, all sin originates in ignorance of God—that is, it is indebted for its existence to the absence of God, temporary or habitual, from the mind—it triumphs most where he is most completely unknown, or forgotten; it could not lift up its deformity, with the hope of being loved, in the strong light of his glorious presence. Because, secondly, were the mind discharged and clear of all the obstructions of sin, it would be only necessary for it to see God, in order to be supremely enamoured of him; the bare perception of his image, as portrayed by Christ, would alone be sufficient to change the soul, by mere intensity of love, into the same image. And because, thirdly, although the mind is filled with hostile influences, it is only necessary for the Holy Spirit to bring him before it, to place his character advantageously before its eye, and the sight attracts—softens—subdues—ceases not to operate, till it has transformed the soul into its own likeness.

Is it, then, producing this saving effect upon us? or is the vast and glorious conception of God inhabiting our minds to no purpose? Shall the knowledge of God, which Jesus Christ came from heaven to impart, remain in our possession, through a whole life, as a dead and useless thing? Have we nothing of less moment to sport with, that we must needs trifle with this? Shall it at last be reckoned our greatest curse, that we knew the blessed

God? We cannot even glance an inquiring look towards him; but Jesus advances to encourage the act, saying, "To know him is eternal life." We cannot place ourselves in the pleasant beams of his light, cannot be conscious of a single emotion of admiration of his character, but Jesus addresses himself to our rising hopes, and says, "You can be like him; you may even resemble the blessed God: Be ye perfect as your Father in heaven is perfect." We cannot cherish a desire, or breathe a sigh for conformity, but the Holy Spirit forthwith begins to transcribe his will on the inner man—to abridge and epitomise his likeness on the heart, in the process of regeneration. God, who commanded the light to shine out of darkness, is willing to shine into our hearts, to give the light of the knowledge of his glory in the face of Jesus Christ.

SECTION II.

CONCERNING HIMSELF.

"I," said Christ, "am the light of the world." He arose on the world an object as wonderful and new in his person and office as the sun when it first took rank among the stars of heaven; and, like the solar light, while pouring a flood of radiance on everything else, he remains himself a glorious mystery. Notwithstanding the diversified dreams in which the world had for ages indulged concerning his person and advent, and all the materials for fancy to work with supplied by the paintings of prophecy, and the significant shadows which Providence had thrown before, his appearance at last took mankind by surprise,—a surprise for which the world avenged itself, by arming against him, and all who should afterwards assume his badge; but a surprise which overwhelmed the church with a measure of gratitude and delight, to which it has ever since been giving expression, and the full utterance of which it reserves for a world where its strains, relieved from all interruption, shall be swelled and aided by all the harps of God.

The supernatural truths by which he is described are so early instilled into our minds, that we ought not to be able to remember the time when first we heard them; and, having become so familiar to us, it requires a considerable mental effort to realize the thought that they were ever original. But though the human mind had been for ages training to receive him, he found himself, on becoming man, a stranger in a world of strangers.

Judging from the conduct of his disciples, the Mosaic economy does not appear to have given them a single correct presentiment concerning him. His character and claims were so perfectly unique, that although their religion was instituted expressly to be his analogue—and it was the only thing in the world which did represent him—yet they did not at first perceive a single point of coincidence. Every truth which he uttered respecting himself fell on their ear with the strangeness of a new revelation, and, instead of being received into their minds with the welcome of an expected guest, had to create a place for itself, or to wait till they could feel themselves reconciled to the novelty. They were not, indeed, wanting in occasional confessions and ascriptions, which satisfied his claims and called forth his approbation; but much of this homage was involuntarily won by some sudden escape of his glory—some surprising display of his greatness; and the frequent inconsistencies in their conduct, by which that homage was, in a sense, recalled or neutralized, shewed that though a new disturbing power was at work within them, it had not yet succeeded in acquiring the dominion of principle and conviction.

Nor was it till after his return to heaven that they began to appreciate aright the claims of the illustrious visitant. Then, when the excitement attending the vision began to subside, they found they had been entertaining the Lord of angels unawares: then, when the Spirit brought all things to their remembrance, when the words of Christ were once more repeated in their ears, and the wonders of his life were made to pass in slow and stately procession before their eyes, they awoke as from a trance, and proclaimed that the Word had been made flesh, and dwelt among us, and that they had beheld his glory, the glory as of the only begotten of the Father, full of grace and truth. At the dictation of the spirit, they proceded to record a sketch of his life; but they laboured at no encomium; they left that life to speak for itself; they felt that in simply uttering the name of Jesus they were repeating a name for all that is transcendant in humanity, and all that is glorious in Deity. Henceforth they sought to atone for their past misapprehensions of him, by confessing and recording those misapprehensions to their own condemnations, —by shewing to the world that he had displaced every other idea of greatness from their minds,—and that if, while proclaiming his worth to others, they were called to die for his sake, it was the highest honour to which they aspired. The vision which John beheld of him, when he saw in the midst of the seven golden candlesticks one like unto the Son of man, was only, in one sense, an image of his surpassing glory, as he was continually present to the minds of them all.

I. Looking at the outline of our Saviour's character, which ancient prophecy had sketched, and comparing it with the more finished portrait which he drew of himself, it is obvious that, even supposing the former had taken full effect on the minds of his disciples, there was yet so much of originality in the additions of the latter that they could scarcely fail to contemplate it without receiving an impression of entire novelty. The pen of inspiration had recorded that his goings forth had been from everlasting: in illustration of this sublime truth, he raised the veil of the past eternity, carried back their thoughts through dateless ages before the world began, towards the unimaginable and awful place where God dwells,—assuring them that there never was a period when he was not there; *there,* as an object of infinite complacency; *there,* in a fellowship of glory with Deity; *there,* in an identity of character and unity of essence, a mutual intuition comprising knowledge which no created mind can be made to comprehend: that he, to whose human voice they were then listening, had *there* seen the cycles of eternity revolve, the ages of time expire, the fathers of their nation, and the lights of their church, many kings and prophets, and righteous men, fill up the measure of their days; and that thence he had actually come forth, and descended, to save the world.

Prophecy, indeed, had accustomed them to expect in Christ a duality of natures, and a consequent mysteriousness of character and person which would entitle him to be called, *Wonderful*. But what imagination was prepared, even by this exciting prediction, for the great reality? It is true, a herald was sent before to call the attention of the world, and to place it in a state of preparation for his coming; but, "should he condescend to speak of himself," it might have been said, " by what mental revolution, what new combination of thought, shall we prepare to understand him? Perhaps, however, he may maintain a reserve on this subject; a regard for our limited capacity, and the peculiar object of his mission, may induce him to hold the mysteries of his nature in abeyance." And he did so. He frequently made it apparent that his object was not to expound the complexity of his nature, but to pour into the heart of the world the entire advantage which that complexity was capable of producing; and that as he had stooped to the low conditions of humanity, he sought not tenaciously to assert the dignity of his superior claims, but considered his humiliation as consisting partly in dwelling on the degradation to which he had stooped. But though he frequently waived the subject in question, yet as often as necessity urged him to advert to it he must be confessed to have uttered "a new thing in the earth." *We* are in the full and familiar possession of his sayings: but had we heard him when first he declared—" No man hath ascended up to heaven, but he that came down from heaven, even the Son of Man who is in heaven"—"Before Abraham was, I am"—should we not have felt that we were listening to a being to whom all space is a point, and all time but a moment—that our thoughts could not keep pace with the rapid and boundless transitions his words required—that he was approaching a subject which the limited terms, and analogical language, of human speech have no signs to represent, no powers to convey; a subject of which our minds, accustomed as they are to the mere parts of things, to fractional thoughts, and fragments of truth, could receive only, at most, an angular point, a very obscure glimpse, and confused impression?

Had we heard him affirm, in the face of his evident humanity, that he was not of this world—that we knew not whence he came or whither he went—that the Father alone, as a being of infinite intuition, knew him to perfection—should we not have felt that we were listening to blasphemy, or else to the only being incapable of blasphemy, because he alone can be the object of it—that a principle of interpretation hitherto unknown to the world must be found and applied to his self-descriptions, a principle which may well be sacred to that purpose alone, since the language of no other being will need its application? Could we have heard him forgiving sins—asserting his right to do so, "even upon earth"—summoning the world to yield up its heart to him, to make its homage to the Father a pattern of its homage to him—could we have heard this without feeling that God must be present in the person of the mysterious speaker,—that the throne of Deity must be, in a sense, removed from heaven to earth? Could we have heard him emphatically call himself the Son of man, and solemnly announce that there is a sense in which the Father is greater than he, without feeling that it was an announcement which a mere creature could never have thought it necessary to make, and wondering at the greatness which could excuse and justify such statements?

Had we been the individuals to whose retirement under the fig-tree he was privy, whose history he disclosed at the well of Samaria, to whose unuttered thoughts he often adverted and replied, as others reply to our words, and to whom he pledged his unceasing presence, wherever we might be scattered, or whenever we might meet,—should we not have felt the natural impossibility of leaving the presence of such a being, and have yielded to the impressive thought, the unavoidable inference, that he who stood before us in mysterious combination with a nature like our own, was, at the same moment, present, in his superior nature, in regions immeasurably remote from earth — the sovereign and uncircumscribed energy of the universe? He defended his alleged breach of the sabbatic law by affirming, that in his providential capacity, like the eternal Father, he knew no sabbath,—that as the soundness of the man he had restored was the result of his healing power, so the repose of the universe was the result of his unremitting activity conjointly with the Father. With the same unaffected simplicity and ease, he both acknowledged inferiority to God and claimed equality with him, and promised to every Christian, in the Father's name, "We will come unto him, and make our abode with him." Now, could we have heard these new and diverse statements from his lips, without feeling that the being who advanced them was a new form of existence,—that in his person, time and eternity, infinity and limitation, laws the most opposite, met and were reconciled—that we beheld in him the grand anomaly of infinite majesty clothed with meekness, supreme dominion rendering obedience, absolute sovereignty exhibiting entire resignation, God manifest in the flesh?

Prophecy had created the expectation of an illustrious Deliverer, for whom a class of descriptive names had been hallowed, and for ages embalmed, and set apart, as sacred to him alone. The *Messiah,* or *Christ*—the *Son of man*—the *Son of God*—were appellations as incommunicable, if not as awful, as the solemn *Jah,* or *Jehovah,* of the Supreme Being; for they described a person and an office of an order so entirely unique as to make all participation or resemblance impossible, by engrossing to itself everything peculiar to it. Jesus came, appropriated these honours to himself as his proper right, and wore them with such an air of accordant ease as to make them his own, with such a port of unlaboured majesty as to translate them into an obvious and sober description of himself. If his right to assume them was challenged, his defence was prompt and complete; he pleaded the sublimity of his doctrine,—appealed to the superiority of his life,—referred to the admitted testimony of the Baptist,—pointed attention to the voice from heaven,—invited a comparison of his history with the prophecies concerning the Messiah, declaring that his life would be found to be a faithful comment on the sacred text,—and called for his miracles a splendid array of evidence, which forced, even from demons, the unwilling recognition of his claims, and left unbelief without any cloak for its sin.

II. Thus warranted by the constitution of his person, and standing on a mountainous accumulation of evidence, which enabled him to speak as from the skies, he proposed himself to our affection and faith as the unveiled character of God. This may be regarded as his grand, original, and all-comprehending claim.

1. Were it relevant to our subject, we might shew, first, that the actions of Jesus evinced the *existence* of God. Had man never previously heard, never entertained the conception, of a Supreme Being, the miracles of Christ would have inevitably suggested and embodied the grand idea. But he appeared among a people with whom this was already a primary truth. Besides, the scripture has nothing to say to the man who denies it; only this, that it is " the fool who saith in his heart, there is no God;" and " that the devils believe and tremble." The existence of the Deity is a truth fundamental of every other; it is the throne of religion: and it would ill comport with the composed majesty and stately grandeur of religion to be constantly proving or protesting that it has a throne. He who denies the divine existence, renounces by that very act his own humanity, falls out of the ranks of rational beings, and courts community and fellowship with brutes. Accordingly, religion, while it condescends to follow him to the outermost limits of rationality, and thus maintains its character for compassion, yet, remembering the state and honours due to its throne, abandons him there, and, proceeding in its onward march through an empire of intelligent beings, receives their homage, and perfects their intelligence, by reuniting it with the divine mind.

2. As the representative of Deity in this lower world, the Saviour, by his incarnation, *embodied the divine spirituality.* " Ye have neither heard his voice at any time," said Christ, " nor seen his shape;" shape, outline, dimensions, he has none; as an infinite spirit he *can* have none. How, then, can we think of him? for unless we can obtain some sensible manifestation, or definite conception, of him, we have nothing around which our thoughts can collect, or on which our affections can settle and rest; he will elude and escape our labouring apprehensions. It is

in vain to allege, that the sublimest material representation can bear no proportion to his glory, no relation to his nature; and, consequently, that it could not fail to impart to the mind unworthy conceptions of his greatness. Without some sensible representation of the divine Being, the understanding can make no approach to him, the affections have nothing to embrace: faith itself, like the dove of the Deluge, has nothing on which it can alight; it finds itself voyaging in an objectless universe, an infinite vacuity: and piety must suffer and pine, as in an atmosphere too subtle and unsubstantial for its present earthly constitution.

This feeling of want, this ardent craving after a definite object which the mind can lay hold of and apprehend, has been the most frequent occasion of idolatry and atheism. The doctrine of an infinite spirit was the only pure abstraction in the human mind: all other things were objects, had their appropriate images, and the power of imprinting themselves upon the mind by sensible impressions: while this, standing in the mind solitary and aloof, subject to the antagonist influence and constant encroachment of material objects, was unable alone to maintain its ground, and in perpetual danger of being displaced and lost from the mind. And hence, instead of making this doctrine a place of rest, men have made it a starting point to one of two extremes: they have either proceeded to refine on the nature of Deity till they have reached transcendental atheism, an infinite nothing; or else, advancing in the opposite direction, they have brought him within the sphere of the senses, and embodied him in the work of their own hands. Every erroneous view of God which the world has entertained was either scepticism, arrived at one or other of its numerous stages in its way to atheism, or else it was idolatry, resting awhile at one or other of its stages on its way to the opposite issue. From the moment that the doctrine of an infinite essence has at any time been deposited in the human mind, it has begun to evaporate; and while the sceptic, on the one hand, rejoiced in the vacuum which ensued, and the idolator, on the other, found or feigned a residuum, which he took and moulded into a god, they both concurred, at least, in this one sentiment— that the theory of an infinite spirit yields no repose to the intellect, nor object for the affections.

Passing by the peculiar provisions of the patriarchal church, we cannot hesitate to regard the Jewish economy, in part, as a temporary but elaborate construction for aiding the mind in its conceptions of a purely spiritual being. All the angelic visits, and supernatural appearances, with which that church was favoured, answered this end. It enjoyed a local manifestation of the Deity: the cloud of glory that dwelt within the veil resided there as a temporary substitute till He should appear in whom would dwell all the fulness of the Godhead bodily; and, probably, most of those devotional expressions in the Old Testament which raise *our* thoughts to Heaven, only carried the thoughts of the Israelites within the veil. The whole of their worship was a presentiment and promise of the approaching manifestation of God in Christ; and not merely a promise of it, but an actual provision to aid them in lifting their thoughts to God, and conceiving of the divine personality, till that more glorious manifestation should take place.

Behold, in Christ, the image of the invisible God! Having left the bosom of the Father, and embodied the attributes of God in an incarnate form, he came forth, and stood before the world, and proclaimed himself the permanent, adequate, apprehensible representation of the invisible Deity. " I am in the Father," said he, "and the Father in me." "From henceforth ye know the Father, and have seen him." "He that hath seen me hath seen the Father also." "I and my Father are one." It is true that he is no longer cognizant to our senses; but, having assumed an incarnate form, he is evermore visible to the eye of faith,—he can never ascend beyond the flight of the sanctified imagination. And if imagination be an attribute of the mind, and Christ be entitled to the homage of all our powers, then to depicture his person and portray his glory is not merely legitimate, but the most suitable and exalted object on which it is possible for the imagination to be employed. When he ascended up, " and a cloud received him out of their sight," were his disciples never more to think of God as manifest in the flesh? They are directed to look at the things which are not seen, to place them before their mental eye in the most vivid imagery; and of all the imaginable and illustrious objects in the temple above, he surely stands central and supreme. In order to inflame our affections, and carry our imaginations with him, he affords us glimpses of his offices and relations in heaven, and prays that we may behold his glory; thus making that glory, henceforth, the appropriate and engrossing object of evangelical faith.

Nor, in thus yielding to the dictates of piety, and the claims of Christ, can we be charged with worshipping his human nature. Though that nature is exalted above the whole creation—though it is crowned with glory and honour—though the fulness of the Godhead is in it—though it forms even a part of the person of God—yet the object we adore is he to whom that nature is hypostatically united, and who stooped to that union expressly that he might become a more palpable and definite object of our love. He invites us to draw near and contemplate this great sight; and, on approaching, we behold the invisible God invested in the robes of humanity, and emitting a glory so softened and subdued that our eyes can rest on it without dismay. In all our endeavours to raise our thoughts to God, the idea of Jesus comes to our aid, like the mystic ladder of the patriarch's dream, and they ascend and descend upon the Son of man. In all our acts of sincere devotion, we behold him by faith, standing betwixt us and the eternal throne, waiting to meet our flagging and half-way efforts, to assist us up the laborious ascent, to raise and present our spiritual offerings: or, if our devotion ascends still higher, to him that sits upon the throne, whom do we there behold but the image of the still invisible God, the Lamb in the midst of the throne. He is the great ordinance by which God and man commune together,— the appointed place of meeting between God and human thoughts; for as all the lines of the divine manifestation converge and meet in him, so all our devotional thoughts and affections centre in him also. And there is, we think, ground to believe that he will sustain this relation for ever,—that whatever may be the modification of the present economy, when, throwing off the accidents and relations of time, it shall retain only the elements and receive the impress of eternity,—yet he, as the light of heaven and the temple thereof, will remain the sole manifestation of Deity, to which every eye will be directed and every heart be drawn,—that no angel or saint will ever know aught of the invisible God but as it is brought forth and unveiled in the adorable person of Christ. Of the future visibility of the divine essence, indeed, we would speak with unaffected diffidence: but the prayer of Christ, that his people may be with him where he is, to behold his glory, while it discloses the chief ingredient of celestial blessedness, makes known also the conspicuous object of heavenly contemplation. By adopting our nature into a personal subsistence with his own divinity, he has given a centre, if we may say so, to the uncircumscribed essence of the Deity, and has prepared a spectacle for the universe, resembling, but ineffably transcending, the angel standing in the midst of the sun.

3. But chiefly did he rest his claims to the regards of the world on the ground that he was *the adequate representative of the divine character.* The condition of the world had rendered the advent of such a being, and the institution of such an office, indispensably necessary. The knowledge of the divine character is the great conservative principle of holiness, and the bulwark of human happiness: and it was the persuasion of this fact which led the enemy of man to make that knowledge the object of his first assault. He knew that, dispossessed of this, we should be divested of all our strength, and be the ready dupes of every artifice he might choose to practise.

And the awful results of his enterprise have proved the truth of his calculations, and must surely have gratified to the full his boundless appetite for human destruction. Planting himself between God and man, he sought to intercept every beam from Heaven, and to throw his awful shadow across the earth: the gloom of his presence fell like a pall over human hope, involving us in darkness that might be felt. It is true, there were many unobliterated traces of God to be found in creation, but these related chiefly to his natural greatness: his moral perfections could only be deduced from his own supernatural disclosures; and these, as they existed among the Jews, were intentionally imperfect. Truths the most vital wore the form of enigmas; the church was local and limited; the moral law was oppressed and borne down by the ceremonial; the sensible was appealed to more than the intellectual, sight more than faith; sin was only ceremonially atoned for; the eternal future was but dimly seen, and the divine perfections only hinted at. Theirs was an economy which professed not to be day, but only the dawn and promise of a day.

The office of revealing and representing the character of the Deity was reserved for him who had been from eternity in the bosom of the Father—the image of the invisible God. What no verbal description could portray—what no image in creation could represent—what the loftiest seraph in heaven would have shrunk from, under a sense of infinite inadequacy,—that Christ undertook, professed, and accomplished, to bless the world with a living, actual, adequate impersonation of the Supreme God. It was expressly for this that he stooped to employ the organs and faculties of a human being; for it was only by adopting that appropriate but humble expedient that he could make himself visible and familiar to our eyes, while working out and embodying the character of infinite love. Arrayed in a body which God had prepared, and not man, he challenged to himself the exclusive power of unveiling the divine perfections. " No man," said he, " knoweth the Father save the Son, and he to whomsoever the Son shall reveal him." He took, as it became him, the highest ground, for he felt that he held the salvation of the world in his hand—that the illumination of mankind was entirely at his discretion —that, at that moment, the fulness of the Godhead was in him—and that had he decided it should remain there concealed, the unrelieved darkness of the world would have been made eternal, and man must have perished in ignorance of God.

That he came to shew us the Father is evident from considerations such as these:—*first*, he claimed to be regarded as the habitation of Deity: " Destroy this, temple," said he, " and in three days I will raise it again;" "He spake of the temple of his body." To constitute a place or a person a temple, the indwelling presence of Jehovah is the primary requisite. The Jews could have had no conception of a temple apart from this; for in the holiest of all Jehovah had dwelt as in his earthly palace, enthroned in veiled and unapproachable splendour: nor could Jesus have intended to claim less than this for the sanctuary of his body, without offering violence to modes of thinking which had become sacred, and to associations the most precious. On another occasion, when standing in the holy place, he affirmed, "I say unto you, that in this place is one greater than the temple;" he said this while perfectly aware that the hallowed object with which he compared himself was, in their eyes, the image of everything magnificent and divine—that it was their heaven upon earth—that they allowed nothing to surpass the temple except the God who dwelt in it; but he could add, *the Father is in me*, in a sense which justified the comparison, and which turned even the symbolic glory which descended at the dedication into eclipse and darkness. Had the vision of Isaiah been repeated, "when he saw his glory and spake of him," it could have made no addition to the greatness he already derived from the personal inhabitation of the Deity. Had Moses and Elijah, attended by all the hierarchal orders of the Jewish church of every age, descended as on Tabor, and laid their official honours at his feet, it would have been only an augmentation of his glory in declaration and appearance. If, on entering his "Father's house," an invisible hand had poured out all its wealth before him—had all its symbols of power and office taken life and form, and settled upon him—had all its priests departed, its fires become extinct, and the last wreath of its incense mounted to heaven—had its ancient shekinah, from within the veil, emerged and enthroned itself on his brow — and had all its angel-guards made themselves visible, and fallen into his train, the enactment of the scene would have been only the homage of a splendid pageant paid to a glory unlimited and divine. The glorious train of the divine perfections had come down and filled the temple of his humility. Truth was seated in his lips; and thence gave forth in abundance unsolicited oracles, such as mortal ears had never before heard, nor the records of heavenly wisdom themselves contained. His heart was an altar on which infinite love could visibly burn, and in which it found for itself a sacrifice as costly and congenial as its soul could desire. Goodness and power employed him to assert their majesty, by bending all things to the further-ance of human happiness. In his breast, mercy may be said to have held her court, and in his looks of com-passion, which were always bent over human misery, to have found the most prevailing advocates and inter-cessors. Holiness could dispense with an ark and tables to contain its laws; for in his life its enshrined glory was made so transparent that even demons confessed him to be the Holy One of God. While justice, which had asked only an equivalent for the wrong it had sus-tained at the hands of man, found that the illustrious victim was the living temple itself—that though reple-nished throughout with the presence of Deity, the whole sanctuary was one entire propitiatory. Like the move-able sanctuary which accompanied the Israelites in the wilderness, he was the *tabernacle of witness;* having been made flesh, he came and set up his tabernacle in the midst of the human encampment, pitched his tent side by side with our tents, to attest the presence of God, to make us familiar with his character, and sensible of his love. The great inscription of Immanuel, *God with us,* was so legible on every part, that the thoughtful and reverent could not raise their eye to Christ without being conscious of feelings of solemnity and awe, like those awakened by the sight of a temple. Even the godless and profane, who armed themselves and went out to destroy this temple, were repeatedly abashed as they drew near, and forgot their purpose; disarmed and ravished at the sight of its divine magnificence, they remained awhile to worship, and then returned to confess their admiration: occasionally, they beheld the shrine of his humanity flooded with light, bathed in the glory of the present Deity—a glory which was obviously attempered and designed to make man in love with God, for it was full of grace and truth.

Secondly, his frequent declarations that he had received universal empire can only be construed as meant to establish his representative claims. Affirmations to this effect he uttered in terms such as these:—" All things are delivered unto me of my Father;—all things that the Father hath are mine;—all power is given unto me in heaven and on earth." Now for what adequate, what assignable reason, could this mighty transfer have been made—this transfer of all things into the hands of the incarnate Saviour, if not for the purpose of employing and making them known? Concealment could not possibly be the object of giving him this infinite treasure; for that end might have been equally answered by allowing it to remain where it had been from eternity—shut up in the bosom of God. But it was committed to him with a commission to make it known; it was given to him, like light to the sun, with a command to shine and turn our darkness into day.

That he was the ordained medium of the divine glory is apparent, *thirdly,* from his "making himself equal with God." The fact that he did this is here assumed; the object he aimed at could have only one alternative;

for it was not to aggrandize himself at the expense of the Deity, to sink the character of the Divine Being in the eyes of the world, and to erect his own pretensions on its ruins; his sole design must have been to furnish an adequate manifestation of the supreme excellence. That this alone was his aim is obvious; for if he ever for a moment intermitted his endeavour to enlarge our views of that excellence, it was only to realize the conceptions which his words had awakened, by giving to them life and form in godlike deeds.

The same end is evident, *fourthly*, from his uniformly referring everything good and gracious he did to the love of God. It is true, that in exalting the character of God, he was virtually magnifying his own; for they are strictly identical. But as far as his own claims, as Mediator, are distinct from those of the invisible God, he laid himself out to aggrandize the paternal character. Take, as an example, the declaration in which he ascribes his advent to the fact, that God loved the world. Had he attributed his coming to his own love, the representation would have been most literally true; but he would have us to see in it nothing but the love of God. Bent on alluring us to God, by filling our mind with a vast conception of paternal grace, he would have us to refer his own incarnation, with all its attendant blessings, entirely to the grace of God. He was content to conceal himself, to merge his own claims, as far as that is consistent with the laws of mediation, that he might occupy the whole of our field of vision with the perfections of God.

And that such was his distinguished office is apparent, *fifthly*, from declarations which are all but express on the subject. In his intercessory prayer, for instance, he declared, " I have manifested thy name; I have glorified thee on the earth; I have finished the work which thou gavest me to do;"—language which intimates that the supreme object of his coming into the world had been to illustrate the glorious character of God; and that, having done this, he considered his work on earth as accomplished.

III. It now becomes an interesting and essential part of our business to trace *his mode of divine manifestation*. As the Word of God, he partly employed the medium of oral instruction. And had he sustained the character of a prophet only, had he added no actions to his words, the clearness, unction, and fulness of his teaching were such, that the most evangelical writers of the Old Testament might have envied a place at his feet, and have exclaimed with the disciples, "Lord, to whom shall we go? thou hast the words of eternal life."

But a verbal representation of the Divine Being, even though it had come direct from the depths of the excellent glory, would have been totally inadequate to the ends proposed; and yet more than this would have been "above all that we can ask or think." Actions alone could adequately set forth the grace of Him whose natural greatness is such, that a celestial alphabet—a glorious arrangement of characters, composed of an infinite number of suns and systems—is requisite to express it. The acts of Christ were a system of sublime hieroglyphics, every part of which stood for some glorious aspect of the divine character; while, of that system, his words were meant to furnish us with the key and interpretation. Actions, it is proverbial, speak louder than words: his actions spoke with a voice which unbelief itself, though it had stopped its ears, could not resist, and which made itself to be heard, even by many who were dead in sin; a voice, which, beginning at his incarnation, went on increasing through all his godlike deeds of power and love, waxing louder and louder through the successive stages of his sufferings and death, his resurrection and ascension, till the Lord went up with a shout; and which still continues to swell in volume and power, as he goes on to work out the character of God, and evolve the glorious purposes of grace, filling heaven and earth, the illimitable temple of the universe, with the echoes of the grand announcement—that God is love.

1. Speaking of the mind by sensible representations was a striking characteristic even of our Lord's ordinary teaching. A memorable instance occurred in his reply to the messengers of John, when they came to inquire, "Art thou he that should come; or do we look for another? And in the same hour he cured many of their infirmities, and plagues, and of evil spirits; and unto many that were blind he gave sight. Then said Jesus unto them, Go your way, and tell John what things ye have seen and heard." He foresaw the moment when these disciples would arrive, and he prepared for it: he knew the object of their visit, and he arrayed his demonstrations accordingly. And what were his preparations? A company of the blind, the deaf, the leprous, the demoniacal, the dying; these were collected around him, and formed the materials on which he proposed to work; this was the selection of misery, the mass of disease and death on which he designed to breathe, and create it anew. The messengers drew nigh, and he made bare his arm: they arrived, and asked him to decide the question of his Messiahship; forthwith they received his reply in a series of stupendous miracles. He spoke, and the deaf heard his voice; he spoke again, and the blind opened their eyes on the blessed light of day; he put forth his hand, and the crimson fever faded at his touch; he looked on the dying, and they

arose and were strong; he called to the phrenzied demoniac, and madness itself fell down and worshipped him. "There," said he, "behold my reply! Go, and tell John what things ye have seen and heard, and abide by the right interpretation of them."

Similar to this was his reply, when Philip requested to behold the Father. "Jesus answered, Have I been so long time with you, and yet hast thou not known me, Philip? He that hath seen me hath seen the Father . . . from henceforth ye know him, and have seen him." The desire of the disciple to behold the sum of all excellence is the last effort, the noblest aspiration, of the human mind. The prompt, detailed, and definite reply of Christ shewed his high estimate of its importance, and his desire to give it a final answer. This he did *by calling attention to himself*: he did not rebuke the desire of being shewn the Father, but instantly and completely gratified it by shewing himself; while the only rebuke which his words conveyed was a tender reproach for that mental obtuseness which could ask for a supplement to perfection, which could look for additions to his own divinity, or think of the paternal character and existence as detached from his own; a remonstrance for the want of that spiritual intuition which should have discerned in him the concentration of the whole moral greatness, *the great name of God.*

The exhibition of the divine character was an end so sublime, that nothing could for a moment divert his eye from it; every action and item of his life was referrible to this, and subsidiary to it. In all he did, he intuitively saw how the Father would have done it, and he immediately embodied and realized the conception. The power which had replenished the universe with worlds and beings employed his human arms, and unbent itself in acts of healing mercy. Omniscience, looking through his eyes, spoke of the future as if it were present, and perused at pleasure the secrets of every heart. As the centre of the Presence which fills immensity, and the seat of the will to which all things are possible, he proved himself present where he was not seen; issued his fiat to distant objects, and received obedience to a mere volition. He made all-sufficience intelligible and familiar, by calling for things that were not, and they came; by making the capacity of the recipients the only measure of his impartations; and by the spontaneous emanations of a virtue which went out of him, and healed them all. Had the star which led the Magi to his feet been actually brought from a distant system, it would only have been a faint illustration of the way in which he brought the perfections of God under the cognizance of man. Those properties of the divine greatness from which previously we had seemed to stand at an infinite remoteness, he brought near, and domesticated, and encouraged us to consider them henceforth as our own.

2. "As the Father gave me commandment, so I do." Such were the significant terms with which the Saviour prefaced his godlike deeds, as, completing one stage in his career of mercy, he advanced and addressed himself to another. "This commandment have I received of my Father;" in other words, "In all I do, I am only consulting the will, and fulfilling the designs, of the eternal Father; so that the history of my earthly life will be the exact record of his purposes towards man, and the adequate manifestations of his divine perfections." Thus interpreted, all have an infinite moral; of which this is the point and essence—that God would vanquish us by love. Did he come forth from the Father? it was to annihilate the distance—to bring us across the gulf which sin had created between God and us—to place us in the domains of mercy, and within

reach of the tree of life. Did he join himself to our nature? it was to shew us that God would have us to be in the closest union with himself, and that as we cannot possibly be happy without him, so neither can his love be satisfied without us; that he is bent on reclaiming a race of creatures who, though they once rejoiced in him, have been lost from his embrace, and of attaching them to himself by a tie as new and astonishing to the universe as it is proof against all the dissevering powers of sin. He lived among us, consuming himself in acts of self-denial and labours of love; it was to teach us that God is always living with us, that he is an inmate of every dwelling, tasting every earthly sorrow, and regarding our wants as the natural channels for his fulness to flow in and replenish.

3. The motto of every divine dispensation to man has been the same, *God is love*. The original apostacy commenced in the disbelief and denial of this truth: for it is only by clearly discerning and cordially believing it that we remain in a state of allegiance to God. But if infinite benevolence was considered problematical by man prior to the fall, by what unimaginable expedient shall the problem be demonstrated to him, now that he looks on everything that comes from God through a medium of enmity? And yet this very truth did Jesus adopt as his motto; this very question he undertook to work out, and set at rest for ever. To convince us, therefore, that there was no dissentient principle in the character of God, that every property of the divine nature consented and subscribed to this declaration of infinite love to man, it remained, that as these perfections had been already displayed separately, they should now be all collected, and concentrated, and put forth in some mighty act of grace, in some definite, overwhelming, all-comprehensive, deed of love. This, and ineffably more than this, was

effected in the decease which he accomplished at Jerusalem. On his way to that ancient theatre of the divine perfections, declarations such as these were constantly on his lips : " As Moses lifted up the serpent in the wilderness, even so must the Son of man be lifted up ; that whosoever believeth in him should not perish, but have eternal life"—" God so loved the world that he gave his only begotten Son, that whosoever believeth in him should not perish, but have everlasting life".—" I lay down my life for my sheep" — " I give my flesh for the life of the world"—" I give my life a ransom for many" " This commandment have I received of my Father." Here was power, nerving his arm, and declaring that it would shew itself in him mighty to save. Here was wisdom, with its unfolded plan of redemption, calling admiration to its amazing details : and faithfulness honouring and accepting its ancient engagements : and holiness pressing to its heart the violated law, and meditating for it illustrious honours : and love, rejoicing to find itself thus supported ; speaking as confidently as if its task were already achieved ; bidding the world look up and smile ; and giving away provinces and thrones in its prospective kingdom.

Having thus taught us to refer his death to the divine benignity, having placed his cross in a line with the light of the divine countenance, so that on beholding the one we may be drawn to gaze on the other, he poured out his soul unto death. He shewed us that, while the hatred of God against sin is strong as death, his love to sinners is yet stronger than death. He brought to an issue the momentous question, which had been kept open since the fall—whether or not God is light and love. The satanic agitation of this parent truth was the origin of human alienation from God : and having once brought it into question in the human mind, and thereby sown the seeds of enmity against God, it only remained for the father of lies to water those deadly seeds, in order to reap the fruit of a continual triumph against the Supreme. Besides, by widening the breach which existed between earth and heaven, Satan might calculate on the possibility of at length realizing his own lie, of wearing out the goodness which only encountered abuse, of extinguishing the last spark of love in the breast of God, and of exasperating justice to doom and destroy the whole species. Every moment of four thousand years, therefore, he had turned to account, in fomenting the aversion of man to God. By a vast, unslumbering, and complicated system, the whole agency of evil had been kept in motion, and made to bear upon man, addressing itself to every passion, and entrenching itself in every heart; so that, in a sense more than figurative, the world, the entire mass of humanity, was subjected to a demoniacal possession.

Under such tutelage, (how could it be otherwise?) every dispensation and event was interpreted against God. Signals of reconciliation were hung out from heaven; treaties were set on foot; but men scowled back defiance, and exclaimed, "Depart from us; we desire not the knowledge of thy ways." Messenger after messenger was despatched to entreat their attention, "but they beat one, and stoned another, and killed another." During the whole tract of time, the principle of human hatred had gone on growing in intensity, collecting its materials for war, and daily augmenting in strength, till it had reached so gigantic and threatening a form, that if it was to be vanquished by love and not by power, it was evident that love must put forth its might in an act unparalleled, unimaginable, and infinite. Such an act was resolved on. Voices from heaven announced it. Calvary was selected for the eventful scene. On the part of God appeared his only begotten Son, wearing the form of a human being: against him came hell and earth; all the nursed and ancient hatred of the human heart, and all the immemorial enmity which had formed the atmosphere of hell, were there collected and concentrated against him. Love and hatred confronted each other. At that moment, of all the passions and principles in the universe, these two antagonist powers alone remained. All the diversified sentiments and emotions of created natures were ranged under, or resolved into, one of these two principles. And while the object of the one was to unite its whole force in a blow which should need no repetition, to throw all its accumulated vengeance into one annihilating stroke; it was the aim of the other, by receiving that stroke, to let the strength of its foe be exhausted, to vanquish it by submission, to reduce it to a state of silence and shame, at finding its powers and weapons all spent, while yet the object of its rage stood unimpaired, and even seemed by wounding to acquire strength.

And what was the sublime result? " Ye know the grace of our Lord Jesus Christ." As the demands of our hatred increased, his love rose with them: we aimed at his heart, and he promptly bared it to receive the stroke; and, behold, it was inscribed with the names of his enemies: we sought his life, " but," said he, " I lay it down of myself," " and he gave up the ghost;" so quick was he in anticipating the fatal blow, that he even forestalled death by the speed with which he voluntarily surrendered his spirit: we demanded his blood, but no sooner had his side been pierced than forthwith came thereout blood and water—a twofold evidence of his death; if not also a symbol of the twofold element of pardon and purity, and an emblem of the fulness with which the treasury of his heart pours forth more than we ask or think.

4. One might have supposed that the cross of Christ, as the great illustration of divine grace, would have been left to stand alone; that even he, whose name is *Love*, would not have thought of enhancing its attractions by any subsidiary aids. As the focal point of his divine benevolence, the cross of Christ is the jewel, of which all the created universe is only the setting: by what possible accompaniments, then, can its attractions be enhanced? He, who can challenge perfection for all his works, whose minutest productions are known by their exquisite finish, would allow no circumstance to be wanting which could grace and complete his master-work. By praying for his executioners, and, still more, by dispensing salvation to the dying malefactor, he shewed that, while dying for all, he was distinctly mindful of the exigencies of each. His cross was surrounded by a mass of the darkest elements of human depravity—a specimen of the gross, the condensed impiety which in every age would collect around it, to deride or to pray; but it became vocal with prayer, and gave forth an element of spiritual life; surrounding itself with an element of light and love which none could approach, without approaching at the same time a personal change. By associating Christ, in his death, with the condemned malefactors, the object of the Jews was to add the last shade of disgrace to his holy name; and had it been their aim to select such as, besides being the refuse of the vile, were the least likely to catch what they might call the infection of his character, they could not probably have selected two human beings more proof against the impressions of moral excellence. By saving one of these, therefore, in the hour of his own death, he created the most affecting and unlooked-for

illustration of the love of God; he shewed that whatever light might then be suffering eclipse, the solar fervour of that love could know no abatement; he caused to meet, in the same moment, the crowning act of human guilt in his own crucifixion, and the crowning act of divine benevolence in the salvation of one of the guiltiest of our race. He thus erected a monument, in the face of the world, to the transcendent love of God; a monument which, from its position, close by the cross, could not fail to be seen by every penitent eye which in after-times should be pointed to the Lamb of God, bearing on it this inscription—" Jesus Christ came into the world to save sinners; even the chief."

5. Had the history of Christ only taught us that sin may be successfully resisted, and the world overcome, even that would have laid us under vast obligation. But having assumed our nature, and espoused our cause, he looked on our enemies as his own; he challenged and assailed them in our name. He laid not down his life, till he could say of the conflict, *It is finished;* he retired not from the scene of blood till he could say to his followers, " Be of good cheer, I have overcome." His resurrection from the dead rolled away the stone from the tomb of human hope. Having carried our nature triumphantly through all the evils that can assail it; having collected at his feet the chains and weapons which were meant for us—all the instruments and spoils of sin —he would have us to know, that henceforth we have nothing to dread from our spiritual foes; since, in the same way, he will carry us triumphantly through all the ranks of hell, and the dominions of the grave, and will bring us into the rest that remaineth for the people of God.

6. Subsequent to his resurrection, the commission which he gave to his apostles, to publish " repentance

and remission of sins in his name, among all nations, *beginning at Jerusalem,* shewed him still inventive of new illustrations of the divine love. It was the act of a most clement sovereign, who, bent on convincing his rebellious subjects of the sincerity of his desire to replace them in his favour, should take some of the most traitorous among them, load them with honours, instate them into the highest offices, and then send them forth into the camp of the revolted, to proclaim his grace to the chief of the disaffected, and bearing in their hands an act of amnesty for all. "Ye have not chosen me; but I have chosen you, and ordained you, that ye should go and bring forth fruit." They had lived in the closest alliance with those who had not only said, "Come, let us kill him," but who had actually perpetrated his death with acclamation, as a deed essential to their happiness. But having reclaimed them from their disobedience, and engaged their hearts, he took them into his counsels, heaped on them his royal favours, shared with them his prerogatives, gave them a joint interest with himself in the success of all his designs of grace, and then sent them forth to his foes with this injunction—that they should first visit the men who had slain him—should let it be seen how affluent he had made them in heavenly gifts, how unlimited the access they enjoyed to his divine treasury; at the same time, exhibiting their commission, and inviting all to a community with themselves of these special privileges and grace.

7. The most affectionate parent can only endow his child with the accidents of fortune, and operate on him by the uncertain influence of education and example. However wise and virtuous he may be himself; and however he may yearn to share his piety with his beloved child, a communication of character is a transference which he cannot make. Everything else he may

succeed in imparting, but here he has no prerogative. Christ not only gave himself *for*, but *to*, his disciples. "He breathed on them, and saith unto them, Receive ye the Holy Ghost." By this emblematic act, he signified, not merely the impartation of miraculous powers, but the *inspiration* of his sanctifying spirit, the vital transfusion of *his own self*, into the souls of his people. He would have them to know that, henceforth, he and they can no more live a divided life; that he will live through their faculties, and act through their organs; and that they must choose with his will, and act with his spirit; that it may be no more they that live, but he that liveth in them. But, in all this, he would impress them with the fact—that he is only giving to them the glory which the Father had given him, that both he and they might be one in God.

8. An original and important part of the Saviour's teaching concerning himself is that which relates to his office of intercession. Perhaps no part of the Jewish ceremonial was more impressive, or calculated to fill the imagination, than the scene in which the high priest passed within the veil on the great day of atonement. Every attendant circumstance—the inviolable sanctity of the veil, which the people dared not to approach, nor even the priests to touch—the fact that only one man of all the human race was permitted to lift that veil, and pass within—the rareness of that occurrence, for to him it was accessible only once a year—and the awful Being, the ineffable mystery, that resided there—all conspired to fill the mind with emotions of the profoundest awe. On the morning of the appointed day, what must his feelings have been, when, having presented the sin-offerings for himself and the people, he took the blood of the sacrifice, and the incense, and, followed by the anxious eyes of the breathless congregation, he proceeded towards the awful

recess—when he reflected that every step took him nearer to the visible presence of the incomprehensible God—when he lifted up the veil with fear and trembling—when the veil closed on him, and left him alone with God—when his eye glanced at the mercy-seat, and saw the glory resting on it—when he advanced up to it, and instantly began to wave the incense before it, that it might forthwith be enveloped in a cloud, lest he should gaze on it, and perish—when he sprinkled the ark with the blood which he had brought in, and remembered the purity of the Being who commanded it, and the sinfulness of the beings which rendered it necessary—what a responsible office, at that moment, he filled! and what vivid, solemn, and lasting impressions must the scene have left on every thoughtful worshipper!

This must have been true, even of that large majority whose views terminated on the passing ceremony, and who did "not look unto the end of that which is abolished." But how much more affecting must it have been to those who remembered that the scene they beheld "was only a figure for the time then present;" and that, solemn as it was, it would eventually give place to a reality inconceivably more glorious. Let any one make the mental effort of transporting himself back into their circumstances, and he will find how impossible it was for the believers of that economy to conceive what the substance of that shadow, the reality of that figure, was likely to be; and he may also apprehend how much more impressive the sign must have been, from the very circumstance of their inability to decipher it. Doubtless "they searched diligently," and pondered deeply, the meaning of the enigma; and numerous and splendid may have been their conjectures of what would possibly be the reality. Of that reality it is our privilege to have been informed: and so stupendous is its nature, that we feel assured the sublimest preconceptions of man could not have come within an infinite distance of it. " We have a great High Priest who is passed into the heavens, Jesus the Son of God." " Christ is not entered into the holy places made with hands, but into heaven itself, now to appear in the presence of God for us." " By his own blood he entered in once into the holy place, having obtained eternal redemption for us."

The most copious account, indeed, of his divine intercession is to be found in the inspired epistles; but the announcement of the doctrine came originally and directly from his own lips. " *I will pray the Father,*" said he, " and he shall give you another Comforter, that he may abide with you for ever." Concerning the mode of his intercession in heaven, it would not be relevant here to enlarge. But, unless the whole doctrine be a mere fiction of mercy, (an idea at which every feeling of piety revolts,) the first appearance of Jesus there, in his new capacity, must have been as invigorating to the worship of heaven as it is encouraging to the devotion of believers on earth. When he went from the place of sacrifice, and stood in the presence of God for us,—when he arrived there, to find that the incense of his offering had preceded him, and had filled the entire temple with its odours,—that, as if impatient for his arrival, his throne was prepared, the hosts and orders of heaven marshalled for his reception, the splendid ranks and hierarchies destined for his future state and retinue waiting to do him homage,—and even the eternal Father himself waiting, with this grant of the world, this burst of infinite love on his lips, " Ask of me, and I will give thee the heathen for thine inheritance, and the uttermost parts of the earth for thy possession,"—from that triumphant moment in the history of grace, the services of heaven must have proceeded with new vigour, and every worshipper there have become conscious of a fresh motive, a crowning incentive, to obedience.

But however this may be, all the encouragement which the intercession of Christ, as revealed in scripture, is calculated to afford, is intended to descend and alight on the heart of the earthly suppliant, as he bends at the footstool of mercy. And what richer encouragement could the avarice of human fear, or our guilty unbelief, desire? What stronger warrant for coming boldly to the throne of grace could God himself supply? A faint illustration of this may be drawn from that part of the former economy to which allusion has already been made—the feast of atonement. Suppose, among the thousands that came up to Jerusalem at that annual solemnity, a penitent Israelite entered the temple with fear and trembling. Like the publican that went up to the temple to pray, he is burdened with a sense of enormous guilt,—he durst not lift up so much as his eyes to heaven,—he smites upon his breast,—he would fain entreat for mercy, but he dreads lest, by doing so, he should be chargeable with presumption. Now, when the high priest went within the veil, how powerfully might this dejected and desponding penitent have been urged and entreated to lift up his voice to God for mercy. "It is true, you are a sinner," a pious friend might have said to him, "you cannot overrate the awful aggravation of your guilt; but then do not underrate the mercy of God through an atonement. Has he not promised that, for the sake of a propitiatory sacrifice, he will certainly forgive our nation their iniquities?—and are not you one of the nation?—and is not our High Priest now within the veil offering the blood of atonement? O then, now, now, while he is there pleading in our behalf,—now, while God is in the act of accepting the offering,—now, ask for remission,—and, as far as the east is from the west, so far will he remove your transgressions from you." What an encouragement was this to pray! The application of all this is obvious. Suppose the intercession of Christ were at present unknown to you—unknown to the world. You have, let it be supposed, just emerged from the darkness of sin into the light of truth. For the first time, you have caught a glimpse of your true condition as a transgressor against God. You feel that you are barely out of hell; your conscience, unused and strange to its office, labours to discharge in a moment the accumulated duty of years,—repeats, and even exasperates, the accents of the violated law,—surrounds itself with an atmosphere as terrible as that of Sinai. But though God is the being whose awful justice you have armed against you, his mercy you must sue for, and obtain, or perish. It is in vain for you to think of compensation, to plead your penitence, to promise amendment: you cannot, in this way, appease his wrath,—you must cast yourself on his free mercy, or perish. Do not think of excusing yourself from this act by pleading that it would be presumption, an aggravation of your guilt, an invitation to ruin: even if this were true, it is also true that to neglect it is destruction. If a single ray of hope be left you, it must come direct from the throne of God.

From what quarter, then, shall we draw the enouragement which shall embolden you to approach the mercy seat? What is the condition on which you would consent to go, at any given hour of to-day or to-morrow, and fall down before God in prayer? Would you promise to do this, could you be assured that, at the moment when you were calling upon God for mercy, you should be accompanied by the earnest intercessions of your family, and of all your friends, in your behalf? You have heard, that " the effectual fervent prayer of a righteous man availeth much;" that the intercession of Abraham suspended, for a time, the descending fire which destroyed Sodom; that, could ten righteous men have been found there, God would, for their sakes, have recalled the sentence which had gone out against it: now, would you deem it a sufficient encouragement to go before God, could we guarantee that, at the time you prayed, every righteous man, every believer in the kingdom, should enter into his closet, and earnestly supplicate God for you? — or beyond this, could we assemble together, in your behalf, a solemn convocation of all the Christian churches upon earth,—could we bring all flesh before God,—could we undertake to engage for you all the power of prayer which at present exists upon earth,—and, carrying the supposition out to the utmost, could we even ensure to you the mightier supplications of the church above, of all its thrones, dominions, principalities, powers, and orders of saints,—were all the created universe to obtain a special audience of God at the same time, and to surround his throne together, for the sole object of entreating him on your behalf,—could you doubt of your success? If he speaks of the combined intercession of "Noah, Daniel, and Job," as all but omnipotent, could you question the efficacy of your entreaties, if you knew them to be thus seconded and urged by the combined importunity of all creation in prayer? But what, if, at the very moment of audience, when the violent were taking heaven for you by force—what, if then you should behold the Saviour himself come forth, and stand at the altar of incense, having in his hand the golden censer,—and what if you should hear him announce, "I will pray the Father for you"? O what a day of hope would instantly arise upon your soul! Would you not at once be shamed out of all your fears and unbelief?—would you not feel that, having him for an advocate, you could dispense with all inferior aid?—that your suit was as good as gained? So far from doubting or dreading the issue of your prayers, you would henceforth feel that the footstool of mercy was the only place of safety and of hope; that if danger impended, yet there he stood between you and it; that if mercy gushed forth, he stood there as the medium to receive and pour it into your soul; that, in his hands, your sacrifice received an infinite accession of worth, and your entreaties, if at all augmented in power, were augmented to omnipotence. But you need no vision to certify the substantial truth of this representation. If there be any veracity in the word of God, there can be no more credible fact than this—that Jesus ever liveth to make intercession for us. You are warranted to imagine and paint the vision to your faith; to believe that you no sooner approach the seat of mercy than you become the client of the great Advocate; that, on the first utterance of your penitence, he espouses your cause, makes it his own, and presents your supplication before the throne as his own desire. Can you doubt or delay to draw near to God after this?

9. It is observable, that our Lord encourages the devotion of his disciples, by placing the *virtue* of his mediation in a striking variety of lights. In uttering the language already quoted, *he pledges himself to the office of their* PERSONAL INTERCESSOR; "I will pray the Father for you." He, who could not see them exposed to destruction without pouring out his life to save them, could not behold them prostrate at the throne of grace, as trembling suppliants, without raising them up and becoming their advocate. He, who has created for them an infinite fund of merit, could not fail to employ it in the way most eminently conducive to their advantage; causing it to ascend, in their behalf, as a memorial before God, at the moment of their entreaties for mercy. It is

to be borne in mind, that, while on earth, he did nothing for himself. Having graciously engaged to be our substitute, whatever he did, he did solely for his people. What, then, has become of the inexhaustible fund of obedience accruing from his obedience unto death? How is the infinite treasure employed? Where is it deposited? By proclaiming himself our Intercessor, he would have us to know that the entire merit of all he did is contained as incense in his golden censer, that he might offer it up with the prayers of his people. Our prayers, then, in their ascent to the throne of God, mingle and blend with the ascending incense of his merit. Our voice, before it reaches the ear of God, falls in and blends with the voice of him whom the Father heareth always. So that, in pledging himself to intercede in our behalf, he is, in effect, assuring us of the certainty of our success.

10. Another encouragement to prayer, which he derives for us from his mediatorial influence, is, *the use which he allows us to make of his name.* " Ask," saith he, " *in my name.*" Were we about to become suppliants to an earthly benefactor, it would be important to ascertain the plea most likely to dispose him to accede to our request. For there is always one argument which affects an individual, and gives us the key to his heart more effectually than all others. How important is it, then, that we, who are daily suppliants to God for blessings on which our salvation depends, should be acquainted with that plea which he most delights to honour. Now the plea most prevalent with him is, beyond all comparison, the name of Jesus. It is the name of his only begotten Son;—it is the name which he has solemnly pledged himself to honour;—it is the name which he himself has conferred in token of his infinite complacency and satisfaction;—it is the name which he has indis-

solubly bound up with his own character and perfections, so that he cannot disregard it without dishonouring his own name. Employ any other name as a plea at the throne of grace, and you insult the majesty of Heaven; —but employ his name, and you instantly attract the complacent attention of the almighty Father, and obtain access to the treasures of his grace.

"Hitherto," said Christ, "have ye asked nothing *in my name.*" Up to that moment, in the history of the church, devotion had been ignorant of its real strength; unacquainted with the extent of its resources and power. Relying simply on the promises of God, it was content to present its supplications, ignorant of the ground on which they were heard; and often sighing, in the paroxysms of conscious guilt, for a days-man and intercessor. But Jesus explained the rationale of devotion; laid open the secret of our success; and thus enabled it to feel the power which it has with God, the *purchase* it has on the eternal throne. "Verily, verily, I say unto you, Whatsoever ye shall ask the Father in my name, he will give it you;" as if he had said, "When you go to the door of mercy, and knock, make use of my name, and you shall gain admission;—make it known that you belong to me, and my Father will treat you as belonging to him;—make it known that there is a mutual affection, a close and indissoluble friendship, subsisting between us, and my Father will take you into his favour, to his heart: tell him that my name is dear to you, and it will endear you to him: so endear you, that, ask what you will,—the forgiveness of your sins, adoption into his family, the sanctification of your nature, the riches of his grace, all, all,—he will give it you: I am so beloved by him, that for my sake he will refuse you nothing."

We ourselves are accustomed to act kindly towards a person, though he be a stranger to us, provided he can shew us that he is related to one whom we love · in shewing him kindness, we feel that we are evincing our affection for the friend who sent him. The Father demonstrates his infinite love to Christ, by receiving and welcoming the friends of Christ as his own friends. He has pledged himself to do so; and he is so complacently delighted with Christ,—so fully satisfied with the atonement he has made,—feels himself so unspeakably glorified by the incarnation and life, the death and mediation, of Christ,—by all that he has done for the honour of the divine government and the salvation of man,—that, if I may say so, he has thrown open his heart and his heaven to all the friends of Christ. They come to his throne; and, on the intercession of Christ in their behalf, the Father lays open all the treasures of his grace for their appropriation and use. "Yea," saith Christ, "ask in my name; and I do not say that I will pray the Father for you; for the Father himself loveth you, because ye have loved me."—" Make use of my name, and that will suffice; my name alone, without any entreaty on my part, would be a certain passport to my Father's heart, and to all the riches of his grace." " Wherefore ask, and receive, that your joy may be full."

Now what a vast acquisition was this to the wealth of devotion; it was supplying it with a key to the divine treasury, and placing it in a position, in reference to the throne of grace, which gave to it an omnipotent influence with him who sitteth thereon. What a prodigious advance was it, in one sense, even on the promise of his personal intercession! By empowering his people to employ the argument of his name, he is, in so far, placing the fund of his merit at their disposal; affording them the profound satisfaction of bringing it into the presence of God, and using for themselves the very same plea which he employs for them; he is, in effect, pleading for them by their own lips, as well as with his own; and thus multiplying the voice and power of his intercession. By investing them with this privilege, he is virtually clothing them with priestly vestments, placing them by his side at the altar, and putting into their hands a censer filled with incense like his own.

II. But further, with a view to promote the devotion of his disciples, *he distinctly engages to answer their supplication:* "Whatsoever ye shall ask in my name, that will I do, that the Father may be glorified in the Son. If ye shall ask anything in my name, I will do it." That the same thing should undertake both to present and to answer their petitions—both to intercede for them and to confer the blessings sought—may appear incompatible; but the offices, though distinct, are perfectly reconcilable. In his conduct at the altar we behold the Intercessor, and in his conduct on the throne we behold the result and reward of his intercession: having become the medium of prayer from man to God, he is rewarded by being made the medium of blessing from God to man;—the Intercessor of human penury is constituted the Almoner of infinite bounty: he is called from the altar of incense, to ascend and dispense from the throne of God the blessings which he has sought for us.

However various the lights, then, in which we behold the virtues of our Lord's mediation, it is evident that one principle explains, harmonizes, and encompasses the whole—the love of God; that they all subserve the grand aim of which we have been speaking—the manifestation of the divine character for human encouragement and salvation. To regard the institution of the intercessory office as necessary to give us success with God, is an injustice to his beneficence, and a misapprehension of the whole economy. "At that day," saith

Christ, " ye shall ask me nothing; for the Father himself loveth you. And whatsoever ye shall ask in my name, that will I do, *that the Father may be glorified in the Son.*" Till our fears are allayed, and our distrust removed, the love of God does not cease to heap up its gifts, and to multiply its grants and appointments. On this principle it is that the throne of grace, though in itself ineffably attractive as occupied by infinite love, is made additionally attractive by the appointment and presence of a benignant Intercessor: as if God did not deem its attractions complete while only invested with the might of his own love, he has placed at the altar before it an Advocate clothed in our own nature. On our way to the seat of mercy, our Intercessor assures us, and asks us to receive the assurance as the only correct interpretation of his office, that if he accompanies and introduces us to God, it is not because God requires it for himself but for us; that the design of his intercession is, not to excite, but to satisfy, the love of the Father—by granting this last favour to our fears. There is a spot in the universe where centres all dignity, authority, and power—the focus of glory; that spot is at the right hand of Deity; and Jesus assures us that he himself is its sole occupant in the capacity of our Intercessor. Yes, he who might have been placing a vial of wrath in the hand of every angel around his throne, with a commission to pour it out on this rebellious world till it was utterly consumed, is standing at this moment at the altar of incense, presenting our prayers for mercy, and officiating there as our great high priest.

" Who then is he that condemneth? it is Christ that died: yea, rather, that is risen again; who is even at the right hand of God; *who also maketh intercession for us!*" This is an argument not to be refuted, a climax to which nothing can be added; leading us upward, step by step, it conducts us to a summit where all is unclouded and serene, and where we can breathe the air of security and triumph. While standing on this elevation, by the side of our Intercessor, and in the light of the throne of God, we feel that no foe can approach, no enemy impeach us—that the universe is at peace with us.

How richly is Jesus entitled to be called the Wonderful! The view, indeed, which has now been taken of his office and excellence is hasty and defective: had it been much less unworthy than it is, it would still have fallen infinitely short of the grandeur of the subject, for we are dilating on a theme on which it is a joy to reflect that perfection is unattainable. But crude and imperfect as our remarks are, they will have answered an important end if they have enabled us to feel this; if they have made us sensible that we are engaged on a theme which we must have eternity to celebrate and comprehend. He has shewn us that even the mysteries of the Godhead admit of increase, for he has added to them the peculiarities of humanity, and adopted the sum of them all into his own person. Besides the predicates which are true of him as God, and those which are true of him as man, by combining divinity and humanity together, he has created, if I may say so, a third class of truths which can be predicated of him, and of him alone; and on these, as they relate to his mediatorial office, hangs the hope of the perishing world.

None, before his advent, had ever succeeded in drawing the character of a perfect man; he not merely described, but exhibited, a specimen of perfect humanity conjoined with Deity; and, while he preserved the characteristics of each nature distinct, he shewed what God is, and what man should be,—became the representative of God, and the exemplar of men. He erected a new order of greatness, of which the laws, conditions, and results — the whole archetype — were peculiarly his own. He gave a new economy to the divine government,—placed himself at the head of a new dispensation, the object of which was to reconcile the prerogatives of justice and compassion; and to do this, not by compromising either, but by honouring both, — by enabling mercy to punish without impairing its clemency or its claims to our love, and enabling justice to forgive without sacrificing its purity or its claims on our awful regards. The rights of justice and the condition of sinful man were essentially hostile,—they had diverged to an infinite remoteness, and stood frowning at each other, as from opposite sides of the universe. He *laid hold on* the nature of man; and, planting his cross midway, created a point of attraction which reached and drew them across the separating gulf back to itself, as to a common centre. Justice moved from its high and awful position on Sinai; and, with all the armies of holiness, brightening and still brightening with complacency as it approached, bowed with reverence at the cross, and said, " It is enough." The sinner, detached by the same magnetic power from the strong confederacy of sin, approaches, relents, and changes as he draws near, till he falls prostrate before the cross, a new creation in Christ Jesus. By giving his heart to sinners, and for them, holiness finds that it has nothing to ask— nothing to do; only to raise the sinner from the dust, and to become the guardian of his new life: the sinner finds that nothing is left him to desire, except that he may never wander from the sight of that cross which has made him the ward of infinite holiness, and is preparing him for heaven. Here God erects his throne, and man adores; to each the cross is ineffably precious, for it is only in its immediate presence that sin can be vanquished, and yet the sinner be saved.

While this amazing consummation was in actual process, the character of Christ evolved an amount of excellence which might have made angelic natures, if capable of the feeling, jealous of the rivalry and riches of earth. The eternal Father himself beheld in it more than an indemnity for human transgression: never before had he contemplated a work in which his holiness appeared so pure, his mercy so amiable, his wisdom so profound; he saw in it the stability of all law—the recovery of man—an infinite augmentation of the splendour which surrounds his throne—an amount of objective glory such as he had never before beheld out of and apart from himself. And, as if this new relation and aspect of the divine nature had been an experiment, the result of which more than answered to his great idea,—as if the advent of Christ surpassed the divine expectation,—the sublime phenomena which it displayed called forth audible and delighted expressions of paternal complacency and love, —the radiance of the divine countenance fell full upon them.

The dedication of the Jewish Temple was an epoch in the history of the earth. All Israel was assembled on the occasion; and, had man done justice to the event, all the world would have flocked and kept festival; for what did it signify, but that the great God himself was become a dweller with man upon the earth. But the dedication of Christ was worthy to be a day of jubilee to the universe. Here human instrumentality was dispensed with, as unworthy the greatness of the occasion; nothing lower than angelic agency was employed; the arrangement and process were wholly divine. His only human herald was directed to announce, "*him hath God the Father sealed;*—he needs no human induction or testimony,—he enters on his office sealed and signalized with all the marks of divinity upon him." He proclaimed himself as "him whom the Father hath sanctified, and sent into the world." The splendid scene at his baptismal inauguration, when the heavens were opened, and the Spirit descended upon him, was only the after-imitation, the faint repetition, of a scene in heaven, in which the eternal Father, passing by all the hosts and hierarchies of heaven, had elected and devoted him to the office of his divine representative, and our mediator,—a scene, of which all the thrones, and dominions, and principalities of heaven stood around the awed and admiring spectators, and in which the only share they took was reverently and joyfully to worship him. God of eternal glory! thou thyself wast never so glorious in thine own eyes as at that moment — never so great in the eyes of thy creatures! Could thine unbeginning and unending existence admit of dates, surely that would stand out as an era in thine eternal round of years. Never was the ocean of thy love stirred so completely to its depths. Never didst thou put forth thine hand on so glorious an occasion as then, when thou didst give up and devote thine only begotten Son to the great work of embodying and bringing thy character into the world, that men might behold it, and live! And thou, co-equal and co-eternal Son, never hadst thou shone more glorious in the eyes of paternal love, nor made so large and unanswerable a demand on the admiration and homage of the universe, as when, accepting thy new and mysterious office, thou didst say, "For their sakes, I sanctify myself." In pursuance of thy voluntary engagement, thou didst come and offer thyself and thy glory to the world, — thou didst withdraw thyself from the grandeur of heaven, and set thyself apart to the wants and sorrows of earth,—and, having set up thy tabernacle amongst us, thou didst keep it consecrated for the indwelling glory and for the worship of man. Ambition never entered it;

the kingdoms of the world, and the glories of them, were brought in perspective before thee; but thou sawest them as though thou sawest them not. Thou couldst, with a single sentence, have flashed light on the darkest mysteries of science; but thou wouldst not spare a moment from teaching that sublimer knowledge—the science of salvation. Thou hadst ears only for one sound, and that was the sound occasioned by sin,—the voice of penitence imploring forgiveness,—the voice of fear and conscious guilt deprecating the vengeance of eternal fire. Thou hadst eyes only for one sight—a wilderness of woe, a captive world, chained to the wheels of the great enemy, and already arrived in the gloomy precincts of hell. This object filled the whole sphere of thy vision—thou couldst see nothing else; and, had all the thrones of earth been vacant, and invited thine acceptance, it would not have induced thee to diverge a single step from the path which led direct to the cross. Thou hadst tears but for one object; and thou didst weep them over lost souls. So fully wast thou possessed with the vastness of thy design, that thou didst value moments, faculties, life itself, only as the means of working it out; and through every step of thy course thou didst bring the whole of thy glory to bear on its completion. Thou hadst not to cast out aught evil from thy capacious mind,—thou hadst not to sweep and cleanse the temple of thy soul from sordid cares, for never didst thou know a thought alien from thine object; and though all the fulness and fire of the passions dwelt in thee, thou didst not waste a single feeling, but didst devote the whole as consecrated fuel for offering up the great sacrifice in which thy life was consumed, and by which the world might be saved.

And how godlike was the object to which he set himself apart! At the altar of God he swore eternal war against the principle of sin,—devoted himself to the work of chasing it from the earth, — of putting it to shame in the face of the universe,—and of achieving this task, not by the arbitrary domination of power, but by merely shewing what God is, by the exercise of omnipotent love. Were we to hear of a design contemplated by God to subdue the rebellion of hell, and to rescue its victims, what a view would it give us of his unresting benevolence, and with what impatient longing should we desire to know the way in which the sun of the divine glory would arise on the blackness of darkness, and how it would paint its lustre on the clouds of perdition. But the importation of the divine character and glory to earth in the person of Christ, however from circumstances we may disparage the event, would bear a comparison even with that; for our carnal mind was enmity against God, like theirs, while we possessed not even the redeeming quality to believe and tremble.

It seems to be one of the laws of mind, that it shall be not merely employed, but employed to the full; and when it becomes conscious of its dignity and powers, nothing less than great objects can satisfy it. Now, what a theatre did the blessed Jesus select—what an object did he adopt in coming into the world! Let us receive it in his own words to the eternal Father—" For their sakes I sanctify myself, that they may be sanctified through the truth;" that he might make truth do the work of power; that he might pervade and transform pollution into sanctity, by merely shewing it the face of truth; that he might erect living temples out of the wreck and refuse of humanity, swept by the besom of destruction to the very mouth of perdition.

Let us hear him repeat the design in other language; " I have declared unto them thy name, and will declare it;

that the love wherewith thou hast loved me may be in them, and I in them." He contemplated nothing less than the conveyance of the love of God to man; to bring it to us as our portion,—entail it on us as our inheritance,—transfuse it through us as our life. Like the prophet emblematically extending himself over the dead body of the child, to convey life into all its parts, the Saviour proposes to shed abroad the love of God through every member of his body, the church, to convey the circulating vitality of that love through every part of our nature, that it may dwell in us as it does in him. But is not this an unattainable design? Is it possible that God can love us as he loves Christ? Jesus himself declares that nothing less than this can satisfy his desires on our behalf; and we may rest assured that, vast as those desires are, they are all defined and accredited by the hand of infinite wisdom,—they are only the pulsations of the heart of paternal love,—they are the desires of one who knows, if we may say so, from actual admeasurement, the length and breadth, the height and depth, of the love of God,—and who knows that as soon as we become united to him, the Father loves us as parts of Christ, as members of that mystical body of which Christ is the glorified head. The tide of the divine love, on its first flowing forth from the heart of God, found its rest in Christ; till, having opened for itself an ample channel through his sufferings and death in our stead, it poured on with unabated strength to reach his people, carrying away all their sins, bearing every obstacle before it, and shedding itself abroad in their hearts; Christ, at the same time, entering with it, and infinitely augmenting it by the accession; and thus realizing his great and godlike design, "that the love wherewith thou hast loved me may be in them, and I in them."

So great was the avowed intention of the Redeemer's

advent, that none but a mind of infinite compass could have formed it; and so amazing the manner in which he achieved it, by the humble organs and instruments of humanity, that, were it not for the immortal interests at stake, we could scarcely wonder at the ancient heresy which taught that the whole of his life was a phantasm, a supernatural illusion of the senses. That God should be manifested in the flesh was truly the mystery which had been hid from ages, and from generations. That, in the nature of a man, God should have been, like light in the sun, enthroned, uttering and unburdening infinite love with his tongue,—beaming divine compassion through his eyes,—illustrating purity and grace by his actions; it is this which renders the person of Christ ineffably glorious above the whole creation; it is this which crowns him with glory and honour. There is nothing like it in the universe: take the wings of the morning, and flee to the uttermost parts of the earth,—ransack the treasures of creation, — visit and behold its brightest glories, — plunge into the depths beneath,—soar to the heights above,—survey and question the blest inhabitants of heaven,—and you will find that the person of Christ, as the manifested glory of God, has no comparison. Bring all that is great into his presence, and it becomes little; bring all that is glorious, and it is eclipsed and lost. Oh! the depth of the riches of that love wherein God hath abounded towards us in the person of his Son. When we begin to speak of it, we instantly feel the poverty of our thoughts, our utter unfitness to approach it. It is a subject in which minds of every order are alike lost—on which human wisdom can say nothing—on which we can only lisp like infants, or acknowledge our helplessness by our silent adoration. Here, then, is the peculiar province of faith and prayer; here is an object in whose presence our wisdom becomes ignorance; here our understanding is completely at fault: God in Christ is an object so stupendous that it cannot be brought into our minds—we have not room to receive it; this truth is a guest so glorious, that our limited mind feels itself both unworthy and unable to receive it under its roof: our faith must go forth, with all the train of Christian graces, and do it homage. Like the apostle, when oppressed in its presence with a sense of its immensity, we can only take refuge in prayer, beseeching "the God and Father of our Lord Jesus Christ, that he would grant . . . . . that we may be able to comprehend . . . . . and to know the love of Christ, which passeth knowledge."

We have already remarked the profound satisfaction expressed by the Father, at the display of his character in the person of Christ; a satisfaction which shewed that he beheld in it the perfect reflection of his own image. On account of this entire identity of character, we often find the apostles speaking of the eternal Father and of Christ in equivalent and convertible terms. Hence, too, the precedence and importance assigned to the knowledge of Christ; and the promise of the Spirit, for the special design of imparting that knowledge; for it is only by acquainting ourselves with the character of Christ that we can arrive at the knowledge of God; our knowledge of the Son is the exact measure of our acquaintance with the Father. The Regenerating Spirit, in all his operations on the human heart, makes the character of Christ the pattern after which he works: he begins by taking of the things of Christ, and shewing them to the eye which he has prepared to behold them; and he ends not till the soul is completely conformed to the perfect model. Believers themselves are enamoured of it, for it is the character of their Saviour; and, as such, every act and feature composing it bears a direct relation to them. They can think of no excellence, can make not the remotest approach to any modification of goodness, of which they do not find the archetype and perfection in him. Turning from every other representation as dim and veiled, they all, as with open face, behold in him the glory of the Lord. A glance at this object fills their minds with a grand and overpowering idea of excellence; it draws to itself the whole depth and mass of their being. They count every part of their moral discipline as lost, which does not promote their likeness to his image; every instance in which the ordinances of grace do not increase their love to him, they regard as a fresh call to humiliation, a fresh provocative to self-examination and prayer; while every act of devotion they deem especially defective which does not celebrate his glory, or implore an accession of " the Spirit of wisdom and revelation in the knowledge of him."

If a life of piety may be considered a life of praise to God,—if man is so fearfully and wonderfully made, that even a discourse on the use of the parts of his body may be regarded as a hymn to the Creator, where shall we find terms fit to describe the tribute of glory to God which accrues from the life of Christ? or, could we appreciate his character in all its perfections, what expressions of ecstasy and delight could do justice to its worth? Nature, from the beginning, had been vocal in her Maker's praise—had been constant and full in an anthem in which every creature bore its part; but the whole creation in chorus could not shew forth all his praise—could but barely hint his excellence. As if conscious of the defect, and anxious to repair it by commencing anew, piety had often restrung her harp, and summoned the creatures to arise and aid her in the infinite attempt — had called on everything that hath breath to join in a full concert of praise to God. But her utmost effort was only a preluding flourish, till he should come to lead the song who had said, " In the midst of the church will I sing praise unto thee." He took up the strain at a point beyond which creation would never have carried it. His voice gave the keynote to the universe. His description of the divine character furnished words for the new, everlasting, universal song. His unconfined power,—his unsearchable understanding,—his holiness, on which no spot, no shadow, could settle, and which the eyes of wickedness could not gaze on for its brightness,—his untiring patience,—his constant community with the general heart of man, which he wept over and bathed in tears,—his meekness clothed with majesty,—his personification of infinite love,—these were the several parts of the harmonious song. All the attributes in him became vocal, and made infinite music in the ear of that glorious Being in whom they eternally reside. Each myriad-voiced rank of the church above, overflowing with joy, took up the mighty, whelming, ocean strain : the church below redoubled, and returned it back again in alleluias to the throne of God ; age after age has heard it swelling on, as lisping infancy, and newly pardoned penitence, and misery beguiled of its woes, and ingratitude charmed into thankfulness, and hope spreading her pinions for heaven, and all the new-born heirs of grace have awoke up their glory, and joined the general choir; and on it shall continue to roll and swell, attuning and gathering to itself all the harmonies of nature, till all space shall become a temple, and all holy being, actuated by one Spirit, and swayed in perfect diapason, shall become one great instrument, sounding forth " praise to God, in the church, by Christ Jesus, throughout all ages, world without end. Amen."

SECTION III.

OF THE HOLY SPIRIT.

It is extremely difficult to discriminate between originality and mere novelty in a public teacher. The multitude are so prone to take their opinions from first impulses, rather than from judgment—inconsiderately and impetuously to ascribe a new and pleasing impression to the highest possible origin, rather than to any secondary cause—that many a public instructor has been invested with the highest prerogative of genius, whose only attraction was, that he had assumed one of the thousand vizors which novelty owns, and wore it gracefully. And what enhances the difficulty of discrimination is, that while it is in the power of an inferior mind to invest a familiar truth with an air of singularity, it is one of the attributes of the highest order of intellect, and an attribute which it delights to exercise, to simplify an original truth, and give to it an air of familiarity; to secure for it an easy introduction into the mind, by giving it, though a stranger, the welcome aspect of a friend.

The difficulty of discrimination is further increased, when the truths to be judged of date back to a remote antiquity; when, by distance of time, which operates in this case like distance of space, the opinions which looked bold and prominent to the near beholder, have mingled and melted into one mass of indistinctness.

We have advanced the claim of originality for many of the doctrines of the Great Teacher; and, were the Old Testament the only witness to be examined, the claim might be easily substantiated. But during the long silence of the divine oracle, during the space which intervened from the last words of Malachi to the coming of Christ, we know not what opinions grew up and prevailed. It is only reasoning on the known principles of humanity to say, that when the living voice of inspiration had ceased to speak, the sacred volume was much more likely to receive the undivided attention of the church than before. And with a volume so seminal of all truth, so constantly whispering in the ear of hope, as the Bible, who can say what approaches were made to many evangelical doctrines—what prophets of hope arose? And when once opinions, to which the wants or aspirations of the soul respond, have been broached, who can say to what consolidation or stability they may attain? The feathered seed, which this year floats in the air—the emblem of volatility—a feather dropped from the wing of levity—will, next year, be found rooted in the earth, dividing with the oak the spoils of the clouds, and rejoicing in the blessings of heaven, itself a seed-bearing plant. And the floating guess of one age becomes the settled creed of a succeeding, its point-like base is forgotten, and men go on building an inverted pyramid whose top may reach to heaven; it is congenial with one or other of the elements of humanity, and, by passing through a thousand minds, it acquires a consistency and power which gives it a place among the realities of our being.

By what process, then, shall we ascertain how much of the gospel is an absolute origination, or how much is a mere adoption and authorization of pre-existing opinions? Taking many other tests for granted, it may be suggested, that the amount of new truth contained in the gospel, or the degree of newness belonging to any one of its doctrines, may be conjectured from the number of errors which have sprung up around it. Truth is antecedent to error, and the measure of it; as is the originality of a doctrine or system, in the same proportion will be the multiplicity of errors following. The whole tribe of error is parasitical, and can only grow by hanging its envenomed weight on the plants of truth. Let the doctrines of Christ be judged of in this way; the plants of the Lord's right-hand planting, and the originality of his teaching, will be apparent to all.

The doctrine of the agency of the Holy Spirit is one of the most original which came from the lips of Christ, and one whose precise degree of originality is most marked and ascertainable. Referring to the records of the Old Testament, we learn the *distinction* of the Spirit in the unity of the Godhead, his *personality*, and his *divinity*. We read of the same divine subsistence as daily replenishing the earth with life and beauty, as visiting and actuating the moral world at pleasure, and as promised to the church, with a frequency, particularity, and magnificence of language, which shewed that the divine Promiser himself regarded the gift as identical with a state of distinguished prosperity, and which led believers to mark it with supreme distinction, by calling it *the promise*.

Concerning the nature of the Holy Spirit, as a distinct and divine person, the teaching of Christ is clear and conclusive: nor can we conceive anything more unwelcome, to those who shrink from applying the personal pronouns to the Divine Spirit, than the valedictory discourse of Christ to his disciples.* If I do not enlarge on this part of the subject, then, let it be understood, that I refrain, not because Christ was silent on it, for he,

---

* On the ineffable promanation or procession of the Holy Spirit from the Father and the Son, though it is a truth which seems necessarily involved in certain parts of that discourse, I presume not to speak.

I repeat, was copious and explicit, but because he had been greatly anticipated by the revelations of the Old Testament.

I. It is worthy of our earliest consideration, both from its native importance and from the peculiar solemnity of the affirmation, that our Lord described the mission of the Holy Spirit as absolutely dependent on his own return to heaven. " Nevertheless, *I tell you the truth*, it is expedient for you that I go away; for, if I go not away, the Spirit will not come unto you; but, if I depart, I will send him unto you." Now, admitting the impropriety of any arrangement which should have combined together the presence of the Spirit and the personal residence of Christ in permanent conjunction on earth, it may yet be inquired why the mission of the Spirit could not have taken place immediately *before* the ascension of Christ, as well as immediately *after?* If the inquirer be sincere, it would be sufficient to reply, " Even so, Father; for so it seemeth good in thy sight." The arrangement may have been founded on reasons of state, reasons which measure with the universe as comprehensive as the divine government, and the issues of which are placed far in eternity. But many of the reasons for this arrangement are apparent; the Almighty evinced by it his reverence for order. He was evolving a plan of infinite magnitude, the unfolding of which had commenced at the fall,—he had arrived at a vital part of it, a part on which he would have mankind in all ages to fix their gaze,—and he therefore caused it to unfold and pass before their eyes in slow and stately procession. He knew that man is easily distracted by multiplicity of objects—is extremely liable to place the cause for the effect, and the effect for the cause—is taught most effectually by example—is prone to disregard a future good, so long as he can retain a present though inferior blessing; on all these accounts, therefore, the mission of the Holy Spirit was withheld until Christ had ascended to his appointed throne. The Almighty would signalize the enthronement of Christ in the eyes of the universe—would impress the minds of believers with the glorious reception which their Head had met with on his return to heaven—would enjoy the infinite satisfaction of hearing the first prayer of that exalted Head for the promised Spirit—and thus demonstrate to them, at once and for ever, the certain prevalency of his intercession; for if his first prayer succeeded in obtaining for us the great gift of the Spirit, how much more shall he secure for us every inferior good. God would shew us in the most impressive manner, by placing the fact in the strong light of the mediatorial throne, that the connexion of the work of Christ with the gift of the Spirit is the absolute connexion of cause and effect.

"He spake of the Spirit which they that believe on him should receive; for the Spirit was not yet given, *because that Jesus was not yet glorified.*" Can we suppose that his ascension to heaven was a silent and private transaction? Shall an Elijah ascend in a chariot of fire—shall the departed spirit of a Lazarus be conveyed by angels to Abraham's bosom—and shall the Lord of angels himself return to his own dominions from the conquest of one world, and the redemption of another, unattended and obscure? No; "The chariots of God," on the occasion, "were twenty thousand, even thousands of angels." At the point where he vanished from the view of mortals, he was joined by the rejoicing ranks of the cherubim and seraphim; he found them arranged to receive him; impatient to commence the celebration of his deeds, and to conduct him in triumph to his glorious throne. His appearance was the signal to begin the song: they called on earth to assist them in the mighty task, " Sing unto God, ye kingdoms of the earth; O sing praises unto the Lord; to him that rideth upon the heaven of heavens." That was the moment when the universe became the vehicle of his glory; when he began to ride on the summit of creation, having all the events and revolutions of time for his chariot wheels. Hitherto, as man, he had inhabited the material parts of the creation; but now he relinquished these, and took possession of the intelligent parts. He began to inhabit the praises of eternity,—not merely the spiritual universe, but even the essence of that,—the life of the spiritual universe, exhaling in the incense and fragrance of praise. He found himself enthroned far above all heavens, with the heights of creation for his footstool.

It had been predicted, and he himself had confirmed the expectation, that when he ascended up on high, he would give gifts unto men. But what gift can Christ bestow rich enough to signalize and grace his accession to the mediatorial throne? Had he collected together all the treasures of the earth, and multiplied them a thousand-fold, and then poured them out at the feet of his people, the gift would have been utterly inadequate to the greatness of the occasion: had all created good been accumulated upon them to the highest possible amount, it would only have disgraced the greatness of the occasion. The unconfined benevolence of his heart impelled him to give something, (for it was the jubilee of heaven,) and if he gave, he would be sure to bestow a gift worthy of himself, answerable to the magnitude of the occasion, honourable to the royalty of his grace. But, if such is to be the character of the gift, the Spirit, the divine Spirit, the converting, enlightening, sanctifying, saving Spirit alone, must be the donation. Because he would give all gifts in one, he gave to them the Holy Spirit.

A very limited measure of this gift, indeed—the mere earnest of the Spirit—had been enjoyed under the Jewish dispensation; but the Spirit in his fulness was not then given, because the framework of that economy was too material to be inhabited and actuated by the Spirit; and because Jesus, for whose bestowment the gift was reserved, was not yet glorified. But, during the whole economy, the influences of the Spirit had been accumulating for that auspicious moment. Prayers had been daily ascending for the fulfilment of "the promise;" and, of all these earnest supplications, not one had been lost—each of them had been turned into the blessing sought for, and had added something to the treasures of divine influence. The church had been incessantly importuning God to hasten the impartation of the gift; and, with profound satisfaction, he had beheld a stream of supplication flowing for ages into the same channel, without a moment's pause, swelling and rising, till it was ready to overflow and pour forth a healing flood of heavenly influence over the world. Nothing was wanting, but that Christ should add his intercession. Nothing was wanting, but that he should ascend his throne, and claim the gift of the Spirit, to pour it out upon his people.

"He ascended up on high, leading captivity captive, and gave gifts unto men." Having reached his throne, the Spirit came down as he had promised—came, like a rushing mighty wind, filling the whole house where the disciples were assembled, filling each heart, filling the whole church—came with a copiousness and a power as if his influences had for ages been pent up and under restraint, and now rejoiced at being able to pour themselves out over the church and the world. And what was the immediate effect of that event? Thousands were instantly converted—the sword of the Spirit seemed newly edged with power, and, bathed in the lightnings of heaven, flashing conviction on human consciences, and piercing to the recesses of the soul. The gospel went flying abroad to the utmost ends of the earth, levying human hearts in the name of Christ, wherever it came. The influences of the Spirit poured over the world like an inundation,—a new deluge, overturning the altars and sweeping away the vestiges of idolatry; and, had the vital flood continued to roll on, the only altar left standing would have been that which sanctifieth the gift and the giver—the altar of the cross. New territories were added to the domains of the church— vast tracts of the moral wilderness were taken into the garden of the Lord. The church beheld her converts flocking to her from all directions, like clouds of doves to their windows: and among the wonders of that period, one was, to see her enemies lick the dust—to see her bitterest persecutors become her champions and her martyrs — to see leopards become lambs, and wolves become kids.

The church became one region of life, of divine vitality throughout; in which whosoever breathed, lived, enjoyed life in perfection. From a state of unsightly barrenness and drought, it was suddenly covered with verdure, like the garden of the Lord. Believers themselves seemed reconverted; if sinners became saints, saints themselves became as angels; thus fulfilling the prophecy which had said, " The weak shall be as David, and David as an angel of the Lord." Every Christian saw in every other the face of an angel—looks of benevolence and brotherly love; one interest prevailed—one subject of emulation swallowed up every other—who should approach nearest to the likeness of Christ—which should do most for the enlargement of his reign. "The whole multitude of them that believed were of one heart, and of one mind;"—the Spirit of Christ animated the whole, became the one heart of the whole community, and every particular pulse beat in concert with it. What a gift was this! The value of a gift depends materially on its suitableness; what could be more suitable to a world dying, dead in sin, than the Spirit of life and of holiness. The world was a valley of dry bones: what could be more welcome than that the Spirit should come and breathe upon these slain, that they might live; that, descending to this moral Golgotha, this place of skulls, he should give a soul to the world, and again replenish it with spiritual life? How munificent was this gift! It was munificent in itself, in its kind, for it was the best; and it was also munificent in its degree, for he poured it forth in a profusion of gifts and graces. It was owing to no indigence, to no niggardliness, on the part of Christ, that his church did not rapidly extend over the world, and that the whole was not filled with the Spirit. He gave with a liberality which shewed that he tasted his own act, enjoyed the godlike act of giving,—gratified himself in the exercise of his benignity. How godlike was this gift! Had man been consulted on the occasion, he would have asked some inferior good; but Jesus, taking the affair entirely into his own hands, poured out his Holy Spirit—a blessing intended to make us holy like himself, happy like himself, and even one with himself;—for, by giving us his Spirit, he may be said to have given us himself,—to have turned himself into Spirit—into a fountain of divine influence, that he may be one with our spirits.

II. The great object of the advent of the Holy Spirit is thus distinctly specified by Christ: "When He is come, he shall convince the world of sin;" an announcement which Jesus himself must have felt as a wonderful truth. Standing as he did at that moment near to the cross, in the shadow of that awful monument of human guilt, he could not have glanced around on the scene of enormous and complicated guilt he was about to leave, and forward to the triumph and agency of the descending Spirit, without feeling, as he uttered this grand prediction, that he was unburthening his mind of a weighty and glorious communication.

An obvious and striking feature of all the divine operations, is the accomplishment of the most comprehensive and important ends by few and simple means. Such is the nice dependence of every part in his government on every other part, and such the entire harmony of the whole, that he only touches an almost invisible chord, and the vibration is felt to the extremities of the universe. How tremendous, then, must that principle of evil be, which can only be subdued by the mighty power of the Spirit—by the advent and accession of the third person in the awful Godhead—by no modified energy, but by the full almightiness of divine power! And tremendous it was! The world had become the grave of piety! If the principle of piety shewed itself vigorous and active, it became the mark for every shaft and weapon of hell; if it was impotent, it soon sickened and sunk under the pestilential atmosphere which sin had universally diffused: angelic piety itself would have found a sepulchre here. Not only was the world destitute of all native, active goodness,—a principle of evil, another Spirit, embodying all the essences of evil, was here, and at work. But did man shew no signs of resistance to this alien Spirit? Not a single indication of spiritual conflict appeared; all was silent, unconstrained submission: for this, to use the emphatic language of inspiration, is "where Satan's seat is."

Now, by what means shall this mass of disorder, darkness, and death, be renovated? The divine benevolence had been prodigal of its means; but, as to any permanent good, they had failed. Experience had shewn that it was easier to crush and destroy the world than to reform it. The Son of God himself had descended; but, as if determined by one desperate act to shut out all further communications from above — as if to intimidate the mercy of Omnipotence, they crucified the Lord of glory. What expedient, then, we ask, remains to be employed? Oh! how boundless are the divine resources! how grand! how amazing the provision! It was not that our world should be the scene of a splendid angelic administration, and be charmed into a love of piety by their graceful exhibition of it;—it was not that our world should be placed in dreadful proximity to hell, and be awed into sullen but silent submission by the sight of worms that die not, and of fires that are not quenched; —it was not that our world should be raised into the precincts of heaven—that a sight of the Being we had rejected, there enthroned in light, and surrounded by the sanctities of heaven, might surprise us into involuntary adoration. "No," saith Christ; "my Spirit alone is competent to the task; *and when He is come, He shall convince the world of sin.* External applications would only produce, at best, a temporary reaction of mind: the agency that shall succeed in transforming it must include the power of coming into immediate contact with it, and of having at command whatever can suitably affect it. I have a cause lying against mankind, and he shall be my Advocate. I have an indefeasible claim on the human heart; and he, the Great Pleader, shall enforce it on the consciences of men. He shall go into all the world, asserting my right, vindicating my claims, and writing my name on human hearts; and he shall pass into every region of the soul, diffuse himself through all its capacities and recesses, throwing light into the understanding, assailing and subverting the fortress of sin in the heart, and taking an oath of allegiance to me from all its redeemed powers."

Accordingly, in the discharge of his awful functions, the Spirit addresses himself to the hearts of man. There is sin lying upon them—enormous sin! and his object is to convince them of it. Oh! how solemn the transaction!—how mysterious the process!—how critical the juncture! The instrument employed may be, in itself, the most simple and inefficient;—hearing the gospel, or reading it, or recalling some truth to mind: but while the eye, or the ear, or the memory, is thus engaged, and all without seems at rest, the Spirit is at work within, bringing the truth forward into the strong light of distinct consciousness, rendering it irresistible, by taking away the very will of resisting; turning it into a living conviction, and incorporating it among the spiritual realities of the soul. There are times, when all sensation seems collected into a point, and we live only in the eye or the ear: and when the Invisible Spirit is at work within, creating a new heart, the faculties and energies of our whole being seem collected into a focal point—the entire soul becomes conscience. Having seated and centred himself there, the whole mass and depth of our being is drawn, slowly perhaps, yet certainly drawn to him, owning his power, and trembling at his presence. He is there, in the name of Christ; there, as the living Law, come down to right itself; and, as he goes on convicting the sinner, piling up sentences of condemnation,—one power of the soul after another wakes, till the whole soul is one region of alarm; and, collecting all its energies into an outcry for mercy, exclaims, " What must I do to be saved?" The prediction of Jesus is then fulfilled; the Divine Spirit has conducted the cause of his illustrious client to a triumphant issue.

And in doing this, observe, no external force is employed—no violence whatever is done to the freedom of the mind; the subject of the operation is never more conscious of mental liberty then when the change is in process. It is true, the change is necessitated; but that moral necessity is the highest form of freedom. It is true that the mind is brought under the authority of a new law; but that law is the royal law of liberty, the law to which the nature of man was preconfigured; and all that the Divine Spirit effects is to bring out and make legible the secret characters of that law originally written on the heart. He comes to the emancipation of the will from a state of slavery; (for sin can only triumph by enfeebling the mind and extinguishing the liberty of the soul;) and hence, from first to last, he carries the mind along with him, employs its own voluntary agency, calls into exercise its noblest powers. Even the expulsion of sin is the act of the soul itself; for no sooner is it thus revisited by its Maker, than it employs against sin those arms and instruments which had hitherto served as members of unrighteousness. In fine, "the only condition on which the freedom of a finite will is possible, is, by its becoming one with the will of God;" and to produce this happy junction is the object of the regenerating Spirit; so that subjection to him is restoration to oneself. His presence in the soul is the first signal and moment of freedom; and the more he puts forth his influence within it, the more spontaneous and vigorous are its own movements; till it utters an instinctive cry for the Spirit, and for liberty, as for an identical good.

III. The same truth appears in another original statement of Christ declarative of the *means* by which the

Holy Spirit should operate on the mind—" He shall take of mine and shew it unto you." Sin is the disease and derangement of the soul, in consequence of which the understanding fails to discharge its appointed function on the heart: the eye of a corpse, as long as its transparency remains unimpaired, will receive the picture of an object on the retina as well as if the organ were living, but there is no corresponding impression produced on the brain; so religious truths may be easily imported into the understanding, but then it has ceased to be a medium of conveyance to the heart; the communication between them is obstructed, and we have the mortification of finding, that to obtain the assent of the one, is no security whatever for the concurrence of the other. To produce this essential coincidence between the understanding and the heart is the province of the Spirit alone.

In a well-ordered family, while every member has his appropriate duties, yet, if occasion require, one will go far in his kind endeavours to supply the deficiencies or absence of another. And though the several powers of the mind, like an exemplary household, have their respective duties, yet, on occasion, will the emotions and excited affections of the soul find an understanding of their own, and anticipate the office of the judgment. Under the influence of the Spirit, the heart is frequently induced to *listen* for the understanding, as well as the understanding for the heart. His entrance occasions a temporary confusion in the household economy of the soul, during which an interchange of friendly offices unconsciously takes place, and which facilitates the necessary preparation for the reception of the King of Glory.

And how alluring the objects, how captivating the means, by which he solicits an entrance into the soul!

It is true that the process of couching the mental, not less than the bodily eye, may be attended with pain; the birth-pangs of the new principle may be severe; but the objects to which he directs the first efforts of the attention are all of the most captivating nature. The first sight which greeted the eye of Adam was the enchanting scenery of paradise, wet with the first dew; and the sight on which the Divine Spirit would have the eye of the new creature first to rest is composed of the selected and arranged glories of Christ. He takes the best of the best, the most attractive excellences of Him who is "altogether lovely," and disposes them so as to engage and receive the first glances of the renewed sinner: infinite love, in the person of the Son of God, looking at him from heaven,—erasing the sentence of his condemnation, —inserting his name in the book of life,—presenting to him a robe of righteousness,—preparing for him a heavenly mansion,—pointing him to the spectacle of the cross as the means of his redemption, and to the crown of life as the end of his faith: these are "the things of Christ," which are placed by the Spirit before the eye of the mind, and along with which he passes in, and diffuses himself through the whole soul. He would silence every other sound but that which emanates from these speaking truths; and cast a veil over all other objects, that the soul might be secluded, and left to the undisturbed influence of this new creation. He would have it awake to the sound of music—to the music of the Saviour's voice of love. He would have it to inhale the knowledge of Christ like fragrance; to imbibe holiness insensibly, as from a surrounding element; and heavenly dispositions, like melodies stealing into the heart from a distance. While "forming Christ within the hope of glory," he would come upon the soul with a grateful overshadowing, and operate only through the medium of the affections.

IV. The absolute necessity of regeneration by the Holy Spirit comes to us under the great seal of our Lord's most solemn asseveration repeatedly affixed; "Amen, amen, I say unto you; I, who not merely *desire* to speak the truth, but who am *the truth*; I, who am the amen, the faithful and true witness; who, having come from heaven, am acquainted with the character of such as are allowed to enter it; I, who hold the keys of that kingdom, I say unto you, Except a man be born of water and of the Spirit, he cannot enter into the kingdom of heaven."

It is the property of every form of created power incessantly to labour to subdue all things to itself. The stagnation of the universe is prevented by this unremitting struggle. The revolution of the planets is maintained by the perpetual contest of two principles, each of which is always equal to cope with, but never able to master, the other. All the activity and life of nature are to be traced to the unwearied contention of its various elements, each seeking to overpower and assimilate the rest to itself, but itself acted on in return by so equal a force, that incessant conflict is made incessant harmony. In the intellectual world, a law of our nature is always at work, striving, by a synthesis of comparison and arrangement, to reduce all knowledge—physical, philosophical, and religious—all to one compact system. The mind (perhaps unconsciously) is labouring after this, by a necessity of nature, in all its searchings after analogies, and attempts at generalization; it acts on the mental instinct, that truth is but one idea, one infinite whole, the product of the one reason; and to this state of unity it is constantly aiming to reduce all its conceptions and knowledge, as the only state in which the whole of its knowledge can be mastered. Now the same representation holds true of the moral world. The will is perpetually aggressive, labouring to conquer and convert all things around it to its own purposes, and to change them into its own nature. But here the conflict, as far as it is instigated by Satan the great rebel, and actuated by sin, is direct hostility against God. It is not carried on in subordination to established law, as the elemental conflicts of nature are; nor in obedience to the immediate mandates of Heaven, as the ministries of angels are; but in direct hostility against God. It arms the understanding against the dictates of revelation,—and the passions against the purity and self-denial of the divine requirements,—and the will against " all that is called God, and that is worshipped,"—it arms every member as an instrument of unrighteousness, and precipitates the whole man into the battle-field occupied by the hostile forces of good and evil.

But happiness is the coincidence of the finite will with the infinite; in other words, it is holiness. And who would wish to be happy at the price of that?—who, what rational or enlightened being, would desire to be happy at the expense of the divine character and government—at the sacrifice of seeing the creature erected above the Creator? But though all the universe should desire the enormity, it could not be; for happiness, we repeat, is nothing more, and nothing less, than the coincidence of the finite will with the infinite. That infinite will, in the person of the Holy Spirit, is come into the world expressly to subdue all things to himself; for shall he alone—he, the Supreme Mind, be inactive,—he, whose every movement is along the line of right, whose every conquest is the recovery of his own, and his every breath the creation and diffusion of happiness? No: he seeks to remedy the errors of the mind, by becoming the one reason of every individual understanding; to correct the selfishness of every separate heart, by becoming the centre and law of all mankind—the one heart for the whole colossal mass of humanity. The primitive church presents us with an instance of his uncounteracted agency—" the whole multitude of them that believed were of one heart and of one mind :" on them his agency took full effect; he became the heart of the whole community, and every particular pulse found its health by beating in unison with it. Until he works, each individual human spirit is striving to be a centre of influence to itself; but harmonious subordination to the Supreme Spirit is happiness—is heaven; and hence the absolute necessity of coming under his subjecting and transforming power, in order to the enjoyment of heaven.

V. The happy *result* of regeneration by the Holy Spirit is the production of a corresponding principle of spiritual life: " that which is born of the Spirit is spirit." That which he *creates* may be material; but that which he *begets* in his proper character, his moral capacity, must partake of his nature and likeness. The possession of an immortal spirit, indeed, is common to all men; for " there is a spirit in man, and the inspiration of the Almighty hath given him understanding." But it is in the power of sin to erect the material part of our nature into a state of dominion over the spiritual; to dethrone the soul, and give it in captivity to the flesh; and, in this unnatural state, the mind is degraded with the name of its material tyrant, and is called a *fleshly mind*. Now, it is the glory of the Divine Regenerator that he turns this flesh into spirit; he becomes a soul to our soul, lifting it out of its materiality, and restores to it again its lost prerogative of dominion. He makes it spirit.

And, in restoring it to the exercise of its peculiar functions, he is said to give it life. As long as it is held in subjection to the flesh, it is represented as being dead while it lives; but, by breathing upon it, he restores it again to the life of God. Henceforth, it not only lives itself, but throws a life into all its spiritual exercises, and is dissatisfied unless God infuses a life into all its religious privileges. In the enjoyment of this new-found existence, it pants after God, can be satisfied with nothing less than divine communications, and seeks to receive its nourishment from the hand of God. One of the distinctive characters of physical life is its power of assimilating materials of different natures to its own substance; like that, the regenerated soul is endowed with the power of converting the various events of time into the mysterious means of its nourishment, and even of turning obstacles into its own form and character. As its divine Author puts forth his power to produce it, so it proclaims its descent, and honours its parentage, by putting forth a corresponding power in its endeavours after holiness. At times, indeed, its possessor may utter a complaint of impotence, " that when he would do good, evil is present with him ;" but so probably he would complain, were his spiritual strength considerably greater than it is. The complaint is often to be regarded, not so much as an evidence of weakness, as a sign of that dissatisfaction with everything short of perfection which is a distinguishing feature of the spiritual life: being born from above, it pants after the perfection of its native region; it essays to rise, and is impatient of everything which impedes its aspirations and detains its flight. It feels the attraction of that supreme central good to which all goodness gravitates; and, like the earth, which is always labouring in its onward course to gain the sun, it is always striving to reach its centre,—to escape beyond all the influences of sin, and to attain the region of heavenly life. And it demonstrates its celestial descent, by persevering in its aim till it triumphs. The divine Spirit, who begot it, will not more certainly triumph over all the array of sin which the world contains, and cast it out, than the new principle of regenerated life will continue to work, till it has expelled sin from the soul, and is conducted, victorious, into the presence of its Divine Parent.

The name which the Divine Regenerator prefers, and by which he chooses most frequently to make himself known, is, the *Holy Spirit*. It is owing to his love for holiness, and his ability to produce it, that he has undertaken the office of changing the human heart. If he were not certain that he should renew the soul, and assimilate it to his own holy nature, he would not come into contact with an object so polluted, and depraved, and unlike himself. But " that which is born of the Spirit, is spirit;" and, as the offspring of infinite holiness, it so completely possesses the believer with a desire for sanctity, that he rejoices in tribulation, accepts the furnace, and exults in the flames, if, by passing through them, he may lose his impurity, and emerge in the likeness of God.

Like its spiritual progenitor, the renewed spirit must have an unconfined range. It is made free of the universe and eternity, and cannot submit its diffusive benevolence to the restriction of limits. Without deserting the concentric circles of self, and family, and party, and country, and contemporaries, it goes forth, expatiating and rejoicing, in a sphere which encompasses all these, and which itself knows no circumference. As an organized part of universal being, it seeks to diffuse and multiply itself through all the mass, by the circulation of unlimited happiness. Beyond the confined range which it labours to fill with its own personal activity, it seeks to be present, not merely in aim and affectionate desire, but by engaging the gracious agency of its infinite Author. Thus it makes an approximation to universal love, imitates the infinity of the divine goodness, and is distinguished by a subordinate omnipresence of benevolence. By drinking of the water which Jesus gives— "this spake he of the Spirit"—it possesses within itself "a well of water springing up to everlasting life." Though it should be cut off from all created streams, it has a fountain of its own, fed from a higher fountain—a perpetual spring, in immediate communication with the well-head of life. Its alliance with the Infinite Spirit raises it to a state of independence of the creature, confers on it a kind of spiritual self-sufficiency. And, finally, as nothing but God could satisfy God, so the renewed soul demonstrates its divine descent by disdaining, as emptiness and insult, less than the fulness of him that filleth all in all.

That, indeed, which is born spirit of Spirit, is necessarily limited in its likeness to God by the natural and straitened conditions of humanity. It has *nothing* in common with *some* of the attributes of its Divine Parent; for, abstractedly considered, they are incommunicable. It has little more than *a name* in common with *any* of his attributes; for the holiness, the wisdom, the goodness, which it derives from him, are infinitely less than the same qualities as possessed by him. But though it does not possess an identity of nature with these attributes, it is its glory that it can boast a likeness, a similitude, which takes in every lineament of his moral image. It is true that his nature obliges him to produce some things in us, in consequence of our depravity, of which there is no archetype in himself; yet even these peculiar features are the counterparts, the necessary impressions, of certain parts of his own character. Repentance, for instance, is one of the first fruits of his renewing operations; but repentance in us answers to holiness in him; it is only the process by which infinite purity is seeking to reflect and behold its image in our breast.

The new creature is an entire impression,—an imperfect and a miniature representation, it is allowed; but still an entire impression of its spiritual Author. All the excellences necessary to make up absolute perfection do not more certainly reside in the character of the Spirit himself, than all the corresponding qualities, necessary to make up the sum of sanctified excellence, exist in that which is born of the Spirit. When the prophet restored the dead youth to life, he did not more carefully extend himself over the whole surface of the body, adjusting his eyes, and mouth, and hands, to the corresponding parts and organs of the deceased, that the whole body might revive, than the divine Spirit joins bosoms, applies himself, in regeneration, to every part of our moral being, to resuscitate and restore the whole. He leaves no dead or palsied part; but, diffusing life and activity through the entire frame, he would have us to develop and work out every principle and function of our new nature in the service of God;—or, to use a scriptural figure, he delivers the soul into a mould from which it cannot fail to receive the unmaimed and entire impression of a man in Christ Jesus.

VI. And our Lord predicted, as the crowning effect of the operations of the Holy Spirit, " He shall glorify me;" a prediction which is realized in various ways. The advent of the Spirit in the cause of Christ, was itself an event which conferred on that cause transcendent honour. Had myriads of angels been despatched instead, to fly through the midst of heaven, preaching the everlasting gospel to the inhabitants of the earth, even that would have given us lofty ideas of the exaltation of Christ: but that the infinite Spirit himself should have come at his intercession, and in his service, this indeed glorifies Christ. That he should come expressly to convince men, not merely that they are sinners, but that they are sinners especially against Christ,—and not merely so, but that the sin of rejecting him is the greatest sin they can commit,—that it is the master sin, the capital offence, of the longest life of impiety, including the essence, and surpassing the guilt, of all other sins combined together,—how unspeakably is Jesus magnified by this act of the Spirit!

He engages to renovate the soul through the medium of truth. Now what honour does he confer upon Christ, that he should pass by all other kinds of truth, and should take that, and employ that only which relates to Christ. Does he not thus teach us, by his own example, to count all things but loss for the excellency of the knowledge of Christ Jesus our Lord? Does he not say to us, in actions louder than words, "This is the sum of all science; this is the only knowledge that can incorporate and mingle with your being; this is life eternal, to know the true God, and Jesus Christ, whom he hath sent;" and all other knowledge is real only so far as it is symbolical of this. He undertakes to change the heart; to produce in the will, where all the strength of man and all the powers of sin are concentrated and entrenched, an entire revolution;—a work so great, that to create a human being is represented as easy in comparison: for it is not merely to evolve *something* out of nothing, but to produce a contrary from a contrary, to bring light out of darkness, love out of enmity, holiness out of essential impurity; and hence, to mark the omnipotence, the infinite outgoing of power, which the work demands, the day in which he does this is called "the day of his power." Now what honour does he confer upon Christ, that without employing any force, without doing any violence to the constitution of the soul, he should effect this mighty change, which angels cannot behold without bursting into a rapture of admiration, by simply taking of the things of Christ, and shewing them to the soul. He asks for no other weapons than these weapons of love—these things of Christ. As if he should say, " Give me these, and I will change the sinner into a saint. Arm me with these, and I will pass into his soul as the antagonist of sin, disturbing and tracking it in all its windings, and expelling it from all its recesses. I will change his pride into humility; his enmity and unbelief into faith and love. And I will do this by illapses so gentle, by a process so natural, and so coincident with the operations of his own mind, that, were not the effects essentially divine, he would deem the agency that effected it essentially human." He engages to conduct the soul to happiness; to merit at his hands the name of the Comforter. How does he magnify Christ, then, by leading the sinner direct into the presence of Christ, as the only method of fulfilling his engagement; confessing, by the act, that, apart from Christ, even he could not give the soul comfort.

In the prosecution of his work, the divine Spirit employs a model to which to conform the renewed soul; for, as he finds the character of man depraved, deformed, and awfully unlike what it should be, he proposes to give it beauty, and excellence, and perfection. What honour then does he confer upon Christ, by making him the pattern after which he works—the model by which he moulds and fashions all believers. He takes of the things of Christ, and shews them to the soul, expressly that it may catch their temper and likeness. He holds before its eye the mirror of the gospel, that, beholding as in a glass the glory of the Lord, it may be changed into the same image. Effacing from the soul the image of the earth, he imprints in its stead the likeness of the Lord from heaven,—nor does he count the work complete till the soul is completely conformed to the perfect model.

And the Holy Spirit glorifies Christ, by rendering him the object of supreme affection and delight to all believers. The uniform effect of his teaching is, that they "rejoice in Christ Jesus." They distinctly see that there never was any righteousness in the world but his—that there is no excellence in the universe except his, and what is derived from him. They feel, therefore, that while there is no sin equal to that of disregarding him, there can be no act which harmonizes with so many of the original and best principles of our nature, or which is so much an occasion of joy, as that of receiving Christ Jesus the Lord. When the Spirit was poured out from on high, the church was flooded with light; but, like the angel standing in the sun, the central object of that light was Christ,—the church was thrown into a transport of joy, but the subject of that joy was Christ,—his name was on every tongue, his love filled every heart. And wherever the divine Spirit operates, the same supreme delight in Christ invariably ensues. He comes to herald the way for Christ—to throw open the temple-gates of the heart for the reception of Christ—to announce the titles, and display the excellences, of Christ, that the soul, beholding the glory of its royal guest, may receive him with acts of worship, and acclamations of delight. And, having admitted Christ, the believer discovers that he has admitted God—the all-comprehending fulness of God. Henceforth he can never lift his eye towards him but his heart assumes a posture of complacent adoration and joy; and when he has been imploring and putting himself under the influence of the blessed Spirit, the name of Christ fills his soul with light and glory. It is a name which has an attraction for everything great and good in the universe. The eye does not more rapidly sweep the midnight magnificence of the starry heavens, than the renewed mind, at the mention of his name, makes the circuit of creation, gathering up all that is glorious in its course, as related to him, and emblematic of his excellence.

But this prediction looks forward to a more glorious fulfilment than any which it has yet received,—a period when the Holy Spirit shall glorify Christ in these various respects, not merely in the conversion of a sinner here and there, but when the sphere of his operations shall embrace the world,—when he shall become the soul of the world, the great animating spirit of mankind, leading them, as with one heart and one hand, to crown the Saviour, Lord of all. But the prediction is of greater compass still; it teaches us to look onward to the period when Jesus "shall come to be admired in his saints, and glorified in all them that believe." He determines that he will reap a large harvest of human hearts, of sanctified affections; and he has sent the Spirit into the world to collect this revenue, to gather up this glory for him: and then the Spirit will have completed his task, will have glorified Christ; for it will then be seen that he has clothed every believer in the righteousness of Christ,— renewed them all after the likeness of Christ,—that, with no other instrument to work with than the gospel of Christ, he has operated on a vast mass of depravity, on a multitude, which no one can number, of sinful souls, and has renewed and made them resplendent, and crowned them with the glory of Christ.

VII. Such is a somewhat connected view of the principal original truths with which the Great Teacher enriched his church concerning the operations of the Holy Spirit. I will point attention, also, to two or three isolated declarations, calculated to shew the importance of receiving his influence, as well as to give a practical application to the preceding remarks.

"Verily, I say unto you, All manner of sin and blasphemy shall be forgiven unto men; but the blasphemy against the Holy Ghost shall not be forgiven unto men. And whosoever speaketh a word against the Son of man, it shall be forgiven him; but whosoever speaketh against the Holy Ghost, it shall not be forgiven him, neither in this world, neither in the world to come." What form of denunciation can be conceived more calculated than this to warn the trifler that he is on holy ground, and to bespeak for the whole doctrine of divine influence the reverence of a prostrate soul. The sin denounced is, probably, *the rejection of the last and greatest evidence of the Messiahship of Christ—the dispensation of the Spirit.* Up to that point of unbelief, the Jews were within the reach of forgiveness. Their blasphemy against Christ,—their rejection of all the evidence arising from his character, his miracles, the testimony of John, and the distinct fulfilment in him of numerous prophecies,—even the act of nailing him to the cross,—all this did not consummate their guilt, and render their condition hopeless. It was, indeed, approaching as near to the edge of the precipice as possible, without actually falling over. It was closing their eyes against evidence which ought to have convinced them that Christ was the Messiah; but still there was further evidence to be submitted to them, and evidence of a superior kind. The miraculous dispensation of the Holy Spirit, attesting, as it would, his resurrection from the dead, and his exaltation at the right hand of God, and bringing, as it would, the right arm of Omnipotence visibly to certify his claims, was reserved for that closing proof. Till that should be found unavailing, their impenitence could not be pronounced final. But should they reject *that*, they would be resisting the last proof that would be given—that Christ is the Son of God, and the Saviour of sinners; with their own hands they would have subscribed the sentence which doomed them to perdition; they would have added the final shade of horror to their condition, anticipating "the blackness of darkness for ever."

But let the specific sin denounced be what it may— and possibly it is left indeterminate, that it may shed a cautionary influence over a larger space,—the denunciation surrounds the doctrine of divine influence with a guard as terrific as the barriers placed about the mount that burned. It has no parallel in the word of God; and is only inferior, in its power to inspire dread, to the awful sentence of the last day. Where all besides is pleasant as the garden of the Lord, it stands out a terrible anomaly—a volcano fast by the tree of life. He who incurs its terrors is henceforth an outcast from grace,—a proclaimed anathema,—devoted to damnation, —the heir of unknown treasures of wrath. Reader, as you would dread to take even the first step in the direction of this tremendous sin,—as you would tremble to think of entering into its mountainous shadow,—trifle with nothing which relates to the agency of the Holy Spirit. That agency is truly "for your life." Sin has brought you into the crisis of the second death; and his is the only hand that can apply the only remedy. In his offers and influence, God may be regarded as collecting up all that is gracious and solemn in the vast economy of redemption, and coming to bring the whole, as far as you are concerned, to an issue; as making his nearest and final approach to your spirit. As you value eternal life, then, let there be no symptom of disinclination to receive him.

But this is not enough: when he spoke of the Holy Spirit, the Saviour would have his disciples to lift up their thoughts, to enlarge their expectations, and form the loftiest conceptions of excellence and grace, declaring that the advent of the Spirit would more than compensate for the loss of his own personal presence. What must be the value of that gift which would supply the place of the orb of day, and make us cease to deplore its extinction? Of infinitely surpassing value must be the gift which could indemnify the church for the personal departure of its Sovereign Lord. Yet such a gift is the Holy Spirit—the soul of the church, and the life of the world; for so much of the Spirit as there is in the world, precisely so much, and no more, is there of life.

In the history of the natural creation, it is recorded that until he brooded upon the face of the waters, the earth was without form, and void; but he infused into it a vital element, and what a world of beauty arose!—an enlargement of heaven—the treasury and temple of the material universe. And, until he came into the new creation, the work of salvation was at a stand. The sacrifice for sin had been offered; the atonement accepted; all the elements of salvation were in existence, but without life; all the blessings of grace were ready, but the Spirit was wanting to convey them into the soul. And when he came, and commenced his office, what glories transpired! The Saviour had not merely foreseen these; his holy mind had often luxuriated in the scene, had dwelt with unimaginable delight on the prospect of the Spirit returned to the world, and employed in its renovation. The valley of dry bones was around him; the place he inhabited was a moral sepulchre; but he saw the Spirit about to become the soul of these slain—to breathe into them a higher order of life than they had yet lived, enabling them to do divine exploits, to defy and triumph over death. Before him lay stretched out, wherever he turned, an ocean of woe, brackish with human tears; the Dead Sea, embittering, poisoning, and turning to ashes the fairest fruits of earth; and exhaling vapours fatal to all human joys. But he saw the divine Spirit—the waters of prophetic vision—issuing forth from the sanctuary of heaven, a new element of life, " going down into the desert, and into the sea, to heal the waters. And it came to pass that the waters were healed, and everything lived whither the river came."

Humanity, to his view, appeared as one body, one mighty growth and stature of sin demoniacally possessed by the prince of the power of the air, and putting forth all its gigantic powers in exploits of evil. But he saw the hour of his exorcism at hand, and rejoiced. "Now," said he, " is the judgment of this world; now shall the prince of this world be cast out." He beheld human nature released from the foe, whose name is *legion*,—renewed in all its powers,—raised to a holy rivalship with angels,—and prepared to be the ornament of a new creation : and all this resulting from the advent and operation of the Holy Spirit. The profound complacency with which he dwelt on the vision evidently shewed that he deemed nothing too great to be expected from the coming of the divine Spirit; and that he desired to communicate to his disciples his own enthusiasm, to fill them with anticipations as enlarged and glowing as his own.

He intimates that, of all the gifts which we can solicit, or he impart, a greater cannot be named than the donation of his Spirit. " If thou knewest the gift of God, and who it is that saith unto thee, Give me to drink, thou wouldest have asked of him, and he would have given thee, living water;" he would have bestowed on thee the gift of his Spirit, extinguishing all thy wants at once, and leaving thee, through eternity, nothing to crave. And who can compute, who can exaggerate, the value of this gift? Had we originally classed with the beasts that perish, as mere animated clay,—and had he then raised us in the scale of being, by adding our immaterial and immortal soul,—we could not have looked back on our brutal pre-existence, or have felt the consciousness of our new-found powers of mind, without standing amazed at the greatness of the gift he had conferred. But here he speaks of a superaddition. He has given to us one spirit; but he proposes to give us another—to make us all the richer by an additional Spirit. He has given a soul to our body; but he would not have us to suppose that his gifts are exhausted, for he offers to give us a soul to our soul. The spirit which he has already implanted is human; but that which he has in reserve is divine. And to excite and inflame our desires, he represents the divine Spirit as his crowning gift,—as rendering any further additions unnecessary, by absorbing all our wants, and comprising the essence of all good.

Were the natural influences of the Spirit to be denied to the material world, who can paint the desolation which would instantly ensue!—its pleasant verdure dried up and destroyed—all its harmonies silenced—its surface strewed with the wrecks of what was life—a sepulchral world, enveloped with a pall of darkness—a wandering star, in which all things were hastening to chaos and desolation. As the Spirit of grace, his agency is the life of the spiritual world. Accordingly, the chief penalty of the apostacy—the most deadly element of the curse—was the suspension and withdrawment of his vital presence; by which the guilty and deserted soul was left to enter at once on eternal death—to begin hell on this side the grave. On the other hand, it follows, that the restoration of the Spirit is the capital blessing of the covenant of grace. As if all the other blessings were represented by this, and included in it, the Saviour magnifies and names the Spirit alone. While in one of the evangelists, we hear him offer *all good things* to them that ask; from another we learn, that, by this all-comprehending offer, he expressly intends his Holy Spirit: thus leaving us to infer, first, that universal good and the Divine Spirit define each other; or, that they are one and the same thing: and, secondly, impressing us with the fact, that the Spirit is the only unchangeable and necessary good. Philosophy teaches us that no material object on earth has a colour of its own; that whatever the hue which apparently belongs to any object, it may be changed, and the object be made to take the hue of all the prismatic colours in succession. This is true, analogically, of all the things and events of this life,—they are not intrinsically good or evil,—do not possess a character and complexion of their own. The same dispensation may prove a curse to one, and a blessing to another—may be an evil to-day, and a good to-morrow—may come as a favour, but be perverted and turned into poison by our depravity,— or may come as a trial, and be converted into food and life by the transforming touch and smile of God. But the gracious influence of the Spirit is susceptible of no such fluctuation. Impassive itself, it is yet capable of changing everything else; while able to impress its own character on the universe of being, it remains itself unchanged and unchangeable,—the only absolute, eternal, and necessary good.

What more can be necessary to turn our whole soul into desire?—to turn all our most ardent thoughts and longings into one channel, pouring forth a copious stream of supplication for the one great gift of the Spirit? Is it possible that we can ask for any inferior good till we have obtained this? Had we an adequate impression of its magnitude, we should forget that any other want existed; our entreaties would rise in energy and earnestness as we moved forward to the attainment of the blessing; our cry would ascend, and peal with ceaseless importunity at the gate of heaven—would go in unto the Almighty, even into his holy place; we should ask, and seek, and knock, till he had bestowed it with a liberality which left nothing for our fears to apprehend, or our expectations to desire.

But is there ground to believe that an earnest application for this ineffable good would be crowned with success? For in proportion as the value and necessity of an object rise in our view, our demand for encouragement to pursue it rises also. Two things are observable in reply. The first is, that the gift of the Spirit, which is the only indispensable good, is the only blessing which is promised with unconditional, absolute certainty. And the second is, that it is the absolute and essential goodness of this blessing which enables the Almighty to promise it unconditionally. If, like all subordinate blessings, its character were mutable, and its value dependent on circumstances,—like them, it could only be made the subject of a conditional promise; the mere mutability of its nature, and the consequent possibility of its becoming an evil, would have made it incapable of an absolute promise. But the intrinsic and immutable goodness of the gift enables the Divine Promiser to say of it, what he can say of no inferior blessing, "Ask, and ye shall receive; seek, and ye shall find; knock, and it shall be opened unto you."

The student of mechanical philosophy is aware that dynamics, or the science of force and motion, enters into nearly every physical inquiry; that it is placed at the head of all the sciences; and that, happily for human knowledge, it is one in which certainty is attainable equal to that of mathematical demonstration. Indeed—what is true of no other branch of physical science—our knowledge of dynamics, of motion and its communication, is only limited by that of pure mathematics. Now let our present subject be denominated *spiritual dynamics*, and the analogy of these remarks will be obvious. The Divine Spirit is the author of all motion in the moral world; the science of spiritual force and motion, originating in him, is at the head of all the doctrines of evangelical religion; it enters into all our religious calculations; and, happily for our hopes and endeavours, it is one in which every step may be taken with absolute certainty. Indeed—what is true of no other promised good—the measure in which we receive his influence is determined only by the measure of our desires after it, or by the limit of our capacity to enjoy it. "Every one," saith Christ, "that asketh, receiveth; and he that seeketh, findeth." He would have us observe that he is not propounding a theory, but stating a fact; that he is expounding a law of the divine government—a law which has established a certain connexion between asking for the Holy Spirit and receiving it;—and that, could we appeal to all who have made the experiment, we should find that this order was never violated;—that, could we interrogate each of that throng without number who have sought the gift, they would testify, with one consent, that they all received to the utmost amount of their desires, and abundantly more.

Prior, indeed, to the act of regeneration,—and, as to the time and manner of that event, the wind itself is not more uncontrollable and free than is the agency of the Holy Spirit,—he illustrates his sovereignty by acting where he listeth;—asserts and magnifies the royalty of his grace by selecting the most unlikely objects, and thus pouring contempt on human calculations. But, in all his subsequent communications, he voluntarily binds himself to act by a rule which man can understand and employ, voluntarily subjects his influence to the call of prayer, and, in a sense, resigns his sceptre into the hand of faith. Amazing condescension! As if only concerned to bring us to the footstool of mercy, and as if fearful lest the recollection of his sovereignty should deter us from approaching, he actually merges that sovereignty; yes, at the tremendous risk of seeing us erase the doctrine of his absolute liberty from our creed—of hearing us deny the sovereignty of his operations, he, in effect, throws up the high prerogative, brings himself under obligation—irrevocably binds himself to answer prayer.

To encourage our application for the Holy Spirit, the Saviour appeals, from the instinct of parental tenderness, to the infinite benevolence of our heavenly Father: "What man is there among you, who, if his son asked bread of him, would give him a stone: or, if he asked a fish, would give him a serpent?" Who would mock the wants of his famishing child? The testimony of universal experience is against the probability of such an act: the thing, indeed, is possible; but so rare, that it has never been deemed necessary to provide a law for its punishment. So deeply does parental affection enter into the heart, that it commonly survives every other benevolent feeling;—it is the last affection which leaves the nature of a bad man. "But if ye, being evil, know how to give good gifts unto your children," said Christ, "how much more shall your heavenly Father give his Holy Spirit to them that ask him?" Could all the parental tenderness which the world has contained, from the beginning of time till now, be all collected and infused into one human heart, compared with the unbounded benevolence of our Father in heaven, it would be but as a drop compared with the ocean. And, therefore, it cannot be that the needy and suppliant soul should plead for the gift of the Holy Spirit, and his infinite goodness refuse to give. Degrade him to a level with sinful humanity, suppose him to be only an earthly parent, still the refusal would be all but impossible. Now what a human father will scarcely ever fail to do, though he is evil, God will never fail to do, because he is ineffably good.

But, that nothing might be wanting to complete our encouragement and crown our hopes, our Lord represents the treasures of divine influence as placed entirely at his own disposal. And where would Poverty and Want have relief deposited, if not in the hands of unconfined Bounty? Like a channel, prepared on purpose to receive and convey the overflowings of a fountain, he receives only to communicate. As well might the sun be charged with niggardliness in the dispensation of light,—though, from the moment of its creation, it has been constantly pouring forth, in all directions, an immensity of light, sufficient to flood with radiance ten thousand worlds like ours,—as to question the readiness of Christ to impart the influence of the Holy Spirit. Let the amazing profusion with which he dispensed it, on the day of Pentecost, testify his grace. Religious ordinances,—means of grace,— a standing ministry;— what are these but channels through which he seeks to pour a constant supply of the river of life for the irrigation of his church?—what are they but pillars which he has reared as memorials of his ascension, to remind us that now we have only to ask in order to receive;—that he can now dispense the Spirit perpetually and without measure;—so that every day might be a pentecostal day —a repetition of his coronation day.

Having become the repository of divine influence, his

only solicitude appears to arise from his not finding recipients to share the blessing. As the heedless and the worldly pass him by, he calls to them in language which shews that they could not find more relief in receiving than he would experience delight in giving; that his benevolent heart is actually burdened with the magnitude of the gifts he has to dispense, and yearns for the godlike gratification of giving them away. " O, if thou knewest the gift of God, and who it is that speaks to thee, thou wouldest ask him, and he would give thee living water. But ye will not come unto me that ye might have life. Ask, and ye shall receive." You cannot open your eye on the light of day, but a thousand rays from the sun instantly enter and illuminate your organ of sight; you cannot inspire, in the ordinary act of breathing, without drawing in copiously the vital air: repair at once to the throne of grace, and you shall not raise a craving look for the blessed Spirit in vain; your eye shall attract him: inspire, draw in, and you shall inhale, at every breath of earnest desire, the influence of the Holy Spirit.

The Christian church is a region, and the only region on earth, replenished with the vital influence of the Holy Spirit: and, by making baptism the initiatory ordinance, the Saviour has significantly taught, that, while all within inhale an element of life, all without are breathing an element of destruction. By appointing the rite to be administered "in the name of the Father, and of the Son, and of the Holy Ghost," he has sealed us to the day of redemption—he has burnt in, and made indelible, the awful signatures of Christian discipleship; reminding us, that as those who have " been born again of water and of the Spirit," he has given into our keeping a new life,—a life supernatural and divine: and charging it on us, as we hope to see the glorious day which is longed for by all creation, that we preserve that life inviolate and ungrieved.

In allusion to the residence of the Divine Presence in the temple, he declares of the Spirit of truth, that " he dwelleth with you, and shall be in you." There is a sense in which all the believers, of all ages, are represented as forming one vast and compacted temple, of which the Holy Spirit is the living soul,—cementing, animating, and pervading the whole. Now if important duties devolve on you, though you are only a fraction, an atom, of the stupendous fabric inhabited by the Holy Spirit, how momentous do your duties appear, when you reflect that you yourself constitute an entire temple. The Jews had an appointed guard to watch their temple, night and day; and, though the guard was numerous, each must doubtless have felt that he was entrusted with a solemn charge. But what would one of them have felt, had the whole trust been devolved on him alone, and that, too, at a time of peculiar danger from a watchful foe: how tremblingly alive would he have been to everything relating to his sacred charge! To you, my fellow-Christian, as to a living sanctuary, the Spirit has been given, " that he may abide with you for ever." Reflect on his divine character and gracious designs, and then conceive, if you can, of a more sacred and weighty trust than that of keeping his temple inviolate.

Had you originally belonged to one of the lowest species of animal life, and had he raised you in the scale of being, multiplying and enlarging your faculties, from step to step, till reason dawned, what a sense of responsibility, we may suppose, would have flashed on your mind as you first awoke to the consciousness of your amazing transformation! To find yourself suddenly endowed and entrusted with an immortal soul,—

rich in affections,—strong in intellectual powers,—boundless in its capabilities and desires,—the perception of your new accountability might well impress you with an awful concern. But a greater responsibility is here. The Spirit of spirits, the Fountain Spirit himself, is given to you, as a principle of new and heavenly life, as a divine in-dweller, and you have to keep for him the temple of your soul. O then, see to it, that your conduct accords with so sacred a trust. He comes to you as the Spirit of truth; study the mind of the Spirit; consult his dictates as your living oracle. By yielding to the dictates of the flesh, your spirit has lost its proper character, its discriminating and determining moral power; but he proposes to rescue and reinforce your spiritual nature— he comes to be your spirit, to turn your very flesh into spirit, renewing your fleshly mind. Do not let it appear by your conduct, as if, having carnalized your own spirit, you would, if possible, carnalize the Divine Spirit also, placing all spirit in subjugation to the flesh. He is the Comforter, the very soul of happiness; do not grieve him whose object it is to solace and bless you. Do not resist him in the execution of his office, while engaged in cleansing and sanctifying his temple. Be not satisfied with merely not grieving the Spirit of God, but aspire to please him, to magnify his office, to enjoy an affluence of his grace, to live in the Spirit as in the hallowed atmosphere of a temple in an all-surrounding element of holiness.

Finally: " He shall not speak of himself," said Christ; " he shall testify of me;" and, as if to reward and provide for that disinterested and emphatic silence of the Divine Spirit concerning himself, our Lord made him the great theme of his own last discourses and promises. And when was he more original and explicit than when dwelling on this subject? What a vast tract of new truth did he add to the domains of faith, all fertilized and enriched with the effluence of the Spirit! On what topic was he more evangelical than on this?—even antedating the style of the epistles, and leaving little if any thing for them to add, either in unction or in fulness. What subject did he equally rely on to console his disciples, and to fill them with expectation in the prospect of his own departure? He was in search of the strongest solace,—and he had an infinite variety of subjects to choose from,—but out of all that multitude the topic on which he chose chiefly to insist, was the promise of the Holy Spirit. And what lofty things did he predicate concerning him? What names of greatness and goodness did he bestow on him? He made him the great promise of his new dispensation! And yet, what doctrine, what *leading* doctrine at least, is less insisted on in the church than the doctrine of divine influence? And, consequently, what promise is less fulfilled to the church than the promise of the Spirit? It is true, an occasional sermon is preached on the subject, just to satisfy the sense of duty,—and an occasional restlessness is observable in parts of the church,—but, alas! it is a starting *in* sleep, rather than an awaking out of it;—like the spasmodic motions of a person who is visited in sleep by the reproachful remembrance of an important duty which he has consciously neglected, it is the involuntary agitations of the slumbering church, convulsively answering to the unwelcome reproaches of the unslumbering conscience. Other prophecies are considered, but the promise of the Spirit, the great unfulfilled prophecy of the gospel, is doomed, by general consent, to *stand over* for future consideration. Other blessings are desired, but this, which would bring all blessings in its train, which is offered in an abundance corresponding to its infinite plenitude, an abundance, of which the capacity of the recipient is to be the only limit,—of this we are satisfied with just so much as will save our sleep from deepening into death. Each falling shower—consecrated emblem of divine influence—the scantiest that moistens the thirsty earth, descends more copiously than the offered influences of the Holy Spirit, and reproaches us with the spiritual drought of the church. And so long have we accustomed ourselves to be content with little things, that we have gone far in disqualifying ourselves for the reception of great things: the *revivals* of the new world are still regarded by many " as idle tales."

The church itself requires conversion. We pray for the conversion of the world, but the church itself, though in another, yet in a sober and substantial sense, needs a similar blessing. The object of conversion is two-fold—personal and relative—to bless us, and to make us blessings. Individual conversion accomplishes the first object, by placing us in a personal and evangelical relation to Christ; the second can only be scripturally effected by the collection and organization of those who are so related to Christ into a church, and by that church advancing forwards and placing itself in an evangelical relation to the Holy Spirit. Now the prevailing sin of Christians is, that they are inclined to stop short at the first of these stages. They are, perhaps, sufficiently alive to the importance of preaching Christ as the author of redemption, for they have their own personal experience in evidence of its necessity; but they are not proportionally alive to the necessity of divine influence as the means of usefulness, for of that they have not the same evidence. Their conversion to Christ, as individuals, was scarcely more necessary to answer the first aim of the gospel, in their own salvation, than their conversion to the Spirit, in their collective capacity, is necessary to answer the second, in the salvation of others. I say their *conversion* to the Spirit; for the change necessary has all the characteristics of conversion: conviction of guilt in neglecting his agency, a perception of his necessity and suitableness, and earnest applications for his heavenly influence.

That the doctrine of divine influence has a place in the creed of the faithful we admit, but it is one thing to assent to its truth and importance, and a very different thing to have a deep and practical persuasion of it. That the Holy Spirit is at present imparted to the church, to a certain degree, is evident from its existence. For every believer is the production of the Spirit,— carries about in his own person signatures and proofs of divine operations,—and thus forms an epitome and pledge of the eventual conversion of the world. But as to the measure in which his divine influence is afforded, who has not deplored its scantiness? From the earliest dawn of the reformation to the present hour, this has been the great burden of the church. What writer, of even ordinary piety, has not bewailed and recorded it as the standing reproach and grief of his day? Look back, and what do you behold? — a procession of mourners, nearly all the living and eminent piety of the time, dressed in penitential sackcloth, moving through the cemetery of the church as through a Golgotha, and exclaiming, in tears, "Come from the four winds, O breath, and breathe upon these slain that they may live." What do you behold?—"the priests, the ministers of the Lord, sanctifying a fast, calling a solemn assembly," lamenting that so few attend the solemn call, and then advancing, a mournful train, casting themselves down, and lying prostrate at the foot of the throne of grace, and, as the representatives of the church, exclaiming, "Behold, O Lord, a poor company of creatures gasping for life! thy Spirit is vital breath; we are ready to die, if thy Spirit breathe not. Pity thine own offspring, thou Father of mercies. Take from us, keep from us what thou wilt, but, oh! withhold not thine own Spirit." Such were the actual terms in which the great and pious Howe led the supplications of a solemn assembly, in his day, convened to cry for the Spirit. And has it not been on the lips of the mourners in Zion, an unbroken procession, ever since? And does it not express the sense of the church in the present day? As we have fallen into the train, and brought up the rear, of the mourning suppliants, have we not deplored the absence of the Spirit as the great affliction of the church, and implored his impartation as our great want, our only remedy?

But "the Spirit will be poured out from on high"—would that the importunity and loud cries of the church warranted the expectation that the event were near! And when he does descend, among the many blessed effects which will accrue, this doubtless will be one—that the teaching of Christ, concerning him, will be hailed and studied as if it were a new revelation,—will be traversed and explored like a newly discovered continent. The reasons of Christ for amplifying the subject, and for laying so much stress on it, will then be felt in the inmost soul; each of his declarations concerning it will seem to expand into a page, and be consulted as a charter fresh from Heaven; promises which we now repeat with freezing accents will then burn on our lips, and be pleaded with an earnestness not to be denied, but which will open the windows of heaven for the emission of still larger outpourings of the Spirit.

SECTION IV.

OF THE DOCTRINE OF THE TRINITY, AND OF A SPIRITUAL CHURCH.

AMONG the subjects comprehended in our Lord's original teaching may be named the doctrine of the Trinity. There is no ground to conclude that, prior to the promulgation of the gospel, this doctrine had any claim on the faith of mankind. The early Christians, indeed, in their eagerness to obtain for Christianity the patronage of philosophy, professed to find the doctrine of the Trinity in the writings of Plato; but had they maintained, instead, a duality, or a quarternity, the same writings would have equally befriended them. The humble pretensions of the Jewish system were satisfied with proclaiming the existence and unity, or oneness of God, in opposition to "the lords many, and gods many," of the heathens; the allusions which the system contained to the triplicity of the divine nature awaited, like so many dormant seeds of truth, the rising of the Sun of righteousness to quicken and draw them forth from their obscurity.

But though the solemn mystery is sufficiently developed in the gospel to demand our faith,—though the Great Teacher held in his hand the entire map of truth, he disclosed only so much of the part in question as related to our path to heaven. In adverting to the abysmal subject of the Divine Essence, he maintained a wise reserve; and he did this, both that he might not entangle us in a labyrinth when we ought to be advancing in the open path of life, and because of our natural incapacity to comprehend him on a theme on which there are no analogies to assist us. " How shall ye believe, or understand me," said he, " if I tell you of heavenly things?" Instead, therefore, of theorizing on the subject, he taught it dogmatically and practically.

The doctrine, in the general opinion of the Christian church, is necessarily involved in various parts of our Lord's teaching. I shall content myself, however, with adverting to his great command—" Go, then, and make disciples of all nations, baptizing them unto the NAME of the Father, and of the Son, and of the Holy Spirit." Whether he intended these words to be a formulary of the rite or not is immaterial to determine. Their obvious import is to describe baptism to be a religious dedication to God, who is known by the manifestation of his NAME—the display of his glorious perfections. Now, as this name is attributed equally to the Father, to the Son, and to the Holy Spirit, it seems inevitably to follow, that the Son and the Spirit are, with the Father, the One God.

Our Lord instituted but two ordinances—baptism and the Lord's supper; he erected but two monumental pillars—one without, and the other within, the church: on the first of these—that which fronts the world—he inscribed the great name of the Triune God; and, as if to render the inscription more impressive, he made it his last act. Baptism is the vestibule, or entrance, to his spiritual temple, the church; so that, before his disciples can cross the threshold, he requires them to receive the print of the Sacred Name: and, by making that one ceremony final, he reminds them that the holy signature is indelible. By baptizing us into the threefold name of God, he would impress us at the very outset of our Christian life with the fact, that the work of our salvation is so vast, that it brings into action every distinction and attribute of the divine nature; that the Father, the Son, and the Holy Spirit, the entire Godhead, find ample scope for the exercise of all their perfections, and employment for all the affluence of their grace. And thus would he put every part and property of our nature, in return, into active requisition in his service; causing us to feel the penury of our utmost love, and constraining us cheerfully to own, that, could we multiply our powers three, or a thousand fold, they should all be his. If, *before*, we considered our obligations infinite, what shall we think of them now, on beholding the Father, the Son, and the Holy Spirit, three distinct subsistencies, actually confederating and concurring together, and embarking all their infinite treasures in the cause of our happiness: what, but that our obligations, which we before considered infinite, are thus multiplied threefold!—a multiplication this which the metaphysics of a grateful heart will allow, if not the severer philosophy of the head. How amazing the thought, that the Godhead, the three glorious subsistencies in the Divine Essence, should be all officially present to receive us in the baptismal solemnity, the porch of the church; that all the Divine Being should be there to enter into covenant relation with us; that we should there be met by the sum of excellence, and have it ascertained to us, that to the utmost extent of our capacity we are entitled to the enjoyment of the whole. An ocean of happiness placed before those whose hearts overflow with a drop! "A presumptuous idea, if our own invention; a lofty one, if revealed to us."

I. Another original subject contained in our Lord's teaching is, the existence of a spiritual church. The grand conception of organizing and erecting a new community, to be distinguished from all the existing forms of civil society in the world, by the spiritual nature and design of its government, could have only originated in the mind of One who had himself seen "the pattern of heavenly things." Under the Mosaic economy, this exalted scheme existed only in emblem. The "church in the wilderness," the Israelitish people, nationally selected, and separated from all the nations of the earth, prefigured an approaching separation of a more select and refined nature, consisting exclusively of "Israelites indeed." Christ came to realize the sublime idea, to be himself the heart of the church, the point around which it should crystallize and form; and, in his own person, (humanity inhabited by Deity,) presented, at once, the image and nucleus of the unearthly society.

II. The voice of prophecy had declared that such would be the spiritual character of his new kingdom. For while some monstrous type, of brute ferocity and power, was deemed an appropriate symbol of each preceding monarchy, as seen by Daniel, the ensign of the Messiah's reign was distinguished by the likeness of the Son of man,—aptly denoting that, while *they* prevailed by the ascendancy of physical might, from *his* kingdom should be banished every carnal weapon and instrument of coercion; and that to him should belong the honour of recognising and erecting the prostrate elements of humanity,—of reigning by the spiritual action of mind on mind, the almighty influence of enlightened reason, of sanctified gratitude and love. It was distinctly predicted that his kingdom, instead of symbolizing with any of the governments of earth, should be to the world an image of his own sufficiency, surpassing and encompassing them all. At first, it would resemble an *imperium in imperio*, a dominion of principle and affection flourishing amidst the kingdoms of the world, like the verdure of paradise set in the desert; but in the end, as Bacon describes the prevalence of a far different principle, "it bringeth in a new *primum mobile* that ravisheth all the spheres of government;" forming, from first to last, in the eyes of the world, an anomaly of government. Accordingly, when Jesus came to erect it, he appeared at a loss for suitable illustrations by which to explain it to the minds of his hearers. " Whereunto," saith he, " shall we liken the kingdom of God, and with what comparison shall we compare it?" None of the governments of the world supplied an analogy: He who is the wisdom of God seemed embarrassed, as he looked around the world of civil society for a similitude, and saw that it contained none.

III. But though the constitution he designed to erect was a new creation, he constructed it in a manner the most unforced and simple. He who asked only the dust of the earth out of which to form a creature of divine lineaments—He, who took the universal law of animal nature, which seeks the propagation of its kind, and, by grafting on it the sacred institution of marriage, made it produce the choicest fruits of the earth, thus converting and consecrating an animal instinct, a principle which man possesses only in common with brutes, into a source of pure and purifying enjoyment, which, more than any other natural means, raises and distinguishes man above the inferior creation—He asked only the elements of our social nature with which to construct " his body," the church. " Wherever two or three are gathered together in my name," said Christ, " there am I in the midst of them." He knew that, in obedience to our social instincts to the law which leads us to seek our kind, we should, in all ages, continue to associate: he saw that, in the kingdom of Satan, familiar intercourse is one of the principal means for extending the contagion of evil, one of the grand ordinances of sin, and he determined to give the same principle sanctified scope and activity, in a sphere where it might prove equally efficacious in the production and reciprocation of good.

IV. His church is the court of holy love, filled with offices and appointments of charity and grace. Bringing into it pity, and kindness, and zeal, he baptizes them with the Spirit of Heaven, assigns them each appropriate duties, and commands them to find and fabricate their happiness out of the happiness of others. Here we are to look on the faults of others, only to pray for, and assist in, their improvement; and to contemplate their excellences, only to admire and imitate. By a law of our nature, like seeks to associate with like; and, in his church, he enables holiness to ally and reinforce itself with holiness; he essays to make the least portion of goodness feel that it is identified with all the goodness in the universe. The fluid which is about to crystallize does not more certainly assume the form of the crystal inserted into it, than believers modify and accelerate the formation of their character by associating in Christian fellowship; and all assimilate to Christ, their common type and centre; according to his prayer, they become one in him.

V. Assimilation is a law of our nature, but the tendency of this principle in the world is to hasten its moral decomposition; whereas, in the church, it is intended to renovate and restore the moral health, and thus render the church the salt of the earth. But, to secure this end, it is evident that the members of his church must possess a character essentially different from the rest of the world. And this radical change must take place prior to their admission: otherwise, there is no guarantee that the world will not modify and absorb the church; rather there is the strongest probability that the principle of assimilation will operate to the triumph of the world, and the destruction of the church.

1. Previous to its formation, therefore, this was the mandate that rang through Judea—" Repent ye, for the kingdom of heaven is at hand;" peculiar elements were wanted to constitute this new society; subjects were called for to enrol under this new form of government; and repentance, transmentation, a change of mind, was the indispensable condition of enrolment. Its divine Founder followed, and, intent on its purity, he not only echoed the same call, but inscribed over its great entrance-gate the memorable sentence, " Except a man be born again, he cannot enter into the kingdom of God." He commanded his disciples to go through the world proclaiming repentance and the remission of sins in his name, baptizing them, (baptizing, that is, such as, being capable, obeyed the call to repentance, and accepted the offer of forgiveness;) these specimens of regenerated humanity, already selected by the divine hand, and baptized with the Spirit, they were to collect, and admit by the door of visible baptism into the Christian church.

2. That his church is to be composed only of spiritual elements—of such only as appear and profess to be the subjects of a divine change—is evident from the power with which he has armed it to expel offenders. " Moreover, if thy brother shall trespass against thee, go and tell him his fault between thee and him alone : if he shall hear thee, thou hast gained thy brother. But if he will not hear thee, then take with thee one or two more, that in the mouth of two or three witnesses every word may be established. And if he shall neglect to hear them, tell it unto the church : but if he neglect to hear the church, let him be unto thee as a heathen man or a publican. Verily, I say unto you, Whatsoever ye shall bind on earth shall be bound in heaven : and whatsoever

ye shall loose on earth shall be loosed in heaven. Again, I say unto you, that if two of you shall agree on earth as touching any thing that they shall ask, it shall be done for them of my Father which is in heaven. For where two or thee are gathered together in my name, there am I in the midst of them."

The whole of this paragraph evidently relates to the same subject, containing the rudiments of church government—forming the only authentic and divine platform of ecclesiastical discipline. We learn from it, first, that mere nominal Christians have no room provided for them in his church; for it is obviously implied that all its members have such habits of charity and devotion to maintain, and such holy offices to fill as the representatives of Christ, and duties to discharge requiring his seal and fiat to give them validity—all of so spiritual and distinctive a character, that they necessarily presuppose the possession of nothing less than vital godliness. Secondly, it implies, that when instances arise in the church calling for the exercise of discipline, the members of the church alone are sufficient to administer the discipline necessary, without the intervention of any civil authority from without. For, thirdly, it might occur, that were a civil arm a part of the organization of the church, that arm might be the very part of the body requiring excision; an hypothesis by no means extravagant, if the spirituality and purity of the church be an object; but, unless the power of excision be lodged in the spiritual community itself, this necessary purification could not take place. And, fourthly, it instructs us that a church, though composed of only " two or three," is complete in itself; that like the human body, it possesses a self-correcting principle, an expulsive power; and is competent to the discharge of all its peculiar duties.

The correction of incidental evils, and the expulsion of offenders, constitute the most delicate and difficult class of duties which a Christian church has to perform. But the task is imperative, and the discharge of it vital to the health and purity of the society : our Lord, therefore, in legislating on this subject, is unusually particular and encouraging. He exalts the duty of Christian reproof into a standing ordinance,—appoints the method, and specifies the several ascending degrees, of its administration, till it has been brought to bear in its utmost force and power on the conscience of the offending subject. Should it prove ineffectual to his recovery, the only remaining step is his excommunication. In exercising this solemn function, this highest prerogative, they are to come into the presence of Christ as the fountain of their power : he declares that he will descend to be a party in the final, awful transaction; that as they discharge the painful task, he will ratify it; that as they pronounce the sentence charged with the terrors of Sinai, he will adopt it as his own, and re-echo it, " as if many thunders uttered their voices," in the conscience of the doomed offender. And this appeal to himself he appoints as final, as the ne plus ultra of church discipline; to appeal elsewhere would be an impeachment of his authority, and treason against his throne.

And let no one speak lightly of his power of rebuke and expulsion. The omnipotence of public opinion, for instance, has almost become a proverbial expression. The world at present acknowledges nothing so mighty, though silent, in its operations. Its slightest whisper is law to a nation. It utters a prediction, and all the powers of society rush to accomplish the prophecy. Unable to endure its censure, numbers seek the asylum of the grave; and, rather than encounter its denunciations, even thrones have trembled and hid themselves in the dust. But, in uttering rebuke, the voice of the church is public opinion in its most concentrated form, borrowing mysterious efficacy from the presence and co-operation of an invisible Agent, and gathering tones of alarm by passing through the avenues of an affrighted soul. As the necessity of punishing the offender springs from the first principles in the divine nature, so the sentence of punishment harmonizes with the first principles of his own nature, meets and coalesces with all the remorse in his bosom, finds a ready and loud response from his conscience, and arms him against himself. Sharper than any two-edged sword, it inflicts a wound on the spirit for which earth has no remedy. It is a flash of that consuming lightning, which, leaving the outward man unscathed, passes direct to its mark within, scorching the conscious soul, and turning all its joys to ashes. It is even an anticipation of the last day, a foretaste of that consummation of terrors,—flashing the fires of the lake that burneth on the face of the soul,—cutting it off from God, delivering it over to Satan as a sealed anathema, an eternal outcast from hope and grace. Such is its efficacy when impartially administered, in connexion with the other branches of Christian discipline, to preserve the purity of the church, that, were it sufficiently known, Christians would no more think of calling temporal aid into the church, than they would of deputing an arm of flesh to guide and assist the bolt of heaven to its destined object.

3. The severe denunciations which Jesus uttered against the Pharisees, for " teaching as doctrine the commandments of men"—discharging all his thunders on the intrusion of human authority into the worship of God, and on the sanctimonious hypocrisy which naturally ensued, indicated clearly the spiritual nature of the church which he designed. He found the world in the

church, but he determined to reverse their relative position, to construct and perpetuate his new society as a church in the world. " Every plant," said Christ, and he spoke prospectively, as well as in reference to existing evils, " Every plant which my heavenly Father hath not planted shall be rooted up." The church is a sacred enclosure taken in from the world,—brought into cultivation by the Divine Husbandman,—and intended to be filled exclusively with the plants of righteousness. On the outside of this enclosure is to be found the spontaneous produce of evil, bringing forth fruit unto death; but all within are meant to be " plants of the Lord's right hand planting," exhibiting in the fruits they bear the essential difference between sin and holiness, and the infinite superiority of his transforming grace over the deadly produce of depraved nature. But if, in defiance of this arrangement, the hand of the world be allowed to interfere, his design is defeated; plants are brought in which are not of his selection; his Eden is degraded into a spot for human experiments, in which the produce of grace is supplanted by poisonous exotics, and overrun with the noxious weeds of human tradition. He designed the church to be his own *peculium:* it is the only fortress which he holds in a revolted world; and he intended, therefore, that no authority should be known in it, no laws acknowledged, but his own; that no parties should obtain admission but those " who are called, and chosen, and faithful;" so that to open its gates for the entrance of any of the revolted, however specious the pretext, is a betrayal of the most sacred trust, and treachery to the great cause of Christ. His high design is, that as Satan has a church, (he himself speaks of the synagogue of Satan,) consisting of the children of sin,—a church in which men have been always labouring to cast off the divine law, and to confound the distinctions between good and evil,—so he would have a church in which these essential distinctions should again be restored and exemplified, and in which the beauties of holiness, seen in their native lustre, should attract the notice, and extort the admiration, of the universe. These are the fruits by which its members were to glorify God,—these the unearthly marks by which all men should know them as his disciples.

But then, in order to the success of this grand design, it is essential that man should not intermeddle: the process is divine throughout. Had Christ taken up his residence visibly and permanently on earth, the impertinence and impiety of interfering with the arrangements of his church would have been too palpable to be attempted. But though he has departed, he appointed the Spirit as his successor, and promised him as more than his equal in the superintendence of the church; the Spirit has come, and, in the scriptures of his own dictation, has presented the church with its only code and charter; so that for man to interfere, is either to impugn the divine sufficiency of the Spirit, or to convict himself of presumptuous impiety. To every such intruder the language of Christ is decisive, " My kingdom is not of this world;" it has no principles in common with the kingdoms of earth,—it refuses all human patronage,—rejects, and casts off from itself, as alien to its nature, the aid of temporal pains and penalties,—and, for a man to put forth his hand, with a patronizing air, to support it, is to endanger its safety, or to peril his own.

Whether personally present or absent, our Lord designed his church to exhibit to the world an image of his own sufficiency;—to furnish to it a standing representation of another world,—of other laws than earth obeys, and of a higher order of enjoyment and power than man possesses, derived from a source independent of all created means. But in order to answer its original intention, its heavenly Founder must be left unimpeded to work out his great idea. If his church is to resemble a temple, let it be built after the pattern of things in the heavens;—let it have the exact dimensions and proportions assigned by the angel-architect, who brought to the work his golden measuring rod from heaven, and it will lift up its head into the light of day, and tower towards heaven, a stately and magnificent fabric, visibly inhabited by the shekinah of the divine presence,—made transparent by the enshrined glory, and radiating around in all directions its dazzling beams, so as to invite admiration, to repel the presumptuous approach, and smite with blindness the profane gaze of irreligion,—finding in its own glory its lustre and defence. If the church is to attain the fair proportions, and to reach the immortal stature, of the body of Christ, let her be fed with the manna which his own hand supplies, and grow as the in-dwelling life shall expand, and be left to the sole guardianship of his own grace, and she shall move in her own light, clad in more than complete steel, having the robes of divinity about her, frowning impurity from her path with a look,—surprising curiosity into blank awe—into involuntary and prostrate adoration, by her noble grace and bearing,—and, passing on in unblenched majesty, she shall perform the heroic works and exploits assigned her by God—a wonder! astonishing heaven and earth—" a woman, clothed with the sun, and the moon under her feet, and upon her head a crown of twelve stars;" being adorned with celestial attire, and crowned with light, instead of seeking to enhance her glory by sublunary ornaments, she evinces her spiritual nobility by treading them under foot. O! had men revered the evident intention of the Great Head of the church, instead of encumbering religion as they have and weighing her down to the dust with a load of earth-made armour, they would have seen her, equipped in the light but indestructible panoply of grace, advance to her appointed conflict, terrible as a bannered host,—carrying with her the sympathies of the groaning creation, whose champion she is,—trampling her enemies under foot, (the earth itself helping her in her straits,)—her weakness doing the deeds of might, deeds which omnipotence might own,—gathering up trophies at every step, —and returning at length from the circuit and conquest of the world, with a train of willing captives which no one can number, of all nations, kindreds, tongues, and people, and laden with many crowns for him whose strength had resided in her right arm, and who alone had caused her to triumph in every place.

4. But the church of Christ, enfeebled and defective as it may be, is that only object on earth on which he bestows his supreme regard. If his attention is divided, it is only between his church below and his church in heaven; but, in his estimation, they are identical—they are only two portions of the one object which constitutes, in his eyes, the glory of the universe. The affairs of the world, indeed, are under his superintendence, but always with an especial view to the prosperity of his church. While he extends his sceptre, and despatches his angels to every part of the world, he engages to come personally into the midst of his church, and to honour their prayers and decisions by regarding them as laws for his own conduct. The church is his mystical body, and he is present as the vital head, living through all its members. It is the theatre of his grace, in which he is making experiments of mercy on human hearts, and effecting transformations so amazing that angels look on with astonishment and joy. Here he is training up a number of those who were children of wrath, and preparing them to take part

in the business and pleasures of heaven. He has it in prospect to collect a large revenue of glory from earth; and his church is the repository in which all that wealth is stored, preparatory to its full and final display. His appointment of her ordinances, the full-souled ardour of his intercessory prayer that she might be with him, *one* with him for ever,—his donation and dowry of the Holy Spirit,—his rich and constant supplies of grace,—his watchful jealousy of all the advances of temporal power,—and the encompassing wall of fire into which his perfections kindle for her protection,—a wall which the gates of hell shall not break and enter,—all concur to shew, that, as the elected bridegroom of the church, he is looking forward to the spousal day, when, having made herself as a bride adorned for her husband, he shall find in her unwrinkled beauty and spotless perfection the solace and reward of all his love,—and in her full happiness the supplement and completion of his own glory. Now he is the centre from which radiates all her splendour; then he shall be the focus to which it shall all return. His voice shall be the only sound to which his church shall listen,—his glory the only object on which her eye shall fasten,—his grace, matchless and untold, the only theme that shall engage her tongue. " Blessed are they who are called unto the marriage supper of the Lamb."

SECTION V.

ON SATANIC AGENCY.

ANGELIC agency, both good and bad, is a doctrine familiar to the Old Testament. That part of the doctrine which relates to the ministry of holy angels, indeed, is there so fully illustrated, that, although the discourses of Christ contain frequent allusions to it, they present so little that is new, except the conspicuous part they will enact in the solemnities of the last day,—and the fact that they are *his*,—that the few remarks on the subject we propose to advance will relate exclusively to " the devil and his angels." Concerning these, the teaching of Christ is more copious, explicit, and original: as if, in compassion to our fears, the full exposure of our danger from hell had been reserved, till he could furnish the antidote to those fears by revealing the counteracting agency of the Holy Spirit.

Having assumed the championship of the world, and being confident of ultimate triumph, our Lord did not hesitate to confirm our worst apprehensions of the numbers, and powers, and malice, of our spiritual foes. He opened our eyes, and, behold! the enemy in full possession of our world. And, as if the seat of the infernal government had been long since transferred from hell to earth, he repeated its princely titles as familiar words, enlarged on its dominion, and pointed out its thrones, principalities, and powers. Among these, he spoke of one as Satan,—Beelzebub,—a liar,—a murderer from the beginning,—the wicked and evil one,—one who, by trampling on law, had acquired the authority of a legislator in guilt,—one who, by signalizing himself as the most daring of rebels, had reached the bad pre-eminence of the " prince of demons."

Of the number of his angels we can form only a conjecture; but the fact, that his " field is the world,"—that he is represented as multiplying himself, through their agency, over the whole field,—and concurring in, if not actually instigating, all the evils which it contains,—warrants the conjecture that they out-number the human race. Let no man, then, hope to escape temptation through any lack of satanic agents. He whose resources enable him to devote a legion to torment a human *body*, cannot be wanting in instruments to tempt and destroy the immortal soul.

Whether sin had ever entered the universe at any dateless period prior to the angelic apostacy, we know not: it is certain that we can only trace its history up to that mysterious event. Speaking of Satan, our Lord declares that " he abode not in the truth:" once he possessed a throne where all is radiant with holiness and joy, but he swerved from his allegiance to " the blessed and only Potentate," and thus lost his first estate. Together with an unknown multitude of associate rebels, he was driven from the presence of God, cut off from the loyal part of the creation, and doomed to be the prey of his own mighty depravity. From that moment he became the avowed antagonist of God; established an infernal empire, and planted the standard of rebellion, around which all the principles and powers of evil might rally and combine. Actuated by that universal law by which each being and principle seeks to conform all things to its own nature, and stimulated by implacable hatred against God, he no sooner found our world created, than he came to efface from it the image of God, and to stamp his own on its breast. In the execution of this dreadful project he succeeded; meriting, by the means which he adopted, and the dreadful results of his success, the titles of liar, the father of lies, and a murderer from the beginning. He impregnated the heart of man with the awful spirit of revolt, and added earth to his infernal empire,—involving the whole species in guilt,—introducing death, (now perhaps first known,) into the dominions of God,—and leading mankind, generation after generation, into the outer darkness of his own proper region. And of all the vast and complicated agency of evil, by which the sinfulness and misery of the world is perpetuated, he is " the Wicked One," the Evil, the great efficient cause. His throne is the rallying point to which all evil looks for reinforcement and support—the centre, from which flows, and to which gravitates, all evil—the heart of the great system of guilt.

The domination which Satan has acquired on earth is called by Christ a kingdom, in which he possesses, by right of supremacy in guilt, the princely titles, and exercises the prerogatives, of royalty. Unable to expel God from his throne, and thus succeed to the homage of man, he had, by a universal system of idolatry, planted his throne between the human worshipper and the Divine Being, intercepting and appropriating the adoration which belonged to God alone. But, in order that earth might not quite forget its rightful Lord, Jehovah was pleased to select a people, and erect a temple, expressly for the maintenance of his true worship. They held their country from God on the express condition of fealty to his throne. From the moment of that arrangement, Satan may be said to have made a descent on Judea: its temple was a memorial of his tyranny—a standing protest against his usurpation; its worship, a national proclamation, daily repeated in the name of Heaven, of his treason and guilt. At different times he seems to have put all the forces of his kingdom into motion to bear upon it: for to shut up the temple of God, to seduce the people to idolatry, to erect an idol in the holy place, was to sit on the only throne of God upon earth—was a triumph which could only be exceeded by ascending the throne of heaven.

For ages previous to the divine advent, the world seemed almost entirely his own. His contest for earthly supremacy, so long disputed by Heaven, seemed crowned with success. His vice-regencies and powers sat in the quiet and unchallenged possession of their thrones. No prophet smote them on their lofty seats, or denounced their usurpations; no miracle reminded them of an omnipotent antagonist. The world appeared to be as completely theirs, to portion out and rule at pleasure, as if they held it by grant and seal from God himself, and were appointed to reign in his name. Nor did Judea itself form an exception to this wide infernal sway; for (short of *formal* idolatry) it belonged to the universal confederacy, and formed one of the fairest and most faithful provinces of the satanic empire. And, as if to exact a terrible compensation, even for this slight nominal deduction from full allegiance, many of its inhabitants were held as hostages to hell by a terrible system of demoniacal possession. Satan had become "the prince of this world." Wherever he looked, the expanse was his own; the teeming population were his subjects; the invisible rulers were his selected agents;—temptation in his hands had become a science, and sin was taught by rule; the world was one storehouse of temptation—an armory, in which every object and event ranked as a weapon, and all classed and kept ready for service: every human heart was a fortified place; every demon power was at its post: he beheld the complicated machinery of evil, which his mighty malignity had constructed, in full and efficient operation; no heart unoccupied, no spot unvisited, no agency unemployed; and the whole resulting in a vast, organized, and consolidated empire. No sooner, therefore, did Jesus begin to attract the attention of Judea, as the " Sent of God," than he became obnoxious to the tyrant's hate. In the usurped capacity of the sovereign of the world, the tempter went forth and met him, asking him only to own that sovereignty, and all the kingdoms of the world should be his, and the glory of them.

But the great object which had brought Christ upon earth was to dispute that sovereignty, to re-assert the original and supreme rights of God to the alienated homage of mankind, and thus rescue man from the grasp of the Destroyer. What the enemy reserved as his last and most powerful temptation—the splendid vision of a thousand provinces—was a sight, we may suppose, familiar to the eye of Christ; though seen by him, alas! under a far different aspect. He beheld in it a scene of woe, which never failed to call forth his profound compassion. On all sides he beheld the blinded victims of satanic cruelty: vast, crowded tracts of spiritual beings—immortal essences—wasted, ruined, murdered, lost;—a captive world, chained to the wheels of the spoiler, and moving along (most of them so beguiled as to be actually pleased with the mock pomp of the gloomy procession) to endless death. While immediately beneath his eye, in the very land where he had taken humanity, he saw legions of fiends in actual, bodily possession of miserable man. Not satisfied with the evil they could inflict by ordinary temptation, he beheld them consummating their cruelty by actually incorporating with men,—turning their bodies into living tombs, engrossing and demonizing all their powers, merging the man in the fiend. Yes, man, who had been created in the image of God, became "the habitation of dragons;" his heart, the fuel consumed by their passions; his senses and organs, the slaves of their rampant impiety; hell brought to him, and begun in him, upon earth; an incarnate demon, his features putting on the image of the legion within him. What a sight for the Lover of souls!—what a spectacle for infinite Goodness to contemplate! The Saviour beheld, and meditated relief. He made bare his arm, and the unclean spirits fled at his approach. He sent his disciples—first twelve, and then seventy—to traverse the land in all directions, each of them armed and charged to cast out devils; and again he repeated the charge to his apostles, when on his way to ascend from earth to heaven.

When vindicating the character of his power from the imputation of the Pharisees, he affirmed that it was of a nature essentially hostile to Satan, and subversive of his kingdom; while the foresight of the redemption his death would achieve enabled him to speak of the future as if it had been present, and to say, " Now is the prince of this world cast out." The voice of prophecy had declared, " He shall divide the spoil with the strong;" and, in fulfilment of that prediction, he planted himself full in the pathway of the destroyer; he may be said to have erected his cross in the highway to hell, that he might rescue sinners from the very jaws of perdition.

Now, as Satan possesses on earth official ubiquity, as he is everywhere present through the medium of his agents, it was not to be supposed that an event so signalized as the advent of Christ would escape his knowledge, or, that, being known, it would fail to call forth his jealous vigilance and utmost opposition. Knowing, indeed, as *we* do, the essential dignity of Christ, we might have hoped that, in deference to his purity and majesty, temptation would have retired from his presence, or have laid its baneful activity to sleep, that the powers of darkness would have left him a free and open passage through the world, and that his disciples would have found in his hallowed presence a certain shelter from the persecutions of hell. But, so far from this, his coming awoke all the original antipathy, the native oppugnancy, of evil against good. He had come into a world in which nothing in human form had ever escaped the pollution of sin; and he had come here, attested by such signal credentials of a divine commission, that from the hour of his advent, through the whole of his earthly course, Satan appears to have called in his agents from every other pursuit, and to have set them in array against him alone; turning away from all ignobler prey, he seems to have made him the sole mark for every shaft and weapon of hell. As if the temptation of Christ were too great an enterprise, a field too momentous, to be left to the power of a common arm, the prince of darkness, himself, undertook personally to conduct the untried adventure. Having drawn out his forces, and entrenched himself in his way, he came into eager and determined collision with Christ on the very threshold of his public life; leaving him to infer, that, if he persisted in his intended course, his progress would be disputed, step by step.

Nor are the eventful narratives of the evangelists wanting in intimations that the threat was made good. In his own express language, especially as that language is afterwards illustrated by the apostles, we can only arrive at one conclusion, that his whole life was a continued conflict, hourly increasing in fierceness and malignity on the part of hell, till it came to the crisis of Calvary. "The prince of this world cometh," said he, "and hath nothing in me." "Now shall the prince of this world be cast out." "This is your hour, and the power of darkness." During that dreadful hour, indeed, no foe could be seen by man but such as the gates of Jerusalem had poured forth. And it is true that, had that been the only foe, the enmity of the carnal mind had that day collected and led out her chosen bands from the halls and streets of the city,—had assembled and crowded around the cross the darkest elements of human depravity. But the *great* Foe was invisible. Often had he assailed the life of Jesus before, but as often had he been defeated; it seemed guarded, like the tree of life itself, by a sword which turned every way. But now, at length, his persevering malice seemed crowned with success; the Saviour was in his toils, and appeared to be abandoned to his fate; he and his cause would expire in ignominy together; and mercy, pierced through his side, and chased from the world, would no more return, but would henceforth relinquish man to the undisputed sceptre of hell.

We cannot but imagine that the thrones and principalities of darkness were there to witness the triumph; that, flocking together from the east and west, the north and south, leaving behind them many an unfinished plot of evil, they came and covered the mount, to celebrate his triumph. And could heaven be absent? No, the angels of God, incapable of repose while such an issue was pending, quitted their celestial seats, and surrounded the scene with horses and chariots of fire. Stars in their courses might have fought during that hour, and have been unheeded. It was more than an era; the junction of all the eras of time: the event of that hour was to determine, whether earth should pass entirely into the hands of Satan, or be again recovered into the hands of God—whether the expiring rays of human hope should be quite extinguished in the blood of Christ, leaving the earth in hopeless night, or whether his cross should henceforth radiate light and life to the universe: it was to draw to a close the great question—to terminate the comprehensive controversy of all ages between right and wrong, holiness and sin. Hell inflicted the decisive stroke; the shock was received and sustained by the heart of the Son of God. Then, and not till then, did the powers of darkness perceive their error: they saw, with unutterable dismay, that, in bowing his head, he was dragging the pillars of their empire to the dust; that he was dying to triumph; that, in effect, his cross was changing into a throne. He exclaimed, "It is finished!" and the gates of hell vibrated at the shout. He entered into the grave for a short space; there attired himself in the robes of triumph; came forth to receive the gratulation and homage of angels and men; and ascended to his new mediatorial throne, "leading captivity captive, and making a show of them openly."

It is by no means unlikely that some persons, on comparing this statement with the moral condition of the world, may be tempted to think, that *if* the death of our Lord is to be viewed as a triumph over hell, we greatly overrate its practical results. To such a suspicion it may suffice to reply, that our language is only the echo of scripture, of the declarations of Christ himself. That "we see not yet all things put under him," we readily admit; that a large proportion of the satanic empire has not yet been even summoned in his name, and that much of the kingdom which nominally belongs to Christ has not really transferred its allegiance from Satan, are facts we deeply deplore. But, first, he distinctly predicted this prolonged activity and power of the enemy;—a consideration, secondly, which should induce us to credit his other predictions of perfect triumph in the end; especially as, in the third place, we recognise in his mediatorial work all the essential elements of that triumph,—the character of God, which Satan had obscured, made more illustrious than before; the most affecting and decisive proof that God, in punishing sin, is perfectly just, and infinitely good; the dignity and happiness of the creature, which Satan had placed in revolt, not only consisting with a state of subjection to God, but depending on it; divinity and humanity, which Satan had traduced and represented as antagonist natures, brought into the close embrace and union of one person; the forgiveness of sin, which the enemy supposed incompatible with the divine rectitude, made more compatible with that rectitude than even the punishment of sin would be; new incentives to holiness, and an infinite augmentation of every previous motive to resist sin; and, to crown all, the almighty agency of the Holy Spirit, to expel from the heart " the strong man armed," and to enthrone in his stead " a stronger than he." And, fourthly, it appears, that wherever these elements of triumph are brought to bear on the human heart, they infallibly achieve success; demonstrating the glorious superiority of Christ to " all the power of the enemy."

The church which he has formed has been reared in the immediate presence of hell in arms; every member belonging to it is a vassal rescued from the empire of sin; many of them were once even the pillars of that empire. As the spiritual erection has proceeded, it has been approached by stratagem, and beleaguered in form; but it is " built on a rock, and the gates of hell shall not prevail against it." When the seventy returned to him, saying, " Even the devils are subject to us through thy name," he received the announcement as a matter of course: his eye had followed them wherever they had gone; and, surveying futurity as already present, had beheld in their success the earnest of a triumph, in which " Satan should fall like lightning from heaven:" looking through all the intermediate clouds and storms of time, he gazed complacently, as in sceptred state, on the serene atmosphere of the world, purged of all its evil elements, and fit to be breathed by the inhabitants of heaven. When surrounded by circumstances of the deepest depression, he said, with the calm confidence of majesty enthroned with all its rivals at his feet, " The prince of this world is judged," " Now shall he be cast out." Even then he saw, in perspective, the completion of his triumph, and beyond: his prophetic ear, even then, caught the distant shout of his redeemed church. He knew that when he should exclaim, " It is finished," the powers of darkness would hear in that cry the knell of their empire; that when his name should be shouted from land to land, as the watchword of salvation, its every echo would shake and bring down the fabrics of that empire.

And now it *is* finished, the work of redemption is completed; all that remains for him to do is perfectly compatible with a state of rest; " from henceforth he is expecting till his enemies be made his footstool." Having fought the battle, he has despatched his subjects to pursue the enemy, to win the victory, and collect the spoils. As long, indeed, as this remains unaccomplished, he will not consider his office fulfilled, or his reward complete. As long as a single principle of evil continues at large, the universe is threatened, the safety and peace of the Saviour's empire are liable to invasion and revolt; " he must reign till he hath put all enemies under his feet." Nor, till then, will his kingdom be in a state to be " delivered up unto God, even the Father;" he has undertaken, expressly, to " gather out of it all things that offend, and them that do iniquity;" to restore it to a state of purity and perfection, worthy to be known as the work of his hands; fit to be accepted, and instated again, as an integral part of his dominions "who is of purer eyes than to behold iniquity." And, as he sits enthroned, with all power in his arm, it is true that, to him, even *now*, is the prince of this world cast out, and the last enemy destroyed. He beholds the prince of the power of the air already in flight, followed in disorder by the routed remains of his once gorgeous and imperial state—thrones, dominations, and powers—the tyranny of six thousand years, sailing through the air, and fading from the view: he looks upon the world— his own world—subdued by love, exorcised of every element and atom of evil—another heaven, catching, and reflecting, and multiplying, his own image; and God is all in all.

And here we should quit the subject, did we not suspect that certain inquiries have been suggested in the course of the essay, some of which, if left unnoticed, might impair the salutary effect which it might otherwise produce, and all of which admit of a practical application.

Concerning the nature of the beings of whom we are speaking, we only know that they are *spirits*; by which, probably, all that is meant is, not that they are absolutely unembodied,—to be only spirit, is most likely peculiar to God alone,—but that they are exempt from the gross materiality of bodies like our own. By calling them spirits, our Lord would probably remind us of the facility with which they obtain access to our minds, and would put us on our guard against the subtlety of their operations. The circumstance, that we are ignorant of the way in which they reach our mind, is no objection whatever to the doctrine that they do reach it: our incapability of tracing many of our sensible impressions beyond the mere sensation itself, leaves the fact of such impressions unquestioned. Besides, à priori, we should have thought it more unlikely that *matter* should act upon mind, that material objects should act on that which seems to have no property in common with them, than that mind should act upon mind—two homogeneous substances on each other. Yet experience tells us, that the former action is always going on in the process of our mental perceptions; and the latter, we presume, is all that is meant, physically, by satanic agency; of which, indeed, a counterpart and illustration is to be found in the action of one human mind upon another.

Nor is the doctrine invalidated by the objection, that we are unconscious of such extraneous influence; this only shews the facility with which the Tempter acts, and is the triumph of his art. He so times and modulates his whispers, that we mistake them for the voice of our own thoughts; so conceals his agency, that while we fancy we are sailing before the impulse, and floating down the stream, of our own free volitions, his hand is on the helm; thus, flattering our pride, scoffing at our weakness, and steering our destiny, at the same time. We ourselves suppose that there is an established order in which our thoughts succeed each other; that, detached and promiscuous as they appear to be, they are linked together with all the strength and sequence of a chain; and the principle which thus unites them we call the principle of suggestion—the law of association. Now, admitting the existence of such a law—a law common to all minds, like gravity to all matter—operating by mental affinity and attraction, it is only to suppose that Satan has mastered this principle—that the result of the experience of many thousand years, in studying the structure, watching the movements, and experimenting on the properties of mind, is, that he knows the universal bearing and operation of this principle; and what a fearful amount of power— what an immense command over the human mind, may he possess in the knowledge of this principle alone.

But whatever the grand secret of his dreadful art may be, the strongest language is but barely equal to express the reality of the power which he wields over the mind. He is represented as actually " entering into the heart ;" becoming the gloomy and fearful inmate of the soul; mingling his very essence with the being of a sinner. " Get thee behind me, Satan," said Christ to Peter, when that apostle acted the part of the Tempter. And " one of you," said he, when speaking of the traitor, " one of you is a devil." Evil is no doubt, at times, attributed to Satan, not because he has directly produced it, but because he loves it; and those who have wrought it have imbibed his spirit, and are employed in his service; such, therefore, may appropriately take their *name* from him, from whom they have derived their nature.

To excite our most solicitous avoidance of the enemy, as well as to describe his nature, he is repeatedly called, by Christ, an unclean spirit. It is not every unclean thing that offends the sight, while the slightest stain upon some things will excite in us deep dislike; the feeling depends entirely on the nature of the thing, and the purpose to which it is applied. We pass by an unclean stone unnoticed; it is unconscious of its state, and was meant to be trampled under foot. But, rising a step higher in the scale of creation, to an unclean plant, we become conscious of a slight emotion of dislike,—because we see that which might have pleased the eye, and have beautified a spot in the creation, disfigured and useless. An unclean animal excites our dislike yet more,—for, instead of proving useful in any way, it is merely a moving pollution. But an unclean human being excites our loathing more than all; it presents our nature in a light so disgusting, that it lessens our pity for him, if he be miserable, and excites in us ideas of disease, contamination, and pain. But an unclean spirit!—it is loathsome above all things,—it is the soul and essence of pollution,—it is the uncleanest object in the universe,—it is a spectacle which excites the deep dislike of God himself. His dislike of it is all the more intense, because, originally, it was pure, and capable of making perpetual advances towards divine perfection; whereas, now, it presents itself to his eye, robbed of all its purity, and defiled in all its powers, a fountain of pollution. It is so utterly unfit for its original employment and state, that the pure and holy God has no alternative, but to banish it from his presence, as a spiritual nuisance, and to consign it to the place which he has reserved "for every thing that defileth." To yield to temptation, then, is to put ourselves into the hands of him with whom contact is contamination: it is to receive into the centre of our being the great spirit of uncleanness, and to let our own spirits be degraded into the sink of essential pollution. How unspeakably precious to the sinner, sensible of his ingrained defilement, is "the fountain opened for sin and uncleanness."

"When the unclean spirit is gone out of a man, he walketh through dry places, seeking rest, and findeth none. Then he saith, I will return into my house from whence I came out; and when he is come, he findeth it empty, swept, and garnished. Then goeth he, and taketh with himself seven other spirits more wicked than himself, and they enter in and dwell there; and the last state of that man is worse than the first." This awful picture of demoniacal possession is expressly stated, by

Christ, to be a parabolical representation of the Jewish nation. But its applicability to a nation warrants the propriety of applying it to certain states of the individual sinner. And what an affecting view does it present of the untiring, encroaching, all-engrossing power of the enemy! how solemnly does it warn us to resist his first approaches! Having obtained a lodgment in the heart of the ungodly, he consults their vicious taste, panders to their depraved appetites, and thus seeks to make himself necessary to their peace. In the sin which most easily besets them he finds his power, and a convenient avenue by which he can always command an entrance and a welcome to the inmost chambers of their souls. They arise in the morning, without being able to say whether he will have gained a fresh triumph over them before night, or not; they have so often yielded, that they feel it will only depend on whether they are tempted or not: if he comes in the shape of their favourite sin, they will surrender again, as a matter of course. They perceive, indeed, some of the evil consequences which will attend it,—they dread his approach,—they foresee that it will occasion them anguish afterwards; but he has only to appear in the form of the tyrant sin, and they throw themselves prostrate at his feet, while he casts his chain around them once more. From the moment he achieves his first triumph, he seeks to make the heart " his house," till, having transmuted it into his own nature, though he should go through the whole world seeking rest, he would find none so congenial as that human house. Circumstances may occur which may induce him for a time to quit his residence. But if, during that interval, divine grace does not seize the throne of the heart, it will again be reclaimed, and re-entered with a large reinforcement of the enemy, and held with a sevenfold power. He will patiently wait, if necessary, till they have outlived the alarm which led to his withdrawment,—wait till they have passed through every downward stage of fear, doubt, indifference, obduracy, enmity,—wait for years, till he is again solicited to return and resume his power. Then does he avenge his temporary expulsion with fearful rigour. Every faculty of the mind is entered and possessed; the serpent-sin coils around the heart, and infixes his fangs, with a power which threatens never to unloose.

Are we disposed to entertain hard thoughts of that arrangement of the divine government which permits our exposure to satanic wiles;—it should be enough for us to remember that God will finally justify, not only this, but all his ways to man. This arrangement, however, is only part of that all-encircling mystery—the origin of evil; so that to notice it here would be gratuitously to misplace it. We will only suggest, therefore, in passing, that the divine Being, in not preventing satanic temptation by the arbitrary exercise of power, is not only acting consistently with the requirements of a moral government—a government which opposes principle by principle, and not by physical force or coercion,—that, as the virtue of good *men* finds an appropriate sphere for action, and is improved, by resisting the influence of the wicked, so it is highly probable the excellence of the holy angels is exercised and advanced by their efforts to counteract the powers of evil,—that the Almighty may be considered as doing everything necessary to vindicate his benevolence, by counterbalancing the agency of the evil by the activity of his holy angels; while, in superadding to their activity in our behalf the omnipotent aid of his Holy Spirit, he is greatly magnifying his grace; that, in securing the final triumph of that kingdom which embraces all the elements of moral good, over that which comprehends everything of evil, he is entitling himself to an infinite revenue of glory; and, finally, that a principal ingredient in the happiness of the redeemed will result from a clear and comprehensive survey of those tremendous powers of evil over which they will have triumphed.

In the meantime, it should be borne in mind, that in no instance in which Satan acquires dominion over the sinner, does he obtain it by force; the means which he employs are perfectly compatible with human freedom; so that the surrender of the sinner is voluntary—he sells himself to work iniquity. If the enemy sow tares in the field of the church, or of the individual mind, it is done " while men sleep ;" if he " cometh, and catcheth away the good seed sown in the heart," it is when the subject of it " understandeth it not"—does not lay his mind to it; or, if he re-enters the soul, after a transient absence, with sevenfold strength, it is only when " he finds his house empty, swept, and garnished," to welcome his return. The sole secret of his power over us is to be found in our own depravity: the soul may be " set on fire of hell," the live coal may be brought from the infernal fires, but the combustible materials were already collected and laid in the depraved soul. And, accordingly, though our depravity is frequently ascribed to " the wicked one," yet his agency is never alleged as an excuse for our sinfulness, but, on the contrary, as its last aggravation.

We have already remarked, that the days of the reign of Satan are numbered; the chain which is to bind him is forged, and the fires which shall encircle him are already kindled; " the breath of the Lord, like a stream of brimstone, hath kindled them." And the day is appointed when they who have lived his willing slaves shall find themselves involved in the coils of the same chain, and enveloped in the same penal fires. The Judge of all " shall say unto them on his left hand, Depart, ye cursed, into everlasting fire, prepared for the devil and his angels." Those who have tempted, and they who have embraced temptation, are the two classes which comprise all the pollution in the universe: as such, the besom of destruction shall sweep them together into one place, as the refuse of sin, the nuisance and leavings of the creation; Gehenna, the receptacle of all the elements of pollution, shall enlarge its capacious bosom to receive them; where, as the appropriate fuel of almighty wrath, they thall " burn together, and none shall quench them."

SECTION VI.

OF THE IMMORTALITY OF THE SOUL; RESURRECTION OF THE BODY.

THAT question in religion which takes precedence of every other—the existence of God excepted—and which gives character and importance to them all, is the ancient inquiry, entailed with unabated interest on each succeeding generation, " If a man die, shall he live again?" Independent of revelation,—if, indeed, any of the human race have ever been quite independent of it,—men have generally anticipated a future existence, as a doctrine harmonizing with their desires and wants, and with the character of a righteous moral governor. The instinctive horror with which the soul recoils from the thought of annihilation—its ardent longing after a perpetuity of life, and its strong presentiment of it—its constant progress in knowledge and power up to the moment of death—its capability of abstracting itself from this world, and conceiving of universal natures, and nobler states of being—the prodigality with which it lavishes its great powers on unworthy objects, owing to the inadequacy of everything earthly to engage them—the necessity of the *hope* of immortality to develop and give scope to its latent powers—and the principles and design of a moral government, in punishing sin and rewarding virtue;—these considerations are so many steps by which men have emerged from the sepulchre, ascended the throne, and, in hope, seized the crown of immortality. Now, throughout the kingdom of animated nature, wherever an organ or faculty is to exist characteristic of the species to which it belongs,—a kind of pre-assurance is given—a practical anticipation that it will, by and by, be developed; nor is this prophecy ever falsified. The most perfect human being is, at best, in this world, nothing more than an unfinished sketch of humanity—a creature full of these pre-assurances and anticipations of future development and final perfection. Unless, then, his instincts and essential principles are a splendid falsehood,—unless the divine signatures impressed on his nature be a forgery, a grave imposture,—unless humanity itself be a lie, a deep-laid conspiracy against all right and happiness, we are warranted in the hope of immortality. Under the government of a righteous Being, we naturally look for an illustration of his character in his works;—we ponder the volume of nature, and find it to contain one vast and compacted argument for the divine perfections; but deny to man a future existence, and the argument is flawed, and the character of God, which it professes to vindicate, stands impeached.

We, however, who enjoy the light of the gospel, are liable to overrate the argument derived from nature, and to forget that, to those who sit in darkness and the shadow of death, nothing short of a divine revelation can give to the hope of immortality stability and repose. For, in that consciousness of guilt which is common to all mankind, a suspicion arises in the mind, that the natural course and order of things have been deranged, a shadow of uncertainty comes over our best-reasoned speculations, and we feel at a loss to say what course the king of a boundless empire may see fit to pursue towards the rebellious subjects of an insignificant province. Here the opinions of a Socrates and a Plato, of a Cicero and a Seneca, though often quoted, are only, at best, the conflicting conjectures of minds alternating between hope and fear. They beheld, with dismay, the human race walking in gloomy procession to the grave; and, as they saw them disappear in the land of shadows, they sought, with strained and untiring gaze, to follow their steps, and learn their fate; and, had not revelation come to our aid, their opinions would have deserved respect, and would have often passed the lips of the dying in the stead of truths. But they themselves were conscious of distressing doubt: while, at one time, they spoke as from the skies; at another, they uttered the language of the sepulchre, according as hope or fear was the oracle of the moment.

Revelation authenticates the hope, and fulfils the obscure predictions, of this great instinct of humanity— an endless existence. It did so partially under the Jewish dispensation: at one time, darkly hinting the doctrine, to magnify the hopes or fears of men; and, at another, portraying it in definite forms, to engage their faith: now despatching a messenger from the unseen world; and now clothing a prophet with the terrors of an unearthly visitant, and planting him in their way to bring them to a stand, by warning them of a fearful something beyond. But the light which it held over the sepulchre flickered — did not burn so strong but that it might have been extinguished by the deadly vapours of the tomb; and hence the views of its disciples wavered also; sometimes speaking in tones of depression, as if their whole horizon were the walls of a charnel-house; at other times, by a kind of lofty divination peculiar to the wise and good of every age, (for every good man is, in a sense, a prophet,) making near approaches to the truth; anticipating revelations reserved for after times; and then, again, seizing their harp, and singing their triumphant song, as if their immortality had already begun.

But the full revelation and proof of the doctrine of a

future state were reserved to grace the mission of Him who, in his own person, is "the way, the truth, and the life." We do not, indeed, conceive these to have been the chief or *specific* design of his advent; though it is a part of the glory of that design that it includes them:— "he hath brought life and immortality to light by the gospel." If he found them problems, he left them axioms; promoted them to the rank of postulates in his system of truth; made them the basis of the whole Christian fabric. Heathen philosophy halted at the grave. Ancient revelation accompanied its disciples a little beyond, conducting them into Sheol, Hades, the unknown state. Christianity comes to our aid in the very moment of desertion; stands to receive us at the very place of parting with every other religion; graciously approaches, and offers its guidance up to the throne of God. If, prior to the coming of Christ, the doctrine of immortality was undefined and unsubstantial,—if, like the spectral phantom of Eliphaz, the believer could only say of it, "It passed before my face; it stood still; but I could not discern the form thereof,"—*He* may be said to have embodied the truth—to have fashioned and impersonated it in his own glorious body. Having rolled away the stone from the sepulchre of human hope, he invites us to look in; and, instead of the dust, and darkness, and loathsomeness proper to the grave, we behold the "linen clothes lying by themselves"—the apparel of the prison-house vacated and left—and angels in white, sitting, to reassure our hope, and point us to the skies.

I. In naming the most original features of our Lord's teaching on this subject, the first in order is the doctrine of an intermediate state. Presupposing the immateriality and immortality of the soul, he frequently employed language which denotes the active existence of the soul between death and the resurrection: " Fear not them," said Christ to his disciples, " fear not them who kill the body, but are not able to kill the soul." Then the soul and the body are distinct existences: the body may be slain and yet the soul escape. But *insensibility* would be virtual destruction to the soul; for we cannot conceive how a thinking being can be more destroyed than by losing the power of thought: then the soul will not cease to think. But the only reason why the soul is indestructible by man, must be its immateriality. The body he can destroy, for that is material; and if the soul resulted from any subtilization, juxtaposition, or combinations of brute atoms, *that* could be apprehended, burnt, divided, exhausted, exploded, destroyed also. " But no," saith Christ, " it is not destructible by man." The suicide has no weapon with which he can reach his soul. Persecution, though it has taxed its ingenuity to the utmost, and has called in the inventive aid of him who is a murderer from the beginning, has failed to devise any instrument with which it could seize and torment the soul,—has felt, and inwardly cursed, its impotence, that, in consuming the body of its victim, it was actually releasing the immortal soul. The soul has nothing to do with death; if persecution will have the body, the soul surrenders it, leaves it behind, drops it in the grave, and passes on to immortality. Indeed, had the contrary sentiment prevailed, there is reason to conclude that Christianity would have had a much smaller number of martyrs to boast; they would have shrunk from death, not to avoid the physical suffering, but the loss they were called to sustain, the dreary suspension of all the enjoyments the gospel had brought them,—*that* would have given to death a new sting. But the fearful apprehension never seems to have visited their minds. A primary article in their martyr-creed was this—" Absent from the body, present with the Lord." They felt that their noblest life had its root in heaven—that their spiritual existence was " hid with Christ in God"—was seated high up, beyond reach, in the very fountain and summit of creation. At thought of this, the apparatus of death became consecrated in their eyes, as the means of their admission to his presence; the instruments of torture glowed with a glory reflected from his throne; the flames were chariots of fire to convey them in triumph to their appointed thrones.

The doctrine of an intermediate existence is recognised by Christ, in the parable of the rich man and Lazarus; where we learn that the former, dying, lifted up his eyes, being in torment; while the latter was straightway conveyed, by angels, to Abraham's bosom. Spirits are evoked by Christ, from heaven and hell, to attest an intermediate state. He would have us to read the doctrine by the lurid glare of infernal flames, and by the radiance of a celestial vision. He taught it also in the light which flashed on the divine declaration: " I am the God of Abraham, and the God of Isaac, and the God of Jacob:"—" God," said he, " is not the God of the dead, but of the living." The Almighty had uttered this three hundred years after the death of Abraham. Now, whatever relation he may sustain to the lifeless body, and to the inanimate creation at large, he can only be said to be a God to the living soul. On the former, he can only bring to bear his natural attributes—can only exercise mechanical power; while, on the latter, he can turn the full aspect of his moral perfections — can bring his transcendental attributes, the peculiar glory of his character—can bring all his nature into active communication with theirs. Whatever he may do to mere matter, he does it to an unconscious object, to a thing which can return him no look of gratitude—no expression of affection; while the soul finds its heaven in his smile, and he beholds the reflection of his image in its face. Wherefore, " he is not ashamed to be called its God;" by which we are to understand, that he glories to be called so: he tells it to the universe, —boasts of the relationship,—is willing to be judged of by his treatment of his spiritual offspring,—is prepared to rest his claims to universal homage on the glorious provision to which he brings them in heaven,—is so satisfied with that illustration of his excellence which he beholds in the present condition of the spirits of just men made perfect, that, could we see their blessedness, he would be content to be known only as their God; and, accordingly, one of the titles which he has adopted, and graven on his crown of light, informs us that he is " the Father of spirits."

Another declaration of Christ, to the same import, is his memorable reply to the expiring malefactor— " Verily, I say unto thee, to-day shalt thou be with me in paradise." The sense of this passage has been made by some, indeed, to turn on a question of punctuation. But receiving it in its general acceptation, (the only acceptation, we apprehend, which common sense will ratify,) we learn from it the capability of the soul to exist independently of the body,—the instant transition of the soul, at death, to the state adapted to its moral character; and the fact, that it there immediately enters on its endless portion.

II. The resurrection of the body was a dogma already familiar to the Jews; but this doctrine our Lord illustrated, amplified, and confirmed. Aware that it formed the key-stone of Christianity, he may be said to have laboured out the *proof* of it, till he brought it to demonstration: " Ye do err," said he to the Sadducees, who denied a resurrection, "not knowing the scriptures, nor the power of God." Here, first, he dismisses the question of its possibility, by placing it at once in the hands of Omnipotence. Secondly, he places around the doctrine a guard of divine declarations; thus reminding us, that if God has said the dead shall be raised, the event is as certain as if it had already occurred and become matter of history. And, thirdly, he alleges, as a reason for the event, the relation which God sustains to his people—" he is their God;" and is bound, therefore, by a pledge voluntarily given, to do everything for them essential to their well-being. But the restoration of their bodies is essential to the integrity of their nature: then his faithfulness is pledged to restore them. Besides, he is the God of the *living*. But a constituent part of their nature is held in captivity by death: then, to vindicate his title as their God, he must effect the redemption of the body, and replenish it, in common with the soul, with immortal life. Agreeably to this declaration, the Saviour elsewhere affirms, "This is the Father's will, who hath sent me, that of all which he hath given me, I should lose nothing; but should raise it up again at the last day." He was commissioned by the Father to accomplish the work of redemption, in a manner worthy of him whose peculiar distinction it is, that "his work is perfect." He holds himself responsible, therefore, for the reproduction of the bodies of all his people: he has set his seal upon each of their graves; and, of all that he holds in trust, he declares that he will lose, not merely not one, but "nothing"— not a fraction—not a particle essential to one of the bodies of his saints. During the short period that he himself remained in the grave, he held his person dishonoured by the bondage; and, till the morning of the resurrection arrive, he regards his people as dishonoured:

the completion of his engagement, and the perfection of his reward, require that "of all which have been given him he should lose *nothing*."

But our Lord did not limit his proof of a resurrection to words; he proceeded to demonstrate the truth by an appeal to our senses. On one occasion, he released an individual whom death had just made his prisoner. On another occasion, he met the king of terrors at the gate of a city, conveying a victim to the grave; and he arrested his march, and reclaimed the prey. And, on a third time, he brought Lazarus forth from the grave, who had been dead four days. On that occasion, he had intentionally delayed to interfere, that the process of decomposition might commence; he had given to death every possible advantage; he had voluntarily kept away, till death should be in full possession—till the monster had not merely seized his victim, but had retired with him into the gloomy dominions of the grave—till he had there closed and barred up the entrance, and fortified himself, as in a stronghold, which none should dare to assail, and where he might reign secure. But Jesus summoned the citadel of death—broke open the enclosure of the grave, and, with a voice which compelled submission, demanded, and restored to life, his deceased friend.

And then, to complete and consummate the proof of a resurrection, he himself arose from the dead. The way in which that grand event demonstrates the doctrine of our resurrection is this:—he came into the world in the high capacity of the Son of God, and the Saviour of mankind. In that capacity he proclaimed, that, having provided salvation for the human race, he would come again, when his plans of mercy were completed, to raise the dead, and to judge the world. To prove that he was what he claimed to be, and that he would fulfil what he predicted, he announced, that he himself would arise from the dead on the third day after his decease. Then said Jesus unto them, " When ye have lifted up the Son of man, then shall ye know that I am he, and that I do nothing of myself; but as my Father hath taught me, I do these things."—" Destroy this temple, and in three days I will raise it up again." He descended into the dreary domains of death; disappeared in the valley of the shadow of death; and, for a time, a darkness, deeper than that which enwrapped the earth at his crucifixion, seemed settling down on the prospects of mankind, and turning his tomb into the grave of immortality. But on the morning of the appointed day he came forth as he had said,—stood at the mouth of the sepulchre, radiant with immortality,—planted the banner of hope on the citadel of death, and called on the world to behold and share in his triumph. Then he *is* the Son of God;—then he *will* come again to raise the dead: here are the undeniable stamp and seal of Heaven that all his representations of the last great day were true, and will certainly be verified.

III. Among the numerous additions which he made to our knowledge of the doctrine in question, we may name, first, the fact, that he himself will raise the dead. " Jesus answered, Verily, verily, I say unto you, The hour is coming, and now is, when the dead shall hear the voice of the Son of God: and they that hear shall live." Whether this prediction related to the approaching resurrection of Lazarus and others, or to the tide of spiritual life which was about to flow through the world in the diffusion of the gospel, is uncertain. Perhaps, indeed, his comprehensive mind may have looked forward to both: it is evident, however, that the sublimity of the prediction, and the solemnity of the asseveration with which he prefaced it, awoke in the minds of many of his hearers vast and awful ideas of some impending event,—ideas which impressed marks of astonishment on their anxious countenances. Remarking that astonishment,—perceiving, by their eager and attentive looks, that they were now prepared to receive a still more stupendous announcement, he continued, " Marvel not at this;" " I perceive that what I have already said has filled you with wonder; and well it might: but attend, and you shall hear still greater things than these: for the hour is coming, in the which all that are in the graves *shall hear his voice,* and shall come forth; they that have done good, to the resurrection of life; and they that have done evil, unto the resurrection of damnation." There was a time when no life existed;—when the earth, just brought into being, presented one universal blank, —no vital motion, no breathing life, upon it. But he spake, and it was done; for his word is the seed of universal nature, the principle of all life. His fiat went forth, and instantly whole orders of sentient beings sprang into happy existence. His goodness opened, and burst forth in a creation; and earth was made the receptacle of his vast overflowing life. His voice was heard; and forthwith the surface of the earth teemed and overflowed with an ocean of living forms. " But by one man sin entered into the world, and death by sin, and so death passed upon all men, for that all have sinned!" Since that tremendous catastrophe, death has reigned upon earth; there is no reason to believe that his ravages are known in any other part of the dominions of God; this is his native seat and throne; here he keeps court and regal state. God has been constantly replenishing the world with new life: but, in every age, death has swept and cleared the stage—has thrown a pall over each generation—has not allowed the grave to be closed— the hatchment of the world to be taken down for a moment—has carried everything before him. We and our contemporaries are the few survivors of the myriads that have fallen, the children of the slain, and we shall soon be added to the number. O, could we see the numberless victims which have fallen beneath his stroke accumulated together, we should behold a mountain of mortality towering to the skies; but he has hid them all in the dust,—has conveyed them all away to his subterraneous caverns—his ever-enlarging prison of the grave.

Now it was not fit that death should thus reign: though we, indeed, had deserved to be left in his eternal possession, yet it did not comport with the benevolent designs and glory of God that death should be thus allowed to enjoy an undisturbed triumph over the work of his hands. He, therefore, who at first had peopled the earth with living beings, again returned to survey the scene, to check the career of death, to repair the waste and ravages which death had made. And what a mournful sight presented itself to his eyes! a pestilential element breathed by death over the whole creation, withering all nature, causing the entire universe of being to languish, and droop, and perish;—the world, *his* world, which was meant to be the pleasant habitation of his creatures, turned into their grave; the shadow of death settled down upon all, and enwrapping it like a funeral pall, signifying that all was his. What a pitiable spectacle stretched beneath his view!—For, remember, he surveyed the whole at one comprehensive glance;—mothers weeping for their children, and refusing to be comforted because they were not,—everywhere groups of mourners collected, weeping over those whom death had seized, bound, and made captive in their presence,—long processions of bereaved relatives, following the car of death, as if to grace his triumph, and uttering their lamentations in their march to the grave; on all sides, the trophies of death, erected in the shape of tombs, and sepulchres, and monumental stones. What must have been his emotions, as the Lord of life and pity, as he walked this field of death, this place of skulls! What were his *emotions?* Did he not shew what they were by his conduct? " He healed all manner of sickness, and all manner of diseases among the people;" in other words, he defeated the designs of death;—drew out the arrows which death had infixed, and healed the wounds they had made. Even had he done nothing to redeem the world, his visit would still have been an era in the annals of mortality;—the Lord of life walking through the regions of death! No wonder the sick and the dying came flocking, and fell down at his feet; no wonder they besought him to shelter and save them from the monster which even dared to chase them into his presence. And did he not save them? He healed them all: death paused, and stood rebuked in his presence—found himself overmatched—discovered, for the first time, that there was one mightier than he. And had all the world brought out their sick and their dying, Christ could have healed them all;—thus famishing death—thus creating a hiatus in the revenues of death. Nor was this all: he called some back into life again; and humbled the power of death, by compelling him to relinquish his prey.

Do we ask what his feelings must have been as he traversed this Golgotha, this land of death? " Jesus wept!"—yes, he stood and wept!—and, as he wept, he resolved to remedy and to save. He advanced to the very gates of death, and proclaimed, with a voice which went pealing and echoing through all the dominions of death, and made even the throne of the king of terrors vibrate and tremble,—" I am the resurrection and the life;"—" I will be known as the antagonist of death;— let my actions prove it;"—" Lazarus, come forth; and he that was dead came forth." There, said Christ, " He that believeth in me, though he were dead, yet shall he live." " That is only a specimen of my designs. I am the great principle of life; if I chose, I could now raise all the dead ;—I could end the reign of death at once. I have only to speak, and all the dead would recognise my voice, and start into life. But wisdom requires me to forbear : this is meant as an instance of my power, a sample of my designs." " Marvel not at this, therefore; for the hour is coming, in the which *all* that are in the graves shall hear the voice of the Son of man, and shall come forth; they that have done good, unto the resurrection of life; and they that have done evil, unto the resurrection of damnation."

IV. In opposition to the Pharisees, the principal sect at that time among the Jews, who taught that the resurrection would be partial, being confined to the bodies of the just, our Lord taught that it would be general. God works by laws, and laws operate universally: every action and every atom in the universe has its own law—is impressed with certain qualities, or endued with certain powers, which operate with all the certainty of a law. It was the appointment of God, that the sin of the first Adam, as the federal head of the human race, should bring in a law of death; and the law has acted universally—all have died. It is equally his appointment, that the mediation of the second Adam, the Lord from heaven, standing in the same federal relation, should bring in a law of life: he was pleased to endue it and impress it with this vital property, or law; and, unless it should meet with counteraction from a mightier law, which is impossible, it must act universally. " As in Adam all die, so in Christ shall all be made alive." It is the perfection of a law that it includes all possible cases that may occur, and has relation to an infinite number of cases that never will exist; so that, had the actual numbers of the human race been multiplied ten thousand fold, the law of death would have swept them all into the grave; and " the law of life in Christ Jesus" would, with an operation co-extensive, have revived them again : " *All* that are in the grave shall hear his voice, and shall come forth."

Besides, it should be remembered that the resurrection is not a final act—it is to take place in subserviency to the divine purposes of retribution; so that the principles of the holy government of God require that it should be universal. Less than the resurrection of all would not satisfy the claims of the righteous Judge. Were one of his people to be lacking, his mercy could not be satisfied; his mystical body would be maimed and deficient in an essential member. Were one of the ungodly to be absent, his justice could not be satisfied. Whether good or evil, all will be raised; every age, every nation, every family, every individual of all the posterity of Adam. Death shall be abolished and swallowed up in victory. Not only shall its operation be arrested, its ravages stopped, but all the victims which it has seized from the beginning of time shall be reproduced and restored. It shall behold all the organized materials which it had dissolved, and scattered, and trampled in the dust, and laboured to efface from the creation, collected, and surrounded, and acted upon on all sides with a principle of life,—and rising, as from a sleep, clothed with incorruption. It shall behold its empire vanish in a moment, by the insurrection of all its subjects, armed with immortality. Many of the greatest empires of antiquity are not only extinct, and their boundaries effaced, but even the seat of their power is only to be known by coloured dust in the desert, or by coloured sand washed up by the waves of a stormy sea; but of the empire of death, not a vestige shall be left—not a particle of dust, if searched for, shall remain for its memorial: life, an ocean of victorious life, shall overflow and swallow it up.

V. We may also infer, from the teaching of our Lord, that the bodies raised will be identical with those committed to the grave: "*They* that are in the graves shall come forth." "Of all that the Father hath given me, I will lose nothing; but will raise it up in the last day." Indeed, the very term resurrection implies this identity; otherwise the bodies produced in the last day would be, not a resurrection, but a creation, like that of the first man. And the design of the resurrection requires it; the purposes of justice demand that the beings, who shall then appear in judgment, should be the identical beings who have been here on probation. To the objection of the sceptic, that the rapid waste and supply of our animal frame, the succession of bodies we may be said to inhabit, renders this identity inconceivable, we deem it sufficient to reply in the language of Christ, "Ye do err, not knowing the scriptures, nor the power of God." It should, however, abate his confidence, if not entirely silence the objector, that, on his principle, neither punishments nor rewards could be *justly* dispensed, even in this life; since the material structure changes so rapidly, that, in the lapse of a few years, not a particle of the primitive body remains. He would not think of asserting, we presume, that he himself is not now the identical individual he was at the time of his birth; that the decrepit body of the aged debauchee is suffering unjustly for the intemperance of his youthful frame; that it would be unrighteous to punish the murderer for a crime which he perpetrated when his body was composed of other particles; or, that he himself, in consequence of a similar change, has no title to property left him a few years ago. His common sense protects him from such absurdities in the affairs of this life; and we will leave him to assign to himself a reason, if he can, why it should desert him only in the province of religion; let him say what is the interpretation to be put on the conduct of him who reserves all his hostility for religion, and who evinces that hostility by availing himself of weapons which he would not stoop to employ against any other object. But among the various triumphs of the resurrection-day, one will be, the triumph of common sense; and let him remember that, even while he has been cavilling, and we replying, the hour of retribution has come nearer; and that the indestructible principle of conscience, the principle which runs through our being, giving continuity and identity to that being through an eternity of existence, has actually gathered strength while we have been thus communing, and increased its store of materials for future joy or woe.

VI. We have already shewn that the doctrine of immortality is not *distinctive* of the Christian system: it is, we think, equally clear, that *the honour of describing the nature, and providing the means, of resurrection to everlasting happiness, is peculiar to Christ alone.* Blind to the fact of their departure from God, numbers are satisfied with believing the bare immortality of their nature: here their inquiries terminate: the *happiness* of that nature they take for granted, as a matter of course; they confound existence with enjoyment,—an error this, which many a heathen would have blushed to own. Though sitting in the shadow of death, *they* were sufficiently enlightened to perceive that an immortality of misery is quite as possible to sinful creatures as an eternity of bliss. They would have regarded him who should have brought to them the *proof* of immortality, as conferring a very equivocal boon, unless he could also sow that immortality with the seeds of happiness; and hence, while they laboured to demonstrate a future state, decidedly the greater part of their endeavours were directed to the task of exploring the character and will of the Divinity, and of descrying the nature of the regions beyond the grave, with a view to provide for their future enjoyment.

Now, while the teaching of Christ *presupposes* the immortality of the soul, to him belongs the grand distinction of having *proved* the resurrection of the body, and *provided* for the endless happiness of the whole man in heaven. Had he not made this essential provision, his instructions would only have illuminated the darkness of the world as with flames ascending from the bottomless pit—would only have painted more dreadful colours on the gloom which has gathered around the seat of the Invisible,—and he himself might be reproached as tormenting us before our time: but having made our happiness and our immortality consistent and co-extensive, what can equally deserve our attention with the way in which he has " brought it to light?"

1. By his essential divinity he possesses the *power* of defeating death, and of opening to the soul unbounded resources of pure and eternal enjoyment. He declared that " he *has life in himself,* so that he can quicken whom he will." " I," said he, " am the resurrection and the life." " I am . . . . . the life." This is language appropriate to the Deity alone; for life, properly speaking, inhabits none besides. Life in him is essence; but of the highest created beings, it can only be said that they live— that they are the offspring, the dependent recipients of his essence. However large their capacities, and replenished with life, still they are infinitely nearer to

nothing than to absolute and essential life. So that he "who only hath immortality," though he hath surrounded himself with an universe of life, still retains to himself the prerogative of swearing, *As I live;* and of announcing, *I am;* and, *I am life;* he only hath immortality in its fulness and essence; and all the oceans of vitality circulating through the universe take their rise in him, " with whom is the fountain of life," " he filleth all in all." But if it belongs to him alone to say, " I am life," when surrounded by " the living creatures," the princes of immortality above, with what a heightened emphasis could he repeat it in this region of death;—here, where life was always conditional, and in jeopardy from the first; here, where comparatively a very small portion of being had been distributed at first; where that little had been invaded, forfeited, wasted; where death was actually in full possession. He came into a land of sepulchres, — found himself standing in a grave, with death for a companion, labouring to tread out and trample in the dust the last spark of human life; and, lifting himself up into an attitude of supreme dignity, he said, with a voice which is still echoing through the subterranean realms of death, " I am the resurrection and the life." " I am the ark in which all the life is contained that shall finally issue to people a world now deluged with death. From me proceeds all the redundancy of life at this moment replenishing the universe; and I will cause a stream of vitality to set in and flood the earth."

2. But power and right are distinct things, and, among men, are frequently opposed to each other. It is, however, the glory of Him who can do all things, that he does only that which is right,—that his power waits on his justice, and takes law from infinite rectitude. Now he had pronounced it right that man should die; how

then can he reverse the sentence without impeaching its rectitude, and appearing to judge himself? And yet Jesus asserts to himself the right of restoring the dead to life, selects for himself a title descriptive of this work, and demands to be known by it, as his most honourable and favourite appellation.

The problem is solved, when we hear him affirm that he had come to give his life a ransom for many,—that, as the good shepherd, he proposed to lay down his life for the sheep. Death was the punishment of transgression; it was in perfect accordance with right that the penalty should be inflicted, in order that holiness might be protected, that sin might be discouraged, and that the divine determination to maintain the law and order of his government might be emphatically proclaimed. If, however, an expedient can be devised by which all these ends can be equally answered, without the infliction of the penalty, right will be satisfied, and concede the exemption. That expedient is found in the incarnation and death of the Son of God. By voluntarily stooping from his glory, assuming our nature, and suffering, before the eyes of the universe, all that humanity, sustained by divinity, could endure, he has answered the very ends which our punishment would have secured, and infinitely more; he has placed the hatefulness of sin, and the holiness of God, in a focus of light which will make itself to be seen by every eye; he has, at once, inflicted a death-blow on the power of sin, given a triumph to justice, secured life, eternal life, to man, and distinguished an attribute which would have been for ever eclipsed had justice taken its original course—the attribute of infinite love. The nature of his reward was determined, predetermined, by the nature of his work; he died, in order to exempt us from death. Having received his reward, having purchased us out of the hands of offended justice, and made us his own property, he may now employ the right he has acquired in us as he pleases. Death, in its judicial character, is abolished. He is at liberty, either to exempt his people entirely from death, to insert an exception in their favour in the universal commission of death; or, permitting the sentence of mortality to take effect, to restore them to life afterwards, and place them for ever beyond the reach of death. His wisdom prefers the latter course. By allowing them to depart from earth in the ordinary way, through the portal of death, he leaves undisturbed the existing arrangements of Providence, avoids many palpable evils, and secures in addition many valuable ends. But while he allows this arrangement to hold, he would have his people to know that it is not forced on him,—that it is the choice of his own benignity,—that he sways an unchallenged sceptre over the whole empire of *hades*,—that in respect to his people, the shadow of death, wherever it falls, may be regarded as the shadow of that sceptre, for at their death " he comes to receive them to himself."

3. But sin involves a spiritual as well as a physical death. We have seen that Christ possesses the *power* of reanimating the body, and that he is invested with the right; but it is evident that these may both be exercised in the punishment of men, " for some shall come forth to the resurrection of damnation." The great question, then, which remains, is, whether or not he possesses the *means* of calling us forth to an immortality of happiness. " I am come," said he, " that they may have life, and that they may have it more abundantly." " Whoso eateth my flesh, and drinketh my blood, hath eternal life; and I will raise him up at the last day." " Whosoever drinketh of the water that I shall give him, shall never thirst; but the water that I shall give him shall be in him a well of water springing up into everlasting life."

"This spake he of the Spirit which they that believe on him should receive." By the agency of his Holy Spirit, he conducts in his people, in the present life, a moral process by which they experience a resurrection to holiness. The hour is not only coming, but *now* is, when the dead hear the voice of the Son of God: and they that hear it live. Starting from the slumbers of sin, they awake to newness of life, and attire themselves in the garments of salvation. Dissevering themselves from their former bonds, they ask to be trained for every duty his service may require, and pant to enjoy all the happiness his kingdom may contain. Conscious that they are once more breathing the only atmosphere in which the soul can live—the complacent favour of God—they feel within themselves an earnest of immortality; feel that the new principle of which they have been made the subjects has nothing to fear from death, that it is made for eternity, that it can smile at the decay of the body, and will soon spring from the bed of death to immortality.

And, from the fact that they have been made the partakers of a divine principle, there arises to believers this new pledge of a resurrection to eternal life,—that Christ has engaged to raise them as a part of his own being. This truth he himself distinctly taught: " As the living Father hath sent me, and I live by the Father, so he that eateth me, even he shall live by me;"— " he dwelleth in me, and I in him;"—" I will raise him up at the last day;"—" because I live, ye shall live also." He became one flesh with us, in order that we might become one spirit with him. Here is a two-fold bond subsisting between Christ and his people; but the former of these they possess only in common with all mankind: it allies him to the species, and, by virtue of it, all the ungodly shall be raised. The *spiritual* bond, however, is peculiar to themselves; it has been tied by his own hand, and nothing shall be able to separate it. By virtue of this union it is that believers shall arise; not merely by an act of his power, for thus the wicked shall arise, but by an extension of his life as their life. To the ungodly he can say, " I am the resurrection;" but to the faithful alone he proclaims, " I am the resurrection and the life." The grave was the prison-house of insulted justice; and, as their Representative, he bowed himself down, and condescended to wear its fetters; but his enlargement and return from it shews that it no longer retains its original character; he has changed it into the peaceful depository of their dust,— the treasury of the skies: they contemplate his grave as the basement-ground whence their nature takes its spring to immortality.

So ample and sufficient are the preparatory measures which Christ has taken for the final extinction of death, that he speaks of it in terms of comparative disparage- ment and indifference. So effectually is it disarmed and mutilated, and so completely at the disposal of Christ, that he speaks of it already as if it were not. " Whosoever believeth in me, shall never die."—" If a man keep my sayings, he shall never taste of death—he shall never see death." In accordance with these repre- sentations, he has given to the state of Death the soft and tranquillizing name of Sleep. This use of the term, indeed, was not unknown to Jewish saints; but, as applied by them to death, it denoted chiefly the silence, darkness, and inactivity, of the grave. The Greeks, too, had long been accustomed to speak of death in the softest terms: the dead they often spoke of as *the departed, the worn-out;* and called their burial-grounds " dormitories," or sleeping places. But this arose partly from the dis- like they felt to allude to a gloomy and unwelcome subject, and partly from a wish to propitiate the deceased, of whom they stood in considerable dread. How superior the sense in which Jesus employed the term Sleep! They used it as a figure, but he turned it into a reality;—they uttered it from fear, but he made it the language of hope and of faith. He used it with the highest authority, for he was about to awaken one of the sleepers from his sleep; and, however protracted the slumbers of his people may be, he knew that they are all finally to hear his voice, and to come forth.

Dense as the gloom is which hangs over the mouth of the sepulchre, it is the spot, above all others, where the gospel, if it enters, shines and triumphs. In the busy sphere of life and health, it encounters an active antagonist; the world confronts it—aims to obscure its glories—to deny its claims—to drown its voice—to dispute its progress—to drive it from the ground it occupies. But from the mouth of the grave the world retires; it shrinks from the contest there; it leaves a clear and open space in which the gospel can assert its claims, and unveil its glories, without opposition or fear. There the infidel and the worldling look anxiously around; but the world has left them helpless, and fled. There the Christian looks around, and, lo, the angel of mercy is standing close by his side. The gospel kindles a torch, which not only irradiates the valley of the shadow of death, but throws a radiance into the world beyond, and reveals it peopled with the sainted spirits of those who have died in Jesus. It descends with us into the low chambers of the grave,—bids us look on its silent inmates; and to look on them with the persuasion that they only sleep. It assures us that death, like sleep, is not the destruction of the living principle, but only a temporary change in the mode of its operation; that, like sleep, it is a state of rest, discharging us from all the concerns of the world; that, like sleep, it principally affects the body, the activity of the soul being meantime continued, and, perhaps, greatly increased; and, most of all, that, like sleep, it will not be perpetual, but only endure for a night. It tells us, that a day will dawn on the world, when Jesus, assuming an aspect of infinite benignity, will say, in effect, of all his sleeping saints, as he said of Lazarus, " I go to awake them out of sleep."

O, how vast the immortal awakening! Who can lift his mind to the greatness of the occasion! Where is the height from which we can command a view of the sublime spectacle? In prospect of it, Jesus said, " The hour is come, that the Son of man should be glorified. Verily, verily, I say unto you, Except a corn of wheat fall into the ground and die, it abideth alone; but if it die, it bringeth forth much fruit." As the first-fruits of them that sleep, he has arisen and appeared before God, the certain pledge of the great harvest-home. " Put ye in the sickle, for the harvest is ripe: multitudes, multitudes, in the valley of decision." The wide earth shall " stand thick," and wave, with that ocean plenitude of life. The produce of the fields, every year, is a renewed triumph of life over death; but the triumph of life on that day will be final and complete, leaving not an atom for which death can contend. It will be a triumph of the highest order, consisting, not in the mere creation of new being, but in the release and reanimation of what had been dragged away from the territories of life;— death itself will be turned into life,—corruption will put on incorruption. The triumph will be enhanced by the circumstance, that it will be achieved on the very spot where death had reigned: if the power of death be confined to this world, what an opprobrium must earth be to all the regions of life, and how naturally may it be pointed at by their inhabitants as the mysterious sepulchre of life,—the dishonour of the universe; but the morning of the resurrection will wipe off that disgrace, will make earth their boast and song; for "there they will be able to say, There death was overthrown; there the great antagonist of life, after wasting the earth for thousands of years, and threatening to push its conquest into other worlds, was expelled from the universe as an evil no longer to be borne. And from that very scene, where death once reigned, heaven has received its largest influx of spiritual and immortal life." And to consummate the triumph, life on that day will be crowned with immortality; it will not merely be restored, but ennobled, exalted to the highest state of security and glory it can sustain. From the ruinous heap of every grave a living structure shall arise, built up into an imperishable monument of " the Resurrection and the Life;" in the stead of corruption, it shall be inaccessible to decay; "for neither can they die any more; they are equal unto the angels, and are the children of God, being the children of the resurrection." In the stead of dishonour, it will be raised in glory, radiating a splendour which shall eclipse all sublunary glory. In the place of weakness, it shall be clothed with the vigour of immortal youth, asking no relaxation or repose, the wings of the soul accompanying and aiding it in all its untiring flights. In the place of a natural body, it shall be raised a spiritual body; the original grossness of its materiality shall be purged away; it shall be refined and etherialized into spirit—a robe of light rivaling the invisible essence of the soul itself; while each of its senses shall form an inlet to floods of enjoyment, and each of its organs be instinct and emulous with zeal for the divine glory.

Earth has been often the scene of splendid triumphs,

the fame of which has filled the world, and reverberated from age to age; but how tame, how trifling, the greatest achievements of man compared with this!—a triumph which not only effaces the remembrance of all that man has done, but even eclipses the glory of the divine exploits—" the former things shall no more come into remembrance." Here man may indulge in wonder without loss of dignity: not to be astonished here would be unnatural! Christ himself is represented, ages before his incarnation, as contemplating this scene with boundless delight—as rehearsing his victory over death from eternity. From the bosom of the Father he looked on through the vista of time, while the successive parts of his great work passed, in slow and stately procession, till he beheld the scene of the rising dead: all the intermediate ages instantly vanished; he saw, in anticipation, the king of terrors disarmed beneath his feet, the world flooded with light and life, the song of myriads of myriads reached his ear, shouting his name as their Great Deliverer; and, with holy impatience to realize the scene, he exclaimed, " I will ransom them from the power of the grave; I will redeem them from death: O death, I will be thy plagues! O grave, I will be thy destruction!" And during the interval till he came in the flesh, did his interest in the prospect appear to have evaporated? What truth did he more frequently or solemnly teach? Thrice, in rapid succession, he exclaimed, " I will raise them up at the last day," as if he sought to find, in the bare repetition of the truth, a solace and compensation for deferring the event. Nor, since his ascension, does his desire to realize it appear to have suffered the least abatement. On the contrary, " from henceforth he is expecting" till this last enemy shall be destroyed. When last he appeared before his church, to close the visions of futurity, the character which he selected for the occasion was, " he that hath the keys of the invisible world, and of death." This is the capacity in which he will next greet the eyes of the redeemed; meanwhile, he is training them to raise, in concert with himself, this shout over the last of their foes—" O Death, where is thy sting ? O Grave, where is thy victory ?"

SECTION VII.

OF THE FINAL JUDGMENT.

We have already had occasion to remark that the resurrection of the dead will not take place as a final event, that it stands in the relation of means to an end, and *that* end, the general judgment, with its eternal awards. Even "Enoch, the seventh from Adam," prophesied of that day, saying, " Behold, the Lord cometh with ten thousand of his saints to execute judgment upon all." And Solomon, when, in the capacity of a preacher, he looked round the universe for the strongest motive to holy obedience—the motive which should render it unnecessary to seek another—took it from the prospect of a judgment to come : " Let us hear the conclusion of the whole matter : Fear God, and keep his commandments : for this is the whole duty of man. For God shall bring every work into judgment, with every secret thing, whether it be good, or whether it be evil."

He who " sees the end from the beginning" has imparted to man a subordinate prescience of the same comprehensive kind, has sketched on his mind an outline of the great system of providence, and filled him with presentiments of the principal events which are to attend the development of that system. The consequence is, that wherever the Bible comes, it finds our nature preconfigured to many of its truths, waiting for an interpreter, and ready to respond to the truth of many a prediction, as a prophecy, or an anticipation, with which it had long been familiar in thought, and for which it only wanted divine authentication, and a name, in order to regard it as a solemn reality. Indeed, in this respect, the work of God only resembles his word; for as in his word he has often disclosed the infinite affluence of his mind by revealing, with all the simplicity of apparent unconsciousness, an eternal principle in a passing word, an infinite project in an incidental allusion; so, in the construction of the human mind, he has traced on it characters and imagery which can only be read by the light of eternity; thrown on it the unsteady shadows of objects which stand yet far distant on the plains of futurity. Of these preintimations we know of none more deeply inlaid in the mind than that of future retribution. That the ancient saints lived in the faith of it we know; for the Spirit of inspiration has recorded the very words in which, in the prospect of that day, they triumphed over their persecutors, and sang of the joy that would crown them in " the day of the Lord." And, relying on the uniformity and immutability of the human constitution, we may safely infer that ancient sinners anticipated it also. There were moments when they possessed the warning of its approach in the restless apprehensions of their own breasts; moments when the fires of that day seemed to rise up in the distant horizon, and to cast a lurid glare on the face of their startled and trembling conscience; when the mention of such a day would have fallen in with the smothered forebodings of their minds, would have aroused an inward monitor, which, however carefully laid to sleep, was ready to awake at the slightest summons, and to bear testimony in the cause of righteousness.

But though the doctrine of a future judgment did not originate in the teaching of Christ,—though, from the earliest ages, mankind had variously received it,—yet the light they possessed, even the revealed light, did but just suffice dimly to shew them the Judge enthroned in clouds, and surrounded with judgments; while, from his superiority to temptation, his greatness and perfection, they inferred that the Judge of all the earth would do right. But the person of the Judge, the pomp and process of the judgment, its most solemn circumstances and affecting results—all this was comparatively unknown to them; and in supplying the information, our Lord has greatly enlarged the original part of his teaching.

1. When speaking of the final judgment, it is observable that he seldom omitted to insist and enlarge on its *publicity*. He thus reminds us, that the end for which there is any judgment at all is best secured by having it held in the presence of all worlds; that piety may be most honoured, sin most abashed, and the government of God vindicated and glorified, on the largest possible scale. In a few descriptive words, he fills the horizon with intelligent beings of all orders and characters. It will not be the judgment of a single individual, nor of a nation, but of a whole world of intelligent and accountable beings. It will not be an assize for sins of recent commission merely; sins committed thousands of years before will be reproduced and examined, with all their circumstances of aggravation, as if they had been only just committed. What a profound impression will that produce of the holy character of God and of the infinite enormity of sin! When his people are crowned, he would not have one of their enemies absent; and when the ungodly are doomed, he would not have one of the righteous absent; he would have them now to forestal that day, to feel, by anticipation, that they are speaking with the universe for their audience, and acting in the great theatre of the judgment; and, *then*, he would have them to depart to their respective allotments, bearing away with them impressions of the hatefulness of sin, and

the beauty of holiness, which shall remain uneffaced through all the scenes of eternity.

2. Pursuing our examination, we recognise in the Judge the person of the Lord Jesus Christ. "The Son of man shall come in his glory, and before him shall be gathered all nations." "The Father judgeth no man, but hath committed all judgment to the Son." He hath "authority to execute judgment also, *because he is the Son of man;*" in his superadded humanity consists the very reason of his appointment. If the Judge is to be seen on that day with our bodily eyes, and if realities are to triumph on that day over appearances, substances over shadows, then it is fit that no illusion should sit on the throne, that he should occupy it who is, "without controversy, God manifest in the flesh." If that is to be the day of final compensation, the day in which all the arrears of reward and honour shall be brought up to all the sufferers in the cause of virtue, then is it fit that the Judge, the Prince of sufferers, and who is set forth as the type of the happiness which holy suffering yields, should receive, in his own person, the amplest compensation; that he who submitted to be arraigned, and who occupied the cross here, should then ascend the throne as his proper reward. If it was right that the work of salvation should be commenced, it must also be right that it should be completed; and if it was fit that Christ should undertake it, then is it fit, that, in order to evince his competency, and reward his toils, *he* also should complete it; that the honour of conferring the last great blessings of his grace, and of giving the final application to the great principles of his dispensation, should be enjoyed by him alone. If it was right in God so to construct the plan of salvation that in all its workings it should be made to yield to believers, as it does, the largest possible measure of consolation and joy, then

must it be right also, that in the person of their Judge they should recognise their Redeemer. It will give an additional value to the crown of life, that it will be bestowed by the hand of Christ; that the very being who died for them, who gave them the grace of repentance, and who awakened in them the hope of salvation, should come personally to realize their hopes, to collect them around him, to wipe away every tear, to receive the plaudits of the universe in their salvation; this will be the only ingredient their cup of bliss will require, and the last it can receive; having that, their joy will be full. And if it be right that his enemies should be vanquished, it seems fit that he should vanquish them; if it is proper that unbelievers should be condemned, there appears a peculiar propriety, that, both for their greater conviction, and his greater exaltation, the sentence of condemnation should be pronounced by him.

And O, what an enhancement of their doom will this single circumstance contain! If a person be conscious that he is chargeable with ingratitude, and with ingratitude beyond forgiveness, he would rather confront his greatest foe than the person he has thus injured. Were any other being than Christ to ascend the throne of judgment, or were he any other than he is, the confusion of the impenitent sinner at appearing in his presence would be less intolerable. But when he shall draw near, and be compelled to look on that injured goodness, his confusion will be complete. When he shall behold him invested in the robe of humanity, that single sight will flash on him the recollection of all that Jesus did in that nature to redeem him—the incarnation, the bloody sweat, the cross, the pierced side—all will rise to view, and penetrate him with an agonizing sense of his ingratitude and guilt. When he shall hear the voice of that injured Being, the voice which he had heard so often in the gospel, inviting, entreating, beseeching him in every tone of gracious solicitude, it will vibrate on his ear more dreadfully than the sound of the archangel's trump which called him from the grave. When the impenitent are represented as calling on the mountains and rocks to fall on them, what is that which they seek to avoid? They ask to be hidden from the face of Him that sitteth upon the throne, and from the wrath of the Lamb—*the wrath of the Lamb*. Had it been the fury of the lion; had it been the wrath of a being who had only created them, given them a law, and left them to obey it or perish,—who had only been known to them as a being of rigorous and unbending justice,—then, however conscious of guilt, they might have attempted to lift up their hardened front in his presence. But it is the wrath of the Lamb; of a Being who has always acted towards them with infinite tenderness and patience; who became the Lamb of God, the great sacrificial victim, suffering and dying to take away their guilt: this is the circumstance which will render his wrath so unendurable, that they will ask no higher favour than to be sheltered from the sight of his face, and would take the weight of the incumbent earth as a blessed exchange.

3. Our Lord very frequently spoke of the pomp and circumstances of the final scene. In painting that coming event, there is, no doubt, a propensity to overcharge the picture with physical terrors; to make it depend for interest, too exclusively, on material splendours; there is a danger of sinking the *moral*, and of leaving the mind unduly occupied with images of material grandeur. And it is, no doubt, true, that in that awful day our spiritual condition will be the great engrossing theme; that a flaming world will have little interest for one who is about to pass into a lake which ever burneth; that the stupendous magnificence of the surrounding scene will

have slight attractions for one whose ear has just drank in the sentence of divine approval, and whose eye is fast filling with the visions of eternal life. But, *till then*, we have the sanction of our Lord's example for introducing, and enlarging on, the physical machinery of that day. He who knew all the avenues to the human heart, knew that the way to engage our attention to the day of doom itself, is to invest it with sublime scenical imagery, to accumulate around it all those circumstances of awful pomp which are known to have terrible attraction for the human heart. " The Son of man shall come in the clouds of heaven, in his own glory, and in the glory of his Father, and of all his holy angels, with a great sound of trumpets."

And who can question that the *truth* of the scene requires this dramatic description ? Had Sinai its apparatus of quailing terrors—its sublime blackness of darkness—its thunders, and tempests, and earthquakes—its sound of a trumpet waxing louder and louder—and its hosts of ministering angels,—did all this appalling machinery attend the *publication* of the law, a mere *national* event, a comparatively private scene, and shall that day, when the law is to assert its high majesty, and man to have his final audit—that day of universal summoning and eternal dispensations—be wanting in circumstantial effect ? Had even Bethlehem its signs and wonders— its guiding star, and exulting cherubim—when He came as in laboured obscurity, could creation even then be hardly restrained from collecting her glories to grace the scene,—and shall she be remiss in her attendance when he will come on purpose to be glorified, when leave will be given her to pour all her splendours in his train? Has Calvary also its tale of prodigious things,—did nature come and weep at his cross, and sympathize with his sorrows, and shall she not come to wait on his throne, and give effect to his triumph? Yes, we believe that the promise which he made, especially to his disciples, is destined to have universal application: that every element and every nature which sympathized in his tribulation will then be promoted to swell his train, or enthroned to share his glory. Whether, indeed, *every* predicted prodigy, every image of terrible sublimity which the scriptures assign to that awful day, will be literally realized or not, it is immaterial to determine. The fact that our Lord's descriptions of it fill the imagination, that in order to aggrandize its interest he has selected and combined every element of greatness, beauty, and terror, warrants us to infer that the machinery will be every way worthy the unparalleled occasion; that if one of those predicted circumstances are wanting, it will only be to make way for another of surpassing power. "He shall come in his own glory," clad in the robe of essential light he had worn from eternity; "and in the glory of his Father," absorbing in his own person all power and office, invested by the paternal hand with all the insignia of supreme majesty, and girt with the sword of ultimate justice, never till now unsheathed; and crowned with the most convincing signs, and glorious demonstrations, of paternal love; "and in the glory of his holy angels;" all the bright inhabitants of heaven, forsaking their sublime occupations, and descending from their lofty seats— ten thousand times ten thousand, and thousands of thousands—shall encircle his throne, and attend his coming. In the presence of that splendour, the sun itself shall wane, and all light be swallowed up. The vast procession, sailing on the bosom of the troubled air, filling the concave of the sky, and flanked with prepared thunder-clouds of wrath, shall open its front on the astonished world. No interpreter will be necessary; it will flash its meaning on every mind, find a key in every breast,—

explaining a thousand presentiments, and realizing ten thousand apprehensions. The sound of a trumpet is heard :—it is the voice of the Judge calling for the sleeping dead,—calling with a voice which is instantly heard, understood, and obeyed: they that are in their graves come forth. Again it sounds; and unnumbered angels, true to the signal, disperse over the four winds of heaven, and collect the whole human family into the area of the great tribunal. Then shall ensue the conflagration of the globe. Forsaken of its inhabitants, all its stores of fire shall be unmasked, every mountain shall be a Sinai, and the flame universal; yet who shall heed the sight? for the great assize will have began. " May the Lord grant that we may find mercy of the Lord in that day."

4. The rectitude which will distinguish the proceedings of the last day is a sentiment familiar to the Old Testament. On this account, I should content myself with barely repeating it, had not our Lord directed our attention to certain particulars by which that rectitude will make itself impressively seen. " Before him shall be gathered *all* nations;" in other words, the judgment will be universal. If it were not, if only one of all the generations of mankind were absent, the whole universe would have a right to complain of injustice. But the judgment will be righteous, so that all will be present; and therefore *you* will be present. However loth to leave the darkness of the grave, you must come forth. However eager to remain in the domains of death, death must deliver you up. However loud your entreaties to the rocks to fall on you, and to the hills to cover you, they will refuse to afford you a refuge. Though, now, you may often compel nature to serve you in your sins, and to conceal your character, then, it will be avenged; darkness itself will reject you—the night will become light about you,—every department and element of

creation, true to its original design, will render service to its Lord in conspiring to facilitate the ends of justice. And so essential to those ends will be the presence of every human being, that if you alone were absent the solemn proceedings would wait, the judgment would stop, for your appearance.

But impartiality requires not only that every individual should be present; it also demands that cognizance be taken of every act. Let a single deed, let a single thought, the most inconsequent and unproductive that ever passed through the mind, be omitted, and, if that thought possessed a moral quality, the universe would be justified in protesting against the omission. But nothing shall be overlooked, nothing made light of; the slightest voluntary exercise of the soul, the very dust of the balances, shall be taken into the account. The two mites —the cup of cold water—the prison visit—the pious wish, on the one hand,—the omitted kindness—the idle word —the unchaste look—the thought of evil—the deed of darkness, on the other,—shall all be brought into the open court. It is in the moral world as it is in the natural, where every substance weighs something: though we speak of imponderable bodies, yet nature knows nothing of positive *levity:* and were we possessed of the necessary scales, the exquisite instrument, we should find that the same holds true in the moral world. Nothing is insignificant on which sin has breathed the breath of hell: everything is important on which holiness has impressed itself in the faintest characters. And, accordingly, "there is nothing covered, that shall not be revealed; and hid, that shall not be known." However unimportant now in the estimation of man, yet, when placed in the light of the divine countenance, like the atom in the sun's rays, it shall be found deserving attention; and as the minutest molecule of matter contains all the primordial elements of a world, so the least action of the mind shall be found to include in it the essential elements of heaven or of hell.

And in order to make good its character for righteousness, it must also be a judgment of proportion and comparison, in which the guilt of each is ascertained according to all its peculiar modifications. In the courts of human judicature, one law, and one measure of punishment, is often applied to a multitude of offences, varying in their shades of guilt. But, in that day, a law will be found for every different sin, and a measure of punishment accurately adjusted to every measure of guilt. It will be more tolerable for some than it will be for others. He who knew his Lord's will, and did it not, shall be beaten with many stripes; and he who knew not, and yet committed things worthy of stripes, shall be beaten with few stripes. The number of talents which each had received will determine the returns which each should have made. It will not be a question merely of guilt or innocence, but a question of—How guilty? The sinner will not merely be convicted of impenitence, but of all the aggravations of his impenitence. He will find himself brought into comparison with those who, though their religious advantages were less than his, succeeded in laying hold on eternal life. He will find himself confronted by the men of Sodom and Gomorrah, of Tyre and Sidon, and Nineveh; the whole heathen world shall rise up in judgment to condemn him. They who *have been* punished will demand—they who *would have been* punished, had they misused their means and mercies as he has done, will demand—the universe will demand, on every principle of impartiality and justice, that the impenitent hearer of the gospel shall not escape, that judgment go forth against him, that he be punished according to the enormity of his guilt.

Were *any* allowed to absent themselves from that tribunal, the hearers of the gospel certainly would not; they form the most important class which will be there arraigned. Could any class of sins be passed by, impenitence under the gospel could not; it takes rank with the highest order of guilt; it will throw every other description of sin into the shade. Were a day of judgment appointed for no other class, the hearers of the gospel are a class so important, that the judgment would be set, and the books be opened, if only for them. They occupy no middle ground. They are either the subjects of faith and repentance, and, as such, entitled, through grace, to the highest glories of the heavenly state; or else, they are the guiltiest, the most inexcusable, of their race, and, as such, deserving the extremest woe. We are to suppose that the most ordinary proceedings of that day will be invested with a more awful solemnity than the universe ever before beheld; but when the impenitent hearer of the gospel shall be arraigned, that solemnity shall deepen, if possible, a thousand fold; while the crimson aggravations of his guilt shall be laid open, the attention of the congregated world shall become more breathless and intense: and when his doom shall be pronounced, the voice of the righteous Judge shall take, if possible, a deeper tone, and speak with a more awful emphasis, as he utters the sentence, " Depart from me; I never knew you."

And to render the rectitude of the judgment perfect, the whole must be conducted according to the *known* laws of the divine government. In other words, the laws to which man is now required to conform are the identical rules to which his conduct will then be brought. Were another standard to be then set up, a new law introduced, man might justly object to its irrelevance, put in a plea of ignorance, and protest against its application. But the rule of judgment will be two-fold: the law of eternal morality, to which our nature was originally adapted, and in obedience to which we should have found perfection; and the law of grace, brought in to suit our lapsed condition, and in compliance with which we may obtain salvation. These, as they are only rules known to us now, will be the only laws adduced then; the consequence of which will be, that *our works*, our present conformity or nonconformity with these known principles, will constitute the great subjects of inquest. "By thy words shalt thou be justified," said Christ, "and by thy words shalt thou be condemned." While he declares that the formula of the final sentence shall run thus:—"Inasmuch as ye *did* it; and inasmuch as ye *did it not*."

In his hands, these laws will become of universal application. He will make it apparent that our conduct has never stopped with ourselves; that it has never stopped at human laws, but has been all related to his divine laws; that everything we have done has obeyed a law, or violated a law, divinely enacted, and either written on our hearts or published in his word. And not only will these laws, in his hands, receive universal application as to persons, but also as to the character of each individual, taking cognizance of all its thoughts and rudiments. If we had eyes adapted to the sight, we should see, on looking into the smallest seed, the future flower, or shrub, or tree, enclosed in it. He will look into our feelings and motives as into seeds; by those embryoes of action he will infallibly determine what we are, and will shew what we should have been, had there been scope and stage for their development and maturity. His law has a magnifying power; and when he shall apply it in that day to human character, the faintest and minutest parts of that character will shew a definite outline, and a determinate quality.

And how easy will it be for him to give the law this magnifying power; or, rather, to shew that it has always possessed it. How often did he do this, in the days of his flesh, for the Old-Testament code. By a single sentence, a passing remark, he sometimes laid open the spiritual interior of a precept, and shewed that in the morality of the ancient book there lay, as in its germ, the whole legislation of his new economy. The last day will be the triumph of law: by a single touch the scales shall fall from our eyes; and what now seems low in the standard of holiness, shall be seen towering away to an infinite height; and what now seems contracted, shall be seen taking an immeasurable compass. God himself will be seen paying reverence to the law; and man shall feel himself pervaded and encompassed by it. Nothing shall seem to exist but character and law: man, denuded of all but character, shall find nothing left him but his virtue or his vice; and the law, in the person of the Judge, applying itself to that character, and making its estimate. The reign of appearances and professions will then be over, and works alone will be in request. Now, men act as though the law called only for words, professions, semblances of right; but then it will be heard calling imperatively for *works, character, works;* and men will find that they have nothing else left them to produce.

5. The necessary result of bringing the human character to this test will be, the division of the whole family of man into two classes—the good and the bad. "When the Son of man shall come in his glory, and all the holy angels with him, then shall he sit upon the throne of his glory, and before him shall be gathered all nations: and

he shall separate them one from another, as a shepherd divideth his sheep from the goats: and he shall set the sheep on his right hand, but the goats on the left." Now, men are distributed into a thousand classes, divided and subdivided by so large a multiplication of social and artificial distinctions, that this greatest of all distinctions, arising from character, is almost confounded and lost in the crowd. But " they that have done good, and they that have done evil," will be the sole remaining distinction then: the multifarious compound of human society will be resolved into these two simple elements.

The student of nature adverts with proud delight to that period in the history of science when, as facts multiplied, leading phenomena became prominent, laws began to emerge, and generalizations to commence,—when the discoveries of a single mind harmonized unnumbered facts, and placed the system of the universe on a basis never after to be shaken. The judgment will be a great process of moral generalization. Wherever, indeed, the gospel comes with power, even now, the process begins. It no sooner obtains a footing amongst a people, than, pouring contempt on all their existing distinctions, it proposes a new classification. It develops the conscience, raises the moral part of our nature into importance, bestows all its attention, and confers all its titles upon that. It essays to separate the precious from the vile, and to collect them into a church; to draw a line of demarcation, on the one side of which shall stand all the good, and on the other side all the bad; and this classification it intends to be all-comprehensive and ultimate. At present, however, numerous impediments operate to prevent the perfect realization of the theory. Approximation is all that can be attained. Tares spring up among the wheat; and, notwithstanding every precaution, the foolish virgins mingle with the wise. But the last day shall behold this simplification complete. By the operation of a single principle he will reduce the chaos to order, " dividing the light from the darkness." By the application of a single rule he will gather " like things to like;" and two classes shall comprise all the infinite varieties. Under one or the other of these, each individual shall find a place—a place so appropriate, that he could not exchange it, even with one of the same class, without doing violence to all fitness and order; and those characteristics on account of which the place has been assigned him will be acknowledged by all to be *specific*, his most distinguishing marks. The universe will confess and admire the justice, harmony, and perfection, of the distribution.

Some, in their impatience, would have the Great Head of the church to effect this separation at once; they would gather out the tares before the time of harvest. As if they despaired of a judgment day, they would fain bring all the plans of Providence within the bounds of time; as if it gave them but little satisfaction to know that a full exposition and justification of the ways of God is to be made in eternity, they would forestall the future, and submit his plans to instant explanation. But, " Nay," saith he, " ye know not what manner of spirit ye are of." " As the tares are left till the time of harvest, and are then gathered and burned in the fire; so shall it be at the end of the world. The Son of man shall send forth his angels, and they shall gather out of this kingdom all things that offend, and them that do iniquity." Thus he signifies that his plans are alraedy formed, formed with an accuracy which admits of no alteration, and on a scale of greatness which excludes all haste. He can afford to wait. Had he any occasion to doubt the issue, he might, at times, be tempted to precipitate the end. But he sees the end from the beginning; sees it so clearly, and awaits it so confidently, that his patience only proclaims the efficiency of his government. If impatience of his apparent delay could have induced him to hasten the final event, if suspicions of his power, if misconstructions of his patience, could have provoked him to rashness, long before this he would have " sworn, there shall be time no longer." But his forbearance serves to illustrate his majesty; and is meant to remind us, that if he does not submit his plans to our present impatience, and compress them into the limits of time, it is because he reserves them for a nobler theatre, and deems them worthy the expanse of eternity.

There are others who construe his apparent delay in favour of the impunity of prosperous vice. " The evil servant saith in his heart, My lord delayeth his coming. And with that he begins to smite his fellow-servants, and to eat and drink with the drunken." " As in the days of Noah, they laugh at the threatened judgment, and eat and drink, marry and are given in marriage." Because the event has been long foretold, but through a series of ages has not taken place, they conclude it need be dreaded no more, and take heart to live on in sin. They forget that his forbearance to the wicked makes part of a vast and gracious plan by which he is seeking their salvation. They forget that one day is with the Lord as a thousand years, and a thousand years as one day; and that when the whole circle of time shall have revolved, they themselves will think it short. They are now in the condition of one who has swallowed some poisonous and fatal draught; the taste may be pleasant, the operation may be slow, and he may begin to flatter himself that it will never take effect; but only wait the necessary time, and it will appear that he has swallowed death. The poison of sin is now sleeping in the veins of humanity; few of its deadly symptoms may at present appear; but in the last day they will all be developed; the destructive element will then appear in its real character, will finish its awful operation in the second death of all who have neglected the divine antidote.

"The angels shall come forth, and sever the wicked from among the just." By this intimation our Lord intended not merely to rebuke the impatience of those who would hasten his judgments, but to denote the perfect accuracy with which the separation will be made. The work will be committed to the highest order of created instrumentality; the process of discrimination will be conducted under the immediate eye of Omniscience. Man, we have seen, in his ignorance and impatience, frequently deems it necessary *now*; God himself, the long-suffering God himself, will deem it necessary *then*. The happiness of his subjects will require that he should gather out of his kingdom all things that offend, and whatsoever worketh abomination; that all whose characters are not congenial with the laws, the enjoyments, the society, of that blessed state, should be removed beyond the borders of his dominions. The stability of his kingdom will require it. Unlike every other kingdom, he declares that his kingdom shall never be moved. He designs it for eternity; but were he to admit into its composition any impure elements, any perishable materials, it would mar his purpose, it would do him no honour, his work would require revision and improvement, it would not be perfect. Like a wise builder, therefore, he will permit nothing to enter as an elementary part of that fabric, but gold, and silver, and precious stones; the wood, hay, and stubble, shall be burnt up. He will secure to it eternal stability by allowing nothing to become a part of it which has not passed under the scrutiny of his omniscience, and received the seal of his approbation.

6. Immediately consequent on this separation will be the final award. "Then shall the King say unto them on his right hand, Come, ye blessed of my Father, inherit the kingdom prepared for you from the foundation of the world." How gracious the language! Every word is fraught with infinite benignity. *Then* shall he say it—*then*, when the universe is assembled, when he is distributing endless life and endless death, when every word he utters is pregnant with fate, when all creation is hushed into the deepest silence, when the spheres, the very stars in their courses, are standing still to listen—then, when no creature is breathing, but all are intensely bending to hear, *then* shall he address to them on his right hand the infinite welcome. He will say to them, *Come;* a word which will place him in the centre of a redeemed universe, which will collect around him all the loyal and sanctified in the creation, which will bring all the blessed into immediate communication, and place them in eternal conjunction with himself. He will say to them, *Come;* and opening his arms of infinite love, their nature shall find perfection, and their love repose. He will say to them, *Come;* and every mansion in heaven shall echo the invitation as if impatient to receive its destined guest.

"*Come, ye blessed of my Father.*" How comprehensive the title! reaching through eternity; causing everything in the universe to cast a benignant aspect upon them; appointing them heirs of blessedness. How efficacious the blessing! not the mere breath of applause, not a faint impotent wish of happiness, which evaporates and is lost in the air, but a substantial, operative blessing, which carries its own fulfilment with it; clothing them with happiness like a garment, surrounding them with it like an element, blending it with their nature, glorifying, or turning them into glory.

If a fellow creature blessed them, it only implied that he loved them; but to be blessed and beloved of God can only be because they are loved. How irreversible the blessing! for, if he blesses, who can curse? the hatred and imprecations of the universe could not deprive them of it. "Come, ye blessed of my Father, *inherit the kingdom prepared for you.*" More than a mansion, a city, a province; a *kingdom* is yours,—honour in its fountain, unbounded resources, freedom and dominion not to be questioned, royalty shared with the King of kings. A kingdom *prepared*, adapted in all its arrangements to your renewed natures; a state in which your lofty aspirations and desires have been amply and expressly provided for. While on earth you evinced the royalty of your descent, you exercised dominion over sin; you sought to give laws to the world—to establish a new reign upon earth; you cultivated the noblest principles; pursued high and regal objects; now realize your most enlarged desires, ascend your thrones, and assume your crowns. The kingdom was prepared for you *from the foundation of the world.* Your happiness engaged the eternal mind before the world began: he purposed it, planned it, secured it, ages before your existence. If wisdom rejoiced, from eternity, in the habitable parts of the earth,—if she shared her delights, prospectively, with the sons of men, while they would be passing their probationary state, how much more would she love to ponder the vision of their final glorification in heaven! If the bare anticipation of providing for their reception on earth, of mingling with them, taking to them blessings from heaven, and seeing them provisionally happy in the low vale of mortality; if the prospect of this filled her with joy, how much more would the completion of all her plans, and the consummation of their happiness, in the crowns and thrones of the heavenly state, engage her care, and enrapture her with delight! Come, possess a kingdom, which existed for you in the divine idea before the earth itself was made.

O, what a welcome this! Yet, vast as it is, he seems only to ease his infinite heart in uttering it. What fragrant breathings of grace, filling the universe with vital odours! What ravishing accents to those addressed! they will feel that till then they never heard the sound of music! Then first will they begin to respire. Then will their glory reach its meridian, to know no decline. Then will their joy attain its full-tide mark, to know no ebb. Less than this would not satisfy the blessed Lord himself. For this he guaranteed, as the reward of his mediation: on this his heart has ever been set. Could he not bring forth, on the occasion, all the reserved treasures of the Godhead, he would account himself dishonoured and defeated. But even he shall be satisfied: even he, as he looks on his people, shall say, both for himself and for them, "It is enough." Glory shall then cast off its last veil; and as it offers itself to their full-eyed view, and looks forth upon them, they shall open to it their inmost souls,—they shall themselves become glory.

"Then shall he say also unto them on the left hand, Depart from me, ye cursed, into everlasting fire, prepared for the devil and his angels." Of heaven it is said, that it was *prepared* for the righteous, prepared for them from the foundation of the world: but it is not said of hell that it was prepared for the ungodly; *that* was prepared originally for the devil and his angels. Hell did not form a primary part of the creation; there was a time when there was no hell in the universe; such a place did not enter into God's primitive design: it was, so to speak, accidental, made necessary by sin; it was an after-creation, forced on the Almighty, that he might provide a receptacle for guilt. Now, if he prepared heaven from the first, it shews that he created man to be happy: and if he did not from the first prepare a hell, it shews that he did not create any for misery. No, hell was not provided, its flames were not kindled at first for man, but for Satan and his angels. Yet, being prepared, the dreadful place can receive any other rebels as well as they; and, as sinners league with them now, and do the works of the devil, they must finally share in the same suffering, in the same place. The sinner renders their place his own; and the sentence of the last day ratifies the awful arrangement.

And who can tell the terrible import of this curse! A curse uttered by God; by the lips of him whose supreme delight it is to bless! What must sin be, that it can force a curse from infinite goodness—that it can move the divine temperament to displeasure—that it can make it an appropriate act, a worthy, becoming, and even god-like act, for infinite love to utter a malediction on the work of his own hands! And such a malediction! Every accent is lightning; every word is loaded with misery—is full of perdition. It is a sentence, every clause of which adds a hell to the misery already denounced, till it reaches the climax of woe—a sentence, in which one vial after another of Almighty wrath is poured out, till the whole is discharged; the wrath of God distilled—a sentence, in which are gathered up, and compressed into one, all the curses of God, requiring an eternity to comprehend and exhaust them. But it is not for tongue to describe it; it is for the heart to ponder —for the imagination to conceive; and muse on it the most fertile conception may, without any danger of excess. Then, first, will the ungodly know what is meant by punishment. Then will they begin to estimate truly the dreadful nature of their situation. And, O! when the prospect shall first open upon them—when they shall find that God himself is against them—when they shall hear themselves outlawed by divine proclamation—when they shall find that on God saying, *Depart*, every thing else, every being, every place, but hell, shall repeat, *Depart;* casting them forth, disowning, refusing them sympathy and refuge—when they shall feel that the curse is made to enter and possess the very centre of their being, that it is not a mere stigma branded on their foreheads, but a substantial curse, written upon their hearts in characters of living fire, burnt in, scorching and consuming their immortality—that they have the wrath of God for a soul—will they not call on universal nature to mourn with them, to aid them in expressing their mighty grief, to assist them in bewailing the immensity and eternity of their loss?

" And these shall go away into everlasting punishment: but the righteous into life eternal." Then the future punishment of the finally impenitent will be eternal. " They shall not see life;" " their worm dieth not, and their fire is not quenched." If they continued to deteriorate here under a remedial economy of grace, is their character likely to be ameliorated in a state where all the elements of universal evil shall be collected and combined together? Whatever may be the punishment inflicted upon them from without, it is certain its sting will be supplied from an angry conscience, and its hottest fervours from the enkindled passions within them; and as these belong to the soul, as they number among its essential qualities, they will be immortal, like the soul itself. And not only has our Lord employed the same term to denote the duration of misery which he has applied to the duration of happiness, thus implying that they will be parallel to each other,—not only has he employed *positive* terms, which, indeed, may be understood in various degrees of latitude,—he has also used negative terms; and a negation admits of no degrees; he has spoken of future punishment as a state of endless privation. He has threatened it as the worst evil, the consummation of all evil; but if it were temporary and remedial, if it meant only a quantum of suffering bearing a relation to eventual happiness, it should rather be spoken of, like the present afflictions of the righteous, not in the language of threatening, but of promise. But " the wicked shall go away into everlasting punishment:" and though it may now be impossible, with our present human feelings and limited faculties, to comprehend the idea, for aught we know, the existence of eternal misery may hereafter be shewn not only to consist with, but to be even the necessary effect of, a perfect government, and of supreme goodness.

But while ultimate justice shall be conducting the wicked away into everlasting darkness, what shall become of the righteous? They will be severed from the heirs of wrath, as far as heaven and hell asunder. Our Lord teaches us that " they shall see God:" whether the bodily eye shall share in the vision or not may probably depend on the degree in which their material part shall be refined and made spiritual; but they shall see him with that which is the true organ of sight in divine things —the renewed heart; they shall behold every feature of his image reflected in the mirror of their purified nature. They shall be " equal unto the angels:" they shall be able to approach as closely to the throne of God, and to gaze as stedfastly on the unveiled splendours of that throne; they will be able to fill every office that angels fill, to soar to equal heights, and to maintain as untiring a flight in the service of God; they will in every way be worthy of the angelic brotherhood, and able to run with them in the race of divine perfection. They shall then " be with him where he is, to behold his glory:" to be conducted by him into the inmost recesses of his glory; to see him throw open and bring out all the glory that is peculiarly his, to be the objects on which that glory shall fall and accumulate, and to have their nature wedded to happiness and him for ever. Then shall his ardent desire be gratified, " that they all may be one in him:" by being one in all, he will make all one; by being all in every part, he will become the unity of the whole; so that they shall ever be viewed, and spoken of, and treated as one with, and a part of, himself. " Then shall the righteous shine forth as the sun in the kingdom of their Father;" in a world where all is splendour they shall yet distinctly shine; shine as suns, for ever and ever.

We shall conclude this section of our subject with two remarks. First, although the revelation of our immortality is not the specific object of the gospel, yet, by combining it with the knowledge of salvation, our Lord has made it, what no mere human philosophy could have done, a guiding principle of life. He has made it the Pharos of the universe: it is true, indeed, that, prior to his coming, this colossal truth existed; but it lay prostrate on the earth, an undefined rough-hewn mass, creating shadow instead of light; while the majority of those who viewed it could only speculate about the uses to which it might be applied. But our Lord, having given it an angel-form, upreared its gigantic stature to the skies, kindled its beacon fire, and placed it in a line with the haven of eternity; that, by flinging its warning light across the dark and perilous ocean of life, it might enable the endangered voyagers to reach the port of futurity in peace. And how many, in every age, by steering in the track of its radiance, have outlived the billows and perils of the deep, and at length " escaped safe to land."

Our second remark is, that in his representations of the last day, our Lord appears to set no bounds to his estimate of his own importance to man. When we hear him announce, " I am the light of the world;" even then we cannot forbear exclaiming, " What must be the dignity of him who can thus stand up and say, in the face of the sun, ' I compare claims with that great source and element of light!' what must be his own conception of his greatness and value, when he can thus seek to eclipse the noon-day sun, and challenge for himself the attention of the world!" But in his representations of the last day, he makes himself the light of both worlds,— the centre of the universe. Now what must be his own idea of his ability and worth, that, having unveiled so tremendous a scene, he should make himself the central object! What must be his own estimate of the saving power of his gospel, that he should select the awful amphitheatre of the judgment in which to try its efficacy —that he should deem it an antidote for infinite terror —the terrors of the last day! Had he supposed its efficacy was limited, he would have made its limit the measure of his disclosures of the judgment day. He would have been silent concerning many of its most alarming features, he would have lifted the veil with a guarded hand, lest, by raising it to its utmost height, he should awaken fears beyond his power to allay. But, in the full confidence of its efficacy to sustain and to save, he rolls back the face of his throne, summons mankind before him, calls for his thunders and the ministers of his wrath, uncovers the mouth of the bottomless pit; and, while justice is in its full career of punishment, he throws over his people the shield of his favour, and canopies them with almighty grace. Well can he afford to disclose the utmost terrors of that day, for he feels that he is able to save unto the uttermost; he knows that even now he can pluck from the mind the sting of conscious guilt, and replace it with a peace passing all understanding, thus enabling his disciples to long and look for his appearing; and he knows that then, while all the guilty shall wail because of him, his people, upheld by his grace, shall rise superior to dismay, and shall only recognise in the pomp and grandeur of the scene the celebration of their own triumph, and occasions for their joy. The saved and the lost will then meet together for the last time in contrast before his throne. And as it will be the last time the righteous will be able to triumph on so large a scale before the immediate eyes of the wicked; and as the scene will be enacted partly to make that triumph complete, we may be assured that every thing present will tend to crown their glory with perfection. Sin will have reached maturity in the wicked, and prepared them for hell; holiness will have attained maturity in the righteous, and prepared them for heaven: and when the purity and beauty, the joy and glory, on the right hand, shall be seen in immediate contrast with the awful array on the left, all will acknowledge that the salvation of his people, as there displayed, is a worthy result of all his stupendous plans, and abundantly exceeds all the lofty things he has spoken concerning them. In that one scene shall be combined the consummation of all the plans of time, the rehearsal of all the glories of eternity. O, who can revere him too profoundly, love him too ardently, or rely on him too confidently!

ESSAY III.

SPIRITUALITY OF OUR LORD'S TEACHING.

I. The doctrine of the spirituality of the divine nature lies at the fountain of all true religion. Accordingly, to assert and preserve it was one of the avowed designs of the Jewish economy. But the frequency with which it became necessary for God to republish and defend the doctrine, shewed how unknown and uncongenial it is to the unenlightened mind of man, and how difficult to maintain it in combination with an economy of carnal ordinances. It is true, indeed, that, for some time prior to the advent of Christ, the Jews had not so entirely lost it as to relapse into the worship of idols; yet, short of this, their views of God were at perfect variance with the belief of his spiritual nature. Divesting him of all the properties peculiar to that nature, the popular creed portrayed him as circumscribed in his essence, and local in his residence, with a jurisdiction which dispensed with the inward homage of the heart, and which only took cognizance of outward acts.

But if, in the prevailing belief of the Jews, the Deity was only *almost*, in that of the heathen world he was *altogether*, such an one as themselves. They had gradually disqualified themselves for all virtue, and prepared themselves for the commission of every vice, by debasing him to a level with themselves, and ascribing to him the attributes of a corporeal being. God, the invisible—the almighty—the omnipresent—the omniscient spirit, was not in all their thoughts. What an awful vacuity! He was excluded from his own world, lost to his intelligent creatures; while his place was occupied with the fictions of human fancy, and beings of material form.

"God is a spirit;" such is the simple announcement by which Jesus dispersed the legions of idolatrous error, and restored God to the world. This was the fundamental principle of his theology. In harmony with its importance, he taught it in every stage of his ministry, and in all varieties of form. The God he proclaimed is all-knowing, and everywhere present, and to whom all things are possible; a being whom no man hath seen nor can see, and who requires to be worshipped in spirit and in truth; whose new evangelical kingdom on earth is to be seated in the human soul, having spiritual laws enforced by spiritual sanctions, and administered by the agency of his Holy Spirit. By thus attesting the spirituality of the divine nature, and making it a fundamental doctrine of his gospel, our Lord lifted the mind of man from earth to heaven, provided against all our tendencies to materialize and debase religion, furnished a motive for every virtue, kindled in his church a central, all-pervading light, and animated all piety with a living soul.

II. Agreeably to the spirituality of the Supreme Being, and the relation in which we stand to him as his spiritual offspring, in exercising the prerogative of lawgiver, he has legislated for the soul. Human laws, for reasons the most obvious, can only take cognizance of outward acts. But even the positive rites of the Jewish code, however carnal in their nature, and temporary in their obligation, were specifically designed and constructed for the soul; while, of the moral law, the soul was the proper sphere, the peculiar province, of jurisdiction; it claims authority over actions only as they are the motions and expressions of the in-dwelling soul. It is, in effect, the voice of God speaking *to* the soul, and *for* it; giving utterance and energy to the enlightened and original dictates of *the man within.* But in entire oblivion, or open defiance, of its spiritual nature, the Jews had "made it of none effect by their tradition." Having dethroned and dismissed it from within, they limited its jurisdiction to the outward life, guarding every avenue by which it might return and resume its seat by a trivial ceremony, or a precarious tradition. And not only so, they bought themselves off at pleasure from even an outward observance of the moral law, purchased a dispensation to transgress it, at the easy price of a little additional punctiliousness in the ritual worship. Thus discredited and disowned, its authority was merely nominal; and the only rank it was permitted to take was below the emptiest superstition.

But Jesus came to its rescue, and restored to it the spirit and office, which, in their hands, it had lost. The tables of the law, prostrate and defaced, and overlaid with the long-accumulating dust and rubbish of rabbinical lore, he drew forth, and again set up; and, retracing their characters afresh, as with the finger of infinite purity, he republished them with an authority and effect which the fire of Sinai rekindled could not have increased. As expounded and enforced by his lips, especially in his sermon on the mount, they not only retrieved their original honours, but acquired a more perfectly reasoned and undeniable title to rule and reign in the heart. He claimed for the operation of the divine law a scope and space as free and unbounded as the divine essence. He shewed that, like the elemental fire, it is not only present where it is grossly visible, but that it is all-pervading; that, with a lidless and unslumbering eye, its gaze is fixed on all the thoughts and ways of the world; that it beholds nothing of an indifferent nature in the whole scene; but that noting, discriminating, and weighing all things, it everywhere and in everything discovers the elements of good or evil, approving or condemning whatever transpires. Opening the dark and secret chambers of the heart, he shewed it there searching for sin; having for its torch the sword of avenging justice, with which it flashed on the face of conscience as it passed, and detected sins which had not yet dared to come forth in action. He shewed it there, discovering and arraigning evil in its first rudiments; rage, in its spark; licentiousness, in its first glance; and murder, ambushed in an unbreathed and unsuspected thought: sin, in its seed, concealing the coming transgression, enclosing the future hell.

So multiplied were the subdivisions, and so minute the gradations, of duty, devised by the Jews, that the *obligations* of holiness were well-nigh forgotten, in endless disputes about the comparative importance and precedence of its several branches. Morality, as a practice, was in danger of being sentenced to wait till morality, as a science, should be complete; till they should succeed in the hopeless task of determining the merits, and adjusting the claim, of its respective parts, so as to give it the scholastic air of a system. Resolving their endless distinctions of duty into two classes, our Lord not only declared which is the first and great command; he shewed them that the principle of all obedience, and the substance of all law, are essentially the same; that *love is the fulfilling of the law*. He taught that "all the law and the prophets," all the duties enjoined from the foundation of the world, are resolvable into this as their life and essence; and that, consequently, wherever this principle exists, though the subjects of it may be ignorant that such duties have been formally enjoined, it would, by the necessity of its nature, unfold and expand, putting forth all the fruits and beauties of holiness; that it is the principle which is in the stead of law, and the fulfilment of all law.

And to the law of God thus explained and enforced, he put the seal of eternity. In the hands of the Jews, it has been made to vary its demands, accommodating its requirements to the changing temperature of times and circumstances; but as the principles on which it rests can know no change, he proclaimed its immutability. " For verily I say unto you, Till heaven and earth pass, one jot or one tittle shall in nowise pass from the law till all be fulfilled." Having raised and restored it to all its original claims, he published it anew as the rule of our spiritual nature; the perfect, universal, and perpetual standard, to which the entire man must be conformed.

III. From his exposition of the moral law, it is only a short and easy transition to the spiritual character which his teaching prescribed for—

1. The worship of God. There is a sense in which spiritual devotion stands opposed to that which is *local*. Among the many restrictions peculiar to the Jewish economy, one was, that after the erection of the temple at Jerusalem, it became impious to perform certain rites at any other place. Hence the difficulty expressed by the woman of Samaria, as to the proper place of devotion. Jesus announced that, by the introduction of the gospel, all such local distinctions would cease, and that believers would offer their spiritual sacrifices wherever, and as often as they chose. On another occasion he declared to his disciples, " Wherever two or three are met together in my name, there am I in the midst of them;" thus

asserting the spirituality and immensity of his divine nature, and harmonizing it with the spiritual character and universal extension of his church: while, by the final commission which he gave to his disciples to carry his gospel into all nations, he abrogated the law of local sanctity, consecrated the wide world to the worship of God, and appointed the whole earth to be " the mountain of holiness."

2. The spirituality of worship which Jesus taught is contradistinguished from ceremonial observances. *God is a spirit*, and the only devotion compatible with his nature is that which flows from the souls of his worshippers. In prescribing the ritual part of a religion, he is to be regarded as consulting not the spirituality of his own, but the materiality and infirmities of our nature; as relaxing the demands of his *heavenly*, to meet the necessities of our *earthly*. But as his only aim, in thus suspending the requirements which are proper to his nature, is to engage and assist our *souls* in his service, so the religion which attains this end with the fewest forms is regarded by him as the most perfect. It is more congenial to his spiritual nature, and less ensnaring to our formality. On this principle it is that the Christian dispensation, which, when compared with the Jewish, ranks so much higher in moral excellence, was assigned to the hands of Jesus to bestow as an incomparably better gift. And of the heavenly state, where devotion is carried to the highest perfection, John informs us that he saw no temple therein: it is dispensed with there as an unnecessary appendage. The worshippers there are independent of time, and place, and circumstance. By such restrictions they would deem their worship impeded and disfigured. Devotion there, divested of all its earthly vestments, is reduced to its pure essential elements. The

soul of religion enters there alone, and hence the superiority and perfection of the worship.

The ritual of the Jews, indeed, prescribed a multitude of perpetually recurring observances. But, though burdened with ceremonies, it was highly significant of all that is spiritual and essential in the present economy. That its rights were not necessary to salvation, must have been evident to the reflecting Israelite, from the fact that many had been saved before they were prescribed. To secure and vindicate the spirituality of the divine worship was one of its chief and avowed objects. For this the Almighty proclaimed himself a jealous God. Hence, too, the rigorous prohibition of graven images,—the certain and awful punishment which followed every lapse into idolatry,—the frequency with which he directed his prophets to correct their formality by partially disparaging the appointed forms of their service, " desiring mercy and not sacrifice, and the knowledge of God more than burnt offerings;" by insisting on the emptiness of ritual worship, unless accompanied by the sacrifice of a contrite spirit,—by reminding them during seasons of captivity and war, when the observance of their rites was not in their power, that if they still retained the piety of the heart, they possessed the essence and core of true religion,—all of which combined to preserve and promote the spirituality of their devotion. Piety, indeed, has always been composed of the same elements, and issued in the same result—the production of spiritual men. For this, the legal economy may be said to have travailed and been in birth. Yet, however laborious the process, and elementary the character it produced, it could be satisfied with nothing less. Disowning and rejecting the formalist as a reproach, it acknowledged for its offspring none who bore not its spiritual impress; and, equally with the gospel, reserved its ultimate rewards for the "Israelite indeed." Over every gate of the temple it may be said to have exhibited this inscription—" He is not a Jew who is one outwardly; neither is that circumcision which is outward in the flesh : but he is a Jew who is one inwardly; and circumcision is that of the heart, in the spirit and not in the letter; whose praise is not of men, but of God."

But though that economy contemplated the pure and cordial worship of God, yet spirituality was not its characteristic. It was light only in comparison with the surrounding darkness of ignorance and idolatry. As viewed from heaven, its devotion must have appeared remote, laborious, and material. Its name, to be descriptive and appropriate, could only be taken from its ritual character; hence it is denominated, " the hand-writing of ordinances;" " the law of commandments contained in ordinances;" " a figure for the time then present;" " which stood only in meats and drinks, and divers washings, and carnal ordinances;" and for a similar reason its disciples called themselves *the temple* and *the circumcision.* Each of the supernatural doctrines it taught was veiled. It contained truth only in the seed or the husk. Its most striking and instructive parts were "only figures of the true." The law made nothing perfect. It left the Adorable himself in shadow. Like its own awful and unapproachable veil, it at once *contained* and *concealed;* investing the spiritual with material forms, and placing the glories in distant obscurity.

But it was only meant for a temporary purpose: " being imposed until the time of reformation" by Christ. In the execution of his office he gradually repealed the whole ceremonial. " Go," said he, " and learn what that meaneth, I will have mercy, and not sacrifice;" thus virtually discountenancing the ritual of their religion, he exalted character into supreme importance, implying its independent sufficiency, and the possibility that under a new dispensation it might exist alone. By dispensing with all pomp and state in his own person, and demanding regeneration as the only qualification for the kingdom of God, he taught that religion was henceforth to prove its independence of forms; that, dismissing all its earthly allies and appendages, it was to rest its claims on its own intrinsic merits—to walk the earth in unattended majesty, indebted for all its attractions and triumphs to the invisible Spirit alone.

His prediction of the entire destruction of the temple intimated the approaching purification of religion. The temple was the fixed and only home of the ceremonial institute. During the earlier history of that institute it had been migratory: "I have not," saith God, "dwelt in any house since the time that I brought up the children of Israel out of Egypt, even to this day, but have walked in a tent and in a tabernacle." The erection of the temple gave to it locality, consolidation, and repose; was the appropriate token and promise of its stability; and, accordingly, around that sacred fane the nation settled and built a home, in reliance on that stability. The unqualified prediction of its fall, then, involved the abrogation of its peculiar rites. The prophecy of its former demolition only involved the suspension of these rites: for it was accompanied, and even preceded, by a promise of its restoration. But Jesus, by announcing the deletion, the utter erasure, of the temple from the face of the earth, without any reserve for the future, intimated the irrevocable nature of its fall, the visible repeal of the religion which dwelt in it, and "the bringing in of a better hope, by the which we draw nigh unto God."

By announcing that he was greater than the temple, he virtually displaced it, with all its contents, and remained himself in the place it had occupied: and by proclaiming himself " the way, the truth, and the life," he intimated that all the typic rites had found their prototype and fulfilment in himself, and that henceforth all the offices of the church would be absorbed and centred in himself alone. Hitherto, the worship of God had been conducted, so to speak, at a distance, believers approaching him only through intermediate forms; but Jesus annihilated that distance, and dispensed with these forms: supplying them with the incense of his own name, he constitutes each of them a spiritual priest, leads them direct to an immediate audience with God, and, placing them around the footstool of mercy, commands them " to ask and receive, that their joy may be full." When solicited to decide between the respective merits of the Jewish and Samaritan rituals, he intimated that the time had arrived when the question ceased to be important, since both of them were about to be annulled and superseded: " The hour cometh," said he, " and now is, when the true worshippers shall worship the Father in spirit and in truth; for the Father seeketh such to worship him."

In harmony with this representation, the disciples of Christ are distinguished as " the true circumcision, who worship God in the spirit." He introduces them into a church from which he has swept every vestige of the ancient rites. He allows them to restore none of these rites, nor to substitute aught in lieu of them, at the awful peril of his displeasure. When they come into his courts, he requires that nothing be laid upon his altar but " spiritual sacrifices;" that nothing appear before him but our spirits communing with his Spirit. He looks for an assembly of human hearts, of naked human hearts; and when he beholds them engaged, delighted, absorbed in his worship, he contemplates an object far more acceptable than the flaming sacrifice of the whole material world.

And the quality of the provision which he has made for his worship perfectly corresponds with the spirituality of its nature and requirements. He has placed it under the entire superintendence of the Holy Spirit, whose aid he instructed his disciples to consider as absolutely necessary and all-sufficient. A convert from Judaism must have felt an amazing change, in passing from its crowded and pompous ritual to the severe simplicity of the Christian church. In a literal sense, he exchanged the gorgeous magnificence of the temple for the bare and unpretending plainness of "an upper room;" and in a spiritual point of view he did the same. But, then, among the new and numerous advantages arising from the transition, it might be said that he found that room to be within the veil. He left the rites to stand in the presence of the God. He emerged from the cloud of incense, to find himself alone with the great Spirit of the new dispensation. "Likewise also the Spirit," he could say, "helpeth our infirmities." Employed by Jesus, the divine Spirit whom he departed to send, compensates for the loss of the material sanctuary by erecting the soul of the believer into a living temple. Having cleansed and made it consecrate, and kindled on its altar a sacred fire, he himself condescends to assume the office of conducting its worship. Acting the part of its high priest and intercessor, he prepares and presents to God the welcome sacrifice of a broken and contrite heart. He calls the thoughts, and affections, and desires, away from the world, and conducts them, like a band of humble worshippers, to the throne of God; constraining the soul, and all that is within it, to bless and praise his holy name.

3. Another species of worship to which spiritual and acceptable devotion is opposed, is that which is prescribed

by human authority. Destitute of that faith which ranges the invisible world, and which makes the interior of the temple above its own, the Jews sought to supply the defect by perpetually multiplying the objects and observances of their earthly temple. Being prevented, by the unchangeable nature of their constitution, from cultivating the science of civil legislation, and, by the intrusion of foreign domination, from the exercise of the highest executive powers, religion was doomed to receive the undivided attentions of worldly ambition; the temple was the great national valve through which that principle, which loves to enact and create, found an escape. But to add to the appointments of God in religion, to legislate where he has been legislating before, is to imply that we understand the wants and niceties of our human, and the requirements of his divine nature, better than he does, and are more concerned to meet them. It is to set up our throne by his throne, and to imply that we possess authority to bind the conscience and control the heart. Besides, so comprehensive and perfect are the divine appointments, however few and simple they may seem, that it is impossible for man to introduce additions without in some way deranging and displacing these prior appointments, and doing violence to some part of human nature. If his petty parasitical additions take root, they gradually shade and overtop the original ordinances of God, depriving them of all that reverence of soul which is the appropriate soil of religion, and which belongs to it alone. If, on the other hand, they incur the neglect their origin deserves, they are likely to involve the religion about which they have entwined in the same undistinguishing contempt. Hence, said Jesus, " Every plant which my heavenly Father hath not planted, shall be rooted up." Arraigning the Scribes and Pharisees, the profane usurpers of religious authority, he demanded, " Why do ye transgress the commandment of God by your tradition?" And having cited a single instance of their impiety, he added, " Thus have ye made the commandment of God of none effect by your tradition. Ye hypocrites, well did Esaias prophesy of you, saying, This people draweth nigh unto me with their mouth, and honoureth me with their lips; but their heart is far from me. But in vain do they worship me, teaching for doctrines the commandments of men."

Piety, or religious obedience, is a virtue in the sight of God only as it is a compliance with *his* authority; so that for man to assume the power of prescribing, is to make virtue impossible; it is to poison duty at the fountain head,—to turn the waters of the sanctuary into an element of impurity and death. To save his purer religion from this deadly ingredient, that is, if any language could have saved it, not only did Jesus institute a more spiritual worship, and one, therefore, less liable to combine with human admixtures, he proclaims its entireness and sufficiency, and his own exclusive authority in the church. To those who would convert his house into a battlemented and frowning fortress he addresses the language of mild remonstrance, and says, " Ye know not what manner of spirit ye are of."—" The Son of man came not to destroy men's lives, but to save them." —" Put up the sword again into its place."—" If my kingdom were of this world, then would my servants fight, but now is it not from hence." Stripping off the tinsel trappings with which men, in their love for pomp and show, would fain adorn his spiritual throne, he reminds them that his kingdom is not of this world. He authoritatively silences the lowest tone, the first syllable, of human legislation in his worship, by proclaiming, " One is your master, even Christ; and all ye are brethren." On conducting the Gentile world into his church, his disciples were to inculcate the observance of his commands, and his alone;—" teaching them to observe all things whatsoever I have commanded." This is, at once, the ample extent, and the well-defined limits, of the evangelical commission. Drawing around his church a line of spiritual interdiction, he requires that, before it be crossed, every badge of authority be laid aside, that every high thing which exalteth itself be left without, and allows nothing to obtain currency and acceptance as devotion within, which does not bear the mintage and impress of his image, the superscription of his name.

4. And the spirituality of devotion which Jesus taught is opposed to that which is formal and insincere. In religion the heart is everything: if the heart be absent from the worship of God, the man is absent; or, what is worse, the Omniscient beholds, in the stead of a sincere worshipper, a piece of solemn formality going through the attitudes and signs of devotion, and even uttering the affecting language of confession, supplication, and praise, but entirely devoid of any corresponding emotions within. He beholds, moreover, in the rites of such worship, an array of spiritual idols; of means converted into ends; of forms erected into objects of trust, supplanting him and substituted in his stead, robbing him of the homage which is due unto his name. The idols of the heathen stood between earth and heaven, obscuring the vision of God, intercepting and appropriating the mounting incense, which should have ascended to the eternal throne. The rites of the formalist are his spiritual idols; instead of leading his thoughts onwards to God, they stand between him and the professed object of his worship, concealing God from his view, engrossing his soul to themselves, and leaving behind them a feeling

of satisfaction, simply because they have been revered and observed.

By attesting the spirituality of the divine nature, our Lord taught that the heart is indispensable in devotion. For if God be a spirit, it follows that our worship, to be acceptable, must correspond with his nature. Accordingly, when we come before him, he requires that the soul, the noblest part of our nature, should do him homage; that our thoughts should relate to him, our affections embrace him, that our spiritual nature should go forth and seek communion with him : nor can he be imposed on by mere forms and semblances; for, being spirit, he is perfectly acquainted with all other spirits : intimately, and always present with them.

If devotion be regarded as the use and application of a spiritual remedy, the Saviour taught the same important lesson, by describing the heart as the seat of our moral disease. "Out of the heart," said he, "proceed evil thoughts, ... these are the things which defile a man; but to eat bread with unwashed hands, this defileth not a man." The heart, then, is the source of moral defilement; not only does it originate all the evil which appears in the life, it must plead guilty to a mass of evil which never comes forth into the conduct; the ungodliness that appears in the life is barely the overflowings of an ungodly heart. It originates many a thought which the tongue never breathes in the softest whisper; and many a desire which is smothered in the birth, as too monstrous to see the day; and purposes without number, for which the darkness of night would be too light, and the secrecy of solitude too public. Well may the prophet exclaim, in allusion to its desperate wickedness, "Who can know it?" It has intricacies which no other creature can penetrate; recesses, which the man himself cannot explore; depths, which God alone is able to fathom. It is there that error takes its rise, as from a fountain, and thence all the streams of error are constantly fed. There it is that sin sows its poisonous seed, as in ground prepared for its reception, and where it is sure to take root. There it is that malice muses its deep-laid projects of revenge—that lust revels in thoughts of sensual indulgence—that treachery plots and cherishes its dark designs. It is in the heart that the fool says, what he fears to utter with his tongue, " No God." There it is that scepticism harbours its hard thoughts of God, and that our natural enmity against him finds a home. It is the treasury of sin, where all its resources are kept against the hour of opportunity;—it is the hiding-place of sin; where it often lurks unknown to us, and whence it frequently steals forth and takes us by surprise;—it is the first place which sin enters, and the last which it leaves; for sin not only takes up its abode in the heart before it appears in the conduct, but how often does it occur that after sin has been banished from the outward life, it only retires back again and hides itself in the heart. Having taken up a commanding position in the heart, and fortified and entrenched itself there, it mocks every effort made to dislodge it, which does not reach and shake the very centre of our being.

Religion, then, the antagonist force which is to expel sin from our nature, must be conveyed into the same seat—must meet the enemy on its own ground—must attack and vanquish it in its stronghold. " Make the tree good," saith Christ, " and the fruit will be good." Our visible piety must be the fruit of a tree whose roots are struck deep in the heart.

The loftiest distinction in his kingdom he reserved for the pure in heart. According to a law in nature, which universally prevails, a change in the constitution of any creature is followed by a corresponding change in his condition. When changed from pollution to purity, his people shall be blessed by purity, be brought into the presence of celestial purity, be beloved by infinite purity, shall ascend to the beatific vision of God as to their original birthright. "Blessed are the pure in heart, for they shall see God."

While leading his disciples into the presence of God, he impressed on them what they were chiefly to implore; they were to solicit that all-comprehending gift, the Holy Spirit,—a gift which, from its very nature, would demand their heart for the place of its reception. And if it be found impossible, owing to a fixed and infallible law of our being, to associate even with a fellow-mortal without receiving moral modification, a degree of assimilation to his character,—how can the supreme, the ever-active and all-assimilating Spirit take up his abode in the midst of our nature without changing the heart and conforming it to his own holiness?

Placing himself between the mercy-seat and the crowd of heartless worshippers that beset it, he shamed their vain ostentation, silenced their endless repetitions, and, lifting up the drapery of the breast, he shewed them to themselves hollow and heartless, and dismissed them with denunciations instead of blessings. Having removed the hypocritical throng, he sought to surround the footstool of grace with Israelites indeed. To engage their affections in prayer, he taught them to call the Being they addressed by the endearing name of Father; thus allaying their fears, and awakening and consecrating their filial instincts to devotion. To call forth the ardour of their souls, he held up a prize of prayer before their eyes—gave to it the most alluring names—called it imperishable wealth—good things—the Holy Spirit—eternal life; or, as though no language could describe the efficacy he would assign to prayer, he assured them that, ask what they would, it should be done for them,—that they should find the treasury of heaven, and all the resources of God, open and accessible to them.

To shew them the triumph of feeling over form, he brought them, by parable, into the temple, and directed their attention to two worshippers: the one, a pharisee, standing erect before God, loud and voluble, with nothing but virtues to recount—the envy of his nation, the pride of his sect: the other, a publican, one of the refuse of the people; bowed, dejected, self-condemned; his eye seeking the dust; his heart swollen even to bursting; his utterance choked; smiting upon his breast, as the seat of all his agony and disease; able only to articulate, " God be merciful to me a sinner." But while the former is sent empty away, he shews them the other returning to his house, rich in the favour of God; forgiven, justified, happy. Thus he taught them that prayer is a sigh; a tear; a look; an act of prostration; a transaction of the soul with heaven; an affair in which the only office of the tongue is to unload the freighted and overflowing heart, and relieve it of its oppressive fulness. He encouraged, and urged them, by his own example, by arguments, by parables, by appeals to the parental affections of their nature, by explicit promises, to ask, to seek, to knock, to set no bounds to their importunity, to give unlimited scope and ardour to their desires; and, that no doubt of welcome and success might obtrude to check the full flow and outpouring of their souls to God, he affirmed it to be an invariable principle of the divine government, that every one that asketh, receiveth;—and, likening his new and evangelical church to a kingdom, and the entrance to it to a strait gate and a narrow way, a defile, in which hell has posted its archers to dispute the passage, he cheered them to the onset; bade them, though at the risk of an eye, a hand, or even life itself, to agonize, to force their way as with a spasm of energy, and seize that kingdom by storm.

Devotion, which to be pure and vital must derive its supplies, like the living stream, by hidden communication with the parent ocean, he found cut off from the great fountain of life, and made to consist in artificial jetworks and devices for proud and public display. Its seclusive character was entirely gone. As if the only aliment on which it could live was publicity, as if its value depended entirely on the degree in which it was seen,—its favourite resorts were the chief seats in the synagogue, the corners of the streets, and the market-place. Tired of the closet, and even of the sanctuary, devotion, or that which passed for it, had brought forth all its symbols and apparatus, which should have been sacred to secrecy, spread them abroad before the public eye, and transacted its high and solemn affairs with heaven at the sound of the trumpet, and in the broad glare of day. Reprobating this shameless ostentation as hypocrisy, he assigned to it its only legitimate reward—the notice of man, the barren applause of congenial hypocrisy, and left it withering under the frown of God. But taking the subject of sincere devotion by the hand, he led him to a hushed and secret recess; and, closing the door, secluded him from the noise and observation of the world, and left him alone with God,—there to forget all things but God and himself,—there to discover, in his connatural affinity and sympathy with God, the hidden and dormant dignity of his own nature,—and thence to come forth, rich in the smiles of his heavenly Father, and, like a priest fresh from a cloud of incense, suffused with the holy fragrance of his divine employment.

IV. But that which formed a prominent feature of our Lord's teaching, and which on that account claims our especial attention, was the spirituality of his new, evangelical kingdom. He came to a people possessed by the demon of national ambition. Having secularized their religion, and thus prepared themselves for the delusion, their early conquests, their miraculous history, and the glowing descriptions of prophecy, combined to foster the expectation of their coming greatness and universal empire; while the galling pressure of the Roman yoke rendered the vision doubly precious, and heightened its splendours, and filled them with a frenzy of impatience to behold it realized. The advent of Messiah alone was wanting to make them a nation of princes, and masters of the world. On his appearing, the nations were to be summoned; and submit, or perish. Leading forth an army of conquerors, the swords of God, he would make the circuit of the earth, and return with the spoils of universal triumph. Judea would henceforth be a land of palaces, the seat of terrestrial power, the very heaven of earth. They lived in the familiar contemplation of a vision in which " all the kingdoms of the world, and the glories of them," were placed at their feet; a vision in which they saw themselves collected and ranged in hierarchal order, gradation above gradation, a towering structure of political grandeur, a living pyramid, whose summit was crowned with the throne of the Hope of Israel, invested with the insignia of universal supremacy, and at whose basement was stretched out in glorious perspective the kneeling and admiring homage of the world. Such anticipation, in substance, was the creed of the nation. It was not peculiar to a visionary few, but was portrayed in vivid and permanent imagery on every mind. Not to believe in its approach was infidelity; and not to pray for it was, to a proverb, not to pray at all. The expectation of it moulded their worship, imprinted itself on their language and on many of their habits, and kept them in a perpetual fever of excitement.

In the face of this sorcerous and powerful delusion, Jesus propounded the simplicity of Messiah's reign. He did this, not merely to dissipate the existing error, but knowing that the principle from which it sprung is native to the human heart, and foreseeing that the great enemy would attempt to employ it against his church, in every form and in every age, he sought to render it, if not impossible, at least utterly inexcusable. His early instructions were devoted supremely, and even solely, to this object. By dispatching his herald to proclaim repentance as the only preparation for his coming kingdom, he essayed to disturb the national dream and to break up the popular delusion. On coming to Jerusalem, he repared to the temple; and by expelling the herd of the worldly that profaned it, he practically taught that in his church, wherever and whenever it might exist, names would be nothing, and character everything. Discoursing with Nicodemus immediately after, he insisted on the regeneration of the heart as indispensable to his kingdom. Then followed his discourse with the woman of Samaria, in which, as we have already seen, he left nothing to the hopes of the secular and carnal, but opened to the spiritual a prospect of unclouded day. Proceeding into Galilee, he took up the burden of the Baptist's preaching, and repeated wherever he came, "*Repent ye*, for the kingdom of heaven is at hand." Arriving at Nazareth, he implied the spiritual design of his mission by appropriating the prediction which described the poor, the blind, the bruised, and broken-hearted as the objects of his peculiar care. Followed by a large and admiring multitude, many of whom had lately beheld him at

Jerusalem when his miracles had divided attention with the temple itself, and all of whom were sanguine of his patriotic designs, he ascended a mount, marked the unholy enthusiasm which fired their hearts, surveyed the phantoms of national greatness which played before their eyes, saw that their ambitious impatience was at its height, and, opening his mouth, by the first sentence which he uttered he laid *their* kingdom in the dust; " Blessed *are the poor in spirit,* for *theirs* is the kingdom of heaven." He corrects their extravagant views, not by branding and denouncing them, but by pronouncing his benediction on sentiments of a very opposite description. He does not require them to relinquish their hopes of a kingdom; he promises a kingdom; but then the kingdom he proposes is spiritual, a state in which their earthly passions will be discredited and unknown, and qualities the very opposite prevail, in which spiritual poverty would constitute the greatest wealth.

Had he delivered no specific instructions concerning the genius of his kingdom, we might have inferred its spirituality from his conduct alone. Had the policy and pride of man been consulted on the means of its erection, they would have demanded that splendour should be seen following in his train, and wealth pouring out its treasures at his feet, and ambition realizing honours and titles at his hands. They would have said, " If a new system is to be proclaimed and established in the world, let the profoundest philosophers of the day be engaged to advocate its merits; let the princes and potentates of the earth be induced to patronize it, and take it under their guardian care; let poetry sing its praises; let eloquence pour forth its most effective oratory in its behalf; let every spring of human power be touched and put in motion, and the gospel may gradually gain a footing in the world." And had it been of earthly origin and character, such instrumentality might have been wise and well. But the spirituality of its nature disdained such alliance. The empire of Jesus was intended to be the great anomaly of the world; and its Founder designed that its distinctive character should be seen in the anomalous means employed to erect it. "My kingdom," said he, "is not of this world;" and forthwith he proceeded to illustrate the truth by laying its foundation in his own death, by erecting a cross for its centre and glory. "My kingdom is not of this world; it came down complete from heaven, and it conducts thither again; it does not contemplate man specifically in his national, secular, or artificial relations, but in his moral capacity as amenable to the invisible and supreme Governor; and it proposes to form him into a subject, and to acquire his allegiance, by laws and influences unknown to the resources of earthly powers, and mysterious as the operation of the wind; an agency derived immediately from heaven." It may impress his image on earthly governments with the happiest effect, but cannot take from them the slightest print without receiving essential injury; it may leave the constitution of a human empire untouched, while it pervades and possesses every member of that state, and renders him a new creature. So spiritual is its nature, that, like its omnipresent Founder, who is always present with his creatures in the same place, without destroying any of the attributes proper to their nature, it is capable of co-existing and co-extending with an earthly state, and of preserving its own separate character, without at all interfering with the functions proper to that state.

Unlike the dominions of the kings of the earth, his kingdom knows nothing of territorial divisions, and geographical bounds. "That which is born of the Spirit, is spirit," and belongs to his domains: so much of the man as is sanctified is native to this state, and no more; and only so much of society as is reclaimed to holiness comes within its spiritual scope and verge. It is a region of light; and, to whatever point its beams may reach, "the kingdom of God is come nigh unto it." It is a dominion of holiness; and he who begins to exhibit the signs of repentance is " not far from it," is approaching its happy confines. The lengths and breadths of Immanuel's land are not capable of being mapped; it is a region too etherial to be subjected to the lines of latitude and longitude; it is commensurate with actual faith, and actual holiness, and knows no limits but where these terminate.

To be the subjects of this kingdom does not depend on birth-place or human relationship. Their great distinction is, that they are born from above; " Jesus answered, Verily, verily, I say unto thee, Except a man be born of water and of the Spirit, he cannot enter into the kingdom of God. That which is born of the flesh, is flesh; and that which is born of the Spirit, is spirit. Marvel not that I said unto thee, Ye must be born again." In their natural state they are flesh of flesh; the depraved offspring of depraved parents. Their spiritual principle —that which principally distinguished them as men, and allied them to God—has become a secondary and subordinate part of their nature. It ought to have reigned, but it has resigned its authority, dismissed its state, and abdicated its throne. It has descended to be a slave where it ought to have been king. The flesh, which should have been only its chariot of triumph, leads it, instead, in degrading captivity. In this degraded state, it is regarded as having forfeited its own name; it is no longer worthy to be called spirit; it even submits to the dishonour of taking its name from the inferior, the fleshly principle. Being immersed in the flesh, and owning the flesh for its master, the mind is animalized, the very mind is turned into flesh, and rendered a fleshly mind; "that which is born of the flesh, is flesh."

Now it is characteristic of all the subjects of the gospel kingdom, that this unnatural order of things has been reversed, and their spirit restored to its proper supremacy and power. Brought out of the grave which enclosed it, and reseated on its native throne, it learns to assert its authority over the flesh. It is not detached from the body; but is enabled to deny the flesh, to hold it in subjection, to give it laws, and to exact obedience. It is not exempt from the influence of carnal propensities; but it struggles with them; and herein consists its spirituality. It will no longer submit to their rule—it will be master—it will triumph over the flesh, and make its new-found royalty appear in a prevailing spirituality. And having thus recovered its authority and birthright, it now again resumes its name—it is spirit. The subject of the change, still taking his name from his ruling principle, is now denominated spiritual, for it is his spirit that reigns: " that which is born of the Spirit, is spirit." And of this spiritual character are all the subjects of the Christian kingdom. God has no moral kingdom on earth, but what consists of such characters; for as the extinction of this spirituality by sin was the extinction of a kingdom, so the reproduction of it by the Divine Spirit is the setting up of a new kingdom; and, except a man be born of the Spirit, he cannot be enrolled among its subjects.

Contrary to the kingdoms of the world, the empire of Christ does not find its subjects, but makes them. This is its specific and exalted object—the production and perfection of spiritual men. Having wandered from the region of holiness, they were accounted dead towards God; destitute of a whole order of life which originally belonged to all their faculties, and was diffused through their nature, constituting its beauty and perfection. "I am come," said Christ, "that they might have life, and that they might have it more abundantly." Being drawn by an unseen hand within the circle of the spiritual region, the life they had lost is again infused; and, in the exercise of its functions, they find themselves capable of the duties of their new empire, and make proof of their allegiance to their new king. Throwing off the yoke of the flesh, they no longer allow themselves to be the sport and victim of whatever sin might choose to assail them; but as the Spirit hath put forth his power to renew them, so their spirit puts forth a corresponding power in earnest endeavours after holiness. Admitted to the presence of their Sovereign Lord, they take their directions from his lips, acquire an expansion and increase of the divine life, until, being changed into the same image, they are translated to augment and adorn his kingdom above.

The enlargement of an earthly kingdom is commonly attended with " the confused noise of the battle of the warrior, and garments rolled in blood;" its boundary lines are drawn in blood. But the progress of his empire is like the silent stealing of light on darkness. " If my kingdom were of this world," said he, " then would my servants fight; but now is my kingdom not from hence." The only panoply he has provided for his militant subjects, is an armour of character; the weapons of their warfare are the love that attracts, the patience that endures, and the union that gives strength. The victories they achieve are all bloodless—the moral conquest of revolted minds. And, hence, like the silent fermenting of the hidden leaven, or the unobtrusive growth of the mustard seed to a tree, the enlargement of his empire is " not with observation;" though it is a leaven which is to pervade and assimilate the entire mass of humanity, and a tree which is to fill the world with its fragrance and its fruits.

The only domains on which his empire aggresses are those of ignorance, sense, and sin; nor does it make any real accession but as it gradually brings them into subjection; so that to accept the patronage, or to seek the alliance of the unrenewed, is to suppose that darkness would combine with light, to introduce a subject of the prince of darkness, and invest him with authority, in the dominions of the prince of light. The primary object of human governments is the protection of property, liberty, and life; the design of the kingdom of Christ may consist with the loss of all these, and yet be perfectly answered, for the enemies and evils from which it proposes to save relate to the soul and eternity. Its sovereign himself asserted his royalty in the presence of death, and endured the cross as the very means of erecting his empire. Qualities which shine most resplendent in the kingdoms of the world, have no place in his; and, while accidents of birth and fortune confer distinction in the former, the latter is an empire in which men take rank according to their piety alone: " whosoever shall do and teach the divine commands, the same shall be called great in the kingdom of heaven." His is a kingdom in which we belong to the higher orders, or the lower, according to our character; in which holiness is the only true nobility; in which it is wealth, accomplishment, and rank, all in one; and the higher our attainments in righteousness, the larger our share of his royal favour, the more unequivocally are we treated as the children of a king. The immunities of his kingdom afford no hope for the covetous, no scope for the proud and restless aspirations of human ambition; they consist of self-dominion, sympathies with heaven, foretastes of perfection, the imperishable affluence of the soul, "spiritual blessings in heavenly places." The laws of his kingdom, unlike the mutable and precarious enactments of men, are unalterable, being founded in his own unchangeable nature, and in the eternal constitution of man; heaven and earth shall pass away before one of them shall fail. And constituting, as they do, a divine and perfect code, they admit of no amendment, accept of no additions, from human legislation. The voice of human authority in his empire is the voice of treason, a fearful approximation to the example of that ambitious spirit whose presumption procured his banishment from heaven. The penalties of his kingdom are all spiritual; within the wide limits of his peaceful dominions he allows no blood to be seen but that of his own atoning sacrifice—no sword to be wielded but that weapon of etherial temper, the sword of the Spirit, whose strokes alight only on the conscience, and whose edge is anointed with a balm to heal every wound it may inflict. If one of his professed subjects offend, the loyal and obedient are only empowered to rebuke the offender, and to refuse him their society: and even of the man who withholds his allegiance, he declares, " I judge him not" during the present dispensation, " for I came not to judge the world, but to save it."

The court of an earthly state is the rendezvous of its pomp, the focus of its splendour; a spectacle which the eyes of its people never weary to behold: his court is invisible: and, though he comes to give audience to his people, and to receive their petitions, his presence is unseen, the object of their faith. Under the dominion of earthly princes, a graduated scale is applied to society, dividing it into ranks, and assigning to each its appropriate elevation and distinction: under the administration of the gospel kingdom, said Christ, it " shall not be so; but he that is greatest among you, let him be as the younger; and he that is chief, as he that doth serve." " For one is your master, even Christ, and all ye are brethren." Under the former, society is a cone, the high places of which are occupied by those who, in proportion to their elevation, speak with authority to the circles below them : under the latter, society is a plane, on which all artificial distinctions are levelled and lost. The rich descending from their elevated station, the poor emerging from their obscure retreats, and, both depositing their respective badges, they are enrolled in his kingdom by one common appellation, enter his presence and encircle his throne on the same low basement. Whatever their distinctions as the subjects of earthly princes, as the subjects of his empire, their wants, and obligations, and destiny, exactly coincide, and place them on a perfect equality : while the only scope they have for emulation is a contest of humility, devotedness, and love—a race of holiness; and to the splendour of holiness, being an order of splendour by itself, no earthly distinction can add a ray of lustre.

And, to conclude this prolonged particular, I will only remark, that, while the subjects of human governments are mortal, and, on laying down their bodies, cease from the dominion of earthly power, the subjects of Messiah's kingdom, as such, are immortal; their departure from earth being only a removal to a higher department of his empire, where their allegiance is undivided, and rendered to him alone, and where their spiritual relations to him are all verified and complete; " Where I am," saith he, " there shall also my servants be." " I appoint unto you a kingdom." And while not only the subjects of earthly states, but the kingdoms themselves, dissolve and disappear, his spiritual empire shall rise on the ruins of them all : having combined with none of their perishable elements, it shall know no change, but that of a perpetual advance from glory to glory; and the moment which shall behold the dissolution of the great globe itself, shall behold his kingdom crowned with perfection, and completed for eternity.

Let the spirituality of the Saviour's teaching, on the great subjects which have passed under consideration, remind us of our proneness and danger to repose in a form of piety, to the neglect of spiritual and evangelical holiness. Created under a law which promised us life on the condition of our perfect obedience, we still retain a propensity to claim the reward, though morally unable to perform the condition. To evade the conviction of this inability, and to maintain unimpaired our pretensions to heaven, we fondly substitute an obedience of forms for the homage and piety of the heart. Besides, owing to the ascendancy which our senses have gained over our minds, it is so much more easy and gratifying to be able to see and recount our religious doings than to attend to the secret duties of the heart, that we would fain lose sight of the spiritual nature of religion, in an engrossing attention to its outward forms.

On these accounts it is that a system of superstition, however torturing the rites it may inflict on its votaries, is able to boast a more imposing array of devotees than the spiritual religion of the gospel of Christ. It is so much more easy to endure bodily torture, than to bend the will and impose mental discipline; there is so much in the idea of personal merit to sustain the endurance of physical suffering, and so much food for complacency afterwards in the review, that Christianity has only to proclaim its acceptance of tortures and penances in the stead of spiritual efforts, in order to enrol among its followers multitudes who now stand aloof in aversion and despair.

Owing to the operation of the same principles it was that the higher and ultimate designs of the Jewish economy became neutralized and lost. Burdened as that dispensation was with ceremonial observances, it was yet highly significant of all that is spiritual and essential in the present economy. But the Jews, while they scrupulously honoured the signs, entirely lost sight of the thing signified. They paid tithe of anise, mint, and cummin; they offered their animal sacrifices; they were even willing to multiply their ritual observances a hundred-fold, provided that, by doing so, they might be spared the irksome task of reflecting, of sustaining a mental effort which should enable them to "look to the end of that which was to be abolished;" this was a duty so much more difficult than to discharge a routine of outward ceremonies, that they utterly dismissed it. In their carnal hands the transparent type became opaque and useless, their speaking and instructive service became an unmeaning enigma, a dumb and tiresome show: and even the glorious temple itself, meant to be the shrine and sanctuary of living piety, became its sepulchre; the mighty mausoleum of a departed religion, in which all that remained to interest was the constant celebration of its funereal rites.

Judea, having proved the grave of religion, became also the scene of its resurrection to a loftier order of life, and clothed in a more spiritual body. Christianity, as compared with religion in its Jewish state, is "corruption clothed in incorruption." And now, we might have supposed, religion is safe from its former fate: its spirituality will now form its protection; and, in addition, it will be guarded by the jealousy of devout admiration; but, instead of this, the very first danger to which it was exposed was that of being divested of its distinctive character, and of being reduced to an affair of forms and ceremonies. Many of its primitive disciples had been born in the shadow of the holy place; had inhaled the incense of the altar with their earliest breath; and had daily walked amidst the solemn and gorgeous magnificence of an economy modelled after the pattern of heavenly things, and adorned by the hand of Deity himself. Proud to be allied to such a church, they had derived their distinctive name from its initiatory rite, and gloried to be denominated "the circumcision." The loftiest conceptions of excellence and distinction, of personal security and future enjoyment, had long been identified in their minds with "the circumcision." And hence, though the superior character of the Christian economy had long since carried their convictions, and won their esteem, yet, true to their early prepossessions, they essayed to insert it as a graft into the Jewish stock, as the infallible means of enhancing the value of its fruits. So far from entertaining the idea that the Christian institute was designed to supplant the Mosaic, they insisted that its saving efficacy depended entirely on its being incorporated with it; that whatever good of a subordinate kind it might impart to others, its ultimate blessings would only accrue to "the circumcision." And accordingly the apostles had early to interpose their authority, individually and collectively, in order to save the new dispensation from being overlaid and destroyed by a favourite and corrupt ritual.

The propensity in question, however, is by no means peculiar to the Jews, whether regarded as professors of Judaism or of Christianity; it is one to which our common nature is prone. What is it that passes throughout Christendom generally for the religion of Christ?—what but an elaborate accumulation of penances and mortifications, of splendid sights and melodious sounds, of fasts and festivals, a constantly recurring round of outward observances? As though conscious of its want of a spiritual life, they have vainly attempted to find compensation in a constant multiplication of heartless ceremonies: as if aware that they had no more of religion than the lifeless form, they have endeavoured to conceal its death-like features by overlaying it with a profusion of costly decorations.

Nor does this propensity confine its pernicious operations to the sphere of our duties alone—of what *we* have to do; but, invading the region of Christian expectation and privilege, how generally has it debased the notions of men concerning the nature of that salvation which God proposes to accomplish for them. By salvation they understand a mere outward deliverance—the bestowment of pardon alone, without remembering that to be pardoned, in the scriptural sense, is at the same time to be renewed in the *spirit of their mind*—in the very soul of their soul. They profess to be infinitely indebted to Christ, supposing him to have accomplished everything for them in such a sense, that now they have only to give their consent, in order to be taken to heaven; not remembering that, before he can be said to have done any thing for them personally, he must actually commence a renovating process within them. They estimate their deliverance from hell as from a place of outward torment; forgetting that sin has created a hell within them; that angry and polluted conscience is a worm which dieth not; that unsubdued propensities to sin are fires which, if now left unquenched, will continue to burn on for ever; that, dying in habits of vice, we shall take them with us as chains of our own forging and imposing, and wear them for ever; and that unless they are delivered from these evils now, by the renewing agency of the Divine Spirit, heaven itself, were they permitted to enter it, would be no scene of joy to them, since everything there would be at variance with their taste, and painfully opposed to their character. And in the same way they are accustomed to anticipate heaven as a spectacle of splendour, and the scene of every refined pleasure which can charm the senses—as the elysium in which they are to find happiness prepared and awaiting their arrival, whatever the state in which they may reach it. They entirely lose sight of the fact, that their present character is creating their future destiny; that their principles and actions, preceding their own departure, have already arrived in eternity, and are there preparing for them a place of reception. They forget, that on departing from earth, that which goes to be examined at the bar of God is the unclothed soul, the naked human character, and that the inevitable test to which it is there subjected is, whether or not it has been formed and sanctified by the Spirit of God. They are blind to the important truth, that the happiness of heaven will principally result from holiness and conformity to God: that so far heaven commences with the Christian on earth; and that, when he leaves the world, he takes the elements of heavenly happiness with him; so that it is only by becoming a subject of the kingdom of holiness now, that he can enter into the kingdom of happiness hereafter.

The principle which leads men to substitute external things for the religion of Christ, is of universal operation: we have seen that it has entered each dispensation, and appeared in every age of the church, obscuring the glory and corroding the very vitals of piety. In the war it has waged with the spirituality of religion, it has succeeded in materializing and debasing it to a degree which has left nothing for the most secular and devoted worldling to hope or desire. It has so consulted his tastes and provided for his wishes, that he can easily serve both God and mammon,—an achievement which was once pronounced impracticable; for while it leaves the heart at liberty for the reception of any guests, it provides that religion shall be satisfied with the attentions of form. It has subverted the whole constitution of Messiah's kingdom; for while it has dethroned him from his seat in the heart, and has turned his laws into prescriptions of empty forms, and the homage which is paid him into an affair of heartless ceremony, of feudal custom, it has left him to sway an impotent sceptre over a kingdom of mere nominal subjects. By anticipation, it has even carried its deteriorating influence into the region of futurity, invaded the upper province of his dominions, materializing the happiness of heaven itself. O, what would that kingdom of which Christ is the author and glory have become, had it been left to be moulded by the hands of man! It would have been made to consist "of meats and drinks;" an assemblage of outward observances, and those of the most trivial description; whereas it is composed of "righteousness, and peace, and joy in the Holy Ghost."

Thus man debases whatever he touches; even the spirituality of the gospel could not escape the contamination. But from this humbling survey of the treatment which Christianity has received at his hands, let me advert, in conclusion, to the divine simplicity of the character which it is intended to form; and advert to it with a view to enforce its necessity.

The great gift of the new dispensation, the promise most frequently on the lips of Christ, and which he evidently gloried to repeat, is the promise of the Holy Spirit. The fulfilment of this promise, which is alike essential to the first and the last step of the Christian life, infallibly transforms its recipients into spiritual worshippers. They speak to God through no indirect or doubtful medium; they approach him by no lengthened process of preliminary forms; through the new and living way, it is their privilege to advance to his footstool personally and at once. They address him with their own lips, and believe that he is listening to every word they utter. They bare their hearts to his inspection, and entreat him to penetrate and pervade them with his grace. Conscience, faithful to its trust, presents the record of its secrets to his eye; and, in the sovereign smile which approves its fidelity, feels reconfirmed in its office, and swears allegiance anew. Their thoughts are busy with the scheme of redemption; and as wonder after wonder rises on their view, they find themselves attracted nearer and nearer to the object of their worship. Their affections, expanding to admit his presence, invite him to enter and ascend the throne. Every part of their spiritual nature is employed; going forth towards him in appropriate acts and emotions, or passively waiting to own the first and gentlest impulses of his hand. Hypocrisy is a mask which they wear not before men; before God, besides its inefficiency, of which they are perfectly aware, it would defeat the purpose dearest to their hearts. They would have every word they utter in the ear of God issue as from the centre of their being. Whatever, while in his presence, diverts their thoughts, or induces them to express an unfelt desire, incurs their displeasure, and excites their regret. Not to hold fellowship with him, not to feel that their spiritual nature has come into contact with his, is to experience a disappointment for which no external rites, however numerous, splendid, or venerable, can compensate; a disappointment like that which we may suppose the high priest would have felt, had he passed into the holiest of all and found the glory departed—the ark, the mercy-seat, and the cherubim gone.

"The Father seeketh such to worship him." He has sought them under every dispensation of religion; but, under the present economy, he has a right to expect that his search will be peculiarly successful. The declaration, indeed, denotes their comparative rareness; and reminds us of the value which God sets on them.

The formal insincere universally abound; but such he disregards—they are an abomination in his sight. But wherever a spiritual worshipper is to be found, there is an object which attracts the divine regard. He entertains the lofty design of translating all his spiritual worshippers to the temple above.

Finally, let those of my readers who belong to the disciples of Jesus be ambitious to exemplify the spiritual nature and dignity of their Christian vocation. Delivered from the shadows and ceremonies of the law, you are placed in a situation pre-eminently favourable to increased spirituality of mind. Disciples of a school in which all human authority is abjured, in which every lesson that is taught is "spirit and life," and in which no limits are placed to the discoveries made by the Great Teacher, you are expected to build up a character eminent for the distinctness of its heavenly features, to become proficients in the art of spiritual-mindedness. Yours is not merely the character of the ancient believer, changed in nothing but in name; it is the elements of which that character was composed, brought from the dimness and distance of a twilight dispensation into the radiance of the divine presence, baptized with the Spirit of Christ, sustained with a purer aliment, and thus developed, expanded, and matured. Looking at the superiority of your spiritual knowledge, the freedom of your access to God, and the fulness of heavenly influence put within your reach, the gospel may be said to have placed you midway between the Jewish economy and the celestial state. Or, as if it had placed you in effect even nearer than this to the privileges of heaven, you are represented as having come to mount Zion, and unto the city of the living God, the heavenly Jerusalem. Raised into this ethereal region, your views are not to be bounded by the sensible horizon of time: urge and erect your souls to take a larger survey; expatiate over the ample fields of revelation; let your eyes range from everlasting to everlasting; you will thus become conversant with objects in whose radiance this world will stand eclipsed, and familiar with scenes and plans compared with which all earth is only a point, all time a moment, all human knowledge an imperfect idea.

If the mind takes its character from the objects which it most contemplates, then yours should be a transcript of all that is great, and pure, and spiritual. You are born spirit of Spirit: you have the mind of Christ; he takes you into daily and familiar converse with himself on the subject of eternal purposes and infinite grace, that he may so transfer you to his own likeness, and send you forth into the world as his spiritual representatives. Your spirituality is, in his eyes, your only glory; it is the only mark by which he distinguishes you from the world, the only part of your nature which he owns for his offspring; you cannot therefore open your souls to the ingress of the world, or leave them unfortified against its influence, without consenting to lose your great distinction, and being guilty of treason against the King of souls.

In effacing from your minds the image of the earthly, his design is to impress on them the image of the heavenly; that you may shew forth his likeness, and circulate his praise in the world. If he admits you to stand in the light of his presence, it is not that you may absorb and conceal it; but that, as prepared mediums, you may transmit the glory of his throne to others. He has made you the subjects of a kingdom which disdains the boundaries of time and place, that your benevolence may know no limits. In approaching his altar as his royal priesthood, you are to speak as intercessors for the race; in offering thanksgiving, you are to be the organ and voice of the gratitude due to him from the world. And having enrolled yourselves as his subjects and servants, you are to apply your hand to the vast machinery of his providence, and to mingle with the operations of his almighty love, in restoring to harmony the disorders of the universe. He has given to you his own Spirit, that even here you may become naturalized to a spiritual element, and be changed into it; and that when you are called to join the great community of spirits, where the body itself is to be sublimated into spirit, you may not be found wanting in any heavenly function, but may enter on it as on the enjoyment of your native state.

ESSAY IV.

ON THE TENDERNESS AND BENEVOLENCE OF OUR LORD'S TEACHING.

In perusing the writings of many a moral instructor, the only abatement from our edification arises from the unwelcome recollection of his character. His statements of truth are forcible, his illustrations clear, his appeals affecting; but the remembrance of the contradiction which existed between his doctrine and his life returns, the spell by which he held us is dissolved,—a shadow falls on the page, and his most arrowy appeals drop pointless and short of our hearts. But in listening to the instructions of our blessed Lord, the recollection of his character is not merely welcome,—in order to do them justice, it is essential. There have been others, indeed, who have owed the success of their teaching partly to their moral excellences; but such is the excellence of his character that, could we only bring to the perusal of his instructions a vivid conception of it, we should no longer have to deplore their inefficacy; could we only come to them under the full influence of that idea, nothing could long resist their power; as often as we returned to them, they would receive so strong a reinforcement of impression from that association, that they could not fail to pass farther and farther into the mind, making for themselves a home in the heart, changing the soul into their own form and quality, and thus verifying his own description of them, that "they are spirit, and they are life."

His original hearers, be it remembered, enjoyed this advantage; whether or not they availed themselves of it is a distinct consideration; they often enjoyed the privilege of beholding his miracles of mercy; and, instantly, on the same spot, they listened to the gracious words which proceeded out of his mouth; while yet they were under the arrest of some new display of majesty, his doctrine dropped as the rain, his speech distilled as the dew. It will not be irrelevant then, if, to place ourselves as nearly as possible in their position, we briefly advert to the excellences of our Lord's character; especially to those which relate to the particular qualities of his teaching, now under consideration. We shall then point out some of his corresponding characteristics as a teacher; and, finally, present examples from his teaching illustrative of his tenderness, benignity, and compassion.

I. In attempting to portray the moral perfection of Christ, we feel that we are contemplating one who is fairer than the children of men; standing in the presence of Him who is altogether lovely. O for the pen of that disciple whom Jesus loved; who selected his Lord's humility and love as themes most congenial with his own taste; and leant on his sacred bosom till he became imbued with the heavenly love which dwelt there! O for the aid of the Holy Spirit, the Spirit of Christ, to unveil his excellences to our view; that, while we are beholding, we may be changed into the same image; may have our taste purified and exalted into sympathy with his transcendant character! Of the early history of Christ, indeed, we have but two or three slight incidental notices; but who can read even these notices, slender as they are, in the light of his after-life, without finding in them a warrant for the imagination to indulge itself with a picture of his early perfection. If his youth and his early manhood corresponded with his subsequent life, how cloudless and blessed must have been the morning of such a day, and how happy they who stood in its light. Unlike the virtues of ordinary humanity, which are grafted, and stunted, and hardly preserved with incessant care, his nature contained in itself the seeds of all worth, and every seed became a fruit; every hour beheld him put forth some additional bud of promise. Like the earth when first it was sown by the hand of God, and held in its bosom the germs of a universal paradise, his nature brought with it all the elements of excellence. Goodness rejoiced in it, as in its native soil. His life was as the garden of the Lord; for there grew in it everything pleasant to the sight and good for food: obedience, which ran at the first call of duty; prudence, rendering the present subservient to the future; sensibility, responding to the softest tones of nature and the clear transparency of truth; and native courtesy and love, that clasped everything lovely to its soul, and became one with it. What wonder was it that, thus adorned and distinguished, he should have "increased in favour with God and man," have become the favourite of heaven and earth. Had the first probation been to be made again, one individual tried as the representative of all the race, and heaven proposed as the prize of success, who would not have thought of him? All eyes would have involuntarily turned to him, all hearts would have confided the great probation to his hands, and have looked on heaven as secure.

Emerging, at length, from the obscurity of his early life, "he came to Nazareth, where he had been brought up: and, as his custom was, he went into the synagogue on the sabbath day, and stood up for to read. And there was delivered unto him the book of the prophet Isaiah. And when he had opened the book, he found the place where it is written, The Spirit of the Lord is upon me, because he hath anointed me to preach the gospel to the poor; he hath sent me to heal the broken-hearted, to preach deliverance to the captive, and recovering of sight to the blind, to set at liberty them that are bruised, to preach the acceptable year of the Lord. And he closed the book, and he gave it again to the minister, and sat down. And the eyes of all them that were in the synagogue were fastened on him. And he began to say unto them, This day is this scripture fulfilled in your ears." Such, then, in his own estimation, was the nature of his divine commission; and he fulfilled it. His whole life was a comment on this text.

If our subject permitted, we should love to linger on the purity of his character; for this, though by no means the most attractive feature to a sinful race, is one of the most remarkable. And here, be it observed, he sought not to preserve his holiness unspotted by avoiding contact with the world; he was not indebted for his purity to the privacy of a recluse. From the moment he became a public character, his field was the world; he domesticated himself, if I may say so, and desired to be numbered as one of the human family; he sought to become the heart of the world; and, in the prosecution of that object, he turned not aside from a personal encounter with the Tempter himself. From everything which the world contained of great and good, his nature selected and drew to itself aliment and life, while it rejected all the pernicious ingredients with which the purest elements on earth are defiled.

He passed through a scene in which, at every step he took, a thousand malignant influences were waiting to dart on him, "Yet he did no sin, neither was guile found in his mouth." He uttered not a single sentence capable of being construed into a confession of guilt, or a consciousness of defilement. He often alluded to his poverty, rejection, and sufferings; and oftener still to the subject of sin, in a variety of forms; but he breathed not a word which could be construed into the most distant intimation that he considered himself less than a being of unsullied purity. On the contrary, he challenged his enemies (and he had but few friends) to convict him of a single sin. The prince of this world came, and found nothing in him, no single thought or feeling, which responded to temptation, or disposed him for a moment to yield to it. He lived for years, and was actively employed in a world in which every condition has its peculiar temptations, so that of all the myriads who have ever inhabited it, not one has escaped the pollution of sin. But, like the sunbeam, which remains uncontaminated whatever the object on which it may shine, the Saviour emerged from this region of guilt, and re-entered the portals of heaven, as pure and unspotted as when he left the bosom of the Father. It was strictly true of him to the latest moment of his continuance on earth,—with perfect sincerity it might have been inscribed on his tomb,—it might have been shouted with triumph as he ascended to the throne of heaven,—" he was in all points tempted like as we are, yet without sin."

Besides his purity, we might specify, not merely his superiority to the age in which he lived, but the absolute contrariety of his character to all existing and surrounding influences; the universality of his plans, which distinguished and left him alone in the earth; the reconciliation and union in his character of opposite excellences, and which formed its perfection and finish. But that which sheds a prevailing hue over the whole character of Christ, and forms its principal feature, is, unquestionably, benevolence. It is that transcendental attribute which ran through all the rest, adapting, baptizing, and turning the whole into grace. What but this could have induced his purity to tabernacle in the midst of sin? It was by no means an indifferent act to him: "he *suffered*, being tempted,"—suffered in proportion to the perfection of his holiness, and the depth of his aversion to sin; but though his residence in an atmosphere of sin was revolting to his purity, though the presence of depravity made his continuance here a perpetual sacrifice, his love induced him to submit—induced him so intimately to associate with the ungodly, that one of his characteristic names became "the friend of publicans and sinners."

We have said that his character was not only superior to all existing and surrounding influences, but quite distinct from them. Others are more or less affected by the circumstances in which they are brought up; however superior to external influences they may appear, they cannot escape entirely the spirit of the age; they hold communion, and enjoy sympathy, with those around them. But the character of Christ had in it nothing local, temporary, or common. It appeared in the world entire, independent, and unique. It was formed for a world which had lost the original pattern of goodness, and had sunk into a state of universal selfishness; the whole of his history therefore is a history of the sacrifice of selfish feelings; his life was calculated and constructed on the principle of a laborious endeavour to imbue the world with the lost spirit of benevolence, to baptize it afresh in the element of love.

The universality of his plans, which left him without any contemporaneous sympathy, must also be resolved into the same principle. He loved man as man, he came to be the light and life of the world. His benevolence could not endure the thought of a single human being perishing; his heart had room for the whole race; and he could not be satisfied with less than a universal offer of mercy.

And benevolence is the principle which harmonized in him the most contrasted qualities. In his mysterious person it had brought into union time and eternity, heaven and earth; and in his character it blended majesty such as God before had never displayed, with meekness such as man before had never shewn. Dignity, in him, was not terror, for he clothed it with a condescension which had before been thought inconsistent with greatness. Temperance and self-denial, with him, were not darkened with austerity, but came softened and recommended by gentleness and suavity. In him were united an indignant sensibility to sin, with weeping compassion for the sinner,—the splendours of more than an angelic nature, with the humility of a little child,—a resolved perseverance in the path of duty which no array of dangers could deter, with a heart so attuned to compassion that the faintest appeal of misery arrested his progress as with the power of omnipotence, and made him stand still. While he seemed to do everything for the future, he yet neglected nothing proper to the present; while he held himself ready to embrace the mightiest plans, and evinced a consciousness that he stood related to the whole species, he yet stooped, without trifling, to the smallest circumstance. Like the Almighty Father sustaining the worlds, yet stooping to succour the falling bird,—he one moment conversed with celestial visitors, and the next he listened to the lispings of infant praise, or meekly bore the obtuseness of his disciples. He, who received the homage of angels, and had all their legions at command, sees wealth in the tribute of a sinful woman's tears, and finds the sweetest music in the dying thanks of the guilty malefactor. Having driven demons from his presence with an awful rebuke, he takes up little children to his heart; and they feel in his looks the security of home, and in his tones an assurance of love, which makes them reluctant to leave his arms, even for the welcome of a mother's bosom. Having portrayed the judgment of the last day, and clothed himself with thunder as the central object of the awful scene, he follows the first beck of misery, or turns aside to weep over the hardness of human hearts. Having proclaimed himself " the resurrection and the life," how easily does he descend from his dignity to mingle his tears with the bereaved mourners! Universal philanthropy did not impair his sensibility to the pleasures of private friendships and domestic intercourse; nor did the momentous interests which pressed on his soul in the crisis of the world's redemption prevent him from thinking of his filial relation, and tenderly providing for a mother's comfort. Never was there a character at the same time so magnificent and unlaboured; so conscious of greatness, and so unostentatiously simple; so full of inspiration to the good, and so free from terror, so replete with encouragement, to the outcast penitent. In his character met the whole constellation of the virtues, each one made brighter by contrast: but one overpowering sentiment softened and subjected them all to itself; one all-pervading law gave unity and harmony to his most opposite actions; interpreting all his words and looks; preventing him, even in the most critical situations, from being at variance with himself, or falling below his professed object;—and that sentiment, that law, was love.

In the history of his miracles, we see almighty power itself consenting to be led by love, and consecrated to its service. Had he only intended to produce impressions of his majesty, or prove the divinity of his mission, he might perhaps have accomplished this sooner by appealing to our fears in miracles of terror and destruction. But the object he aimed at, and the truths he taught, were both of a benevolent nature; and the miracles he performed in confirmation of those truths partook of the same character. He refused but one application to his miraculous power,—when his disciples rashly desired that fire might descend from heaven on their enemies; but he reminded them that he came " not to destroy men's lives, but to save them." On the night of his apprehension, he touched the wound of an enemy and healed it; for, with him, power and kindness were the same thing. Wherever he came, disease and suffering fled from his presence. His path might be traced from place to place in lines of life, and health, and joy. Where he was expected, the public way was thronged with forms of helplessness, disease, and woe. Where he had passed, the restored might be seen making trial of their new-found powers; listeners formed into groups, to hear the tale of healing; and the delighted objects of his compassion rehearsing with earnestness what had passed, imitating his tones, and even trying to convey an idea of his condescending ways. His voice was the first sound which many of them heard; his name the first word they had pronounced; his blessed form the first sight they had ever beheld. And often, at the close of a laborious day, when his wearied frame required repose, the children of affliction besieged his retreat, and implored his help. And did they ever seek in vain? Wearied and worn as he was, " he pleased not himself;" he went forth, and patiently listened to all their tales of woe, tasted their several complaints, raised each suppliant from the dust, nor left them till he had absorbed their sufferings, and healed them all. He went through the land like a current of vital air, an element of life, diffusing health and joy wherever he appeared. Had the spiritual object of his advent permitted the continuance of his abode on earth, he would have become the shrine at which all disease would have knelt, the centre to which all suffering would have tended as by a law; to him the world of the afflicted would have gone as on pilgrimage; and would it not then have been equally true, that " he healed them all?"

Jesus of Nazareth! who can declare thee! thou wast the heart of infinite love, beating and bleeding for human happiness! How didst thou consult our wants, and adapt thyself to our condition! Among the ignorant, thou wast the light of life; when surrounded by the needy, thou wast the fulness of the Godhead. When didst thou disregard the cry of suppliant misery? Thy daily path, like the radiance left by one of the splendours of the firmament in its midnight path, was marked with simple but sublime glory; for, with thee, the close of one act of beneficence was the commencement of another; thou didst dispense thy blessings so profusely, as if thou hadst forgotten thou wert a man upon earth, and didst think thyself still on thy throne. Why did sorrow come to thee to have its tears wiped away! and conscious guilt fall at thy feet with an uplifted eye of hope! Why did unsheltered weakness run, as by instinct, to take sanctuary in thy presence! and penitence lay bare its wounds to catch the balm that fell from thy lips! Blessed Jesus, thou hast a balm for every wound.

Thou hadst come to seek companionship with sorrow; yet didst thou not frown upon the social amenities of life, but didst affably partake of them. Every action of thine was inlaid with grace; even aversion, with thee, was not hatred, but only sorrow heightened into concern. Thy mercy was not proud and imperial in its blessings; thou didst condescend and love to be thanked; and, O, if gratitude melted into penitence, thou didst proclaim a jubilee in heaven, and invite the universe to share thy joy.

And why wast thou thus benignant? It was not because thou hadst been surprised into a career of mercy, and couldst not draw back; for thou hadst looked into the darkest recesses of depravity in the human heart, and sounded the lowest depths of human misery, before thou camest to expiate and relieve: it was not that, as man often will, thou didst compromise with sin, or indulge compassion at the expense of truth; for thou wast a martyr to fidelity, and a sacrifice for sin: nor was it that thy character was all yielding and undistinguishing softness; for while thou wast as an altar at which the lowliest could kneel, like an altar also thou didst check the profane look, and command veneration from the passer by: nor was it that the world caressed thee; thy injuries might have taught patience itself to blaspheme; yet didst thou remain meek and lowly in heart, and persist in turning the tears of the world into smiles.

Jesus of Nazareth! who can declare thee! In thee wisdom and goodness were in conjunction with holiness and power. All who treated with thee tasted of goodness, of divinity; thine actions, if distributed over the course of time, might have formed its eras; thy virtues were dowries sufficient to enrich a world; thy character was glory set in grace.

II. With this impression of our Lord's benignity, let us, secondly, proceed to some of the circumstances which evince his benevolence as a Teacher.

And here we may as well, at once, dispose of an objection;—and it is, I believe, the only shadow of an objection which can be found, in the whole compass of the evangelical narratives, to the tenderness of Christ, in the capacity of a Teacher; arising from the reason he assigns for speaking in parables. On one occasion, "the disciples came, and said unto him, Why speakest thou unto them in parables? He answered, and said unto them, Because unto you it is given to know the mysteries of the kingdom of heaven, but to them it is not given . . . . . . therefore speak I unto them in parables: because they seeing, see not; and hearing, they hear not; neither do they understand. And in them is fulfilled the prophecy of Isaiah, which saith, By hearing ye shall hear, and shall not understand; and seeing, ye shall see, and shall not perceive: for this people's heart is waxed gross, and their ears are dull of hearing, and their eyes have they closed; lest at any time they should see with their eyes, and hear with their ears, and should understand with their heart, and should be converted, and I should heal them." From this reply, many have inferred that our Lord addressed the Jews on that occasion in parables, that they might *not* understand; an inference which was probably suggested by the apparent severity of the quotation from the prophet. But let us only remember the canon—that it is common for God to speak, by his prophets, of events that would happen, in a manner as if he had enjoined them—and all appearance of severity will vanish.

That the employment of parables was not meant, by Christ, as an act of judicial severity, is evident from the following considerations:—First, it was an ordinary and prevailing mode of instruction. Secondly, the question with which he prefaced his parables, " Whereunto shall we liken the kingdom of God?" evinced a gracious anxiety to make himself understood by selecting similitudes adapted to their capacity. Thirdly, there is every reason to conclude that, had they gone to him afterwards for an exposition of the parables, he would have shewn delight at the application, and have promptly met their inquiries. Fourthly, he continued the parabolic strain to his disciples after the multitude had retired; a proof that he had not adopted that strain in anger. Fifthly, he frequently spoke in parables at other times, when his only object was evidently to allure and instruct. Sixthly, the contrary supposition is at variance with all we know of his benevolent character. The motive of our Lord for speaking in parables on this occasion, was, no doubt, to avoid the malice of his enemies; for his subject, which related to the progress of his kingdom, would call forth all the ingenuity and activity of that malice. And hence the reason he assigns for adopting this mode is, that their wickedness had disqualified them for listening to more explicit teaching, and deprived them of it. His speaking to them by parables, then, so far from being an act of judicial severity, was a device of kindness, the recourse of compassion. They could not look on the open face of truth, and he veiled it. Their morbid sensibility and malice left him no alternative, but to be indirect on this particular subject, or entirely silent. Displeasure would have chosen the latter, but compassion adopted the former. Rather than be quite silent, he addressed them by parable; for to have taken the truth out of this casket would have been casting pearls before swine. It is true that, in its effect, it operated as a judgment, for they disregarded its meaning; but we are not, on that account, to disparage his grace, any more than we impeach the conduct of the sower, some of whose seed fell where it took no root. Life itself is a parable, a course of instruction by events; each of which, if rightly construed, is found to contain a useful lesson; but neglected, it leaves us in ignorance and aggravated guilt; and yet who does not see that it is a mode of instruction consistent with kindness, and even dictated by love? We might therefore, without any refining, place the conduct of Christ, on this occasion, among the illustrations of his benevolence as a Teacher.

But other and superior illustrations demand our attention. Had the object of Jesus been merely to leave in our possession a revelation of the will of God, he would have dispensed with that tender solicitude which marked his conduct, and have confined himself exclusively to the design of his mission. But he came to enlighten, only that he might save; and, like a wise and kind instructor, he clothed himself in love, that he might gain for his instructions a place in our heart. To this end it was that he chose to move in the humbler walks of life. Every condition of society was open to his choice, and human taste would have selected a state of wealth, and rank, and worldly influence: but this would have removed him from the society of the people; whereas his object was to make himself one with *them*. He selected others to assist him in preaching the kingdom of heaven; but he asked not philosophy to argue in its defence, or poetry to sing its praise, or eloquence to pour forth its oratory, or royalty to clothe it with state, or arm it with power. The instrumentality he employed was of the humblest order; was, like himself, "raised up from among the people," and, therefore, adapted to gain the attention of the people.

He regarded himself as specially "anointed to preach the gospel to the poor." Had human pride been consulted on the subject, it would fain have had splendour follow in his train, and wealth pour out its treasures before him, and ambition receive titles and honours at his hands. It would have had his gospel patronized by the great and mighty of the earth; and then it would have mingled among them, and enrolled its name among his followers. But the great distinction of his ministry, and the fact in which he gloried, was, that the *poor* had the gospel preached to them. This was a stretch of philanthropy unknown to the philosophers of Greece and Rome. The transcendent idea of propagating a universal religion—a system which should include the multitudes who throng the highways and thoroughfares of life, which should convert religion into daily bread for the poor—was reserved for Him who came to seek and to save that which was lost. He could not look on the exigencies and evils peculiar to their condition, could not witness the neglect and scorn to which they were subjected, and of which in the present day it is not easy to form an adequate conception, without feeling his compassion stirred within him. Among the most civilized and polished nations, they were prostrate in the dust. For them philosophy disdained an interest, as utterly beneath her notice, as having nothing sufficiently vulgar for their taste. For them the law had no protecting arm, justice no balances: right, if it spoke at all, spoke in a voice scarcely to be heard; and kindness, if it deigned a look, regarded them with a countenance which indicated a heart at ease and devoid of sympathy. For their darkness, religion—that is to say, the religion which prevailed—had no ray of light, nor did a drop of its consolation fall into their cup. Even in Judea itself they were treated as the refuse of society, and as cut off from the favour of God. "This people that knoweth not the law," said the proud Pharisees, "are cursed;" this ignorant and contemptible class are forsaken of God, and doomed to destruction. Now it was to rescue them from this oppressed and degraded state, to plead their cause, to redress their wrongs, to wipe away their tears, to raise them to that level which they ought to maintain, as heirs of immortality, in common with those around them, that Jesus preached his gospel to the poor. Numerically considered, even, they might have claimed his chief attention, for he saw that they formed the large majority of every land: but their condition, more than their numbers, touched his heart. He came down from the throne of his glory, and mingled with the despised and neglected poor. He delighted their ears with assurances of the divine regard. He invited them to rest their heads on the bosom of Providence. He sought to lighten the burdens of their heart, and to support their steps with the staff of the divine regard. He aimed to give them the wisdom which maketh wise unto salvation. While he shewed them that sin is the most grievous poverty, that sin had robbed and stripped them of all their spiritual wealth, he taught them the art of happiness, the secret of amassing imperishable wealth, and of treasuring it up in heaven; "and the common people heard him gladly."

In the same spirit of surpassing benevolence he taught gratuitously. Though the knowledge he imparted was beyond the price of rubies; though, at times, he had not where to lay his head; though weary and way-worn, he had to solicit a cup of cold water from the hand of a stranger; yet he laboured without money and without price; the only reward he desired was the tear of penitence, and the cordial reception of his message.

And the mode of instruction he adopted was of the most simple description. He taught no abstract theories, inapplicable to the affairs of life; no philosophic systems, incomprehensible to ordinary capacities; dealt in no cabalistic lore; sanctioned no distinctions of philosophical teaching. Jewish pride would have dictated, that if a new dispensation was to be given, it should be proclaimed immediately from heaven; that, amidst the splendours of another Sinai, it should be delivered by the ministry of angels. Had the taste of Greece been consulted, it would have required that the gospel should be announced in all the studied beauties of composition, supported by the ingenious reasonings, and accompanied by the airy speculations, in which their philosophers were accustomed to propound their flimsy abstractions. But the Great Teacher would not thus debase his gospel, and frustrate his design. He sought to make himself universal—to speak to humanity. His tongue was only the interpreter for his heart; and he aimed to render his teaching a contact of hearts. The " key of knowledge had been taken away," by those who should have held it only for the people; they had " shut up the kingdom of heaven" from the poor, and left them to perish: and, while he charged them with this awful fraud on the well-being of man, he hastened to supply the perishing with superior means of salvation. " He sought out, and set in order, acceptable words." His leading topics were few, that he might not confuse; but so personal and important, that they found a response and an interpreter in every bosom. He simplified knowledge, and reduced it to its elements; now removing the veil from an ancient prophecy, now uttering a touching parable, now a graphic illustration from familiar life, now an easy precept or weighty truth, and presently returning again to place the same truth in a new light. Though all the science of eternity was hid in his mind, and the unspeakable words which it is not lawful for a man to utter could have flown from his tongue, he delighted to be known as the teacher of babes. He lowered himself down to their capacity, waited on their dulness, tasted knowledge for them, and fed them with food convenient for them. He went about as the bread of life.

And the simplicity of his teaching was only in accordance with its compassionate design—to console the wretched. The effect of sorrow is to reduce our nature to its elements; to suspend our intellectual powers, and resolve us into creatures of mere feeling; to shut up every avenue but that which leads to the heart. He knew that grief thus simplifies our nature, and he provided a remedy equally simple. He imparted truths to which the heart listens, and which the heart alone can understand; for he held the heart of the world in his hand; and knowing the secret of all its sympathies, he communed with its weakness and sorrows by methods peculiarly his own. Sorrow was, in his eyes, among the most sacred things he found on earth; and had it not been so before, the reverent attention with which he honoured it, and the simple and sympathetic terms in which he addressed it, would have made it hallowed. He knew also that the time of affliction would be the season when numbers would first direct a look to the gospel for relief; when help, if it came to them at all, must come without effort; when the staff must not only be provided, but actually put into their hand. And knowing this, he published his gospel as a system of consolation for the miserable; and they who know it best are the readiest to confess how fully it answers to the character: after the trial of ages, it maintains its prerogative of binding up the broken in heart.

Even the *places* in which he taught evinced his condescension. If he discoursed in the temple, it was not from any regard to its vastness, splendour, or circumstantial sanctity; for, in his eyes, it was only the mausoleum of piety, the tomb of a departed dispensation; but because he could there teach " before all the people;" could there, especially at the great festivals, when it became the centre of attraction, meet with, and appeal to, the *heart* of the nation. But during his ministry, it could be said literally, " Wisdom crieth without; in the chief concourse of the people." The ship, the strand, the desert, the mountain, were as eligible, in his view, as the city and the temple, for the work of saving souls from death. By his godlike indifference to time and place, in the work of religious instruction, he consecrated the practice of itinerant preaching. He embodied the conduct of the good shepherd in his own parable of the lost sheep, traversing, with unwearied zeal, the moral wilderness of Judea, in quest of " the lost sheep of the house of Israel."

Wherever he found a multitude disposed to listen, he was prompt to address to them the words of eternal life. Some present object, some late occurrence or familiar incident, was the point from which he led them, step by step, up an easy ascent, to themes of heavenly altitude, of infinite importance. He was always ready to gratify the inquirer, provided his inquiries were made with sincerity, and were such as he could solve with propriety. Though he often enjoined his disciples to tell no man where he was—for in his life were combined the active and the contemplative in perfect proportions—yet the eager suppliant who should succeed, at such times, in discovering and penetrating his retreat, never encountered a repulse, even though " he came to Jesus by night." Over the door of his most sacred retreat may be said to have been inscribed, " Knock, and it shall be opened." When his disciples came to him in private, to request an explanation of the statements he had been making in public, he was always ready to descend to their low capacities, and to gratify their desires. When Peter replied to his inquiry concerning his personal claims, " Thou art the Christ, the Son of the living God," like a teacher charmed with the progress of his pupil, and anxious to encourage him, he pronounced him blessed, and rewarded him with an animating promise. He watched the progress of his disciples, however slow, with more than parental delight. He spoke in accents of encouragement to piety of the weakest pulse; feeding it with line upon line, and invigorating it with promise upon promise.

Lessons unwelcome to our depravity, but important to our happiness, he not only repeated often, but even devised the most condescending expedients to make them live in our minds. His disciples had often contested the question of precedence in his kingdom. He could at once have rebuked their ambition with a denunciation of wrath, have withered their pride with a frown: but, in accordance with his characteristic benevolence, he chose to admonish them by an affecting sign which they could not easily forget. How beautiful, affecting, and instructive the sight! The Lord of glory folding in his arms a helpless babe, as an emblem of the humility which adorns his kingdom. Humility, from that day, needs to plead no other sanction for her lowliest acts.

Often had he inculcated the condescending offices of brotherly love; for well he knew that, like the ligaments and arterial net-work of the human frame, the health and happiness of his body—the church—depended on their binding power and reciprocating influence. But by what new expedient can he deepen the effects of his past lessons? " Jesus knowing that the Father had given all things into his hands, and that he was come from God, and went to God; he riseth from supper, and laid aside his garments; and took a towel, and girded himself, and washed his disciples' feet." When he was about to ascend the seat of universal empire; when the cross alone remained between him and the government of heaven, earth, and hell; even " then he took a towel and girded himself, and poured water into a basin, and washed the disciples' feet, and wiped them with the towel wherewith he was girded; saying, Ye call me

Master and Lord : and ye say well, for so I am. If I, then, your Lord and Master, have washed your feet; ye also ought to wash one another's feet;"—to condescend to the lowest office of Christian beneficence and love. Beyond this, he might have said, ye cannot go.

But, O, there was another lesson to be taught,—the highest, and the last; a lesson comprehensive of every other; and he sought to steep it in the essence of his tenderness and love. He, who had laid aside his garments to wash his disciples' feet, had laid aside his robes of celestial light, and taken upon him the form of a servant, that he might become obedient unto death, even the death of the cross. "The same night, therefore, in which he was betrayed, he took bread: and when he had given thanks, he brake it, and said, Take, eat: this is my body, which is broken for you: this do in remembrance of me. After the same manner also he took the cup, when he had supped, saying, This is my blood of the New Testament, which is shed for many for the remission of sins: this do ye, as oft as ye drink it, in remembrance of me." Thus tenderly did he seek to impress us with the great love wherewith he had loved us; to remind us how essential he is to our happiness, and to live in our devout affections. By this touching rite, he would have us to erect his cross in our minds, that we may hold personal and perpetual communion with his dying love. He gives into our hands the doctrine of his atoning sacrifice, charging us to keep it—by all that is sacred in his death, precious in his love, valuable in our own happiness—charging us to keep it embalmed in his own blood. He gloried in his cross, as the pillar of human hope—the column on which he desired that his name might be inscribed as the great memento of his love to man, as that single act by which he is content to be known, and on which he desires to rest his claim on the eternal gratitude of the world. Knowing the power which it would give him on human hearts, he has made his cross the depository of all the doctrines of salvation.

III. But, thirdly, our professed object requires that we should present examples from our Lord's teaching illustrative of his tenderness and benevolence. "Learn of me," said he, "for I am meek and lowly of heart; and ye shall find rest unto your souls." This is the character which he gave of himself as a teacher, and the only instance in which he laid claim directly to human excellences. And who will not accord to him the amiable qualities which he here claims? When first he opened his lips in the synagogue of Nazareth, the audience wondered at the gracious words which proceeded from his mouth. And the description of his benevolent commission, which he then read from the prophet, and distinctly appropriated to himself, seems intended to throw forward a tender and mellowing light on the whole of his after course. By informing us at first of the gracious character he meant to sustain, he seems to seek to disarm our opposition, to invite our confidence, to ask us to meet his tenderness with a corresponding feeling of affectionate reliance. From a certain date, too, in his public ministrations, his teaching must have acquired a very affecting character, from his frequent allusions to his approaching sufferings and death. "*From that time forth* began Jesus to shew unto his disciples, how that he must go unto Jerusalem, and suffer many things of the elders, and chief priests, and scribes, and be killed, and be raised again the third day." Up to that time he had but obscurely alluded to the subject: but suddenly he lays naked to their view—the cross; he speaks of coming sorrows, approaching sufferings, impending death; he paints a scene in which he appears the principal object, bending under the weight of a cross, spit upon, scourged, crucified, the victim of human and infernal malice. Most probably, as often as he adverted to the topic, his voice took deeper and more tender tones, and his countenance assumed a more solemn aspect: but whether they did so or not, his teaching, which had always been grave and pathetic, had from this time infused into it a new element of solemnity and pathos. Henceforth he stood in a shadow, which threw on him a tender and solemn grandeur—the shadow of the cross; and while speaking from that position, his promises became more gracious, and his commands more affecting and binding than ever.

1. The first sentence he uttered, in his first recorded discourse, is a sample of the spirit he breathed in all his subsequent addresses; "Blessed are the poor in spirit, for theirs is the kingdom of heaven." To bless men, to make them happy, was the great object for which he descended from heaven. He came into the world, expressly, to bless whatever he could, to encourage and promote it, and to rescue from earth whatever would accord with the purity, and enhance the glory, of the world from which he came. Instead of using the lofty and imperative style of positive command, he seems to dismiss the state of supreme authority, to lay aside the character of the legislator, and to appear only as the Saviour and the Friend: in the most gentle and engaging manner, he insinuates his will, and our duty, by pronouncing those blessed who comply with it. Blessing after blessing follow each other in quick succession; every sentence comes from his lips loaded with grace; like the gushing forth of a fountain long sealed up, they shewed the fulness of benevolence which possessed his heart.

Rejecting the minions and favourites of the world, he selected those whom the world disowns. The poor in spirit, the meek, the holy, the sorrowful and broken-hearted, the merciful, the sincere, the peaceful, the persecuted; the orphans, the disinherited, the rejected of the world; such was the large family on whom his blessings fell, and to whom he opened his arms, and welcomed them to the shelter of his heart. Each of the virtues which he here implies may be regarded as a separate and essential feature of Christian excellence; and, as he adds one lineament to the portrait after another, he surveys it with delight. He sees wealth in this spiritual poverty, more ample and enduring than all the treasures which earth can boast; a majesty in this meekness, to which pride can never erect itself; and, in this Christian sorrow, he beholds the seeds of joy, the blossomings of glory. He contemplates it in reference to another state of being; and though the world in its blindness may hold this character in contempt, he knows that it is such as angels will bless; that the great God, seated on the throne of heaven, pronounces it blessed, repeats over it all the divine beatitudes. He would have us to know that, when it departs by death from this earthly scene, he raises and welcomes it into his own kingdom; and that, when every mere earthly embellishment shall have faded and disappeared, he will proclaim it happy in the presence of the universe, and crown it with glory and honour; that it is a character whose blessedness eternity itself will ratify and augment. As if the benevolence of God had forsaken every other vent, to find a channel through his lips, thus freely and copiously did he pour forth his divine benedictions.

And may we not affirm, without a paradox, that it was in the exercise of this same benevolence that he uttered those denunciations of woe—if, indeed, they are not rather to be regarded as exclamations of pity—recorded in the twenty-third chapter of the Gospel of Matthew.

The compassion which brought him from heaven dictated these denunciations; for he uttered them in the defence of the oppressed and the wretched. Having identified himself with the victims of injustice, he stood forth in their behalf, as one who felt himself personally insulted and dishonoured by their wrongs. He would be known to the avaricious, the proud, and unjust, as the Patron of injured humanity; taking misery within the pale of the divine law, and extending over it the shield of his divine protection. But even his denunciation, of "Woe! woe!" ending in that affecting apostrophe, " O Jerusalem, Jerusalem, ... how often would I have gathered thy children together, even as a hen gathereth her chickens under her wings, and ye would not!" Like the thunder-cloud, which, having discharged its bolt at the earth, weeps itself away—exhausts itself in a healing shower, which closes the rent it had made,—so his pity commiserates, and pours itself forth over those whom, in the same breath, he had felt himself called to rebuke.

2. In the same discourse which opens with the beatitudes, and pervaded with the same compassionate spirit, we meet with the exhortation, " Therefore I say unto you, Take no thought for your life, what ye shall eat or what ye shall drink; nor yet for your body, what ye shall put on. Is not the life more than meat, and the body than raiment? Behold the fowls of the air: for they sow not, neither do they reap, nor gather into barns; yet your heavenly Father feedeth them. Are ye not much better than they? Which of you by taking thought can add one cubit unto his stature? And why take ye thought for raiment? Consider the lilies of the field, how they grow; they toil not, neither do they spin; and yet I say unto you, That even Solomon in all his glory

was not arrayed like one of these. Wherefore, if God so clothe the grass of the field, which to-day is, and to-morrow is cast into the oven, shall he not much more clothe you, O ye of little faith?" &c. Matt. vi. 25—34. This is one of the beauties of scripture. Had it no other recommendation than its felicity of illustration, and its graces of composition, it would deserve our warm admiration; and indeed it has received the tribute of admiration from men who were only in pursuit of literary beauties. But it has higher qualities of excellence than these; it speaks to the understanding and the heart, on themes of deep and universal importance. It contemplates the world labouring, restless, fevered, about the petty provisions of the present life; causing their cup of sorrow to overflow, by holding it with an unsteady hand; anxiously looking onward to the future, borrowing the distresses of the morrow to aggravate those of the present day; loading themselves with burdens of grief which do not belong to them, and which they are not required to bear: and, surveying this scene of overtoiled labour, and sleepless anxiety, and wasting solicitude, in which mortals are embroiled, the voice of Jesus, the friend of man, the tender sympathizer with human woe, is heard, rising in tones of the kindest compassion, above the sighs, and plaints, and groans of the multitude, and saying, " Peace, be still; mourner, dry thy tears; ye who are laden with the self-imposed burdens of worldly care; deposit the heavy load: ye destitute, who count yourselves outcasts of the world, for whom no one cares, know that you have a Father, and that the God of providence is he. Come, learn of me, and I will give you rest; I will allay your anxieties, and lay your hearts to rest on the bosom of that paternal providence which cares and provides for all it has made; for everything, from the meanest herb which it feeds with the precious dews, up to the immortal soul on which it pours the immediate influences of the divine Spirit."

It is true that the books of pagan morality abound with counsels against grief. The cup of sorrow is so constantly in circulation, passing from hand to hand, through the whole family of man, and every individual has so surely, sooner or later, to drink a portion of the bitter draught, that there is no subject which is more popular, or on which men speak more frequently and feelingly than on that of human exigence and sorrow; and none which it is more easy to reason against, shewing the folly, the uselessness, and injuriousness, of excessive solicitude. But the reasonings of Christ on the subject have this vast distinction of superiority; he does not unfeelingly and gratuitously disparage the wants and the trials of life; he does not seek to degrade our nature by divesting us of feeling, and reducing us to a state of brutish insensibility; he would have us to believe that our earthly cares are of sufficient importance to engage the attention of the Divine Being; and, in that persuasion, he would have us to devolve the entire burden upon him. He does not propose to give us freedom from care, merely for its own sake; nor does he seek to disengage our hearts from the world, without filling the vacuum with a new object; he would replace the perishing trifles of earth with objects vast as our wishes and permanent as our being; and would discharge us from all the corroding anxieties of time, only that we may be free to put forth all our unincumbered strength in the pursuit of heaven. He knows that our whole nature is reduced to a state of exigence; not the body merely, but also the immortal, imperishable soul; and, with the deep anxiety of true friendship, he sees that our extreme solicitude about this life entirely disqualifies us for attending to the eternal exigencies of the soul; he would fain, therefore, relieve us from the pressure of the present, lest we should lose the substance in grasping at the shadow. Accordingly, he assures us, in accents of gracious concern, that if we will but seek supremely " the kingdom of God, and his righteousness," we shall, from that moment, find that God is our Father; that, as we advance from stage to stage in our way to his kingdom, we shall find the necessaries of life ready, and waiting our arrival; and that rather would he move all nature, and put all his miraculous agency in operation, than dishonour his paternal relation, or disappoint the confidence we repose in his word.

3. " Come unto me, all ye that labour and are heavy laden, and I will give you rest. Take my yoke upon you, and learn of me; for I am meek and lowly in heart: and ye shall find rest unto your souls. For my yoke is easy, and my burden is light." Among the numerous illustrations of our present subject, which spontaneously rise to our recollection, this passage is one of the first, and claims our attention by its pre-eminence of grace.

A message from the Baptist, which is related at the opening of the chapter, had led our Lord to advert to that prevailing impenitence and unbelief which had resisted both the preaching of John and his own ministry and miracles. " Woe unto thee," said he; or, " Alas for thee, Chorazin! alas for thee, Bethsaida!" He might have called down fire upon them, like that which desolated the cities of the plain; for he affirmed that their guilt exceeded that of Sodom and Gomorrah. But though he seems, at the moment, to have taken a wide survey of human depravity, and to have been deeply affected at the sight, he prayed for no vengeance, breathed no desire to relinquish the work of saving ungrateful man. On the contrary, as if he feared that, by upbraiding the people for their unbelief, he had been placing himself in an unwelcome light; as if, by glancing at the topic, he had been actually doing violence to his own benignity, repressing for a time the current of benevolence which constantly flowed through his heart; as if he now felt all the Saviour return again into his breast, he exclaimed, with divine compassion, with an irresistible kindness that would not be denied, " Come unto me, and I will give you rest." To add force to his appeal, he prefaces it with a declaration of his divine relation to the Father, of the identity of their character, and of the fact that, as our Redeemer, all things are delivered into his hands. Therefore, saith he, " Come, and partake. All things are mine; come, and share them. I have received them for your enjoyment and use: come, and let me confer them upon you. I am made the Treasurer, the Almoner of all the riches and resources of the divine nature; and you are to be made the happy recipients; come, and let me make you the richer by the free gift of eternal life."

Had the invitation been addressed to any one class exclusively, how invidious an office would it have been to proclaim the gospel; and how mournful the feelings with which many would retire from hearing it; for they would find that it was not meant for them. But it knows no such exclusion. It addresses us by a description which is common to humanity; its boast and glory is, that it is intended for all who need it, all who labour and are heavy laden. It does not even pry into the cause of our restlessness; it does not ask what occasions our distress; it only inquires whether or not we are the subjects of disquietude. If we can look within, and pronounce all calm and tranquil there; if we can look around on the various circumstances and relations of life, in which we are concerned—and backwards on the history of our past life—and forwards into the eternal future which we are rapidly approaching; if, on taking this survey, we can see no cloud in the whole horizon to disturb our repose, then may we take it for granted the invitation was not meant for us. Or if we can point out one whose heart is corroded by no care, restless after no object, disturbed by no apprehension, we have discovered an individual uninterested in this appeal. But till then, it admits of no restriction, its application is universal.

In uttering it, our Lord undoubtedly selected language which would meet the condition, and fall soothingly on the ear, of every man. He had surveyed on the morning of creation, the vast and disordered abyss of chaos; and he had silenced its tumults, and reduced every element to order. He had sailed with his disciples in a storm which threatened them with destruction, and had calmed it to rest: but when he surveyed the condition of man, he beheld a storm more furious and deadly than that which raged on the sea of Tiberias, and a scene of confusion more appalling than that which chaos presented on the morning of creation. His eye travelled over scenes and wastes of human woe, scenes in which he saw the chains of captivity; the pains of superstition; the struggles of poverty; the disappointments of ambition; the misgivings of the self-righteous; and the exhausted efforts of the sinner, lashed by the reproaches of an angry conscience, and aiming to escape from a load of guilt. He heard the thickening cries of misery; his ear caught a sigh, or a sound of woe, from every habitation, every breast of man; a never-ebbing tide of the sounds of anguish, strife, and death. His omniscience penetrated every heart, and saw the tooth of care corroding the peace, not merely of the poor and the afflicted, but preying alike on the learned, the wealthy, and the mighty of the earth. He beheld a storm in which every one was seeking for shelter, without knowing where to obtain it; and, voluntarily exposing himself to all its horrors, he pressed forth into the midst of it, and exclaimed, with a heart which felt and bled for them all, " Come unto me, and I will give you rest."

This is an invitation from which no peculiarity in our character or condition can possibly exclude us. If any such exception could be named, it must be the peculiar accumulation of our guilt, or the amount of our misery; but this, so far from excluding, brings us more completely within the scope of its grace. Were it possible for a man to unite, in his own individual person, all the wants, and guilt, and capacities of the whole human race, the invitation would only address him in a more personal manner, and with a deeper emphasis of compassion. And shall all this benevolence be lost on us? In the name of all that is tender and gracious, he urges us to come. He addresses us as if we had never offended him, nor had rendered it necessary that he should suffer on our account; as if, in contemplating our wants, he had actually forgotten our depravity and guilt. Indeed, had he himself been the offending party, and had entailed on us all the evils we suffer, he could not have employed language more affectionate, nor have manifested greater solicitude to relieve us. Had he descended from heaven to announce only this single invitation to our guilty race, it is so graciously adapted to our condition that it would have fully justified the important mission, and ought to have endeared him to every human heart.

4. If the gospel be regarded as a temple of spiritual truth, the parables of our Lord may be compared to paintings with which he has adorned the walls, and by which he seeks to arrest the wandering eye, and to please while he instructs. Among these, the parable of the prodigal son never fails to attract and impress. The errors of the wanderer, his sufferings, his bitter tears,

his penitential return, the melting heart of that indulgent parent who ran to welcome to his arms, and weep over, his long-lost son;—how many eyes have looked at it till they filled with tears; how many a heart has melted before it; how many a penitent has it first inspired with hope. It makes an appeal, which finds a responsive chord, of one kind or another, in every bosom. It is always fresh, and always welcome; equally affecting us in infancy and old age.

But what is the secret of its subduing influence? It is not that it embodies any profound philosophic truth; it evinces no desire to affect; it is a specimen of unlaboured simplicity. Much of its power is, no doubt, to be ascribed to that graphic minuteness of detail by which we seem placed in the midst of the scene described, and to become spectators of all that transpires. But it appeals to more than our sympathy; it draws in our heart, and creates in it all the interest of a personal event. The truth is, it is a picture of the prodigal and ruined world come to itself, lamenting its wretchedness, and retracing its wanderings back to God. It represents the meeting of misery with compassion: the communing of penitent wretchedness with all-sufficient grace; of our lost humanity with that infinite love which received and embraced our guilty nature, and even adopted it into the person of Christ. The parable is an epitome of the spiritual history of the whole church; so that every individual member beholds in it an image of the most affecting parts of his own life.

And what an insight does it give us into the depths of our Lord's benevolent character! We feel that we are listening to a party concerned; he presents us with his heart in almost every sentence; nor is it easy to conceive that he uttered it without tears. And the view which it gives us of his benevolence is further enhanced, when we think of the object for which he uttered it: he sought to promote repentance, to encourage that change by which the sinner comes to himself; not merely by depicting the paternal compassion of God, but by representing it as an occasion of joy to angels, and to every order of holy intelligence in the universe. From a perusal of this, and the two parables connected with it, he would have the penitent to believe, that in going to God for mercy he is occasioning a joy which, beginning at the centre of all benevolence—the heart of the eternal Father—circulates through all ranks of holy existences, to the utmost circumference of the spiritual creation.

5. There are numerous passages in our Lord's discourses in which, as the representative of his people, he describes himself as personally affected by all that befals them—a sentiment which can only be resolved into that enlarged benevolence which identifies him with all piety. He reproved the errors and sins of the Jews with the indignant sensibility of one who felt himself personally wronged and dishonoured by them. He spoke of the weakest believer as his other self; resenting his wrongs, and adopting the favours shewn him as his own. After often repeating this sentiment, and presenting it in various lights, he raised it to a climax in the declaration that, in the last great day, he will pronounce concerning every action relating to them, "Ye did it unto *me;* or, ye did it not unto *me.*" If sympathy is to be regarded as a kind of substitution, by which we are put into the place of another, and affected in many respects as he is affected, then what shall we think of the sympathy of Christ, which never allows him to remain an indifferent spectator of anything his people may suffer? Virtue cannot receive the slightest wound, of which he does not instantly feel the smart. He is the great sympathetic nerve of the church, over which all the oppressions and sufferings of

his people distinctly pass; nor does that mysterious instrument of sensation in the human body convey more correctly to the sensorium a sense of the condition of the extremest part of the frame, than the benevolence of Jesus, who is the sensorium of the spiritual universe, apprehends, and sympathizes with, the least emotion of suffering in his body, the church.

6. " And when he was come near, he beheld the city, and wept over it, saying, If thou hadst known, even thou, at least in this thy day, the things which belong unto thy peace! but now they are hid from thine eyes." Often had he approached Jerusalem before by the same road, and gazed on it from the same spot; and never, we may suppose, had he looked on it but with emotions of unutterable concern: for, O! Jerusalem was endeared to him by ties unimagined by man. But now he was approaching it for the last time; and he paused to take a final look. He knew that his entrance within its gates would be the signal for filling up the measure of its guilt; and therefore he lingered a moment, as if to respite its doom; the sun of righteousness lingered a moment on Mount Olivet, as if to prolong for it that day of grace made by his own immediate beams. He had before asked for it "another year," that he might make on it fresh experiments of mercy; and now he graciously vouchsafed it another moment. And as he stood and gazed on it, his mind filled with affecting recollections of the past; the future rose to his prophetic eye, crowded with scenes of guilt and woe; while both became aggravated by the afflicting thought, that all his generous efforts to save it were defeated, and would only serve to enhance its doom.

His comprehensive mind reverted to the past; he remembered the days of old, " when Israel was holiness to the Lord." He could not forget that Judea had for ages been the ark of religion, where the knowledge of Jehovah had been preserved and cherished when lost by all the world besides; that it was filled with the mementos of prophets and miracles; that it had been the birthplace of men of whom the world was not worthy; that its paths had been trod by angel-feet; that its dust was hallowed, its very soil sacred to God. He thought of the temple, where devotion had for so many ages felt itself nearer heaven; where the bleeding sacrifice had daily testified of human guilt and divine placability; where successive generations had communed with God from off the mercy-seat; and multitudes had found the gate of heaven. But these recollections, pleasing in themselves, were embittered by the remembrance of the guilt they necessarily recalled—ages of accumulated guilt. The Lord had sent unto them his prophets, " rising early and sending them;" but " they beat one, and killed another, and stoned another." It could not be that a prophet should perish out of Jerusalem. It was saturated with " the blood of all the prophets, down to the blood of Zacharias, son of Barachias, whom they slew between the temple and the altar." And, now, he knew that it was thirsting after his own blood. For more than a thousand years it had enjoyed the peculiar regards of Heaven; yet, with all his compassion for it in lively exercise, the benevolent Jesus could not but see that it was the grave of hope, the vortex of all piety. For three years now, he himself had come seeking fruit, and finding none. During that period, his preaching and miracles had but this one object—the instruction and salvation of its thankless and disobedient people. How solemnly had he warned them, how graciously invited them, how anxiously laboured to convince them that he was the Hope of Israel, their promised Messiah. For them he had toiled, and travelled, and interceded, and spent himself in self-consuming privations. For their sakes he had made himself of no reputation, and had taken upon him the form of a servant. When driven from Jerusalem by persecution, exiled by bitter hate, he carried their welfare with him in his heart, and soon he returned to them again with a kindness which seemed increased by ingratitude. They formed the sole object of his tenderest solicitude, the essence of his daily thought. For them every pulse of his heart had beaten, and for them that heart was ready to pour forth its vital blood. He had done everything that could be done, consistently with his own perfections and with the liberty of accountable creatures,—but in vain. On them the object of his mission was entirely lost. He knew that at that moment they were passing his destruction into a law. He looked down on the guilty city; and, behold, it resembled a vast cauldron filled and fermenting with all infernal passions, of which he was to be the devoted victim.

But with the self-denying love of a patriot, and the grace of a Saviour, he looked beyond the spectacle of his own sufferings, and fixed his eye upon theirs; he could view them only through an atmosphere of compassion. And, O! what an appeal to his pity was there. Clouds of wrath were gathering over Jerusalem from every quarter of heaven, fraught with materials of destruction such as none but a divine hand could collect; his own blood, by which he had graciously meant to wash away their guilt, calling with a voice not to be denied, for the ministers of justice to arm; all things on earth and in heaven mustering and disposing for their doom. He looked again; and lo, the city, *his* city, was beleaguered and lost; Jerusalem lay bleeding at his feet; the harpy nations had taken their prey; her dwellings of holiness were laid waste; and the sound of her expiring lament, drowning even the voice of justice itself, pierced his heart, and drew from him words in which all his soul came forth : " If thou hadst known, even thou, at least in this thy day, the things which belong unto thy peace! but now they are hid from thine eyes."

The exclamation, regarded as a sentence, is interrupted and incomplete; but who does not see that it is both interrupted and completed by tears—tears, which are the natural language of compassion, and which express its intenseness beyond all words. But he not only thought of the past, and surveyed the future, he evidently glanced also at a pleasing picture of what the present might have been; and then the *hiatus* is to be regarded as filled up with a silent reflection on what would have been the happy results had Jerusalem accepted his mission. The lingering contemplation of the same blessed possibility is apparent also in his subsequent exclamation : " O Jerusalem, Jerusalem, thou that killest the prophets, and stonest them who are sent unto thee, how often would I have gathered thy children together, even as a hen gathereth her chickens under her wings, and ye would not !" Had the nation appreciated his character, and sympathized with his mission, how different, we may suppose, his conduct would have been, and how changed the history of his earthly life. The Jewish economy might have died a glorious death, full of days and full of honours. Instead of entering the temple to denounce and to scourge, he might have gone to explain, and to apply to himself, its ancient rites; to make known the termination of its service; and to pronounce, in the hearing of the great congregation, its funeral eulogium. Instead of being hated, persecuted, and ignominiously put to death as the victim of malice, he might have assembled the tribes by proclamation; have lifted up his voice, and explained to their breathless attention the doctrine of the atonement; have opened their understanding, and disclosed the amazing fact, that the principle of vicarious suffering, which ran through the whole of their economy, was now to terminate and triumph in his own piacular death for man: and then, amidst the tears and sympathies of the world, he might have ascended Calvary—or even the altar of sacrifice itself—and there he might have been visibly smitten by the immediate sword of justice; while angels, bending over the mysterious scene, would have pointed each other to his blood, and said, "Behold, how he loved them." Instead of retiring into Galilee when he arose from the dead, he might have shewn himself openly to all the people; he might once more have entered the temple, where "Moses and Elias," as the representatives of the Jewish church, might have resigned into his hands the trust which it had held for the human race; and, investing him with the insignia of prophet, priest, and king, have hailed him as the Hope of Israel, and the Surety of the world. "O that his people had hearkened unto him, and Israel had walked in his ways!"

It is true, the contrary was foreseen; every step he took was calculated and arranged on the distinct foreknowledge of his rejection; the wickedness of his enemies was interwoven into the texture of the Divine plans concerning him. But his rejection was necessitated only by their own depravity. Had their blinding unbelief permitted them to "know him, they could not have crucified the Lord of glory." The morn of mercy would have arisen cloudless on the world. He would have made the temple the cradle of Christianity, the rendezvous of piety to all nations, the sanctuary of the world. Jerusalem should have arisen as a stately palm, towering to heaven and seen to the ends of the earth, distilling balm for the healing of the nations, and wafting its fragrance as incense through the skies; religion should have built her palaces in its shadow; it should have been the joy of the whole earth.

How often would he have done this, and more than this, for his beloved Jerusalem; gathering her children under his fostering care, and making her the abode of heavenly glory. But, alas! this was only a vision—as the name *Jerusalem* imports, *a vision of peace;* and now it was both hid from her eyes, and vanished from his. He would have turned the vision into reality; but she would not; she thrust him from her. Painful indeed is the situation of the patriot who is condemned to watch the exhausted struggles of his country; to tend it during its alternate paroxysms of raving and intervals of lethargic stupefaction, till one by one the lingering symptoms of life have disappeared, and it lies prostrate in corruption, and trodden under foot of the nations. But here was more than a patriot called to mourn over the desolation of his land, and to witness the frustration of all his plans for saving it; here was the friend of sinners, the lover of human souls, called to contemplate the spiritual perdition of a whole land, and that land the immediate scene of his godlike labours. He could not fail to be deeply affected by the prospect of its temporal sufferings; but what were they, compared with its impending spiritual fate? He knew the history of sin; he had seen it in its awful origin, expelling the angels from heaven, and preparing for them a hell; his omnipresent mind had all the endless consequences of sin present to his view. And knowing and deploring as he did the eternal results of the least sin, how inconceivably great must his emotions of grief and compassion have been at the sight of a whole nation of human beings, for whose welfare, at any moment, he was ready to become a curse, destroyed by the vials of Almighty displeasure, and perishing under a charge of guilt, only inferior in aggravation to the guilt of the angels that kept not their first estate. His benevolent nature recoiled at the idea; he felt as if he could not give them up, could not see them consigned to such irretrievable ruin; as if even now it was not too late to save them; as if he could almost have saved them even against their wills. The consideration of their continued aggravated guilt had, we might have supposed, drained the whole passion of pity from his nature; but at the sight of that coming woe, a new fountain of compassion opens in his heart, and pours itself forth in an unexampled gush of sympathy; at the prospect of that dreadful scene, that type of the terrors of the judgment day, he hears not the acclamations of the surrounding multitude, hailing his entrance into the devoted city,—thinks not of his own impending death, but abandons himself to sympathy; his whole nature dissolves into compassion, which can only find vent in an exclamation in which he poured forth the tears of his heart, " O that thou hadst known, even thou, at least in this thy day, the things which belong unto thy peace! but now they are hid from thine eyes."

Pitiable, indeed, must be the state of that mind which can find itself at ease to debate a question of metaphysical divinity in the presence of the Redeemer's tears. Yet there are men whose creed has no place even for his sacred grief; who are actually annoyed at these tears wept over perishing sinners, as at heterodox variance with the divine decrees; who frown at this precious distilment of infinite love as inconsistent with their views of divine inflexibility. There are those who would rather these tears had never been shed, or that the record of this burst of divine compassion should be expunged from the sacred page, than that it should remain as an obstacle to their logical views of the Divine purposes. But we linger over it with delight; we love to remain within the softening influence, the hallowed contagion, of the Redeemer's tears; we bless him for them; we regard the melting scene as only inferior in pathos, in tender and solemn grandeur, to Calvary itself.

The compassionate exclamation of Jesus, on this occasion, intimates that the salvation of the Jews would have been more agreeable to his benevolent nature than their destruction; that, notwithstanding this, there were sufficient reasons why his omnipotence should not interpose to prevent that destruction; that, in the same act, justice, awful and unbending justice, may denounce destruction against the sinner, while benevolence sympathizes in his misery even to tears. When Jesus afterwards turned to the mourning daughters of Jerusalem, as they followed him to Calvary, and said, " Weep not for me, but weep for yourselves," he sought, by that admonition, to impress them with the magnitude of the calamity which awaited them; a calamity so pregnant with woe, that had all the tears shed from the creation been reserved for that event, had all the universe joined and aided them in the mighty grief, it would not have equalled the greatness of the occasion. But his own tears should affect us more deeply with the greatness of the calamity, than the sight of all creation in tears. To think that Jesus wept, that tears fell from his eyes, the eyes of incarnate perfection; how great must have been the calamity which occasioned them, the calamity of souls lost, immortal natures perishing under the frown of God. And he would encourage us to infer, that, making the necessary allowance for the difference between his earthly and his heavenly state, his nature is still the same; that no sinner perishes unpitied, unlamented. He would have the ministers of his gospel to mingle their appeals and warnings with tears, and to assure the impenitent that, if they finally perish, they descend into perdition bathed in the tears of his divine compassion.

7. What an affecting illustration of the tenderness and

benevolence of our Lord's teaching do we find in his valedictory discourse to his disciples on the evening prior to his crucifixion.* He was about to leave them. He had so far advanced in his earthly course, that he was now only a step from the cross; a few hours more, and the pang of parting from their Lord must be endured. Tender as his conduct, and gracious as his intercourse had always been, he had evidently reserved the outpouring of his heart till now. He sought to prepare them for the approaching trial by shewing them that, though he died, he died with them in his heart. Addressing them in terms of gracious endearment such as they had never listened to before,—and such as, considering the circumstances under which they were uttered, they could never forget,—he took them into a new region of truth, expatiated over fields filled with the products of infinite love, ranged over ground which they had only before beheld dimly at a distance, ground which brought them within sight of the gate of heaven. Often had he spoken to them as never man spake, descanting on topics which it had not entered into the heart of man to conceive; but he now led them into a higher department, an inner chamber of truth; he now conducted them into the treasury of his love, displayed before them his resources and affluence, pointed out the costly gifts which he meant for them, and even invited them to select and appropriate his choicest treasures. He drew them close to himself; afforded them the nearest inspection of his character; unbosomed to them his inmost designs; shewed them his very heart, with all their names engraven there, and all their interests bound up and made one with his dearest purposes, and with the glory of the Father.

His avowed object in thus addressing them was, that

* John, xiv., xv., xvi.

"his joy might remain in them, and that their joy might be full;" that the same exalted views and principles which had sustained and actuated him might descend to them; that they might inherit the very same spiritual property; that it might be entailed on his church for ever, and yield to his people in all generations as large a revenue of joy and peace, as, in proportion, it had brought to him. And, as if to increase the pathos of this touching discourse, he invested it with circumstances of irresistible tenderness and love. He uttered it in the presence of the symbols of his death, and while the melting sentence, " Do this in remembrance of me," was yet sounding in their ears; and he immediately followed it with a prayer such as, till then, heaven had never received from earth—a prayer in which he seemed unconscious of mortal presence, and spoke as if he had never left the bosom of the Father—a prayer in which he asked with the largeness and confidence of one who felt that he had established a claim on the divine resources, that, having so nearly reached the cross, he was entitled to ask what he would; and all he asked was for his disciples; all his new and unmeasured influence at the throne of grace was employed for them, that they might enjoy an interest in all his perfections, a share in all his glory—a prayer in which he pleaded as if he had already reached the altar of incense above, and had actually entered on his office of intercessor there; and in which he clasped the eternal throne as if he would save his people by prayer alone. By means such as these did he aim, not merely to prepare them for the trial of his approaching departure, but to leave his image impressed on all their hearts, to bind them fast to himself with the cords of love, to assure them that, henceforth and for ever, he and they were one.

8. There are numerous declarations interspersed through every part of our Lord's discourses, concerning

the object of his advent, in which he invites us to listen to the highest strains of benevolence. " I am come," saith he, " that they might have life, and that they might have it more abundantly. I am the bread of life. I am the good shepherd, and lay down my life for the sheep. Whoso eateth my flesh, and drinketh my blood, hath eternal life; and I will raise him up at the last day. As Moses lifted up the serpent in the wilderness, even so must the Son of man be lifted up: that whosoever believeth in him should not perish but have everlasting life. The Son of man is come to seek and to save that which was lost; to give himself a ransom for many; to shed his blood for many for the remission of sins." These passages form part of a numerous class; and we have reserved them till now, as exhibiting the benevolence of Christ, in its highest and most comprehensive form; for they disclose both his purposes of grace and the costly means by which he effects them.

They teach us that, in saving man, he is obeying the spontaneous dictates, and gratifying the compassionate yearnings, of his own heart. He assumed life for the express purpose of laying it down. He shewed that his heart was full of a purpose formed from eternity. No scene of trial could take him by surprise; no hour of suffering found him unprepared. He saw as from a height the whole array of duty and trial which awaited him; and the only emotion he evinced at the sight was a self-consuming ardour to reach the cross which stood at the end of his path, a holy impatience to be baptized with that baptism of blood. And when his hour was come, the mysterious manner in which he surrendered up his life on the cross—breathing it forth—giving it up —parting with it as a freewill offering to God—evinced the truth of his own declaration, " No man taketh it from me; I lay it down of myself."

"For their sakes," said he, " I sanctify myself;" and he did so: he devoted himself exclusively to the cause of human salvation; it occupied his thoughts from the first moment to the last of his continuance upon earth. All the paths of human ambition were open and accessible to him, but he passed them all by. All the kingdoms of the world, and the glory of them, were laid at his feet, but he saw them as if he saw them not. With a single sentence, he could have flashed light on the darkest mysteries of philosophy; but he would not thus debase his mission, he would not spare a single moment from teaching that higher science, the knowledge of salvation. He had ears only for one sound—and that was the voice of penitence imploring forgiveness; the voice of fear and conscious guilt deprecating the vengeance of eternal fire, and crying for relief. He had eyes only for one sight—and that was the misery of man; the spectacle of a world invaded, ruined, lost, and moving along in chains to the pit of perdition. This object filled the whole sphere of his vision; he could see nothing else; and had all the thrones of earth been vacant, and invited his acceptance, it would not have induced him to diverge a single step from the path which led direct to the cross. He had tears but for one sorrow; and he wept them over lost souls. He valued life itself but for one object; as it enabled him to present it in sacrifice for human redemption.

The key to all his conduct is love; this is the principle by which he invites us to interpret all his earthly history; and which is found to explain it all, while itself remains inexplicable. Such is the property of sympathy, that, even in ordinary cases, it impels us to enact a kind of mental substitution, imparting to us the feelings, and placing us in the situation, of the party with whom we sympathize. But such was the power of the Saviour's compassion, that it impelled him to enact a real substitution! it gave him our nature. Under its mighty impulse, he took our place in the universe; invited the government of God to treat him as the representative of the human race; absorbed our interest; opened his bosom, and welcomed to his heart the stroke which we had deserved. And having thus answered our liabilities, and honoured the claims of injured justice, he is rewarded with all the means and the power of salvation. Having offered to God a perfect sacrifice as the substitute for man, he is now to be regarded as offering a perfect salvation to us as the substitute for God. And in making these overtures of infinite grace, every word he utters breathes of compassion that will not be denied.

9. In further illustration of the tenderness and benevolence which distinguished our Lord's instructions, we might adduce the universality of his offers of mercy. He could not contemplate, without deep solicitude, the exclusion of any from the blessings of his grace; to satisfy the cravings of his benevolence, all must love him, and be beloved by him. He might refer to the relations which he represented himself as assuming and sustaining; for in him the tenderness of the shepherd, the affection of the parent, and the grace of the Saviour are combined. We might point to the attractive epithets which he applied to the blessings of his grace; not contenting himself with merely announcing those blessings, but aiming to excite our desire to possess them by describing them in the most alluring terms. Nor should we omit to mention, for the same end, the characteristic tenderness of the topics on which he delighted to dilate. He loved to dwell on the paternal character of God; it was a view which formed his own consolation and joy through every stage of his earthly course, and he essayed to

conduct his people to the same fountain of delight. Prayer was a subject frequently on his lips. His heart was set on bringing about an interview between God and man: for he knew it must lead to the reconciliation of the parties; he knew that if he could but bring us to the footstool of mercy, all would be well. Hence the attractions with which he has invested the throne of grace,— assuring us that we go there invited and expected as his friends; hence the unalienable charter of prayer, which, sprinkled with his own blood, he has placed in our hands,—promising to it all the good within the compass of Omnipotence to bestow, and urging it in terms of gracious encouragement, to which nothing, consistently with the divine dignity, could be added. How evidently was he gratifying his own mind, while expatiating on the doctrine of divine influence; offering the Holy Spirit as the free gift of God; promising his presence as the abiding Comforter; and enlarging on the great and certain advantages of dwelling in the element of his light and love. How visibly congenial to his taste was the topic of brotherly love; it formed the subject of his new command, of his frequent admonition, and occupied a principal part of his intercessory prayer. He might justly have engrossed the love of his people to himself; but, no, he waived his own right, and said, "Love one another." Such is the superiority of his claims on their hearts, that no other being could justly demand a share, until they had rendered to him his due; and this would never have been. But he graciously dispensed with his own interest, consenting to take the love they owe to him in the form of love to each other. Like a father looking on his assembled children, while kissing and embracing each other in the first fond essays of love, he is content, for the time, to *witness* their mutual regard, without being the immediate object of it. He loved to contemplate his church as a community of hearts, cemented by attachment to a common object, and thus rendered one. For this he prayed with an earnestness that would not be denied, "that they all might be one;" that they might form a church in whose capacious bosom there should be but one heart to sway all its motions and direct all its actions, emulating the harmonious movements of the blessed; a heart which should beat in concert with heaven, and whose every pulse should diffuse life, and health, and joy, to the remotest members of the body.

10. Nor were the tenderness and benevolence of Christ abated, either by the lapse of time or the perseverance of human ingratitude. His kindness exhibited no tendency to degenerate into mere professional sympathy; nor had the malice of those who seized his outstretched hand, and nailed it to the cross, any other visible effect than that of inducing him to hasten the work of saving them from themselves and from hell. The superiority to ingratitude which some exhibit, arises from a defect in the constitution of their nature, by which they are armed with a degree of insensibility to wrongs sufficient to blunt the weapons of unkindness. But the sensibilities of Christ were of the most acute description; for in him were harmonized all that is great in mind, noble in sentiment, and delicate in feeling; his nature exhibited the perfection of humanity. And, during the whole of his continuance on earth, his sensibilities were all in excitement and activity; for wherever he looked he saw man was perishing; and yet wherever he turned he saw man, the object of his tender solicitude, requiting his compassion with a fixed frown of hostility and defiance. The conduct of man made a constant demand on his forbearance, a perpetual drain on his pity, sufficient to exhaust every heart but one which was daily replenished at the fountain of compassion itself. He endured, at times, paroxysms of anguish so great, that no compound of mortal elements, unless supernaturally sustained, could by any possibility have outlived them. There is abundant reason to believe that his course would have been much sooner run, that he would have fallen exhausted in body and mind before the cross was reached, had he not lived in immediate communication with a hidden source from whence he drew daily reinforcements of strength. Thus supplied and sustained, " he failed not, nor was discouraged;" his affections maintained their freshness and youth; his tender and feeling eloquence, and his holy sensibilities, went on increasing even to the last.

On arising from the dead, it appears as if his first concern was to convince his apostles of his undiminished regard for them; to prove to them that he had returned from the grave with the same heart with which he had died. Often had he spoken to them before, as if he would not merely win their souls to him, but breathe his soul into them; and now he actually did so: " he breathed on them, and said, Receive ye the Holy Ghost;" he imparted to them his own Spirit. He had been accustomed to call them his disciples and servants. On the evening prior to his crucifixion, as if his affection for them increased the nearer the hour of separation approached, as if he desired to draw closer the bands of affection before he left them, he called them his friends; " Henceforth," said he, " I call you not servants, but friends." And, then, it was not till after his resurrection that he drew the cords of love still closer, and called them his brethren; " Go, tell my brethren," said he, " that they meet me in Galilee." " Go to my brethren, and say to them; I ascend to my Father and your Father, to my God and your God." Thus he reserved the tenderest appellation for the last; as though he would provide against all their suspicions and fears that he would forget them as he rose in dignity and power, by shewing them that he loved them the more, the more he did for them, and the more he became capable of blessing them; that whatever the dignity to which he might be raised, he would value that dignity chiefly as it gave him the power of blessing them, and of raising them to a joint participation of his glory. "And he led them out as far as to Bethany, and he lifted up his hands and blessed them. And it came to pass, *while he blessed them*, he was parted from them, and carried up into heaven." This divine *arrangement* was undoubtedly meant to be as significant as the gracious benediction he was pronouncing. It taught his disciples that he carried their interests with him to heaven; and that his occupation there would be only a continuation of his employment here—the godlike work of blessing them. He meant to cheer them with the impression that his departure to heaven, so far from terminating his ability to bless them, would augment that power; that the intercession which he had begun on earth, he went to carry on and complete in the immediate presence of the eternal throne.

His kindness to his disciples only corresponded with the grace of his conduct towards the guilty city. He commanded them, " that repentance and remission of sins should be preached, in his name, among all nations, *beginning at Jerusalem.*" Could tears have washed away the crimson guilt of its inhabitants, they would now have needed no remission; for over them the Man of sorrows had dissolved into grief. Could kindness have melted or moved them, they would not now have required an exhortation to repentance; for his last anguish on the cross included a pang of compassion for them; and for them he had saved his latest breath, to pray, " Father, forgive them; for they know not what they do." But their impenitence was triumphant. Yet no sooner does he find himself in a capacity to bless, than he exercises the prerogative in blessing them. We might almost as soon have expected that he would have sent his gospel to be proclaimed over the mouth of perdition as to Jerusalem, the hell of earth. At least, we should have expected to see it making the circuit of the earth before it came there; to hear him directing his apostles to wait till his immediate enemies had descended to the grave—to visit Jerusalem last. But the course of his grace admits not of human calculation; for he sends them to Jerusalem first. While the eyes of his enemies are yet gleaming with the fire of triumphant revenge, he commissions his apostles to hasten and open the charter of redemption within sight of Calvary; to let them know that, whatever they might have drawn from his heart, his love for them remained there still; to assure them that there is one mode of inflicting on him greater pain than even that of employing the cross—by obstinately refusing the blessings which his cross has procured. But, O, there is an exalted sense, in which this act of grace to Jerusalem is only to be regarded as a type of his benevolence to the world at large; an affecting rehearsal, on a limited scale, of that great dispensation of mercy which selects for its objects the chief transgressors of every age, and traverses the world in quest of those whose lives have been spent in "crucifying the Son of God afresh, and putting him to an open shame."

Accordingly, his last injunction to his apostles was, to preach salvation in his name to every creature. His final act on earth was to make the world the heirs of his grace; to leave behind him in trust the conveyance of his salvation to all mankind. He had now contemplated man from various and affecting points; and, from each point, the aspect presented to view was calculated to try his love in a new and peculiar manner. From heaven he had beheld us falling by myriads into perdition; but awful as the sight was, it was only the natural result of guilt so great as to make even the earth itself to loathe us. He clothed himself with love, and descended into the midst of us, offering himself and his glory to the service of man; but he had beheld us instantly league and arm against him, making common cause with hell in the work of his destruction. He had earnestly gazed on us from the cross; and what was the spectacle he beheld immediately before him, but a group of maniac fiends, yelling a song of triumph at having compassed his death. And now, at the moment of his departure, as he pierced the future, he saw his humiliation continued and perpetuated through every succeeding age, and in every variety of form; he beheld the enmity of the carnal mind, true to its character, daily enacting afresh the ignominious scenes of Calvary down to the close of time. Yet, with all this infinite guilt lying distinctly like a map before him, he commended and sent his love to every creature. He remembered only that we were perishing, and felt only that he could save. He found himself in possession of the gift of eternal life, and he sent it in messages of grace over all the earth. By connecting this embassy with an act of special benediction on those whom he honoured to fulfil it, he significantly taught them that he set them apart to a work of blessing; that they were to go from under his uplifted hands to bless mankind, as he had blessed them; to issue forth from under the canopy of his blessing, propagating and diffusing that blessing to the ends of the earth: and, as they were the only agents he employed, he thus intentionally taught us that henceforth he devoted himself to the office of saving us,—that he engaged no agency, owned no agency whatever, but for this purpose,—that henceforth his only communication with man would be in streams of unmingled mercy, the ocean of his grace pouring its fulness into our emptiness; that while he needed no destructive agency whatever, he should require all the benevolent agency of heaven and earth to be put into motion, in order to do justice to the purposes of his love. Having died for the redemption of the world, he felt that he had made the world his own; and, embracing all its dearest interests, he pressed them to his heart.

But fascinating and enchaining as this subject is, we must now hasten to a close. Casting our eye back on the ground we have passed over, what a miracle of moral portraiture do we behold in the evangelical history of Christ! What transcendent wisdom! What divine benevolence! What perfection! The character of Jesus stands alone; it has no archetype in history; no analogy in nature; no model in all the worlds of imagination: as portrayed in scripture, it could only have been drawn from a contemplation of the living reality. It was the conception of an infinite mind. It was the triumph of mercy, aiming to condense in the same being the evidences of divinity, adequate illustrations of divine love, and the power of winning the souls of men to salvation, and transforming them to holiness.

The character of Christ forms a distinct proof, an invincible demonstration, for the truth of the gospel. When we remember that it received a tribute of homage from fallen spirits, we shall the less wonder that it has extorted expressions of reverence from some of the worst specimens of fallen humanity. Men, who have sported with the sanctity of everything else that religion owns, have passed by the character of Christ in respectful silence: this was conscience, recognising in his perfection a likeness which it felt it ought to be familiar with and adore: such is the awful power of goodness on natures preconfigured to its image. Some have been entirely restrained from violating the sanctuary of truth by the same guardian influence; the character of Christ, like the presence of a shrine, protected it. As the house of Obededom was blessed for the sake of the residing ark, so religion has often escaped evil, and received homage from its foes, for the sake of the character of Christ. Men who have destroyed, in intention, every other part of the temple of truth, have paused when they came to this—have turned aside, and desisted for awhile, from the work of demolition, to gaze and bow before it; have not merely left it standing as a column too majestic, or an altar too holy, for human sacrilege to assail, but (it was the only redeeming act in their history) have even inscribed their names on its base, and have been heard to burst forth in admiring exclamations approaching to love.

The peculiar excellences of the character of Christ, as an argument for the gospel, are, that it tends to attract and invite inspection; for it is the perfection of moral beauty; it is level to the apprehension of all; for it makes a direct appeal to some of the first principles of our nature, to our natural perceptions of goodness, and our instinctive approval of it: and it not only convinces, but transforms; engaging and carrying with it at once the understanding and the heart. While some, who were in the last stages of depravity, have been allured by it to the pursuit of excellence; others, who have been sitting in despondency at the gates of perdition, have beheld it, and conceived hope. And though the best specimens of our race have, in every age since his appearance, been labouring to imitate, they have not been able to equal it. The character of Jesus challenges the affections of all intelligent beings, leaves the impression of its image on every object it touches, and is destined to collect around itself all the sanctified passions of the universe.

But, besides being an evidence for Christianity, the character of our Lord is to be regarded as an example. " I have given you an example," said he, "that ye should do as I have done unto you. Learn of me. A new commandment I give unto you, That ye love one another; as I have loved you, that ye also love one another." Thus he seeks to augment the value of his own character, regarded as an argument for the gospel, by multiplying the copies of his excellence in the lives of all his people: he would render each of his disciples like himself—a living demonstration for the truth. All the wealth of moral power which the wise and the good have ever possessed is summed up in him, and infinitely augmented, and brought to bear on the hearts of his people; that, by living as under the focus of all excellence, they might be transformed into the same image. Having turned all his infinite nature into grace, having dissolved into a fountain of healing mercy for the recovery of the world, he would now employ the hearts of his people as consecrated channels for the diffusion of its streams: he would have their natures, like his own, changed into tenderness and love. It is true, his example can never be equalled, for it embodies infinite goodness; but with so much the greater force does it oblige us, in our humble measure, to attempt the imitation. Having adopted our humanity, when it was only related to him, like other natures, by creation, he is surely entitled to expect that we should love our own flesh, that we should seek the welfare of the nature which is essentially our own, by diffusing the greatest possible happiness among those connatural with us. Having died for the good of man, the least he is authorized to expect is, that we should live for the same benevolent object. What do we behold in his history, but a whole life of humility, one continued act of condescension, a vast and unbroken descent from the heights of heaven to the form of a servant, the life of an outcast, the death of a malefactor? The least use, then, we can make of his example—we who have it not in our power, as sinners, to practise great condescension, since we are all on a level in the dust already—is to assist each other to arise, aiding the infirmities of the weak, and breathing a spirit of sympathetic tenderness for all. As far as religion is practical and relative to others, he has made benevolence its life and essence; not merely a part of the Christian character, but the character itself.

And how eminently is the tender compassion of Christ calculated to encourage all to repair to him! When the more prominent parts of his history are made to pass before our eyes, if we are not destitute of all sensibility, how softening and hallowing the effect they produce on the mind! How impossible is it for the most timid spirit to picture the serenity of that brow which no evil passions ever disturbed, to mark the benevolence which beamed from his eye, and to listen to the tones of that voice which soothed and cheered the most fearful and sorrowful, without feeling itself drawn gradually nearer and closer to his side. Wherever his grace is scripturally displayed, it secures the attention of the most thoughtless, it melts the hardest and subdues the proudest heart, and inspires the most fearful with hope. The apostle declares, that had the princes of this world known him, they would not have crucified him; had they known the principle of love which brought him from heaven, they would have been disarmed of their enmity against him, and, instead of condemning him, they would have paid him homage as the prince of the kings of the earth. Had those who were most eager to hasten his crucifixion, and most delighted with his death, caught but a glimpse of the love which dictated every action of his life, their cruel malignity must have yielded and given place to unfeigned penitence and love.

The character of Christ is the character of his dispensation; it is the dispensation of the still small voice; and the secret of its power is love. His ministers, therefore, are to win souls, to persuade men, to beseech them, to mingle their instructions with tears; and the more deeply they are imbued with the mind of Christ, the more tender will be their address, the more affectionate their message. They have only to consult their own experience to learn that the public exhibition of Christ, as the Saviour of sinners, constitutes the most welcome and profitable topic on which they can enlarge; that, whatever their subject may be, like John the Baptist pointing abruptly to his passing Lord, *that* cannot be a faulty digression which directs their hearers to *behold the Lamb of God*.

The fact that Jesus was peculiarly his own subject, teaches us that he ought also to be ours; and that aspect of his character which he most delighted to exhibit must be the feature to which we should give especial prominence: and what was that but tender compassion for the souls of men? Approach, then, and look upon him: the nature in which you behold him clothed is truly your own; he has assumed it that he may dissipate all your fears: that he might taste death for you; that he may absorb and carry away all your sorrows; that he may claim kindred with you; that he may discharge for you all the kind and beneficent offices of brotherhood; that he might make it impossible for you to doubt his love. Approach, and behold his hands and his feet; those are the wounds which he received when he was wounded for our transgressions, bruised for our iniquities, when the chastisement of our peace was upon him, that by his stripes we might be healed. Urge nothing in excuse for not coming to him; lose not the time necessary to utter it; for whatever your guilt or weakness, your wants or unworthiness, may be, his grace overrules and provides for the whole. He knows the value of a religious principle too well, as well as the dangers to which it is exposed, to despise it on account of its weakness; he does not wait for a time, to see whether the spark of piety will increase or vanish; but he watches it, and solicits, and feeds it, until it rises into a pure and steady flame of devotion towards God. He does not disregard the piety of the poor and destitute, because they are unable to advocate his cause, or to contribute to its support more than two mites, or to adorn it with earthly splendour; the arms of his love embrace alike the obscure and the more useful; and if you are only conscious of a desire to love him, a concern to please him, you share a place in his heart in common with the angels around his throne. When the backslider relapses into the state from which he had been rescued, and seems even to prosecute his sinful course with renewed avidity, he does not, as man commonly does, regard him as lost. He goes after him into the wilderness; sends afflictions in pursuit of him; and waits to see the effect which trial and reflection produce. And if, like the prodigal, the sinner should come to himself, and say, "I will arise and return," and actually begins to retrace his steps, the Saviour delays not in order to see how far he will return—he sees him yet a great way off, and runs to meet him; he is delighted at the first indications of penitence, anticipates his intention, assists him in returning, and rejoices over him as one who was dead and is alive again. We ourselves can trace the mightiest occurrences back to sources the most insignificant; and, with intuitive ease, the Saviour beholds, in the first emotion of the penitent, the first symptom of an endless life, the first step in a career of glory, honour, and immortality. He does not, therefore, despise the day of small things. And how many thousands of the blessed, who are now surrounding his throne above, are constrained, on looking back to the weakness of their early religious impressions, and the hesitation with which at first they advanced in the path of life, to bless him that he did not break the bruised reed, nor quench the smoking flax. O that you knew the unutterable interest which he takes in every serious emotion of your soul, you would love him more, and resort to him oftener, and repose in him all the confidence which he asks.

Finally; let those of my readers who have been hitherto regardless of the ineffable compassion of the Son of God, remember the melting tones of remonstrance with which, when looking round upon such as you, he said, in all the grief of defeated mercy, "Ye will not come unto me, that ye might have life." You can go to *others*, and inquire the way to happiness; you can believe what *they* say; you *do* follow their advice; but to Him who has laid out himself for your welfare, who alone could make the vast provision necessary for your immortal happiness, and who has made it at the expense of an infinite sacrifice, to him you will not come. He has to complain of you, that while you have been always ready to yield to the solicitations of the world, to follow the first beck of temptation, to accept of any invitation in the shape of worldly pleasure, yet his call you will not obey. He has to complain of you, that you put him off with mere professions, and make him to serve with the mere semblance of friendship; that though you have for years frequented his house, and heard his invitations, and been pressed to accept them, you still remain on terms as cold and distant with him as ever; that you never come to his footstool as suppliants, nor to his table as friends, nor walk in his ways as devoted disciples. But he will not let you go:

though he feels your obstinate refusal to come to him, feels it as an insult to his grace, feels it as a deep disappointment, a grievous frustration of an object on which his heart was set, yet once more he comes to you; and, O, mark and admire the gentleness of the terms in which he expostulates — it is the melting rebuke of mercy chiding you into its embrace—" Ye will not come unto me, that ye might have life." There is a sense, perhaps, in which, owing to your prolonged and stony indifference to his claims, you may be said to have closed your hearts against him; but he seeks to surmount even this obstacle; " Behold," saith he, " I stand at the door and knock." He knows what unholy guests are within, what sins are entertained and regaled in the chambers of your hearts, while he is kept standing without and refused admission. But still, by the instrumentality of his gospel, if by nothing else, he continues to knock and to urge you to come to him; or he tenderly upbraids you that you will not.

But why does the blessed Jesus thus expostulate? " It is not," saith he, " that I receive honour of men; it is not that I seek to be gratified with the barren applauses of men, or that I hope for human requital; but these things I say unto you, that ye might be saved." Yes, Saviour of sinners, this is thine only object, that they might be saved; the object of all thou hast said to them, and of all thou hast done for them; the object which is always present to thy mind. For this thou hast surrounded thyself with convincing proofs of thine appointment and power to save; and, O, surpassing grace, thou even consentest to wait for their decision till they have examined the evidence of thy claims in detail. For this thou hast withheld nothing, not even thy blood, thy life; thou hast done so much for them, that infinite love can do no more.

HIS TENDERNESS AND BENEVOLENCE.

Behold, then; behold, in the boundless love of Christ, a sufficient inducement to repair to him at once. He may be regarded, at this moment, as standing before you, with the hoarded love of eternity in his heart, offering to make you heirs of all its wealth; nor is it in your power to grieve him more than by disregarding the gracious overture. He fears nothing but your neglect; deprecates nothing but your inattention. The first look you direct towards him would not escape his notice—the first step you take towards him would bring him more than a step towards you. All things are ready for your reception; he will meet your weakness with his almighty strength, your emptiness and poverty with his inexhaustible fulness.

ESSAY V.

THE PRACTICAL NATURE OF OUR LORD'S TEACHING.

A VARIETY of circumstances seem to concur, in the present day, auspicious to the study of the gospel as a practical science. Two or three of these circumstances may be named.

1. The great error of religious polemics, hitherto, has consisted in arguing from compound dependent truths as if they were *ultimate.* The application of the inductive method of investigation, however, has taught us that, as in philosophy so in theology, we as yet possess but few ultimate truths; that principles on which parties have been accustomed to rely with the greatest confidence, may be easily carried to a point where they break down, and fail us; that where two truths appear thus to clash, it is evident they cannot be ultimate; but that each of them having been affirmed by the God of truth concerning the same thing, there is no doubt whatever of their eventual coincidence in one comprehensive and axiomatic truth. In the meantime, we feel that we must wait patiently, pronounce less confidently, inquire more diffidently, look at each other more charitably, and, leaving the polemics of piety in which we differ, unite in the practice of piety in which we agree.

2. Religion has been regarded as the great monopolist of mystery; the popular ignorance of the wonders of natural philosophy has favoured this error, and the consequence has too commonly been that the neophyte has brought to religion a speculative spirit, and has spent

that breath in disputing which might otherwise have been spent in the race of holiness. It is a subject of congratulation, however, that as natural science advances, she is throwing a light on many of the dark things of scripture, and at the same time, multiplying her own *incredibilia;* so that wonder and scepticism will have to transport their throne from the region of Religion into the province of Science. And thus much of the strength which would once have been wasted in speculation and controversy, is now more usefully employed in biblical criticism and the enforcement of piety, in acts of obedience to God, and in deeds of benevolence to man.

3. The present day is pre-eminently distinguished, in every department, social, national, and universal; civil, political, and philosophical, by *practical activity.* Religion, also, is up and doing. In everything proper to her peculiar province, she leads the van. Once more she appears before the world in her appropriate character, militant and aggressive. Hushing their mutual feuds, she is leading her followers forth to the conquest of a world. To fall into her train is to swear obedience to the laws of Christ.

4. Another characteristic of the present day, whether for good or for evil we stay not to inquire, is its *cui bono,* or *utilitarian* spirit. By this test, religion glories to be examined. Godliness is profitable for all things. It can call witnesses from all classes of the community; bring evidence from all parts of the earth; and constrain even its enemies to speak well of it.

It is the boast of philosophy, that any accession to our knowledge of nature is sure, sooner or later, to make itself felt in some practical application and benefit. Every additional truth which the gospel has brought, is an additional principle of holiness, a fresh element of virtue; it is, in effect, the addition of a new *mechanical power* for accelerating the motion of the world towards God. It is the pride of physical science, that it can lead the very elements captive, subduing the most powerful energies of nature to its purposes, and employing them in a variety of useful ways. Spiritual triumphs, analogous to this, are familiar to the gospel. It is the power of God unto salvation to every one that believeth. It gathers grapes from thorns, and figs from thistles. It turns the wrath of man into a song of praise worthy the harps of heaven. It takes the passions, the most intractable and unapproachable human passions, yokes them to the car of duty, and henceforth they run in the way of obedience, proud to grace its triumphs. From elements of vice and wretchedness the gospel forms *a new creature*, instinct with God. These are its ordinary effects; but not only does it retain all its original applicability and power unimpaired, it only waits occasion to develop energies of unimagined value, and to fill the world with wonders of grace.

Do we admire its practical utility and power? Then the Saviour turns on us a look of personal application, while he repeats, " Whosoever heareth these sayings of mine, and *doeth* them, I will liken him unto a wise man." " If ye know these things, happy are ye if ye do them." His sublimest doctrines were all practical. He would not have revealed any one doctrine contained in his word but for its moral effect. He measured beforehand the power of each to sanctify, and according to its tendency to illustrate the holiness of his divine nature, and to restore sanctity to our human, he assigned it an appropriate place in the system of truth. The moral of each separately, and of all combined, is simply this, " Sin no more." Reader, such are the beauty and excellence of the seal; what is its impression on your heart and life? The character of the Christian should be monumental, commemorative of the great facts and truths of the gospel: how many of these facts and truths could be learnt from your character, or transcribed from your life? "If ye love me, keep my commandments."

I. Considered as a teacher of holiness, our Lord Jesus Christ exemplified his wisdom, not only in the light which he imparted, but also in what he withheld.

1. Pretenders to a divine revelation have seldom omitted to infuse into their systems of error a large proportion of the marvellous. Calculating on the credulity and ravenous curiosity of the multitude, they have been graphic and unsparing in their disclosures of the invisible and future. Besides pandering to the prevailing passions of mankind, they have aimed to establish their dominion by stimulating and engrossing the imagination with wonders; and, having raised the veil of mystery to its utmost height, they proceed to measure the infinite, to paint the inconceivable, and to materialize and subject the spiritual to the senses.

But he who came forth from the bosom of the Father, and who could therefore have dazzled and astounded the world with celestial visions, practised a wise and gracious reserve. He came, not to astonish, but to instruct and to save; and to instruct solely with a view to save; and, knowing that to feed curiosity is only to increase its appetite, that to impart a particle of knowledge more than is essential to our advance in the path of holiness, would operate as a diversion from that path rather than an incitement in it, he limited his communications to the exact measure of practical utility. He kept his hand, if I may say so, on the pulse of conscience, and administered only so much of the exciting element of knowledge as would subserve the health and holy activity of the soul.

In order to estimate the gospel aright, it is necessary to bear in mind, that it is not meant for intellectual beings as such; it is not addressed to man in **his** mental, but in his moral capacity; it contemplates him as a lapsed and ruined creature, to whom the only knowledge that is essential is a knowledge of the way of deliverance. If, besides containing this vital information, it also ministered to his unsanctified curiosity, he would, undoubtedly, prior to his conversion, value it the more highly; but, from the moment he opened his eyes to a perception of his guilt and danger, he would as certainly account that very circumstance a great defect. His first solicitude and employment then would be, to disentangle and detach the plain and simple prescriptions of mercy; and, bestowing on these, and on these alone, the name of *gospel*, he would cast the remainder away as refuse, as an insult to his anguish, a mockery of his woe. However unnatural his cravings before, nothing now but the unadulterated bread of life can satisfy his famishing soul.

Accordingly, at the hazard of displeasing the speculative and inquisitive, the Saviour confined his communications to the wants of our condition. Repelling the curiosity of his disciples, how often did he turn their prying inquiries into occasions of solemn practical appeal. When they sought to pluck from the interdicted tree of knowledge, he graciously presented them with the fruit of the tree of life. They found every avenue closed, but the narrow way that leadeth to life eternal: every fountain sealed, but the fountain of the water of life. While the heavenly Oracle was prompt in answering even the mental and unuttered inquiries of the devout and humble, the inquisitive received a rebuke which contained a blessing. Having come to seek and to save that which was lost, to open a way from the mouth of that fearful pit around which we had gathered, to the gate of heaven, he caused all the light of revelation which he shed to fall on that path alone: that we might not be tempted to wander from the highway of holiness, he left it skirted on each hand with original darkness; while from whatever part of the spacious firmament of truth he brought the beams of revelation, he caused them all to converge and rest on that strait and narrow way.

2. But if we admire the wisdom of the Great Teacher in thus limiting his discoveries to the measure of our wants and interests, we cannot withhold our complacency at his legislation, in delivering a code of pure and simple morality entirely unencumbered by the clogs of an onerous and elaborate ritual. Discharging his disciples from the cares and vexatious obligations of the ancient ceremonial, he has laid aside for them every such weight, and left them free for the race of holiness to heaven. The rites of baptism and the Lord's-supper are too simple and spiritual to be treated as exceptions to this fact. Instead of wasting the powers, and exhausting the vigour of the soul, on outward observances, he holds it disengaged and fresh for the upward path of holiness. Economizing our energies and passions, he points us to a sphere of duty in which angels might engage with honour, and commands us to put forth all our strength, adorning ourselves with all that is fair, emulating all that is great, overtaking the excellences and embodying the perfections of heavenly natures. Having touched and given impulse to all our spiritual powers, instead of impairing that momentum by calling us to surmount the obstacles of preliminary rites, he collects and compacts its force, and dismisses it in a line direct for heaven. Treating our nature with a divine respect, the code which he enacts is one of generous authority, taking off every depressing weight, only pre-

scribing what is absolutely necessary, and actuated in doing so by the aim of building up our character into a goodly fabric of spiritual beauty and perfection.

II. If it comported with our design to specify the subject of our Lord's discourses, we should unhesitatingly say, that *his most favourite practical topics were, humility before God, and a spirit of forbearance and love towards man.* In the inculcation of morals, by uninspired teachers, novelty is the last quality to be desired, since it could scarcely fail to be error; but the practical instructions of Jesus had this distinction, that their peculiarities were excellences. One of these marked peculiarities consists in his taking under his special protection certain dispositions which the world had consented to brand and cast out, had conspired to frown out of existence; in restoring them to the rank of duties, and proclaiming them graces of the kingdom of God.

1. Humility is a habit of mind which has never been in favour with the world: in every age it has been degraded into the footstool of vanity, and conceit, and enthroned pride; but, in direct opposition to the unanimous verdict of mankind, he raised it out of the dust into which it was trodden, pronounced it a favourite of Heaven, and clothed it with the garments of salvation. "Blessed are the poor in spirit, for theirs is the kingdom of heaven."

Since the fatal moment when man aspired to "be as a god," his great quarrel with his Maker has been, a determination to assert a power of independence altogether alien to his nature and condition. The standard of revolt was then erected; and the history of all his subsequent conduct has been the history of an insane endeavour to construct an empire, governed by laws, and replenished with resources, independent of God. The idolatry and sensuality, the unbelief, irreligion, and all the multiform sins of man, are resolvable into this proud and infernal attempt. Now, before God can do anything towards our personal recovery, it is obviously necessary that we should be disabused of the idea of our supposed self-sufficiency; that, descending from the pedestal our pride has erected, we should cast ourselves down at his feet, and await his pleasure. The true value of humility consists in its inducing us to desire and welcome the assistance we need, to abandon ourselves cordially to the divine direction, to return, and descend, and gratefully to occupy our proper station at his footstool, as pensioners on his bounty and grace. "They that are whole need not a physician, but they that are sick;" and they only will apply to him for aid.

Alas, for man, that his humility should have to be accounted a virtue; that, by simply conforming his views to his condition, and taking a just estimate of his state and character, he should render himself an object of congratulation to man, and of peculiar complacency to God; what a depth of depravity does it imply, what a reproach on our nature does it convey, that for a blind and insignificant creature to believe his infinite Creator, for a guilty and condemned criminal to accept of pardon, for a man in the act of perishing to submit to be saved, —that this should be esteemed a virtue! and should be lauded with a warmth which denotes its rareness! "This is indeed a lamentation, and shall be for a lamentation." But, condescending to our condition, our Lord inculcated humility as a cardinal grace, promoting it to the highest place in the catalogue of virtues. He repeatedly intimated, that while a spirit of self-exaltation shall finally be smitten with a blow which it cannot survive, that while the Almighty will array against this avowed antagonist all the forces of his wrath, and will not rest till he has driven it far from his presence, into outer and endless darkness, humility shall be raised from glory to glory, till it has reached the loftiest throne in the kingdom of God.

But that which gives peculiar emphasis to his inculcations on this subject is, that humility is inseparably connected with the cordial reception of his gospel; so that, in enjoining it, he is infallibly preparing the way for the enlargement of his holy kingdom. Humility is the conservator of the virtues; nor is there an act or office peculiar to Christians in which its influence is not vitally felt. As portrayed by him, on entering his evangelical church it is a little child, to whom belief is natural, an emblem of candour, simplicity, and faith; when hearing his word, it sits at his feet, and is all docility and attention; on entering the presence of God, it throws itself prostrate, or smites on its breast, and dares not lift up so much as its eyes to heaven; when it is free to take the highest seat in the assembly, it voluntarily selects the lowest, and is taken by surprise if called up higher; in the presence of superior excellence, it is praise and imitation; associated with fellow-Christians, it is willing subordination, emulous of no distinction but that which arises from preeminent service; it declines to be called " master," and lays all its honours at the Saviour's feet; and when, at length, he shall ascend his throne, and enumerate its godlike deeds, he describes it as filled with self-abasement even there, and diffident of receiving his divine award. Under the reign of holiness, it is the office of humility to lay a foundation for universal obedience, by filling every subject with gratitude for the blessings he enjoys, and making him feel that the lowest situation is a post of unmerited distinction, held by a grant from sovereign grace.

2. Benevolence—meaning by that term the most enlarged exercise of forbearance, forgiveness, and love—

was another despised and unworldly obligation, which he rescued and enforced by the highest sanctions. Under the disorganizing influence of sin, the tendency of the world is to a state of universal misanthropy. Having lost its original centre in God, it attempts not to find any common point of repose, but spends itself in fruitless efforts to erect an infinity of independent interests. Every kingdom and province, every family, every individual, discovers a propensity to insulate himself from the common brotherhood, and to constitute himself the centre of an all-subordinating and ever-enlarging circle. Such is the natural egotism of the heart, that each individual, following his unrestrained bent, acts as if he were a whole kingdom in himself, and as if the general well-being depended on subjection to his supremacy. He would fain be his own end; himself the reason of all he does. On this ungodly and unnatural experiment the Saviour laid his sovereign interdict. He places it in every light, takes us to view it from every point, in order to shew us its flagrant sinfulness; and no sooner do we place ourselves at his disposal than we find ourselves restored and related to all around, and engaged in a career of godlike benevolence: we " remember the words of the Lord Jesus, how he said, It is more blessed to give than to receive."

He sought to neutralize the maxims of the world in favour of selfishness and revenge, by bringing into currency opposing maxims of forgiveness and love. He would have it impressed on us, that we owe to every man a debt of affection which is never discharged; that we owe it to him as one of our own kind; and that no conduct of his, however personally offensive, can ever release us from the obligation of seeking his welfare. He would have us to honour all men; to pay respect to human nature; to aim at the general good of that human family into which we have been born everlasting members. " Peter said unto him, Lord, how often shall my brother sin against me, and I forgive him; until seven times? Jesus answered, I say not unto thee, till seven times, but until seventy times seven." And, when we have done this, he points us to the conduct of our heavenly Father, and renders the duty of forgiveness infinite, while he says, " Be ye merciful, even as your Father in heaven is merciful." He meets us on our way to the throne to obtain forgiveness, and he assures us that, however costly the gift we may be about to lay on the holy altar, God is not to be bribed to do that for us which we refuse to do for others; that there is no access to his presence, no audience, nor hope, until our friendship for man is entire. He supposes us to have even reached the altar, to be standing in the immediate presence of God; he supposes the religious service to have reached that juncture when the Deity is actually waiting to receive the offering; what now can be of sufficient importance to stop the service? He teaches us that the exercise of forgiveness is that important thing, and that while that is performing, the Majesty of heaven and earth consents to wait. And, to save his disciples from all reservation and delusion on this subject, he taught them to pray that the measure in which they forgive might be the standard by which God would dispense his grace to them; thus leaving to revenge no alternative but instant reconciliation, or the imprecation of revenge on its own head.

He represents our Almighty Father as conceding his high prerogative, merging the consideration of the infinite difference between our offences against his majesty, and the offences of a fellow-mortal against our insignificance, and offering us pardon for pardon, grace for grace, " if we from the heart forgive every one his brother their trespasses." He would have every man proclaim a general amnesty; an act of oblivion of all injuries; a year of jubilee; and that jubilee he would have us to make perpetual.

The world has no notion of vanquishing enemies, except by the employment of outward force, by the exercise of revenge, and the infliction of punishment. Jesus Christ has brought into operation a new power for subduing an enemy. He enjoins his disciples to try the efficacy of love; not to content themselves with mere negative benevolence, or, *not* avenging themselves; but to breathe back love for hatred, and blessings for curses. He points them to the triumphant effects of this principle in the hand of God; and, taking out of their hands the weapons of revenge, he would have them to make trial of it also. And is it possible for them to survey the unconfined goodness of God, to entertain the great conception of infinite goodness, to have their minds possessed with so vast and glorious an idea, without receiving corresponding impressions? They will be led by a necessity of nature to imitate that diffusive goodness, to act the god, if I may say so, in their small and limited spheres—to exercise the divine prerogative of mercy, to wield that power before which all opposition is destined to give way—the omnipotent power of love.

As a spiritual being, man is the offspring of the Father of spirits; this is a relation and an honour which he cannot lose; and in this high capacity, the Saviour, having further dignified us with his own love, proposes every human being as a magnificent object of affection to the whole species. Taking us from that small circle, that point of selfishness, which we have made our home, and where, in building ourselves in from the incursion of outward evils, we have at the same time shut out the sight of the great, the spiritual, and the future, he conducts us to a mount of vision from which all the territorial lines and artificial distinctions of society are no longer visible, and where the living landscape presents us with the view of one vast community of immortal beings, claiming the same distinguished origin, involved in a common danger, invited to one grand deliverance, and passing together into the unseen state. While surveying this comprehensive and affecting scene, he would have us especially to remark the mutual action, the certain relation, by which, like the interdependence of the planetary system, the interests of each are commingled and blended with the welfare of the whole. From this elevation he points us to the infinite resources he has opened for us in God; reminding us, that we have access to more than we want, in order that we may go and instrumentally minister to the wants of others. Then, dismissing us again into the vale of life, he would have us to descend and mingle with our race, surcharged with a benevolence like that which brought himself from heaven, and which induces him still to identify our interest with his highest glory.

He would have his disciples to combine in a god-like endeavour to disarm the species; to gather out of his kingdom all the weapons and instruments of revenge, casting them far into the territories of Satan, from which they came; to bring the art of mutual destruction into disgrace and disuse; and to prove their descent from the great Peacemaker of the universe, by binding the whole family of man into one vast confederacy of mutual assistance and brotherly love. "Blessed are the peacemakers, for they shall be called the children of God." The ancient distinction between neighbour and enemy he has annihilated; his disciples are to know no enemy; the very term is banished from the Christian vocabulary, or to be inserted only as obsolete. He would have them to supersede the *visible* employment of angels under the present economy, by becoming themselves his angels and ambassadors to man. By commanding them to imitate his own love, he would have them not only supplant but surpass angelic ministrations; like an orphan family, whose members have attained an age and state of active affection in which the foreign helps they enjoyed in childhood are made unnecessary, by their mutually caring for and aiding each other. The friendships which are cemented in adversity are commonly of a more tender, disinterested, and lasting nature, than those which are formed in any other circumstances: that friendship between man and man of which he has laid the foundation is to be eternal; and therefore would he see it cemented as closely as possible, by having it commenced while they are here in a state of trial, and commenced (how wise, how worthy of himself the divine arrangement!) in a reciprocation of Christian offices whose issues shall reach through eternity. For not only does he charge them to do all the good they can to each other themselves, he takes them to the throne of God, and invests them with the office of mutual intercessors, empowers them to touch and set in motion an almighty agency for each other; he even puts into their hands the means of mutual salvation, making it at once their honour and office to assist as subordinate agents in training and conducting each other to eternal life.

III. Much of the preaching of Jesus was occupied in *adjusting the claims between heaven and earth:* so frequently did he return to this theme, and so conspicuous a place did he assign to it in his discourses, that it may be said to be one of their distinguishing features. A prevailing characteristic of man, as portrayed in scripture, is an inordinate attachment to the world. Sin having expelled from his heart the love of God, the love of the world has rushed into the vacuum, and made it impossible for any but Omnipotence to dislodge it. Having lost that organ of spiritual vision, which, by keeping another world in view in rivalry with this, would have preserved the balance of his affections even, the present is left to tyrannize over him with all the advantage of a power which is ever visible, ever at hand, soliciting him, and making itself necessary to him in a thousand different ways; while the only rival which it has to dread is not only invisible, but incalculably remote: and having thus sustained the loss of a world, having thus become reduced in spiritual wealth by the loss of a whole order of ennobling objects, he not only pours out his affections on the unworthiest things that offer, but he has literally idolized the most contemptible. Most graphically is he represented in the word of God as bearing the image of the earthy; his very mind has become materialized: instead of being pictured over with celestial imagery, it only contains the portraiture of the world; in all its chambers of imagery are depictured and burnt-in the debasing abominations of earth. The mind, which with one sweep of its pinions should have reached the stars, settles down in the dust; his affections, which were meant to rise and be diffused over an infinite circumference, of which God is the centre, let themselves down, and labour to accommodate themselves to an indivisible point, a fugitive atom. As if an anchor were fixed in the centre, his bosom is enchained to the earth. The material particles of which the globe consists do not obey the law by which they cohere more constantly than man endeavours to accommodate himself to the world as his centre of moral gravity.

Now the Saviour addressed himself to the task of correcting this evil. Entering the mart of the busy world, where nothing is heard but the monotonous hum of the traders in vanity, he lifts up his voice like the trump of God, and seeks to break the spell which infatuates them, while he exclaims, " What shall it profit a man if he gain the whole world and lose his own soul? or what shall he give in exchange for his soul? Were all sublunary glory laid at your feet, let a few years expire, and death would force you away from your world; and then a few years more, and your world, and all that is in it, would be burnt up; but your soul, your immortal soul—what can compensate for the loss of that!" He calls for that nobler world they had lost from their hemisphere, and brings it again within the range of their vision. He takes them to the threshold of the infinite, and shews it flushed in one part with living glories, and in another burning with the fiercest flames of wrath; while he assures them that in one or the other of these states they will shortly be fixed for ever. " Watch, therefore," saith he, " for ye know not when the time is."

Having thrown open to view that interminable duration, and compelled them to see that they are actually approaching it, he proceeds to adjust its momentous claims in harmony with the duties of the life that now is. It might have been apprehended that the vision of eternity, if once beheld, would utterly incapacitate us for the affairs of time; that the infinite grandeur of the future, having suffered so total an obscuration from the littleness of the present, would have taken revenge on that littleness, by henceforth engrossing our every thought. But the Saviour did not come, as the avenging champion of eternity, to annihilate time and its appropriate interests. Having deposed it from its usurped supremacy, he takes it by the hand, and assigns it its place and its duties as a subject. He aims to impregnate every moment of life with endless results. Having weeded life of its vanities, he commands us to cultivate it with all that is useful and precious as fruit for the heavenly garner. He would have every moment of life to be so passed as to fructify into an age of pleasant recollections.

That eternity might not be an object of mere barren contemplation, he has so revealed it that its hallowing light falls upon fields of activity and usefulness which before were involved in darkness; everything conducive to our real interest, in every relation of life, receives its countenance, and rejoices in its sanction. If he finds us lost in indolent musing on the future, he breaks up our vacant-eyed reverie by the startling monition, "Why stand ye here all the day idle? Work while it is day, for the night cometh wherein no man can work." That eternity might not overwhelm us by its solemnities, he has not only softened its aspect, and made it welcome as the face of a friend, he also engages our attention to daily duties which hold us in a state of healthful activity. Our life, in his hands, is converted into a lamp, which, like the virgins of the parable, or the priests of the temple, we are to keep bright and burning. Our various endowments are so many talents, which the Lord of all expects us to multiply by constant use. He calls us to be the almoners and agents of providence, to " the poor who are always with us;" models of correctness in all the relations of life; and centres of light and usefulness wherever we move. It is necessary that celestial observations should be taken in order to construct a terrestrial chart; and having a chart to consult thus accurately formed, the skilful mariner is prepared to navigate the wastes of ocean with tranquil confidence. If the view we entertain of eternity disqualifies us for the duties of life, it is not to be traced to the gospel of Christ; he meant not that it should haunt us as a terror, but accompany us as a guide: nor will he accept the convulsive service which it may occasionally extort from us, by alarming us into a spasm of fear. He calmly inquires, " Are there not twelve hours in the day ? Does not the day of life, short as it is, contrasted with eternity, contain time sufficient, if properly employed, for all that is truly valuable?" And having engaged us in his service, and pointed out our duty, he gives us a glimpse of eternity to quicken the pulse of activity, and expects us to distribute our agency as equally as possible over the remaining hours of time.

But the liability of eternity to paralyze the active duties of time is not to be named, as a danger, compared with the fatal and universal propensity of men to subordinate the claims of the future to the affairs of the present. While their enlightened judgment compels them to concede the point of superiority to Heaven, their depraved heart is for giving the practical precedence to earth; and the result of this variance is an attempted compromise between the two claimants. But against such an accomodation the Redeemer enters his protest: appealing to the tribunal of common sense, he exclaims, " No man can serve two masters, whose interests clash." The experiment has been made and repeated in every form, and in every age; and he solemnly avers, with the confidence of one who knows that it has failed as often as it has been made, and will prove eternally impracticable, " Ye cannot serve God and mammon." Passing into the sanctuary, and marking the worldliness of the assembled hearers, he shews how necessarily, in such soil, the seed of the kingdom must prove unfruitful. Visiting the place of gain, and contrasting the burden of thick clay which the worshipper of mammon carries, with the narrowness of the entrance to the way of life, he exclaims, in accents of deep commiseration, " How hardly shall they that have riches enter into the kingdom of heaven !" Penetrating into the inmost circle of domestic life, and arresting the inmates in the midst of their household cares, he calls them to his side, and turns on them a look of pity as he reminds them, that while they are careful and cumbered about many things, "one thing is needful." He even lifts the curtain of eternity, and bids us approach and listen, while the voice of Dives from the deeps of hell, and the replies of Abraham from the realms of light, pronounce the moral of the tale of life. And taking his stand on the highway of the world, and surveying the busy crowds as they pass and repass, each one as eager as if he had just discovered the secret of happiness after a thousand failures, and were about to give it an instant trial, he points them upwards, and reminds them that the good they seek is there,—that there is one thing to which everything else desirable is appended; and *that* he exhorts them to "seek first."

It is the misfortune of some to be afflicted with that kind of defective sight which prevents them from seeing to an ordinary distance; they are unable to distinguish the most towering and colossal object if placed at a short remove, while the merest atom brought close to the eye is magnified as with the power of a microscope. An affliction analogous to this in the moral sight, but pregnant with incomparably greater danger, is the universal malady of mankind; and our Lord insists on the urgency of its removal. He finds them mistaking phantoms for realities, and realities for phantoms; calling an atom a world, and a world an atom; practising on themselves an endless succession of delusions; and he gives them the alternative of a remedy or death. He finds them absorbed in providing for the temporal future, and he urges them, as they respect their own rationality, not to omit eternity from their reckoning. He approaches them while gazing on the near perspective of time, and, by raising and extending the point of sight he adds eternity to the view, and leaves them lost in the contemplation of a boundless futurity. In all his addresses on the future, he does not forget that we are mortal; but neither will he allow us in our attentions to the present to forget that we are immortal. As the worshippers of mammon make religion subservient to the world, so he requires the worshippers of God to subordinate the world to religion. Instead of exhausting ourselves in efforts after the bread which perisheth, he reminds us that there is angels' food, and urges us to put forth our chief endeavours after that. He finds us in the midst of a spacious repository, crowded with an infinite variety of objects; some of which are adapted to the body only, while others might form a rich dowry for an immortal soul; some of them things that perish in the using, and others of them things that form the gold and currency of heaven, — things on which God has stamped his image and superscription, and inscribed an infinite value. But however diversified their character, he finds them each soliciting the first and highest place in our esteem; and aware that we are in danger of lavishing our affections—those precious things which if given to God would bring us heaven in return—of wasting them on less than nothing and vanity, he draws near and expostulates, and entreats us that we cheat not our souls of eternal happiness by providing for them only an earthly portion, but that we select for them a good spiritual and immortal like themselves, suited to supply its immortal wants, and to gratify all their large capacities. "Lay not up treasures on earth," saith he, "where moth and rust doth corrupt, and where thieves break through and steal: but lay up for yourselves treasures in heaven, where neither moth nor rust doth corrupt, and where thieves do not break through and steal."

And, by exhorting us to establish our principal interest in heaven, he actually consults our peace on earth; " For where your treasure is," he adds, " there will your heart be also." By choosing a heavenly treasure, our character and hopes, which are invariably modified by the object of our paramount regard, will partake of its celestial attributes; for it is both ennobling in itself, and is lodged in the only part of the universe which is exempt from calamity and change; so that, while others partake of the littleness, agitation, and debasement, which belong to their earthly gods, we shall receive, by anticipation, an impress of the greatness, and security, and stability, of heaven; while, at the same time, our temporal mercies will be enjoyed with a superior relish, since we should feel that the loss of them would leave us still in the possession of our real treasure entire and secure. In the prospect of a national convulsion, it is not uncommon for the wealthy to transmit their property for security into other lands. And, O, were there a country on earth perfectly exempt from all the changes which endanger property, that would be the envied land in which all would aim to invest their riches. But that blessed region, not to be found on the face of the wide earth, actually exists in the kingdom of God. Yes, by throwing open to us the gates of a heavenly commerce, he would give scope to our loftiest aims, security to our choicest treasures, and objects to our most capacious desires. Here, the affluent may embark their abundance: instead of living for themselves, let them live for God, and they will be remitting their property to a world where it shall accumulate with abundant interest; they will be laying up a store for the future, on which they may live splendidly and gloriously for ever; they will be placing uncertain riches in a safe repository, and transmitting them into certain wealth. Let them acquit themselves as faithful stewards of the great householder; and, as they dispense their wealth, it will direct its flight towards heaven, bearing on its wings the prayers and benedictions of those they have benefited. Having made to themselves friends with the mammon of unrighteousness, when they die, those friends will welcome them into everlasting habitations. Here the humblest believer may employ his penury:—and he will find eventually that his single mite, his cup of cold water, or his one talent, consecrated to God, has augmented into a treasure exceeding his powers of computation. For every sacrifice we make in his service, he guarantees to requite us,—not indeed as of debt; this the magnitude of the requital shews; but of his own exuberant munificence—he promises to repay us a hundred-fold in the present life, and in the world to come life everlasting. Every struggle against sin, every effort in the cause of benevolence, every holy principle exerted for God, he pronounces an element of future blessedness, and constitutes a claimant on his grace at the recompence of the just. Whatever is transmitted by the soul to the world above, is placed under the guardianship of Omnipotence, is laid up securely by the throne of God. His seat is the centre of a circumference, within which nothing that impairs or destroys can by any possibility intrude, and which itself remains unmoved and immutable, while all besides is fluctuation and change.

It is not easy to speak of the claims of heaven and earth as needing adjustment, without seeming to countenance an erroneous impression, that they are naturally at variance. But let it be borne in mind that originally they were one. The only quarrel which eternity can have with time, is, when it usurps an ascendancy which, by inverting all order, and doing violence to the first principles of our nature, renders the happiness of the soul impossible. Let the present defer to the future, let it fall into its proper place as the handmaid of immortality, and instantly they are one again; each is seen reciprocating its influence, and lending its aid to the other, to secure to us a blessed futurity, and to prepare us for it. But though all hostile opposition terminates with this new adjustment, it is not to be denied that difficulty still remains,—the natural and unavoidable difficulty of keeping the world from that dangerous domination which, having once enjoyed, it is ever impatient to regain. New habits are to be formed, powerful propensities are to be held at bay, old and indulged inclinations are to be denied, and enemies which we had fondly thought we had laid dead at our feet, suddenly starting into hostility again, are again to be coped with and vanquished: this is attended with a disheartening sense of difficulty, which some have no sooner tasted than they have declined the contest, and surrendered themselves at discretion.

Now, while our Lord, in various ways, takes cognizance of this struggle—for one of his great excellences, as the founder of a new religion, was the most transparent simplicity and candour—while he even enlarges on the conflict, presents his followers with a plan of the battle, points out its imminent hazards, and exhorts them, before entering on it, to " count the cost," he, at the same time, assures them of such supernatural succours as shall enable their weakness to do the deeds of omnipotence, and make perseverance infallible success. While he takes them to an eminence, and shews them the vast confederacy of evil arrayed against them, he reminds them that they struggle for an invisible world, that they fight in fellowship with all the children of the light, that more than angels are in their ranks, for he promises them the abundant aid of the Eternal Spirit. Their infirmities may be numerous, their sins may be mighty, their ignorance may seem invincible, but an almighty agent is employed for the special purpose of piercing that ignorance, overpowering that sinfulness, and surrounding them with an element of light and holiness.

And even beyond this, as he leads them to the field, he proclaims, " *Be of good cheer, I have overcome the world ;*—your leader is a conqueror; advance to victory." The history of the first Christians proves that he did not utter this inspiring address in vain. By this sign they conquered. Though the world within, and the world without, were in arms against them, they could not be depressed. They fought in the presence of an invisible world. They surveyed the whole array of evil, looked calmly in the face of every foe, considered all that might happen—but to this triumphant conclusion they came— " Because he lives, we shall live also." Like the earth on which they trod, and which continues to roll on in its orbit unimpeded by the earthquakes which rend it, and carrying all its atmosphere of storms along with it, so they, animated and impelled by the love of Christ, advanced in the course he had assigned them, as steadily and cheerfully as if no ills within, no storms without, assailed them,—as if each step they took were across the heavenly threshold, and in sight of their appointed thrones.

IV. In entering on any of the offices or relations of life, it is an obvious advantage to possess a view of the duties peculiar to that sphere, in as brief, clear, and comprehensive a form as possible; indeed, if they could all be adequately described in a single sentence, they would be so much the more acceptable. It is the distinguished excellence of the Great Teacher, that, in the inculcation of morality, he preferred *comprehensive rules* to a distinct specification of duties; though he took the most enlarged of human obligations, he generalized and enforced them by a few compendious laws, instead of separately legislating for each particular duty. Had he adopted, or rather attempted, the latter method, descending to a minute enumeration of duties, it would have involved this serious evil—that every duty which might have arisen *below* the point of enumeration would have been in danger of being treated as unobligatory, because not inserted in the specification. Glad of the plausible excuse arising from the omission, men would have regarded every duty not enjoined as omissible, and every sin not prohibited, as allowable. But, in the hands of Jesus, the science of morality is simplified and complete. A single prohibition is so planted by him, that, like a piece of ordnance, it may be said to enfilade and sweep a whole territory of sin ; nothing can come within its range without challenging its thunder, and courting death. A single rule is found to contain laws for an indefinite number of actions; for all the possible cases, of the class described, which can ever occur. Like the few imaginary circles by which geography circumscribes the earth, he has, by a few sentences, described and distributed into sections the whole globe of duty; so that, wherever we may be on it, we find ourselves encompassed by some comprehensive maxim ; and, in whatever direction we may move, we have only to reflect, in order to perceive that we are receding from or approaching to some line of morality.

By thus generalizing morality, he has consulted the weakness of the most impaired memory; presented us with a map-like view of the wide region of duty, which a single glance can survey ; provided rules for all the possible varieties and contingencies of human action ; while the consciousness it affords his followers that they are able to sustain the particulars of their life upon great first principles, enables them to advance in the path of holiness with an erect, assured, and dignified carriage of mind; and the demand which it makes on the higher capabilities of their nature, in calling them to comprehend such measures of greatness, and to sympathize with such perfection, raises and ennobles them to themselves, and possesses them with the feeling that they are allied to God.

To give a single exemplification, let me advert to the axiom known by the names of the golden rule and the universal law of equity : " All things whatsoever ye would that men should do unto you, do ye also unto them ; for this is the law and the prophets." The Saviour himself ascribes to this rule the condensed and comprehensive character for which we have cited it; he pronounces it an abstract of all that had been prescribed by the law and the prophets; all they delivered on the subject is reducible to this ; so that, were their writings lost, this summary might be expanded into all they uttered. Notwithstanding its conciseness, it is a maxim of so generic a kind, that, encircling the whole sphere of social virtue, it embraces *all things whatsoever* that sphere contains. No injury can be done, no reasonable kindness be omitted by man to man, which is not a violation of this royal law; nor can any duty be performed which it does not virtually enjoin. If it needed any other quality to recommend it, we might easily shew that it has numerous excellences fully answerable to its comprehensiveness. It is a rule as *portable* as our *self-love* and identical with it; for what is it but the love of self applied to the destruction of selfishness, by being pressed into the service of universal benevolence? It is the measuring rod, which is never out of the hand of self for its own purposes, legalized, and applied, to mete out the same measure for the good of others. It seeks to equalize vicissitude; to make a community of our joys and sorrows, by distributing them as nearly into equal parts as if we knew not the portion which would fall to us. It aims to transform self into an impartial judge, by giving it an interest in all the decisions which it pronounces on others. By compelling our selfishness to do the work of destruction on itself, it makes us content to number as one—as a mere unit in the sum of the species, and to seek the welfare of the whole, as the shortest and the only way of promoting our own individual interest. Let this infallible law be understood and applied, and the trade of the casuist would be gone in the department of social life; for self-interest, prompt, and even intuitive when it sits in judgment for its own ends, would have only to imagine a momentary self-transmigration, and to transfer its judgments for the advantage of others.

We might extend this representation to another particular of a similar kind, shewing the comprehensiveness of our Lord's maxims concerning the omission of duty. The line which divides his kingdom from the empire of sin is so fine, that, like the line of geometry, it is length without breadth; it occupies no part of the territories which it defines; it creates no border land, no neutral ground. "He that is not with me, is against me; and he that gathereth not with me, scattereth abroad;" a sentence which separates the world into two great classes; assigning over to the dominion of Satan the lukewarm with the hostile; and leaving them to discover, that, whereas they had expected to find themselves standing at least on neutral ground, they are actually and considerably within the frontiers of the kingdom of darkness.

How large a proportion of those whom custom and courtesy agree to call Christians live and die in self-complacency and hope, from the persuasion that they have been *harmless,* or, because they have *done nothing.* It seems never to occur to such, that to spend threescore years and ten on a field of conflict, the listless spectators of a strife in which Heaven every moment importunes them to take part, is disobedience and guilt. But, for this large sum of human ciphers, this aggregation of figures, whose total is nothing, the final sentence is already prepared. Having never aspired to Christian activity, or positive excellence, the doom which will consign the whole class to their own place will descend on them with this fearful formula, " Inasmuch as ye did it *not.*" Now if human guilt is reducible to a graduated scale of demerit, by thus inscribing condemnation at the least and lowest degree on the scale, how unavoidable is the inference made that greater condemnation is reserved for every higher degree of sin; if the mere absence of activity, the negation of friendship, for Christ, be denounced, it follows, of course, that activity against him, that positive hostility, being superior guilt, has nothing to hope for. Thus, by recording a sentence against the omission of duty, the Divine Teacher has not merely destroyed the plea of harmlessness, and proscribed the whole tribe of the useless,—he has tacitly comprehended and denounced the hostile and persecuting, leaving them to infer that to doom them formally would be superfluous.

V. Another excellence of the morality which Jesus inculcates, is, that it extends to the thoughts and operations of the heart. To legislate for a small department of the outward life is all the power that is accorded to human authority. In speaking of the spiritual character which the law assumed in the hands of Christ, we shewed that it is his prerogative to prescribe for the heart. " He knew what was in man ;" and he knew the connexion between that hidden source and the visible life to be the relation of cause and effect; he sought, therefore, to purify the streams by cleansing the fountain. He denounces the murder and adultery of the heart; sins which were unknown to the popular code of Jewish morality. "Out of the heart," said he, "proceed evil thoughts and every thing that defileth;" and, accordingly, he laid his hand on the hidden machinery of pollution, and essayed to destroy it in its springs. He sees evil there in its type; and aims to crush and annihilate it in its mould. He does not wait till sin comes out into the life, an overt act; but, passing into the heart, he begins to exert the authority of law, much earlier and higher; he meets the sin in its native home—detects it before it has become any thing but thought, or desire, or intention.

By repeatedly asking his auditors, as he did, "Why think ye evil in your hearts?" he, in effect, proclaimed that the busy and populous world of thought is subject to divine jurisdiction; that his eye is on all its most silent pulsations and hidden movements; and, consequently, that these would furnish materials for a future judicial process. And if it exalt our conceptions of matter to know that, by man, it is absolutely indestructible,—that of all which has ever existed not an atom is lost,—that, however it may be modified and dissipated, it cannot be destroyed,—and that the whole is destined to pass through the final regenerating fires,—then, what is the amount of solemn importance which should invest the slightest movements of our minds, and what the degree of intense solicitude with which we should control and watch them, when we know, that of all the infinite myriads of our thoughts, not one is lost; that they are accumulating fast for judgment; that over the least of them all a solemn inquest will be held, by God and his empannelled angels: and that their verdict will turn it into an element of endless joy or woe. Yes, the moment will come when the slightest movement of the mind will be deemed inexpressibly more worthy of attention than the aspect of the starry heavens in their solemn midnight magnificence —the most august spectacle of nature; for it will be seen creating for us our eternal state: and why should we not deem it so now? To cleanse the air, under certain circumstances, philosophy has divised a method of straining, and even searching, that subtle element for every particle of matter injurious to life: did we duly care for the health of the soul, the morality of Jesus would teach us the nobler philosophy, the more vital art, of subjecting the inner atmosphere of the soul to a process of examination in which the faintest rudiments of evil would be detected, and rejected as seeds of death.

VI. But the morality which Jesus inculcated penetrates deeper than to the thoughts: it goes down to that which originates and gives character to thought itself—to motive. Conscious that the vilest motives may co-exist with the fairest actions, men have ever made it a favourite object to have their character estimated by professions and appearances. But the morality of Jesus will accept nothing for virtue which is not pure in its origin: it proposes to restore the reign of motive: "Except your righteousness," said he, "shall exceed the righteousness of the Scribes and Pharisees, ye shall in no case enter into the kingdom of heaven." The radical defect of their piety was, that it was only superficial—a robe of light assumed to conceal the fiend of darkness. Their actions were the outside of the platter, burnished and clean; but their motives were the inside, polluted with their excesses. Their professions were " like graves which appear not, and the men that walk over them are not aware of them." Their piety was the "whited sepulchre, which indeed appears beautiful without;" the motive which produced it was the corruption and death within. They gave alms; but it was only when the trumpet sounded, to attract the notice of the public; and, from this ostentation, the Saviour took occasion to convey this important truth—that, in the kingdom of God, the reward of a laudable action never rises above the level of the motive which produces it; if it originates, as theirs did, in a thirst for *human* applause, it must not look for the *divine* approbation; its motive is the measure and arbiter of its own reward.

But not only did he reprobate impure and selfish motives; he specified and even provided the motive which holiness demands—the principle which fills the bosom and sways the actions of God himself—*love*. Like a perfect legislator, having prescribed the sublimest rules of life, he proceeded to furnish the most generous and glorious principle of obedience. He died for us. As if determined that a sense of obligation should overpower and absorb every other incentive to duty, he made the obligation infinite by laying down his life for our redemption. He died to secure us from the penalty of the law we had broken, that he might bring us under irresistible obligation to obey the law which he enacted. In the place of the two tables of stone, he substituted the cross, inscribed with the memorials of his love, and of our duty. He erected his cross; and constituted it at once the seat of legislation and the altar of sacrifice. "When Moses had spoken every precept to all the people according to the law, he sprinkled with blood both the book and all the people, saying, This is the blood of the testament which God hath enjoined unto you:" when Jesus had completed his code of divine morality, he sprinkled it with his own most precious blood, saying, "If ye love me, keep my commandments. Greater love hath no man than this, that a man lay down his life for his friends: ye are my friends, if ye do whatsoever I command you."

It is true that, while inculcating his divine precepts, the piacular and vicarious nature of his death was not understood by those whom he addressed. But not only were his injunctions copiously interspersed with allusions to his grace, and descriptions of his remedial relations to man; he required faith in himself, whatever he might do or become, as the great work of God: " This is the work of God, that ye believe on him whom he hath sent;" a command which was anticipatory and prospective of his approaching death, for it foresaw that their faith in him would have shortly to contemplate the amazing fact of his death for the remission of sins, and would thus possess them with that love which is the great evangelical motive to obedience. On the foresight of this approaching event, he required of his disciples that love should be the ruling motive of their conduct, as though his death had already transpired. Whatever they did, they were to do it in his name, from a principle of obedience to his will, and obligation to his grace. If they received a disciple, they were to do it in the name of a disciple; making the fact of his discipleship, his relation and resemblance to Christ, the object of their regard. " Whosoever shall receive one of such children *in my name, receiveth me.* Whosoever shall give you a cup of water to drink in my name, because ye belong to Christ, verily I say unto you, he shall not lose his reward. Whosoever shall lose his life *for my sake and the gospel's,* the same shall save it."

Now, considering the depraved condition of our nature, the appointment of love as the moving principle of our obedience might seem to exceed in boldness the loftiest flight of the most romantic theorist. But he, who knew all the workings of our mysterious nature, foresaw that his miraculous death for our redemption would give rise to a cause fully commensurate to the proposed effect. And the history of his church, from that period to the present, is a comment on his wisdom and benevolence; it demonstrates that his death gave a new motive to the world; brought into operation a principle which, meeting and uniting with every other principle of virtue in the human heart, and assimilating to itself all that is foreign to its nature, turns everything it encounters into an accession of power, and holds the soul for Christ, and in cordial allegiance to him. Like the great but unobtrusive operations of God in nature, it is silently but constantly at work, achieving the mightiest effects in the soul of man, converting his human into divine, and raising him, from a state of close companionship with demons, to the society of the blessed, and the vision of God. Issuing from the cross, it has more than the power of moral gravitation; for, while it retains the Christian in the orb of duty, it propels him forward at the same time. And if, in mechanics, the strength of a particular power is displayed in the number of opposing forces which it overcomes, what must be the potency of that principle which overcomes the world, wrestles with satanic agency, conquers the love of life itself, and which makes its way through a host of adverse powers, mastering them all; a principle, whose lowest degree of operation results in acts of heroism and triumph, and which generates all the obedience God receives from man.

VII. But not only do we need an actuating principle; being put into a state of activity, we also require an end to aim at; accordingly, the morality of Jesus, having supplied us with a principle which allies us to God, points us to an object, and gives a direction to that principle which terminates in God—the glory and enjoyment of the Divine Being. Uninspired morality, the offspring of ignorance, or passion, or pride, refers us to inferior objects; to the indiscriminate love of pleasure, the avoidance of pain, the dictates of nature, or to the greatest present advantage; (and if I do not enlarge on these various theories of human ethics, it is only from the fear of desecrating the divine morality of Him who is soon to sit in judgment on us all;) but the ethics of Jesus include every allowable inferior object, by proposing an end above and beyond them all.

Having shewn us the character of God as the first good, and the first fair, he makes it evident that our happiness consists in the imitation and enjoyment of that infinite excellence. He does this, generally, by requiring us to make the will of God the rule of our conduct; for it is not in our power to render greater honour to God than by thus placing our immortal interests in his hands. "Blessed are they that hear the word of God, and keep it." And, more particularly, he prescribes the divine glory as our end and aim, in declarations such as this—"No man can serve two masters; for either he will love the one and hate the other; or else he will hold to the one and despise the other; ye cannot serve God and mammon;" thus, by inference, erecting the glory of God into a supremacy, before which every other object must fall down and do homage. And how emphatically did his own conduct inculcate the same sentiment: "I came," said he, "not to do mine own will, but the will of him that sent me. My meat is to do the will of him that sent me, and to finish his work." And when entering the shadow of that hour of darkness in which his life of suffering and reproach was to be consummated in a death of ignominy and agony, he fixed his eye on the glory of God, and exclaimed, "Father, glorify thy name."

It is no valid objection to the loftiness of this object, that, being pure, it is only adapted to a state of sinless perfection; it is addressed to our imperfect nature as one of the means of restoring us to that perfection for which we are destined. And, besides the agency of the Holy Spirit, of whose help we have yet to speak, the gospel, unlike the law, while it demands and provides for our ultimate perfection, and could be satisfied with nothing less, is yet satisfied, for the present, if it sees us advancing in holiness. It infuses into our nature a motive adapted, by its very loftiness, to sustain its office; for were it less exalted, the depressing influences of sin would draw it down to their own level, and destroy it; but now, though it meets with many a check, and mingles with much pollution, it remains uncorrupted as light, and never fails eventually to triumph, leavening humanity with its own purity. It proposes, for our aim, an object fitted by the infinity of its excellence to engage our pursuit—for that object is final; had an inferior end been set before us, we should have had a pretext for discontent, for we should have felt ourselves capable of a higher aim than was assigned us. It strengthens our principles by simplifying them; expelling some from our hearts; and reducing those that remain under the sway of a reigning affection, which gives to the soul the harmony, simplicity, and singleness of intention of "a little child." But this sanctification is a *process*; and, like that change of one political government for another, that setting up of a new kingdom in the heart, to which it is compared, it encounters many an obstacle, and asks time for adjustment and consolidation.

It is, indeed, impossible to say whether, in the present state, the great motive of the gospel ever exists pure and uncompounded. Principles of action are too subtle for analysis; they elude our most anxious, but coarse, attempts to reduce them to their elements. The motive which, to our eye, looks pure as light, might, could we examine it through a moral prism, prove, to our astonishment, to be many-coloured. The aim which we regard as in a straight line to the glory of God, might, could we obtain a comprehensive view of its course, appear like a stream meandering to the ocean, touching at every accessible point, and taking every object in the way, consistent with reaching its final destination. But indirect and compounded as is the best principle of human action, the Great Teacher would have us raise our eye to the highest point, and aim at the loftiest mark in the universe. Unhinging us from the centre of self, on which we have turned, he supplies us with a common centre in God. The eye which has glanced at the unclouded sun is unable, for a time, to recognise the most familiar objects of earth; he unveils to us the splendours of the eternal throne—and the grandeur, and wealth, and most attractive objects of the world fade and vanish from our view; he calls us away from the limited and sordid pursuits of time, takes us into the counsels of God, invites us to join hands with Providence, to mingle in the operations of almighty love in renewing, and beautifying, and making happy, a world of immortal beings.

Without destroying the rotatory principle of self-interest, by which every man resembles the diurnal motion of the globe, he gives to us a momentum, and assigns to us an orbit, of which God is the centre, and which transports us, in effect, into the most distant parts of the universe, placing us in relationship to every part, and blending us with the great whole. He directs us to pray that earth may copy the example, and rival the obedience, of heaven, where the glory of God is the point from which every action starts, and the goal at which it terminates. "Sacred to God" is to be inscribed on all our possessions, in the use of which we are to consult his honour and acquiesce in his arrangements. He invites us to take part in a concert of praise which ascribes "kingdom, and power, and glory," to God supreme; a concert in which earth is once more to chime and chord with heaven, and which is finally destined to be universal, when "everything that hath breath shall praise the Lord." In the meantime, like the solar splendour, our light is so to shine before men, that they, seeing our good works, may glorify our Father who is in heaven; may be constrained to take part in the divine concert. Opening before us a career of glory in which angels are our competitors, he would have us to stop short at no attainment till the will of God be done on earth as it is done in heaven; he would have us be satisfied with no reward, till we can mingle the radiance of our crowns with the emanations of the paternal throne.

VIII. The holiness which the ethics of the gospel inculcate, acknowledges no standard but God. Man is an imitative creature. Having lost his original likeness to God, he involuntarily discloses the insufficiency of his nature, and a sense of the loss he has sustained, by looking out of himself for precedent and example in all he does; while the facility with which he lets himself down, and adapts himself to the low circumstances into which he has sunk, reveals the awful entireness of the revolution his nature has undergone. But, if his character is to be a copy, how important that the model should be of the best description, of a description which is likely to elevate and improve his nature, to develop its powers, and fill it with all the excellence of which it is capable. But where was such a model to be found? where, among all the specimens of virtue which earth has owned, and even all the ideal forms of worth the imagination had portrayed? Man had lost even the *idea* of moral perfection. Such excellence can be understood only by sympathy; but for this sin had disqualified him; and hence the necessity of his regeneration into the divine image before he can understand what that image is. To have selected the best, the least imperfect, of human characters for imitation, would have been therefore to erect a defective standard; and of this, the part which, most likely, would have been first copied into his nature, would have been its faults and imperfections. Besides, the period might have come when he had succeeded in equalling his model; the resemblance is complete; but he feels himself capable of higher attainments still; where now is the pattern for him to copy? He wants one whose excellence knows no limits, but which shall continue to enlarge as he approaches it, and to unfold new beauties as he becomes capable of appreciating and imitating them, in endless progression; in fine, the only example suitable to our nature is a perfect example.

The blessed Saviour supplies this necessity; "Be ye perfect," saith he, "even as your Father in heaven is perfect." And what an honour does he confer on our nature, by simply exhorting us to attempt so high an example! Whatever of excellence the universe contains is only a faint resemblance copied from Deity. All created goodness, in heaven and earth, is derived from him as its only fountain; and could all this excellence be collected and concentred in one being, that glorious being would still fall infinitely short of the Supreme Perfection. In exhorting us, then, to attempt the remotest imitation of him, the Saviour was putting an honour on our nature which, of itself, should be sufficient to lift us out of the world and sin, and to fill us with high and heroic aims. And, to encourage us to engage in this great endeavour, he not only reminds us that God is our Father, thus appealing to our filial love—for one of the earliest characteristics of a child is, that he attempts to imitate his father, and any action carries with it a sufficient recommendation in his eyes if his father does it—but, in order to bring the divine example within the scope and compass of our feeble endeavours, he humanized and embodied it in his own life. "He that hath seen me," saith he, "hath seen the Father also;" hath seen the character of the eternal Father acted out and submitted to human imitation. And so softened and subdued is that example, as seen in him, that the babe in Christ beholds in it features which he hopes and aspires to resemble; so attractive is it, that all the family of God, in heaven and earth, have their eyes habitually fixed on it in holy and delighted contemplation; so perfect is it, that the least deviation from it is sin, and the least approach to it a step towards holiness; and so great and glorious is it, that the spirits of the just made perfect, and the angels before the throne, have higher conceptions of it at this moment than they have ever had before; and so their conceptions of it will go on perpetually enlarging, and their admiration constantly increasing, while they will always feel that there is in it an unfathomed excellence, an infinite perfection, still remaining.

The Divine Redeemer, by thus making the character of God exemplary in his own life, has graciously adapted it to universal imitation. Uniting in his person the extremes of wealth and poverty, majesty and abasement, power and weakness, his example, in one or other of its aspects, is accommodated to every variety of condition. It teaches the highest, that there is an order of greatness distinct from all that earth can confer, and superior to it; and it reminds the lowest, that they can invest their state with grandeur, and finally attain an elevation of excellence from which all the inequalities of life will appear on a level; while, to every intermediate condition, it presents a phase especially suited for study and imitation. And what a motive to imitation arises from the fact, that he who has thus become our exemplar is himself occupied in the perpetual inspection of our conduct. " Lo," saith he, to his disciples, " I am with you always." By moving in the presence even of a man of a vigorous and commanding character, we gradually imbibe his spirit and opinions: on this principle it was, that a heathen philosopher advised his disciples to imagine themselves constantly acting under the eye of some ancient sage renowned for virtue; we can never lift our eye without encountering the look of our Divine Master. We never move out of his presence, nor does he ever withdraw his eye from us: and as, in copying the productions of ancient genius, the admiring artist takes up his station before his model, and, that he may not omit a single line or shade, raises his eye every moment to scan the original, so we are to avail ourselves of his perpetual presence, by recurring in thought to his divine example preparatory to every step we take; and as the soldier in actual conflict is instantly nerved with additional vigour on catching the glance of his leader, so we shall be braced to redoubled energy in the field of duty, while conscious of the presence of the Lord of hosts, the Captain of salvation.

Were the world to lose the idea of the character and example of God, it would forthwith rapidly retrograde towards the lowest point of depravity; earth would from that moment begin to compete with hell, in a fearful enterprise and rivalry of sin. The possession of this idea, as it is exhibited and secured to us in the gospel, is the safeguard of all morality, the germ of all real excellence. Barely to apprehend it, even, is an era in the understanding; but to conceive the desire of copying it, is a lift in the scale of excellence which gives us the sympathy of angels, and places us, as at a bound, within sight of the gate of heaven. It ventilates the human breast of everything sordid, grovelling, and impure; and turns through it a cleansing and invigorating current of heavenly influence. The student in art is sent to refine his taste, and exalt his genius, by the patient investigation of the great masters of antiquity; the student in holiness is referred to him who is the exemplar of all that is good, the original of all that is fair; and no sooner does he begin to admire, than he begins to partake; he is " changed into the same image from glory to glory." Possessed with the idea of God, he is enamoured of all he meets with that is beautiful and good; but, instead of resting in any fragmentitious excellence, it only sends him in thought to the great Archetype, with whom, by an instinctive act of the mind, he compares it, and so estimates its worth.

In the universe of intelligent beings, the character of God is the centre to which all that is virtuous and obedient gravitates; the authority with which every enlightened conscience is in constant intercourse; the appointed rendezvous from every part of creation, to which all the hosts that have retained or resumed their allegiance resort, to renew their oath, and to reinforce their strength. And, in the heart of every individual believer, this exalted conception of the divine character reigns supreme. It is a principle and a power which awes every other fear, expels every rival authority, and commands him to fear that Being only who can cast both soul and body into hell. It is a nucleus, around which " whatsoever things are honest, just, pure, lovely, and of good report," collect and crystallize. " If there be any virtue, and if there be any praise," this is the point about which they form, and brighten, and acquire their splendour. Claiming the entire homage of the heart, it receives the subjection of every thought, and beholds every other name of power withdraw and vanish: while, capable of perpetual accretion and aggrandizement, it comes at length to fill the soul, and to constitute the sole principle of holy action.

IX. We must not omit to notice the advantage which the preaching of Jesus derived from the simple and authoritative manner in which it was delivered, and the sanctions in which it was invested. In putting a man on any given course of action, it is important to his progress and perseverance that he should feel unlimited confidence in the wisdom and authority of his patron. If the instructions he receives are couched in ambiguous terms, or delivered in a tone of uncertainty, or enforced with the verbosity of a special pleader, the methodical clauses and measured distinctions of the logician, the endless exceptions and provisoes of the jurist, or the misty filmwork and cold abstractions of the metaphysician, he will most probably suspect that his instructor has yet to form a definite idea of his own wishes; or, that he doubts their practicability, or feels that their questionable propriety requires the protecting veil of a disguising sophistry; and the probability is, that, possessed with these very natural suspicions; he will never attempt to carry the instructions into practice; or will waste the feeling and passion necessary to action, in harassing alternations between right and wrong; or will construe the first obstacle he encounters, in the course proposed, into a providential intimation that he is not in the path of duty, and should instantly turn back.

The injunctions of Jesus were clear, determinate, and imperative; combining, at once, the simplicity of a father directing his child, and the authority of a king whose will is law. Taking his stand on the firm, broad, uncompromising principles of morality, he spoke, as conscience itself speaks, concisely, energetically, and to the point. The only logic he employed was the logic of the heart; his only auditor, common sense. Loading every sentence with meaning, he levelled it direct at the breast. His style seems not merely to breathe a solicitude that it may be understood; it seems to burn with a resolution that it *will* be felt, that it will make itself to be remembered. This is true of the style of all his commands; but there are some of them which go even beyond this, they not only effect for themselves a lodgment in the memory, but when once there they defy oblivion,—nothing can dislodge them.

The unauthorized precepts of other moralists are only guesses at right, and should, therefore, be uttered with diffidence, and received with discretion. But he spoke, as the organ and oracle of God, for the universe, and for eternity. He knew that his precepts are to constitute the laws of the last day; and that each of them is to sustain the everlasting awards of myriads of immortal beings. If any one could hear them enjoined, and yet refuse to them unbounded regard, his miracles came to his aid, collected and clustered around to abet and confirm them. He called in the terrors and powers of the world to come, to augment their sanction. If we consider his character and office, his relation to man and to the invisible world, we shall feel that, while propounding his laws, he occupied a position more imposing than that of the mount that burned; that he legislated as in an amphitheatre filled with the attendant thrones and dominions of heaven, with the judgment seat in perspective, the rewards of glory piled up in sight, the penal fires of perdition flaring up at intervals and darting forth volcanic flashes from an unknown depth, and God meanwhile corroborating his authority in accents of thunder, and saying, " This is my beloved Son; hear ye him."

X. How unspeakably superior is the holiness of the gospel to that of mere human moralists, not only as it raises the standard of excellence higher, even up to an imitation of the blessed God, but also as it supplies the necessary hope and help to obedience. They only tell us what they conceive to be our duty, and there they leave us in our helplessness; but Jesus provides us with motives, sets before us the incentive of his own example, points us to the throne of grace, and engages to meet us there with the aid of his Holy Spirit. When the mind is first awakened to a consciousness of its guilt, it is inclined to look at those things most which serve to corroborate its fears, and deepen its gloom; the intrinsic evil of sin, the immutable requirements of the divine law, the aggravating peculiarities of its own transgressions, these are the fearful aspects of its condition which concentrate its attention, and augment its dismay. Revolting at the thought of aggravating its guilt by looking to the general goodness of God, it turns away from him who would give it encouragement from that source, as from a sophist and a foe. It derives a morbid satisfaction from nourishing its anguish; and whether or not it will ever essay a first step in the way to heaven depends on the practicability of inspiring it with hope.

To this crushed and overwhelmed state of mind the Saviour draws nigh, and ministers the balm of consolation. " Blessed," saith he, " are they that mourn; for they shall be comforted. Blessed are the poor in spirit; for theirs is the kingdom of heaven. Blessed are the meek; for they shall inherit the earth." Though less than nothing in their own eyes, he tells them that in his estimation there is a wealth in their poverty of spirit more ample and enduring than all the treasures of earth; a majesty in their meekness, to which pride can never erect itself and attain; and, in their sorrow for sin, in every tear they shed, an immortal seed, the fruit of which will be peace and unending joy. Though the world in its depravity and blindness may continue to hold their character in contempt, he assures them that the great God, seated on the throne of heaven, pronounces it blessed; that the dowry which falls, even now, to its portion, contains the blossomings of celestial life; that as often as the partakers of it depart by death from this earthly scene, he raises and welcomes them into his own kingdom; and, when every earthly embellishment shall have faded and disappeared, he will, with his own lips, proclaim them happy, and in the presence of the universe, will crown them with all the beatitudes of heaven.

He informs them that he came into the world to seek and to save that which was lost; that his commission extends to the mouth of the bottomless pit; and, to shew them that he goes to the extreme of his commission, he points them to those whom he rescued at the awful brink, and who accompanied him about as the specimens and trophies of his grace. By his parable of the prodigal, his encouraging views of the paternal love of God, his inspiriting invitations and promises of grace, he sought to make despair impossible, and hope the first emotion of their penitent souls. He assures them, that so far from being unnoticed, they no sooner turn their faces in the direction of heaven, than their Father beholds them yet a great way off; that their first incipient desire for aid brings an almighty agent to their side; that, during the hour of their first application for mercy, the place of audience is kept peculiarly for them; and that, on the tidings of their repentance arriving in heaven, whatever may have engrossed the angelic harps till then, instantly and joyfully the theme is changed to the celebration of this new event. Having allured them to the footstool of mercy, he stretches forth his hand from the throne before which they have fallen, and lifts them up, places them on their feet, and points them to the duties and encounters which now await them.

To calculate on miraculous interposition in the ordinary affairs of life savours of presumption and romance. But, in the sphere of Christian hope, Jesus has made the extravagance of romance impossible, by promising to exceed all hope; he has given a wing to our expectation which disdains all limit, for he has declared that whatever we ask in his name we shall receive. He meets the desponding objection to which the survey of our duties and difficulties would give birth, and he destroys it before it can be uttered, by engaging, " Ask, and ye shall receive." He thus gives us immediate access to the treasury of the divine benevolence; so that, even in this world, we can not only ward off and suspend around us every evil, but we can draw around us every good; as though we possessed an omnipotent charm, we can create around us an atmosphere of peace and joy. He grants us introduction to the armory of God, and to all his resources of strength; so that, like the angel who had the key of the bottomless pit, and a great chain in his hand, we can fetter the operations and restrain the power of the prince of darkness; or we can enter the field of conflict, and overpower him. To put us in progress towards heaven, he even guarantees the assistance of the Holy Spirit; this is help to which nothing *can* be added, for it is all-comprehensive; and nothing *need* be, for it is all-sufficient. It infuses omnipotence into our feeblest effort, and renders us, while moving in the line of duty, invincible and irresistible.

And he not only inspires hope by supplying the necessary aid, he also quickens our activity in the path of holiness by exhibiting its ultimate reward. Instead of taking it for granted that we should be enamoured of duty for its own sake alone, he evinces the kindest consideration for our fallen condition, by accompanying his commands with appropriate promises and blessings. Thus, in his sermon on the Mount, while inculcating the virtues peculiar to the Christian character, he associates each with a divine beatitude; graciously alluring us to cultivate the tree, by engaging that all its fruit shall be our own. And frequently, to give an access of fervour to our zeal, he unveils the prize which he has promised to holy perseverance, and places it distinctly before our eyes; he brings out all the crowns, the regalia of heaven, and suspends it from his throne, reminding us that it is placed there to be won.

XI. But, however perfect the morality of the gospel may be, and however delightful the task of thus expatiating on its excellence, it is necessary to remember that, like its heavenly Author, it has not escaped the tongue of calumny; though the painful shock which this recollection inflicts on those who know the gospel best, may be regarded as a sufficient refutation of its foes. Numbers, indeed, who have withheld their admiration from the Son of God in every other respect, have yet accorded the highest praise to his precepts; they could not advert to these without soon exhausting the powers of language in eulogy and delight; and to such, therefore, we might justifiably refer the impugners of his code, to receive the answer they need, and the reprobation they deserve.

But we would not leave his morality to be precariously defended by the enemies of his cross, though we can now advance only a word in its behalf.

1. Is it objected that, wherever the gospel has come, dissension has more or less invariably ensued? It is time for such objectors to know, that there is an important difference between an incidental occasion and a direct cause; that, of whatever evils the gospel may be the indirect occasion, it is the cause only of unmixed good. Like the sun, it cannot rise and shine without being *the cause* of light, and life, and happiness, to the world; though there are some fatal spots on which it cannot look without *occasioning* pestilence and death.

2. Is it alleged against the gospel, that it maintains a profound silence on the subject of friendship as a duty? This is its wisdom. For until it can be shewn that friendship is a virtue, whatever the kind of characters it may unite; that it is a good abstractedly and for its own sake alone, whatever the effects it may produce; and that, although its formation depends on the sympathetic attraction of twin-like dispositions, on the nicest balancing of feeling and concurrence of circumstances, yet all in every situation enjoy the means of cementing it; he who should enact it as a law, and enforce it as a duty, would betray his ignorance of human nature, and evince that, from whatever quarter his credentials were derived, he was no legislator sent from God. But, though Jesus has not prescribed friendship as a proximate duty, he has done what is far more consonant with our nature, and infinitely more conducive to our well-being. In the amiable qualities which his gospel produces, and the acts of relative kindness which it prescribes, he has laid the foundation of a friendship, sanctified and eternal. So far from being indifferent to this union of souls, he has not only set us

a most attractive example in his own conduct, but, by commanding his followers to collect into a church, he has consecrated the social instinct, and built a home for friendship to inhabit: he has shewn that it is only within the sacred pale of Christianity that it can exist in perfection; only in the soil of religion that this plant of paradise, this scion from the tree of life, whose root is grace, and whose fruit is glory, can bloom with freshness and vigour. Having redeemed it out of the hands of the ungodly, he has sprinkled it with his blood, breathed on it his own spirit, and given to it a life which passes uninjured through the gate of death, and emerges in the kingdom of God; where those who are the subjects of it approach and fall down together before the eternal throne, and receive from his approving smile the only element wanted to crown it with perfection—the element of immortality.

3. Equally futile is the charge which some allege, that the gospel is silent on the subject of patriotism. All, however, that can be really meant by such an objection is, that it says nothing of a tendency to fortify and build up a nation in its selfishness: that it confers not on one state a right to forge fetters for another; that it kindles no brand to ignite those popular passions which nature has already made sufficiently inflammable, and to which a vicious education has added the dangerous tendency of spontaneous combustion. But, as far as consistent with his ultimate and unearthly aim of establishing the universal kingdom of God, our Lord has prescribed every general rule on which the welfare of a country depends; and it would be easy to shew, that no evil could possibly befal a state, either in its internal or external relations, which had not arisen from the infraction of one or other of his divine laws.

Besides, it should be distinctly remembered, that *love of country* is a phrase of very uncertain value; that the period may come when it will fall into comparative disuse, since it depends even for existence on the continuance of the present condition of the world. Only let the great society of nations harmonize and blend— only let knowledge go forth in its might, as it is promising to do, and throw down the barriers of conventional prejudice—and patriotism will enlarge and lose itself in philanthropy. This is a fact which is beginning to force itself on the conviction of the most reluctant. Even science cannot touch on this theme without becoming loud and prophetic. It refuses to entertain any project less than the amelioration of the species. It undertakes to convince mankind that every true interest must be universal, that good is indivisible, so that to be enjoyed in perfection by one it must by conferred upon all. But, what Science *says*, the Gospel will *do*. In prosecuting the march which it has commenced, it consults the map of the world. As the sun of righteousness ascends in the firmament, our moral horizon enlarges: those whom we had seen by the brand-light of ignorance disfigured into phantoms which it was thought merit to hate, are shewn to be men whom it is pleasure to love; and thus all kindreds, people, and tongues, are drawn into the close relationship of a family compact, preparatory to their final assembly in heaven.

But, while the gospel aims at universal benevolence, it does not overleap any of the inner and smaller circles of duty; and, as one of these, it takes up, directs, and sanctifies the love of country. In the conduct of our blessed Lord we behold a holy patriotism personified, the love of country embodied. Where did patriotism ever exhibit a nobler burst of sorrow than on Mount

Olivet; when "he beheld the city, and wept over it, and said, O Jerusalem, Jerusalem, how often would I have gathered thee, as a hen gathereth her chickens under her wings, but ye would not?" Whose patriotism ever endured what his did? He had but twelve offices to bestow; but then they were the highest out of heaven, and these he bestowed on twelve of his countrymen. He had but one gift to impart; but, oh! it comprehends every other—the gift of eternal life; and this he directed to be offered to his country *first,* "beginning at Jerusalem."

4. But we will not prolong our defence of evangelical morality, though the examination of every fresh objection could not fail to repay us with the discovery of unforeseen excellence. We may confidently assert for it the claims of divine perfection, and tranquilly rest them on an appeal to its practical effects: " Men do not gather grapes from thorns, nor figs from thistles; the tree is known by its fruits." Concede to Christianity the benefit of this criterion, and its triumph is complete. Follow it in its progress from place to place, and, as it was with its heavenly Author while here on earth, its path may be traced by the song of gratitude, the acclaim of joy, which it leaves behind: whatever form of misery and vice it may overtake, nothing but purity and peace is in its rear. If it gains introduction to a community already civilized, it takes all that it finds there, of wise and good, under its special protection: it gives new motives to duty, new sanctions to law; arms justice with a new and keener sword, and presents her with more perfect balances then she possessed before; throws its shield over oppressed and prostrate virtue; and becomes the rallying point, from every quarter, for conscience, and truth, and hope, and right. Engaged in a per-

petual conflict with evil, it invites all ranks to enlist under its banners; by giving them an interest in the result of the struggle, it urges them to arise in a body, to make common cause against the common foe; and, not merely to chase it over the borders of their own community, but to give it no pause till it has descended into the pit from which at first it issued.

If the gospel, in fulfilment of its universal commission, visits a barbarous people, its advent among them is like the bursting forth of a fountain in the heart of a desert— the waste is changed into the garden of the Lord. From that moment they find a place on the page of history; and from having been tethered to the limits of a wilderness, and knowing nothing of their fellows beyond, it calls them to take rank in the commonwealth of nations, opens to them a commerce with heaven, and makes them free of every part of the universe. It not only lifts us out of the grossness of barbarism, by acquainting us with the secret of our real birth-right; by the new and ennobling employment which it gives to thought, it raises us also in the scale of intelligent beings; so that many in finding it have found a mind, have exhibited the first symptoms of intellectual consciousness and power. Yes, thousands, whom ignorance and selfishness had branded as the leavings and refuse of the species, if not actually akin to the beasts that perish, are at this moment rising under the fostering care of the gospel, ascribing their enfranchisement to its benign interposition, taking encouragement from its smiles to assume the port and bearing of men, and, by their acts and aspirations, retrieving the character and dignity of the slandered human form. But these are only blessings accidental to religion, the shed blossoms of the tree of life, the dust of that diamond which constitutes her crowning gift. In giving light to the eye of the mind, and objects of spiritual purity to the affections, and immortality to the hopes, in shewing us that there is nothing too great for us to expect, or too good for us to attain, it is only fulfilling its trust and calling us to perfection.

Of every other system it may be said, that it only actuates a part of our nature, leaving the rest, like a palsied member of the body, unnoticed and unused; to Christianity alone belongs the high prerogative of calling every latent principle of our complex nature into action, giving appropriate exercise to every function, and proportion to every part; of animating, and maturing, and circulating, like an etherial fluid, through the whole, and bringing it to the perfection of "a man in Christ Jesus." Wherever it comes, it creates a capacity for true enjoyment, and puts all the universe in motion to gratify that capacity. It makes us feel that we exist under an obligation to be happy. Perfect itself, it pants to behold perfection in everything else; and, since it finds it not already existing, it puts forth all its efforts to produce it. Perfect from the beginning, it has remained unchanged, while the arts and sciences, and systems of a dateless antiquity, have yielded to the demand for improvement. It has seen everything human, contemporaneous with its origin, renovated and changed again; but, like the Jewish legislator, when he had survived his generation, its eye is not dim, nor its natural force abated. It maintains its post in the van of improvement, and points the way to enterprise and hope, as the anointed leader of mankind. And however untried the paths, and high the distinctions which await them in their onward course, it will still be seen in exemplary advance, beckoning them on to the goal of perfection. No living springs of good shall gush from their hidden depths in human nature, which have not been smitten into existence by this rod of heaven; no forms of excellence shall arise to bless the world, of which it is not the parent and the perfect type. Only give the gospel room to plant its moral apparatus, and let it obtain the necessary fulcrum for its powers, and it will employ a lever which shall move the world from the dark vicinity of hell, and lift it into the sunlight and neighbourhood of heaven.

XII. However incredible the statement may appear to those who are unacquainted with the chimeras of error, there is a class of persons who, under the presumptuous pretence of enjoying an intimate acquaintance with the mind of Christ, and of magnifying his grace, profess to glory in the gospel as a dispensation from holiness. That such a dispensation would be highly acceptable to the children of disobedience we can easily imagine, but that its advent should be ascribed to him whom hell itself acknowledged to be the Holy One of God, must be regarded as a masterpiece of impiety which bids defiance to imitation, as the last **triumph of** infernal art. Compared with the **advocates of this blas**phemy, he who only charges on the gospel a defective morality is a mere venial trifler; *he* only alleges that it is wanting in some of the elements of a perfect excellence; *they* claim for it as a peculiar glory, that it dispenses with all excellence. For, by affirming that it discharges them from the law as a rule of life, they virtually declare that it legalizes vice, that it grants them a patent to sin under its own broad seal, that it naturalizes the alien and eternal outlaw, sin, and makes it a denizen of the kingdom of God. *He*, by pretending dissatisfaction with its unfinished excellence, is guilty of abating the ardour and expectation of the thirsty inquirer after the water of life;

they, by adulterating the vital element, by infusing their own poisonous distillation, turn the very chalice of salvation into the cup of perdition. He wears no mask, he bears the mark of his master visibly stamped on his forehead, and takes on himself, so far at least as the character of the gospel is concerned, the undivided responsibility of his sin; while they, under the treacherous guise of an alliance with Christ, affiliate their monstrous enormities on his holy gospel, and throw its hallowed skirt over the nakedness of their pollution.

This, it must be confessed, is a "doctrine of devils;" it partakes of the infernal too palpably to be mistaken; like a stream of volcanic lava, it may be traced directly to the mouth of the pit which disgorged it, to scorch and desolate the earth in its progress. If demons can rejoice, the successful introduction of this error into the church must have furnished them with an occasion for exultation not less triumphant than that of the first transgression: it taught them that the paradise of the new creation is as accessible as the original Eden, that the upas can be grafted on the tree of life, that they might confidently repose on the success of this experiment, and regard it as final, secure that, after this, there is nothing too monstrous to be believed, or too good to be perverted, when human credulity and depravity are the materials to be employed. If he of our race who lent himself to be the first vehicle of this deadly sentiment, had aspired to the bad pre-eminence of eclipsing the first sinner, of enacting another fall of man, he could not have adopted a more effectual expedient. Beyond all proportion of demerit, he has purchased for himself the first place in the classification of the heretics, and troublers, and monsters of the church. Judas betrayed his Master to the cross; but *he* has betrayed the cross itself, and all its loaded blessings, into the hands of the enemy of God and man; his name, like that of the Iscariot traitor, deserves to be the synonyme of all that is exaggerated and enormous in guilt.

XIII. Instead, however, of humbling the gospel by putting it on its defence against such an enemy—indeed, an apology is due to common sense, and to the most ordinary piety, for having adverted to the topic—I shall draw to a conclusion by adducing a few illustrations of the supreme importance attached to holiness in the preaching of Christ.

1. Every reformer of ancient abuses, every benefactor of the species, must expect, on entering on his godlike career, to be assailed by two antagonist forces. He passes to his work through two opposing ranks; the hosts of prejudice draw out, and assail him as an Abaddon, a reckless destroyer of everything covered with the dust of antiquity: the lovers of change congratulate themselves that, at last, they have found a champion to defy and destroy whatever is. In this predicament stood Christ: but to silence suspicion, and to leave the minds of both parties at liberty to accord to his doctrine undivided attention, he stood on the threshold of his labours, and made known, that, so far from assailing the fundamental principles of law, upon them he should take his stand as upon the *terra firma* of morality, that he should make them the foundation of all he built, the basis of a superstructure which should survive the dissolution of heaven and earth.

2. Whenever holiness came into comparison with any of those objects which the world is inclined to idolize, he omitted no opportunity of assigning to it a place infinitely above them. Knowledge is one of these objects:

so powerful are its attractions to many, that they cordially sacrifice property, and health, and everything, in the pursuit of it. But had we mastered all the branches of human science, laid open all the secrets of nature, and expounded its most hidden and comprehensive laws; could we recal the past, control the present, and, by a wide range of philosophical induction, foretel the future; were we able to descant familiarly on the remotest regions of the universe, and, in the wantonness of that power which knowledge confers, to yoke the imperial elements of nature, and compel them to labour for us; still he would impress us with the fact that the science by which a defiled heart may be made holy, comprises the sum of all wisdom. " This," said he, " is life eternal, to know thee the only true God, and Jesus Christ whom thou hast sent." But he valued even this knowledge only as it prepared men for heaven by regeneration; " Sanctify them through thy truth; thy word is truth."

3. He foresaw that the time would come, when a splendid profession of piety, and the possession of superhuman endowments, would be objects of envy in his church. But, in order to correct our estimate of their value, he would have us to understand, that although we could speak in every dialect of heaven and earth, rob futurity of its secrets, lay open all mysteries, and grasp all knowledge; though our faith could enable us to move the everlasting hills; though we possessed, what to our apprehension is the greatest distinction of a miraculous nature which a human being can enjoy, the power of casting out demons, of detecting their presence and commanding them to depart, of defying their power, and compelling them to submit; though, like the apostles, we could invade the infernal region, and add it to our Lord's unearthly conquest; though our benevolence disdained

less than the sacrifice of our whole property; and though our martyr-zeal impelled us into the flames,—the absence of evangelical holiness would render the whole nugatory and useless. " Not every one that saith unto me, Lord, Lord, shall enter into the kingdom of heaven; but he that doeth the will of my Father who is in heaven. Many will say to me in that day, Lord, Lord, have we not prophesied in thy name? and in thy name have cast out devils? and in thy name done many wonderful works? And then will I profess unto them, I never knew you: depart from me, ye that work iniquity."

4. Our Lord foresaw that, in every age of his church, his professed followers, true to the bias of depraved humanity, would be in danger of substituting the appendages and accretions of religion in the place of piety itself. This pernicious propensity began to disclose itself under his own eye. For on a certain occasion, when he had been delighting his hearers with an effusion of heavenly wisdom, a woman of the company lifted up her voice, and said, " Blessed is the womb that bare thee, and the paps which thou hast sucked." Now of all the conceivable substitutes for personal piety on which human indolence might seek to repose, that of kinship to Christ seems the most natural, and the least liable to general abuse. But he saw in this outburst of maternal feeling, however natural, a principle involved, capable of general application, and pregnant with danger; and, therefore, in order to take off our attention from every inferior distinction, and fix it on the true theory of blessedness, he instantly rejoined, " Yea, rather, blessed are they that hear the word of God, and keep it."

5. On another occasion, his mother and brethren, actually presuming on the ties of kindred, wished to

interfere with his labours, and expected that he would shew them some public mark of deference. "But he answered and said, Who is my mother? and who are my brethren?" thus plainly intimating that, in his official capacity, he knew no affinity but that which originates in faith, is cemented by love, and puts forth the fruits of holy obedience. He detected the hydra of religious formality in this chrysalis of natural feeling; and, therefore, at the hazard of appearing severe to his earthly kindred, he cast it from him, and smote it with the sword of his mouth. But "stretching forth his hands towards his disciples, he said, Behold my mother, and my brethren; for whosoever shall do the will of my Father who is in heaven, the same is my brother, and sister, and mother."

6. Were we to quote every part of the practical instructions of Christ, our citations would amount to at least two-thirds of all he is recorded to have taught. In his first discourse on record, that which he addressed to Nicodemus, he describes himself as having kindled a light in the midst of the world; and that while all the children of the day delighted to feed and strengthen their spiritual vision at its beams, the doers of evil, all the progeny of darkness, feared to come forth from their dens of night to encounter its rays, lest it should flash condemnation in their face.

7. His Sermon on the Mount, the most detailed specimen of his preaching we possess, is practical throughout. Unlike many a modern discourse, it is not merely guarded and finished with a border of practical application, that it may not be quite unuseful, the material and texture of the whole piece consist of the most serviceable and enduring principles of duty. So perfect is the character which Jesus requires of his disciples, that the infidel has

pretended to see in it nothing but the unattainable beau-ideal of romance, and to read in its very perfection its own refutation. He knew not that celestial aid is offered for the attainment; and reflected not that to erect a standard professing to be divine, and yet short of perfection, would have been representing the holy God as making a compromise with sin. The morality of Jesus gives no quarter to vice; allows not a moment's truce to any sinful propensity. Every member and instrument of sin is to be severed and cast away with an unsparing hand. His people are to turn every act into devotion; to make every meal sacramental, a token and pledge of infinite love. The termination of one duty is to be only a signal for the commencement of another; their life is to be one continuous act of obedience. Though, for the sake of civil government and order, they may comply with many of the forms which yoke men to duty, and keep them in allegiance to virtue, they are yet to consider themselves bound by superior obligations; their heavenly Master has taken them to his cross, and sworn them to holiness over the symbols of his death; henceforth they are to live on oath.

8. And their piety is to be diffusive: bursting the limits of their own life, it is to multiply itself in the lives of others. He offers a premium to eminent piety by proclaiming that, when sinners, aroused by its active and unsparing aggressions on vice, shall league and arm to destroy it, the gates of bliss shall be thrown wide open to welcome the martyr-spirit in its ascent from the field of conflict, and great shall be its reward in heaven. His people constitute the salt of the earth: the advent of his gospel was the introduction of a new restorative principle into the world; it arrested the progress of corruption, renovated much that had fallen into a state of moral

decomposition, and infused into it the permanent vitality and strength of holiness. His people are the depositaries of this principle; and by their holy activity they are not only to suspend the tendency of the world to a state of general demoralization, but to save it for God. They are the lights of the world; they have been kindled to irradiate the surrounding gloom; they are placed in their respective orbits to catch the radiance of his throne, and transmit it to a world immersed in the shadow of death. In order to sustain their office with effect, he requires them not merely to shine, but to burn, to be resplendent with holiness and zeal.

9. When an eastern monarch contemplated a journey through a distant part of his dominions, he prepared for the expedition, and made it memorable, by sending harbingers to level a road, and announce his coming. The regal progress of Jesus through Judea was preceded by the command, " Prepare ye the way of the Lord, make his paths straight." The impediments to be removed, and the mountains to be levelled, were moral obstructions; and by issuing an edict for repentance, a call to universal reformation, he would fain have signalized the epoch of his mission, by sweeping the land of its mountainous iniquities, preparing it for the free and unobstructed commerce of goodness, and filling it from one end to the other with the paths of pleasantness and peace.

10. And this holiness he wills to be universal. In requiring us to yield our supreme affection to God, and to love our neighbour as ourselves, he was prescribing for earth the elements of celestial felicity; for it is by doing this that angels are happy, that heaven is the region of blessedness which it is; nor could its happiness survive this duty for a moment. But in directing us to pray, that " the will of God may be done on earth, as it is in

heaven," he would open before us the prospect of unbounded progression and improvement; he would inspirit us to enter on a career of emulation with angels; to despair of nothing, to hope for everything, in the moral advancement of the world; to stop at no point short of universal holiness; and to call in, at every step, the almighty agency of God. Heaven, it is true, is in every divine excellence immeasurably in advance of earth. Truth is the food of the soul; and there, in the clear revelations of the eternal mind, the spirit is perpetually feasted with fresh discoveries of truth. Obedience is the activity and exercise of the renewed soul; and there it is its privilege to serve him day and night in the noblest acts of duty. Holiness is the beauty of the soul; and there it is robed in that "fine linen, white and clean, which is the righteousness of the saints." Happiness is the health, the well-being of the sanctified spirit; and there it imbibes felicity, at will, at the fountain-head. The specific employments of the blessed we know not; but we are told that every earthly impediment to duty is to them unknown, and that in every act of obedience they put forth all the mightiest ardour of the most intense devotion. Every motive to holiness acts on them with a force to which earth at present has no parallel. So directly does their happiness flow from their obedience, that they would deplore a pause in their duty as a suspension of their bliss. Holiness is always at its standard there; and happiness at its full-tide mark.

But that state of blessedness, instead of depressing us by its superiority, becomes, in the hands of the Great Teacher, a spring to hope, and a motive to imitation. He knows that, in every condition of our nature, the best way to ensure excellence is to aim at perfection; on this principle he renders the perfection of the heavenly state subservient to the improvement of this. Aware of the capabilities of earth, when pervaded by his Spirit, and blessed with his fostering care, he has pledged himself fully to develop its best properties, even all its possible excellences; and, for this end, he has raised its aim to the highest point, elevated its endeavours to the loftiest pitch, by shewing it the fairest specimens of created excellence as seen around the throne above. He has brought the throne of God within sight of earth—he has directed all flesh to come and collect around it; and, that we may not ask a blessing unworthy of the greatness of the occasion, he instructs us to request that we may rival angels in the perfection of their obedience; in order that we may not retire from the throne unblessed, through the poverty of our desires, he aims to make us jealous of the inhabitants of heaven, and incites us to ask to be admitted into a full community of excellence and happiness with them. Yea, more; by urging us to make this request, he would fain induce us to move God himself to jealousy, for the honour of his holy name; for what is it, in effect, but the presentation of a memorial to the King of kings, setting forth that, in this distant dependency of his empire, though its capabilities are great, though it might be made to yield him a revenue of glory which should compete with the treasured homage of heaven, yet his laws are dishonoured, his glory defrauded, and his will left undone; what is it, in effect, but a petition founded on this memorial, that heaven may not engross to itself all the immunities of loyalty and obedience, but that earth may add its full tribute to his throne, and receive its quota of his royal regard; that Righteousness, looking down from heaven, may behold her image reflected back again from the earth, as perfectly as it is mirrored in the crystal sea which circulates around the eternal throne.

O, thou divine Instructor and Redeemer of mankind,

what tongue can suitably speak the sublimity of thy precept, the vastness of thy benevolent designs for man, and the happiness that would flow from the fulfilment of them. How graciously wouldst thou animate us to heroic acts of virtue, by intimating that it is possible for us to equal heaven; how wisely wouldst thou guard us from presumptuous self-reliance, by referring us to Him for help to whom all things are possible; how like thyself dost thou act in saving us from a romantic expectation of the end without the means, laying on us every necessary command, and thus making us instrumental to the accomplishment of our own desires! Would man but yield himself up to thy directions, the hosts of the blessed should have to gird on their zeal afresh, in order to maintain their ancient ascendancy; heaven and earth should become convertible terms, and, as seen from the height of thy throne, should appear equally active in thy service, and radiant with thy glory. O, Holy Spirit of God, glorifier of Jesus, and renewer of the world, give thou the necessary impulse, and soon shall it be transformed into a paradise again—a paradise, in which the virtues of heaven shall be emulated, and its divinest pleasures be foretasted—in which the noblest exercises of a coming eternity shall be antedated and rehearsed, and into which God himself shall descend from heaven, bringing the peace and joy of heaven with him.

THE END.

www.ingramcontent.com/pod-product-compliance
Lightning Source LLC
Chambersburg PA
CBHW052137300426
44115CB00011B/1420